Franziska Fecher
ARCHAEOLOGICAL INVESTIGATIONS
IN GUADALUPE, NORTHEAST HONDURAS

FAAK 19

DEUTSCHES ARCHÄOLOGISCHES INSTITUT
Kommission für Archäologie Aussereuropäischer Kulturen

FORSCHUNGEN ZUR ARCHÄOLOGIE AUSSEREUROPÄISCHER KULTUREN 19

Herausgegeben im Auftrag des Instituts
von Jörg Linstädter und Christian Reepmeyer

DEUTSCHES ARCHÄOLOGISCHES INSTITUT
Kommission für Archäologie Aussereuropäischer Kulturen

Franziska Fecher

ARCHAEOLOGICAL INVESTIGATIONS IN GUADALUPE, NORTHEAST HONDURAS

Interaction Networks during the
Late Pre-Hispanic Period (AD 900–1525)

HARRASSOWITZ VERLAG · WIESBADEN

Autor/*Author*: Franziska Fecher (ORCID iD: https://orcid.org/0000-0002-6633-4965)

Titel/*Title*: Archaeological Investigations in Guadalupe, Northeast Honduras. Interaction Networks during the Late Pre-hispanic Period (AD 900–1525)

Reihe, Band/*Series, Volume*: Forschungen zur Archäologie Aussereuropäischer Kulturen, 19

Reihenherausgeber/*Series Editor*: Jörg Linstädter, Christian Reepmeyer

Herausgebende Institution/*Institutional Editor*: Deutsches Archäologisches Institut, Kommission für Archäologie Aussereuropäischer Kulturen, Bonn

XX, 275 Seiten/*Pages* mit/*with* 223 Abbildungen/*Illustrations*

This publication is a modified version of a Thesis presented to the Faculty of Arts and Social Sciences of the University of Zurich for the degree of Doctor of Philosophy, Zurich, October 27, 2020

Bibliografische Metadaten/*Bibliographic Metadata*: https://zenon.dainst.org/Record/003017260

Peer Review: Dieser Band wurde einem Peer-Review-Verfahren unterzogen./*The volume is peer-reviewed.*

Verantwortliche Redaktion/*Publishing Editor*: Kommission für Archäologie Aussereuropäischer Kulturen, Bonn
Redaktionelle Bearbeitung/*Editing*: H. Prümers
Prepress: le-tex publishing services GmbH, Leipzig
Buchgestaltung und Coverkonzeption/*Book Design and Cover Concept*: hawemannundmosch, Berlin
Umschlagfotos/*Cover Illustrations*: M. Reindel

Druckausgabe/*Printed Edition*
Erscheinungsjahr/*Year of Publication*: 2022
Druck und Vertrieb/*Printing and Distribution*: Dr. Ludwig Reichert Verlag Wiesbaden • www.reichert-verlag.de
Druck und Bindung in Deutschland/*Printed and Bound in Germany*

© 2022 Deutsches Archäologisches Institut
Otto Harrassowitz GmbH & Co. KG, Wiesbaden · https://www.harrassowitz-verlag.de

ISBN: 978-344-7-11941-2

Bibliografische Information der Deutschen Nationalbibliothek: Die Deutsche Nationalbibliothek verzeichnet diese Publikation in der Deutschen Nationalbibliografie; detaillierte bibliografische Daten sind im Internet über https://dnb.de abrufbar./*Bibliographic information published by the Deutsche Nationalbibliothek: The Deutsche Nationalbibliothek lists this publication in the Deutsche Nationalbibliografie; detailed bibliographic data are available online at https://dnb.de.*

Digitale Ausgabe/*Digital Edition*
Eine digitale Ausgabe des Werkes wird zwei Jahre nach Erscheinen der Druckausgabe auf iDAI.publications zur Verfügung gestellt/*A digital edition will be available at iDAI.publications two years after the printed edition has been published* (DOI: https://doi.org/10.34780/qof1-zo68).

Contents

List of Figures

List of Tables

„Zwei Dinge sollen Kinder von ihren Eltern bekommen: Wurzeln und Flügel."
— unbekannt

Ihr habt mir beides gegeben, wofür ich euch auf ewig dankbar bin.
Für meine Eltern.

Preface

The Commission for Archaeology of Non-European Cultures (KAAK) of the German Archaeological Institute (DAI) was founded in 1979 as the "Commission for General and Comparative Archaeology." It aims to conduct comparative archaeology in Asia, Africa, America, and Oceania to better understand the history of prehistoric societies worldwide. On the one hand, the objective is to give an overview of the continents' archaeology; on the other hand, exemplary research projects are to provide detailed insights into the archaeology of each region. While the commission's early years were characterized by editions of survey works and selective thematic research, it soon initiated its own field research projects.

In the Americas, field research projects initially focused on the Andean region of South America, such as the excavations in Montegrande, Peru, directed by Michael Tellenbach, or the settlement archaeological studies in the Topará Valley, Peru, led by Wolfgang Wurster. Later, projects were added in the Bolivian lowlands under the direction of Heiko Prümers and in southern Peru under the direction of Markus Reindel. In 1990, Wolfgang Wurster began a long-term cooperation with Oscar Quintana to explore Maya sites in the lowlands of Guatemala. The latter work now also covered a second focus of ancient American research, Central America.

After the end of the KAAK's research activities in Guatemala with Wurster's retirement in 2000, the two research foci in South America, Bolivia and Peru, were continued. Central America, however, was not represented in the research agenda for several years. In order to ensure the continued presence of KAAK archaeological research in Central America, Markus Reindel initiated a research project in 2012 at the Maya site of Copán in western Honduras. Together with Jennifer von Schwerin, he led the interdisciplinary project MayaArch3D, funded by the German Federal Ministry of Education and Research (BMBF). The goal of this project was to use modern digital methods to develop a web-based digital 3D documentation system for complex archaeological sites. Existing data from many years of research in Copán was used, but new data was also collected and evaluated.

While working with highly technical methods in Copán, the most intensively researched site of the Maya culture that represents one of the most developed so-called complex societies of ancient America, it became clear that the many other pre-Hispanic cultural developments in Honduras that could not be assigned to the Maya culture had received far too little attention in research as of yet. This observation generally applies to research on Mesoamerica at large, that is, the region where stratified social systems and large settlement centers with monumental buildings and writing systems developed. Research on Mesoamerica is far more advanced than that on Southern Central America, which includes parts of Honduras and El Salvador, Nicaragua, Costa Rica, and Panama. The deficit of research on Southern Central America is increasingly recognized, as the region represents an important communication zone between Mesoamerica and the Andes, both of which have been studied more intensively to date. Throughout several periods of cultural development in Southern Central America, influences from adjacent regions were absorbed, and in addition to its own autochtonous developments it served as a conduit for technological and cultural innovations that originated in the Andes or Mesoamerica. Many details of such cultural influences, such as fine-grained data about the first settlement of the continent, the domestication of plants, the development of social systems, or metallurgy, are only rudimentarily explored in Southern Central America and therefore represent an urgent research desideratum.

In order to fill this research gap, regular expeditions to eastern Honduras were already carried out during the implementation of the MayaArch3D project. In particular, northeast Honduras, an important culture area between Mesoamerica and Southern Central America, has hardly been explored archaeologically. Together with project partners from the Honduran Institute of Anthropology and History (Instituto Hondureño de Antropología e Historia, IHAH), several regions in northeast Honduras were systematically surveyed, sites were registered, and their potential for more intensive future research was evaluated.

Guadalupe was chosen as the excavation site for several reasons, which are explained in detail in this book. The project was carried out as a cooperation of the German Archaeological Institute with the University of Zurich and the Museum Rietberg Zurich. It was financially supported by the Swiss-Liechtenstein Foundation for Archaeological Research Abroad (SLSA). The SLSA thus continued its commitment to the archaeology of Latin America. The SLSA had already previously supported the projects led by Markus Reindel in Ecuador (La Cadena) and Peru (Nasca-Palpa), thus making an important contribution to archaeological research in these countries.

Cooperation with the Swiss partners proved to be extremely successful, not only with regard to the exchange of knowledge and international cooperation but also concerning outreach work, which was implemented in an exemplary manner in the form of an exhibition thanks to the expertise of the project's co-director, Peter Fux, of the Museum Rietberg. Lastly, the scientific evaluation of the results of the excavations in Guadalupe could be secured through the employment of Franziska Fecher at the Department of Prehistoric Archaeology of the University of Zurich, headed by Philippe Della Casa.

Franziska Fecher had already gained experience in Honduran archaeology in the previous project MayaArch3D and wrote her bachelor thesis on the research history of Honduran archaeology and her master thesis on the definition of the southern limits of Mesoamerica, using information technology methods in archaeological research. She had been involved in the reconnaissance, preparation, and implementation of the Guadalupe project from the beginning. She also coordinated the excavation and analysis work during the five field campaigns of the Guadalupe project. Thus, she was fully prepared to conduct the final analysis of the fieldwork results and place them in the context of archaeological research on Mesoamerica and Southern Central America.

Excavation in humid tropical regions is not an easy task. Due to the regularly recurring saturation of the soil by periodic heavy rainfalls, archaeological features are often not as clearly defined as in other regions. Organic materials are subject to more severe decomposition than in colder or drier areas. Both the excavation itself and the subsequent evaluation of the excavation results are therefore subject to particular difficulties. Scientific evaluation is further complicated by the fragmentary state of research in northeast Honduras. The chronology has been worked out only in rudimentary form. Publications covering the material are sparse and only include a few sites, hindering the comparison of finds with already published objects.

One of the analysis focuses of excavations at Guadalupe, therefore, had to initially be on the fundamental work of documenting the excavation results and find material in detail. Even when classifying the finds, Franziska Fecher could not rely on established interpretation schemes. The challenge was precisely due to so little being known about the region. To which period should the excavated finds and features be assigned? To which pottery sphere did the large quantities of pottery recovered during the excavation belong? What exchange relationships could be deduced from the various find materials? How were the settlers of Guadalupe organized? What did their houses look like? How did they bury their dead?

Franziska Fecher has pursued all of these questions in her remarkable and extremely detailed analysis. In the process, she has achieved astonishing results. She presents the most comprehensive documentation of an excavation in northeast Honduras to date. She analyzed the large quantity of pottery finds in detail and thus considerably expanded the typological basis for the classification of the pottery of the Cocal culture (AD 900-1525). Through the analysis of the recovered obsidian artifacts, together with specialists Geoffrey Braswell and Luke Stroth, it was possible to determine the extensive networks of the pre-Hispanic inhabitants of Guadalupe, which served to obtain raw materials for the production of artifacts. Insights into economic relationships were supplemented by studies of mollusks by Nayeli Jiménez and Annkatrin Benz and analyses of greenstone by Ulrich Glasmacher, as well as metallurgical analyses by Andreas Hauptmann. Finally, the discovery of burials in the periphery of the settlement mound of Guadalupe allowed the excavation site to be identified as a central ceremonial site, where feasts were carried out in connection with funerary rites. Initial anthropological analyses by Luisa Mainou and Julio Chi Keb, as well as pertinent comparisons with corresponding burial finds, indicated that the burial practices at Guadalupe followed a tradition found at other sites in Southern Central America. In this way, a fascinating picture of the living conditions of the inhabitants of Guadalupe emerged from the extensive and multifaceted analyses.

The results of the analyses ultimately provided an answer to the question posed at the beginning about the cultural affiliation of the region. The inhabitants were indeed integrated into superordinate networks that reached into Mesoamerica and Southern Central America and even the Caribbean. However, the cultural characteristics of both the finds and the lifeways and customs suggest that the region was more culturally oriented toward Southern Central America. Franziska Fecher has thus succeeded in making a valuable contribution to the knowledge of the pre-Hispanic history of northeast Honduras in an environment that can only be described as difficult due to both the excavation conditions and the state of research. Many questions about this transitional region between Mesoamerica and Southern Central America could be answered, but at the same time, the foundations for future research could be laid, which is certainly still necessary to shed more light on the significance of this important research area.

Markus Reindel

Acknowledgments

I would like to thank the editors of this book and the Commission for Archaeology of Non-European Cultures (KAAK) of the German Archaeological Institute for the opportunity to publish the results of my doctoral research. I express my thanks in particular to Burkhard Vogt, Jörg Linstädter, and Heiko Prümers.

The doctoral research, which serves as a basis for the present publication, was conducted within the framework of the Archaeological Project Guadalupe, which is a cooperation between the German Archaeological Institute (DAI), the University of Zurich (UZH), the Museum Rietberg Zurich (MRZ), and the Instituto Hondureño de Antropología e Historia (IHAH) with additional funding from the Swiss-Liechtenstein Foundation for Archaeological Research Abroad (SLSA). I would like to express my deepest gratitude to all of these institutions, without which the work presented here would not have been possible. My thanks also go to the UZH Alumni's Research Talent Development Fund (FAN) that supported me by financing the last year of my doctoral program. I greatly appreciate that this support gave me the freedom to focus on my dissertation.

I would like to thank the supervisors of my doctoral research Philippe Della Casa and Markus Reindel, who have accompanied me along the way with guidance and support and have always kept me on the right track. Many thanks for your time, encouragement, and valuable advice. My sincere thanks also go to Peter Fux, who has devoted himself to the project despite challenging circumstances. On the Honduran side, I want to sincerely thank the Instituto Hondureño de Antropología e Historia for the permits and the always pleasant cooperation. Special mention goes to Oscar Neil Cruz Castillo and Tania Guardado for their guidance, infrastructural support, and interest in the project. I would also like to thank the German Embassy in Tegucigalpa, which has always been helpful in the organization of permits and the field campaigns.

I cannot express enough thanks to the team of the Archaeological Project Guadalupe, without whom this work would not have been possible. My special thanks go once again to Markus Reindel and Peter Fux as project directors for their guidance and commitment and for sharing their valuable knowledge with us, to Mike Lyons for the creation of an endless number of 3D models, for managing the GIS and providing me with maps, and especially for the invaluable and careful English correc-tions, to Marlisa Schacht for the excellent organizational support and for always keeping track of things, to Jill Mattes and Timea Remsey for their incredible patience in drawing and photographing uncooperative ceramic sherds and Jill for her painstaking help in preparing the ceramic drawings, Paul Bayer for the immensely helpful thoughts on ceramic analysis, for the analysis of the ocarinas and the inspiring yoga classes, Kevin Engel for his patience with the stones and loving care of the pets, and to all the other Guadalupeños who participated. Thank you so much for sharing your enthusiasm for Honduran archaeology with me and that even long hikes through spiny bushes in scorching heat did not discourage you! My special thanks also go to Christine Busch; your incredible strength is an inspiration for me. For that, I thank you. I am especially grateful for the support of the Honduran students Fiama Hernández, Raquel Otto, Nabil Mejía, and Jorby Tejada. It was a great pleasure meeting you, and I wish you all the best in your archaeological careers.

The following people supported me in creating the drawings, photographs, 3D models, and redrawings of ceramic sherds and other find material: Mike Lyons, Brigitte Gubler, Paul Bayer, Jill Mattes, Judith Bucher, Timea Remsey, Marlisa Schacht, Jorby Tejada, Nabil Mejía, Fiama Hernández, Raquel Otto, Kevin Engel, Jeannine Langmann, Marcel Müller and Niklas Hoge.

It is also very important for me to mention the people from Guadalupe, who welcomed us with open arms and have grown very close to our hearts over all of this time. I am especially grateful to Mildred Fernández for always standing up for our project, Iris and Ricxi Puerto for taking care of our culinary well-being, and the Payes family for sharing their knowledge and their passion for archaeological sites with us. Thank you to all the workers who always supported us with full strength, enthusiasm, and cheerfulness. Thanks to Tito Ever, Oscar Serrano, and Aníbal Maldonado for accompanying us on all of our trips and becoming part of our little Guadalupe family and to Hans Weller and Edgardo Ortega for welcoming and guiding us on Guanaja.

My thanks also go to all the experts who shared their knowledge with me and gave me valuable advice. Special mention goes to Brigitte Gubler, who taught us so much in such a short time, Nayeli Jiménez, who was always there with full commitment, Annkatrin Benz, Geoffrey Braswell, Luke Stroth, Hubert Mara, Julio Chi Keb, Luisa

Mainou, and Ariana Aguilar Romero, as well as Luis Barba Pingarrón and Marlene Rodríguez. I would like to thank Ulrich Glasmacher and Andreas Hauptmann for the analysis of the greenstone and metal samples.

A huge thank you goes to Andrea Peiró Vitoria for the corrections of the Spanish summaries. I would like to thank Christine Woda, Luke Stroth, Christopher Begley, Paul Healy, Carrie Dennett, Whitney Goodwin, Jill Mattes, the Museum Rietberg Zurich, and the Museo de Antropología e Historia de San Pedro Sula for their permission to use their images.

I would also like to express my gratitude to the Prehistoric Archaeology team at the UZH. I am incredibly thankful to you for welcoming me so warmly and for allowing me to work in such a great team. Your mental and moral support has been a great help to me. My special thanks go to my office colleague Judith Bucher for her help with ceramic drawings and design issues, the stimulating conversations, and simply for being such a great companion.

I would also like to express my sincere thanks to Albert Lutz and Jo Siegler and team. You accompanied us during a particularly challenging time and captured our experiences in Honduras in moving pictures so that we can always remember them and bring the Caribbean atmosphere back to our homes.

Lastly, although they should be first, thank you to my family and friends, who accompanied me along the way with all its ups and downs and were always on my side. An especially big and warm thank you goes to Tasos, who shared his easiness with me and made sure I didn't lose my confidence, and to Hannah and Emilia, whose precious friendship is a source of calm and strength.

1 Introduction

1.1 Introduction to Northeast Honduras

Northeast Honduras has a rich history. Columbus first encountered the American mainland here in 1502. The colonial period was marked by conflicts between the European conquerors and the indigenous population, resulting in the decimation and dislocation of indigenous groups. In the 18th century, Garifuna people were deported from the Caribbean island St. Vincent and settled along the coasts. Privateers made the Caribbean coast unsafe until the 19th century. At the beginning of the 20th century, the U.S. fruit companies used the region around Trujillo for the extensive cultivation of banana plantations. Today, the area struggles with land conflicts and drug trafficking but is also defined by its cultural diversity and the coexistence of different ethnic groups. Little is known about the history of this vibrant area before the arrival of the Spanish. However, available evidence suggests that this area was already highly complex[1] in pre-Hispanic times and that the inhabitants of the region were integrated into various cultural, economic, and sociopolitical networks. Today, we know that northeast Honduras was at the intersection of three major culture areas: Mesoamerica in the northwest, the Caribbean in the northeast, and Southern Central America in the southeast (Figure 1). Nevertheless, Honduras is considered one of the archaeologically least explored countries in Central America, and many questions of pre-Hispanic cultural history remain unanswered. This is especially true for the eastern part of the country, where fundamental questions about pre-Hispanic cultural processes remain unresolved. This is mainly due to the assumption that this area lay outside the developments of "complex societies" that were represented in western Honduras by the Maya and the emblematic city of Copán. Curiosity about the southern extension of the Maya culture attracted the interest of researchers early on, while the eastern part of the country was considered less compelling and was neglected for a long time. To understand the cultural processes in northeast Honduras, basic research is needed to expand our knowledge base and allow conclusions to be drawn about pre-Hispanic times.

The work presented here aims to contribute to the reconstruction of the cultural history of this key region. The questions guiding these investigations include the following: How can this region, at the intersection of many different culture areas, best be characterized? What did the material culture look like, and what were the characteristics of settlements? What were the relationships and interactions between the inhabitants within the region and with the inhabitants of the surrounding regions, and which effects did changes in these areas have on the inhabitants of northeast Honduras? What role did northeast Honduras play in the exchange of objects and ideas between the major culture areas of Middle America? Of particular interest are the last 600 years before Spanish arrival since it is assumed that the interaction with the inhabitants of the surrounding regions increased during this time. Ethnohistorical sources are also available for this period, opening another window into the past.

1.2 Research Design

Until now, northeast Honduras has mainly been considered from the perspective of its location between different culture areas, and investigations have focused on the region's relationships to the societies in the north and south. The present study chose northeast Honduras for investigations due to this unique location since it represents a fascinating situation. However, during our activities, it became clear that the prevailing approach of culture areas and their relationship to each other is not an appropriate approximation to the understanding of the study area. This is a top-down approach that starts with defined entities of culture areas, tries to identify their influences on northeast Honduras, and then defines northeast Honduras based on these influences. Although recent studies have helped change this view, the discussion of influences and connections with the surrounding areas remains a focus, while considerations of autochthonous developments have received little attention.

---

1 For a definition of the term "complexity" in the present work, see chapter 3.2.2.4.

1   Culture areas in Middle America. The frontier between Mesoamerica and Southern Central America is indicated by the dashed line (F. Fecher, M. Lyons).

However, the new research presented in this work makes it clear that northeast Honduras should be considered something of its own, and if we want to get closer to the reality of the people who lived in northeast Honduras during pre-Hispanic times, a new approach is needed. It can be assumed that relations to distant regions or culture areas do not shape everyday life or constitute social identity, at least not to a great extent. Instead, interactions in the immediate environment, on a local and everyday level, are what shape a society (Gamble / Gowlett / Dunbar 2015). Therefore, the approach taken in this work is a bottom-up approach, starting with interactions detectable in the archaeological context on the smallest geographical scale and building on these to investigate connections to more distant regions. It is also important to note that the present work examines interactions that represent reciprocal actions rather than passively received influences. Interaction cannot be unilateral; it always requires at least two parties. Autochthonous developments thus come into focus, and the inhabitants of northeast Honduras are assigned an active role.

Network theory is applied to address the complex situation in northeast Honduras while ensuring the study area itself has its own significance and that an active perspective supplants the passive approach. This approach understands archaeological settlements and their inhabitants as nodes of a network and aims to reconstruct the relationships that existed between these nodes. This approach brings interaction to the forefront of investigations and allows for the study of interaction

on different geographical levels: local, regional, and interregional. Network theory also allows the neutral observation of interaction and thus provides a way to circumvent the implicitly evaluative dichotomy between "complex societies" in the west and the supposed "periphery" of northeast Honduras.

This work's foundation is formed by the research of the Archaeological Project Guadalupe, which took place between 2016 and 2020 on the north coast of Honduras. The project is a collaboration between the University of Zurich (UZH), the German Archaeological Institute (DAI), the Rietberg Museum Zurich (MRZ), and the Instituto Hondureño de Antropología e Historia (IHAH). It is directed by Prof. Dr. Markus Reindel and Dr. Peter Fux. The project's core comprises the excavations in the Cocal-period (AD 900–1525) settlement Guadalupe and surveys in the surrounding area. Guadalupe is located directly on the Atlantic coast of Honduras, in an area of clearly visible but as of yet unexplored pre-Hispanic settlements.

The present work understands Guadalupe as a node that had connections to other nodes and thus formed part of one or more networks. The aim is to explore and understand the central node of Guadalupe as thoroughly as possible. The excavations, for example, provide information about economic and cultural aspects of the local society. They suggest that feasts were held in Guadalupe that represent a special form of social interaction that includes connections to the deceased. Based on observations we made in Guadalupe, connections to other settlements are reconstructed. Since networks are reconstructed mainly via objects in the form of material networks in archaeology, the presentation, illustration, and analysis of the finds are a major focus of the present work. Ceramics play a special role as they represent an especially diagnostic find category, and thus a new classification scheme is developed for them. Networks are reconstructed from the bottom up, starting with the identification of regional networks followed by the examination of interregional interaction. While Mesoamerica and Southern Central America have been well-considered as influential areas, this work assumes that relations with the Caribbean also existed, and evidence for such connections is discussed. The temporal focus rests on the period between AD 900 and 1525 as this was presumably a highly dynamic period in which relations intensified and exchange along the coasts took on a significant role.

1.3 Organization of the Text

The text begins by covering the environment and surroundings in which northeast Honduras is situated. The definition of adjacent culture areas has strongly shaped how northeast Honduras has been perceived throughout the history of research. Such definitions are essential to understand the current prevailing perspectives on northeast Honduras and are presented below. While previous research has primarily focused on the connections to Mesoamerica and Southern Central America, this work includes the Caribbean as well. How the respective culture areas were defined is also examined. This is followed by a brief outline of the cultural history of each area, including a characterization of the state of current research and a presentation of the open research questions. The next chapter presents an introduction to the period from AD 900 to 1525 and the major events that archaeological and ethnohistorical sources tell us about. The following section introduces the study area of northeast Honduras. It begins by providing an overview of the geographic context and the history of its archaeological research. This is followed by a brief overview of the available linguistic and ethnohistorical data for the region, which are used to complement the archaeological data in the analysis. The section concludes by outlining the traditional views on northeast Honduras, including an examination of definitions and theoretical conceptualizations that have been applied to the area so far.

This contextual consideration produces the research questions that are formulated in the following chapter. These questions will be discussed and answered in the present work. As a theoretical approach, network theory is used. This decision is based on a discussion of other potentially relevant theories for the investigation of intercultural interaction that explains why they are not suitable for clarifying the presented research questions. Subsequently, the network approach, its basic assumptions, and its analytical possibilities for archaeological research are outlined, and the adaptations and definitions for the reconstruction of networks in northeast Honduras are presented. The extent to which network theory can offer alternative perspectives on controversial concepts such as complexity and culture areas will be explained.

Chapter 4 deals with the research results in Guadalupe and the surrounding area on the north coast of Honduras and the Bay Islands. The methods and results of the data collected during the investigations of the Archaeological Project Guadalupe are presented in detail in this chapter. The definition of the research area, the results of the stratigraphic excavation in Guadalupe, and the survey of Guadalupe and the surrounding area are addressed here. The excavation results include data on the stratigraphy, dating, and chronology of the site and features, and their relation to each other, all of which are important for interpreting the site. In addition to the stratigraphic excavations, surveys were carried out to familiarize ourselves with Guadalupe's surroundings and enable the determination of its role in the settlement structure and its integration into various networks. The results of this survey are presented, which concentrated on the coastal strip between Betulia and the Guaimoreto Lagoon, the Aguán Valley to the south, and the island of Guanaja to the north. A comprehensive presentation of the finds follows. Stylistic and scientific analyses are applied to investigate possible links to other settlements and regions. The methodology for the find analyses is also outlined here. A new classification scheme for the ceramic finds is developed based on the classification method by Iken Paap (2002). Other groups of finds discussed in this research include obsidian, greenstone, ground stone, metal, and zoological material. Along with the analysis results, preliminary comparisons and connections to the surrounding regions are shown, which later form the basis for the discussion.

The following chapter contextualizes and discusses the presented results using the concept of network theory. First, the local society of Guadalupe is examined. Guadalupe forms the central node from which relationships to other nodes are studied, and thus networks are reconstructed. Aspects of the local economy, architecture, culture, and sociopolitical organization are considered, including the practice of holding feasts in connection with burials. Based on these observations, different spatial levels of networks are analyzed in which the inhabitants of Guadalupe were involved. Networks at a regional level comprise a coastal interaction system that includes the coast, the adjacent islands, and the Aguán Valley. In a further step, the relations with the other settlements of northeast Honduras are examined. In the next level, interregional networks are observed. The motivation for and types of relations with the surrounding regions are examined, including those with Mesoamerica, Southern Central America, and the Caribbean.

Finally, directions and strategies for future research are outlined based on the current state of knowledge. The paper closes with a summary and synthesis of the previously considered and discussed points. The appendix contains an acoustic analysis of ocarinas by Paul Bayer, the Raman spectroscopy of greenstone artifacts by Daniela Oestreich and Ulrich Glasmacher, as well as a list of museums that house collections from northeast Honduras.

2 Culture Areas and Cultural History in Middle America: Current State of Research

Northeast Honduras is located in an area of overlap between the three large culture areas of Mesoamerica, Southern Central America, and the Caribbean. This location is significant and greatly impacts the perception of pre-Hispanic northeast Honduras. In order to understand the influence that the definition of these culture areas had on archaeological research in northeast Honduras and to understand the cultural-historical context in which the inhabitants of this region found themselves, we look at the culture areas relevant to our research region and address the questions of how these culture areas were defined, which assumptions underlie their definitions, and how the archaeological research of these regions can be characterized. A brief outline of the cultural history is also given.

2.1 Mesoamerica

The culture area of Mesoamerica was first defined by the German anthropologist Paul Kirchhoff (1943). Geographically, the area extends northward to approximately the level of the Rio Lerma, where it is limited by Arid America. Kirchhoff defined the southern border as extending from the mouth of the Rio Motagua to the Guanacaste Peninsula in Costa Rica. Its definition was based on the assumption that all of the inhabitants of a given area shared the same cultural tradition and certain cultural characteristics united by a common history. These cultural characteristics include elements related to subsistence, such as the cultivation of maize as a staple food, the preparation of cooked maize with ash or lime, or the cultivation of cocoa. Other elements include the construction of pyramids and ballcourts, the use of writing and ritual calendars, and rituals involving human sacrifice and auto sacrifice. The Mesoamerican culture area is further characterized by the development of so-called "complex societies" (defined by Kirchhoff as *cultivadores superiores*), which developed a state-organized sociopolitical order early on. In the 1940s, Kirchhoff's understanding was mainly based on linguistic, ethnohistorical, and ethnographic data that presented the situation as it was during the arrival of the Spaniards. Later, verifiable chronological data based on archaeological research became available, adding historical depth and showing that the culture area's boundaries fluctuated through time.

Of the three regions reviewed here, Mesoamerica can certainly be considered the best explored. By the middle of the 19th century, early adventurers and explorers were attracted to the impressive ruins in the rainforest. Especially in Mexico, nationally managed and organized archaeology has seen significant development. From the beginning, the main areas of research consisted of the Central Mexican highlands and the Maya region. Less attention was paid to the north and south frontier regions, except for investigation of the Mesoamerican culture area's southern extension (e.g., Lothrop 1939). Only when questions of interaction between state-organized and non-state-organized societies arose in the 1980s did these areas garner more attention from researchers. During this time, several projects developed to investigate the so-called Southern Mesoamerican Periphery or Southeast Maya Periphery. This zone includes areas of western El Salvador and Honduras and is characterized as a transition zone (Schortman / Urban 1986).

Mesoamerican cultural history is characterized by overarching horizons that repeatedly radiate over large areas. The widespread use of common traits and features clearly indicates that the societies were in close contact with each other since the earliest periods. The cultural history is divided into four major periods: Archaic, Formative (or Preclassic), Classic, and Postclassic (Figure 2). The Classic period, between AD 300 and 900, was named as an analogy to the classic cultures of the Mediterranean region, which directly relates to the long-held belief that the Postclassic period was a period of decline. This division is thus partly characterized by an evolutionist understanding.

Research questions related to the Archaic period mainly concern when and where the domestication of plants and the process of sedentism developed. Much of the data on this comes from the Tehuacán Valley (MacNeish 1967–1972), where plant domestication began around 5000 to 3400 BC. Towards the end of the Archaic, the domestication of plants became increasingly important, and authors speak of a semisedentary lifeway (MacNeish 2010). In the western Honduras, cores from Lake Yojoa show that the region was inhabited and exploited by humans by at least 3000 BC (Rue 1989).

	NE Honduras	Mesoamerica	Southern CA
1500 AD	Late Cocal	Late Postclassic	
	Early Cocal		VI
		Early Postclassic	
1000 AD			
	Transitional Selin		
		Late Classic	V
	Basic Selin		
500 AD	Early Selin	Early Classic	
0	?	Late Preclassic	
			IV
500 BC			
		Middle Preclassic	
	Cuyamel		
1000 BC			
		Early Preclassic	III

2 Chronology chart by culture area (F. Fecher).

During the following Formative period (2000 BC–AD 300), many foundations developed that would later shape the Classic and Postclassic societies. Settlements and agriculture became widespread, and irrigation techniques saw early use (Evans 2008). The Olmec culture emerged with its center on the Mexican Gulf Coast (1200–500 BC). For the first time, monumental architecture and sophisticated stone monuments were produced. The exchange and control of resources played an important role, and iconography revealed a complex cosmology. In modern times, in many regions of Mesoamerica, objects are found that are described as Olmecoid, which display a very similar iconography. However, the nature and consequences of the exchange relationships remain unclear and subject to intense discussion (Grove 2010). The beginnings of Maya culture arose in the centers of El Mirador and Nakbé in the Maya lowlands, Kaminaljuyú in the Guatemalan highlands, and on the Pacific coast. In western Honduras, excavations in Puerto Escondido show that pottery production began here as early as AD 1600 (Joyce / Henderson 2001). Burials from Playa de los Muertos indicate a clear social stratification (Popenoe 1934), and monumental architecture emerged

in Los Naranjos and Yarumela around 1200 BC. Finds from the Cuyamel Caves and the Cueva Hato Viejo are some of the most remote examples of Olmec influence (Cruz Castillo / Juárez Silva 2006; Healy 1974a). It is still a matter of discussion as to whether these objects indicate a direct influence or if they found their way to Honduras by down-the-line exchange.

In the Classic period (AD 300–900), the southern Maya lowlands were among the most densely settled regions in the world (Santley 2010). They were dominated by competing city-states ruled by godlike kings. In the Central Mexican highlands, Teotihuacán was the dominant center with widespread influence throughout Mesoamerica. Other large centers were Monte Albán in the valley of Oaxaca and Matacapán on the Gulf coast. In western and central Honduras, the Classic period is characterized by population growth. In AD 426, the southernmost Maya dynasty was founded in Copán. Copán was probably a multi-ethnic settlement from the beginning, which was connected to the Maya lowlands and central Honduras. Especially in the early phases, relationships with Teotihuacán can also be seen (Fash 2001). In several settlements in western Honduras, cultural changes are visible that researchers attribute to the influence of the Maya. The center of Gualjoquito was rebuilt during the Early Classic period to echo the architectural layout of the center of Copán (Ashmore 1987). In the Naco Valley, La Sierra became the dominant center during the Late Classic period with 468 visible platforms. In the El Cajón region, between AD 500 and 1000, a clearly visible population increase occured, and a hierarchically structured settlement pattern developed. In western and central Honduras, the Late Classic Ulúa Polychrome style was widespread, the design of which is reminiscent of the polychrome ceramics of the Maya lowlands.

At the end of the Classic period, the large centers lost power, and many competing polities began to emerge due to the resulting power vacuum. The central and southern Maya lowlands were affected by a phenomenon known as the "Maya collapse", a somewhat misleading term since the collapse did not concern the society but rather the political system, which had been characterized by the central authority of a godlike king until this point. The phenomenon started in different areas at different times but culminated in most centers being abandoned by around AD 900. How and why this process took place are still important research questions in Maya archaeology (Sharer / Traxler 2006: 505-513). One of the most plausible explanations is famine caused by agricultural limits being reached due to overwhelming population growth, which undermined the rulers' authority. In 8th century Copán, there are signs of a famine resulting from the valley's excessive exploitation and deforestation, which led to the collapse of the central authority in the 9th century when the center of Copán was abandoned (Fash 2001: 171-179). Centers to the west of Copán were also in decline at this time. La Sierra and Gualjoquito were abandoned by AD 1000. Growth and decay were closely connected to developments in the Maya region. Similar observations are made for the El Cajón region and the Jamastrán Valley. Evans (2008: 398) speaks of a domino effect, suggesting that the loss of Copán as an important and regulating center impacted the other centers in western Honduras. Simultaneously, new centers, such as Cerro Palenque and Tenampúa, were emerging, which may have been facilitated by the power vacuum. Their elevated location and fortifications indicate that these times were not without conflict (Dixon 1987).

The Postclassic period (AD 900–1521) is largely characterized by migratory movements and changes to the economic system. In the Central Mexican highlands, Tula emerged as an important center of the Toltec around AD 1000. Other important sites include the center of Cholula and the competing city-states of the Mixtecs and the Tarasks in western Mexico. In the Late Postclassic period,

the Mexica group established itself in the central valley of Mexico. Extensive trade relations, markets, and *pochteca* merchants played an important role in the tribute empire. In the Maya region, the population had shifted to the north, with Chichen Itza dominating the scene during the Early Postclassic. It is assumed that Chichen Itza was no longer ruled by a divine ruler but by a supreme council. It was also an important religious center for the cult of the feathered serpent Kukulkan (Quetzalcoatl), which spread throughout Mesoamerica during the Postclassic (Evans 2008). Mayapán replaced Chichen Itza as the dominant center during the Late Postclassic. A second center of Maya culture was located in the highlands of Guatemala, where groups of K'iche'-Maya competed with one another. Little data is currently available regarding the southern Mesoamerican periphery. The most well-known site is likely Naco, which is characterized as a trade center and Nahua enclave based on mainly ethnohistorical data (Henderson 1978). The end of the Postclassic is marked by the Spanish conquest of the Aztec capital, Tenochtitlán, in AD 1521.

2.2 Southern Central America

Throughout history, different concepts have been used to define the Southern Central America region. Roughly speaking, it includes the southern part of the Central American land bridge, i.e., the eastern parts of El Salvador and Honduras, Nicaragua, Costa Rica, Panama, and, depending on the definition, parts of the South American mainland (Colombia and Venezuela). Gordon Willey (1959) was the first to define the region as a coherent culture area, which he termed the Intermediate Area. This designation mirrors how the area was perceived at that time. It arose from the necessity to define the gap between the adjacent "complex civilizations" in Mesoamerica and the Andes. Especially in early research, the region was viewed as transitional and marginal to the complex societies in the north and south, and it was believed that cultural developments were strongly influenced by the neighboring civilizations. A later concept, coined Lower Central America by Claude Baudez in 1963, excludes the South American part. For a long time, researchers neglected the region, with few exceptions. The lack of development of "complex civilizations" made the research area appear unattractive to archaeologists (Sheets 1992). However, this view changed by the 1980s (e.g., Lange / Stone 1984). John Hoopes and Oscar Fonseca (2003) developed a new definition based on the region's common elements and coined the term Isthmo-Colombian Area. The geographic definition roughly ranges from northeast Honduras to Colombia but has permeable borders. The concept is primarily based on the linguistic unity of the Chibcha languages, which make up the largest language group in the region defined above. The second important criterion for the definition is the production of gold and *tumbaga* objects, which played a central role in this area. Hoopes and Fonseca (2003) show that linguistic and genetic data suggest that the region they defined was characterized by fewer migratory movements and external influences than previously assumed. On the contrary, endogenous dynamics and an extended continuity of inhabitants are currently assumed. Another concept on which Hoopes and Fonseca's idea is based is the concept of "diffuse unity," which means that smaller independent groups are united by shared iconographic elements in which a unifying worldview is reflected. While the terms "Intermediate Area" and "Lower Central America" have been criticized for their negative connotations (Sheets 1992), I prefer to use the term "Southern Central America" here, as it describes the region in a neutral geographical sense and avoids the conceptualization as a culture area (see chapter 3.2.2.4).

Until the 1980s, the main research focus was on chronological questions. After that, other topics were addressed, whereby the intensity of research differed from country to country and was strongly related to the respective political circumstances. For example, in Costa Rica, which has been governed by a relatively stable democracy, the national archaeological framework is well-developed. At the same time, large parts of Nicaragua are hardly researched due to the civil war making archaeological work impossible for many years (Geurds 2018: 5). In general, there is a clear concentration of research on the Pacific coast, which is likely connected to infrastructure but also influenced by the assumption that it had stronger connections to Mesoamerica throughout prehistory.

In contrast to Mesoamerica, no overarching horizons for the pre-Hispanic cultural development in Southern Central America have been recognized. Even today, it is still assumed that no state-organized societies had developed. Questions regarding the emergence of cultural complexity and why it did not occur in Southern Central America, therefore, resonate in many research projects. Cultural history is marked by great cultural diversity, a "highly complex cultural mosaic"[2] (Hasemann / Lara Pinto / Sandoval Cruz 2017: 41). Some researchers see this fragmentation as a result of geographic conditions. Nevertheless, some cultural similarities serve as the basis for defining cultural regions within Southern Central America. Among the most

important are Greater Nicoya, Greater Chiriquí, Greater Coclé, and the Darién (see Figure 1). In the past, researchers believed that the Central American land bridge served as a corridor between the continents for people and that events were strongly influenced by the neighboring societies in Mesoamerica and South America. Today, we know that people were closely networked among themselves (especially neighboring regions), but "surprisingly buffered from events and processes in continental areas" (Cooke 2005: 164: 164). Technologies were adapted, and goods were produced locally; they were adjusted to local needs and world beliefs. Not many objects were imported, and their reuse and transformation indicate that the raw material was probably more important than the notions of exoticism and foreignness (Cooke 2005: 162).

A concept for the subdivision of Southern Central American cultural history was developed as a result of a seminar on Central American archaeology (Lange / Stone 1984). With the aim of periodization independent of Mesoamerica and as neutral as possible, a chronological framework consisting of six phases was created, which is designated by the Roman numerals I–VI. Periods I and II cover the time from Central America's first settlement to 4000 BC and correspond to the Archaic period. Cores from Yeguada Lake in Panama prove that human populations had modified the environment early on and probably already practiced slash-and-burn agriculture around 6000 BC (Ranere 2008: 200). One of the earliest known sites is Cerro Mangote in Panama, which was settled from the 5th millennium BC onwards (McGimsey 1956). Period III (4000–1000 BC) is characterized by the introduction of ceramics. The oldest known pottery in Central America comes from Monagrillo in Panama and dates to 3900–1250 BC. The similarities to early pottery styles in Ecuador (Valdivia) and Colombia (Puerto Hormiga) are a subject of debate (Cooke 2005: 142f). Furthermore, movement away from foraging economies towards dependence on plant cultivation is evident. Again, cores from lakes show us that, by 2000 BC at the latest, agriculture was widespread in Southern Central America (Ranere 2008).

Period IV (1000 BC–AD 500) saw the emergence of social hierarchy and was associated with population growth in many regions. In Nicoya, graves were furnished with greenstone objects and finely carved metates (grinding stones). Beginning in 500 BC, an increase in production and exchange of objects is evident, and the archaeological record became more diverse (Geurds 2018: 7; Solórzano 2009: 219). Concerning pottery, the so-called Zoned Bichrome Style was predominant in

---

2 Translation from Spanish by the author.

many regions. Towards the end of the period, widespread use of prestige goods can be observed, and special cemeteries for elites developed. One of the most valued raw materials was greenstone, but by the end of the period, gold processing was introduced from South America. The emergence of regional centers can be seen in sites like Barriles in Panama, which stand out due to their size and the presence of large anthropomorphic stone statues.

In Period V (AD 500–1000), significant changes are apparent in many regions. They are observable in settlements, architecture, burial customs, and material culture. In Greater Nicoya, the so-called Polychrome Period began, which indicated a stronger connection to Mesoamerica. The relocation of settlements to the coast and increased exploitation of marine resources can also be observed (Willey 1984: 350f). In the highlands of Costa Rica, the changes in architecture, burial customs, and ceramic styles indicate an influence from the south (Snarskis 1984: 219f). The settlement El Caño and the neighboring cemetery Sitio Conte in Panama indicate a strong social differentiation. Gold introduced in the previous period had taken on a new significance and was displacing jade as the most valued prestige item. Period VI (AD 1000–1550) witnessed a rapid increase in the number of settlements. In the highlands and the Atlantic coast of Costa Rica, large ceremonial centers such as Guayabo de Turrialba, Las Cabañas, and Las Mercedes were emerging. In Greater Nicoya, elements that show a clear influence from the Mexican highlands that had been traditionally associated with migratory movements of Mexican groups were present. When and how these migrations took place, and the extent to which they shaped the local culture is a topic of ongoing debate (McCafferty 2015; Steinbrenner 2010).

Questions regarding migration and the direction of cultural influences have played a major role from the very beginning and still greatly influence today's research. It is striking that cultural changes are repeatedly attributed to influences from various external sources, without providing a more precise source for these influences. Closely linked to this issue is the question of social complexity. Why did state-organized societies develop in Mesoamerica and the Andes, but not in Southern Central America? The concept of chiefdom as a form of sociopolitical organization plays a major role here and is frequently discussed. Simultaneously, some Caribbean archaeologists have dismissed this concept because they feel that it is more problematic than helpful when comparing societies due to it overgeneralizing the issue (Wilson 2007: 111). Another related question is the role of subsistence in the emergence of social hierarchy, in which the domestication of maize is paramount. In recent decades, researchers have begun to focus more on local developments, such as the interaction of coastal settlements and their hinterland or the complexity of coastal systems. The definition of culture areas within Southern Central America has not yet been agreed upon, and the definition of the culture area of Southern Central America itself will continue to be debated.

2.3 Caribbean

In a geographical sense, the Caribbean covers all landmasses bordering on or within the Caribbean Sea. In the west and southwest, the Caribbean is enclosed by the Central American mainland. In the south, it is limited by South America and, in the east and north, by numerous islands. Julian Steward (1948) defined the Circum-Caribbean Area, which includes the islands and the mainland. In the following years, however, research traditions took different directions and led to Caribbean archeology dealing mainly with the cultural history of the Caribbean Islands. These directions can be divided into three groups: 1) the Greater Antilles, including Cuba, Hispaniola, Jamaica, and Puerto Rico, 2) the Lesser Antilles, including the islands south of Puerto Rico, from the Virgin Islands in the north to Grenada in the south, and 3) the Bahama Archipelago. Although the Bahama Archipelago is geographically located in the Atlantic, it is considered a part of the Caribbean in cultural terms. In addition, there are numerous other Caribbean islands not covered by these three groups, including some islands off the South American mainland and the Bay Islands off the north coast of Honduras.

This research is characterized by regionalization with roots in geographic conditions. Research questions and related strategies differ across the islands due in part to the many nations involved in this research and their different political backgrounds. Similar to Southern Central America, archaeological research in the Caribbean has seen a boom in the last 30 years. Until the 1990s, the focus was on the creation of ceramic chronologies through small-scale excavations. Today, the chronological framework is widely known, and questions about sociopolitical organization, processes of cultural change, economic strategies, and iconography can be asked (Fitzpatrick 2015; Wilson 2007). Also, the idea of a Circum-Caribbean area and related questions about connections between the islands and the American mainland are being increasingly discussed (e.g., Geurds 2011; Hoopes 2017; Rodríguez Ramos 2013; Rodríguez Ramos / Pagán Jiménez 2006).

At the beginning of the 20th century, the cultural history of the Caribbean was divided into three phases (Fewkes 1922; Hatt 1924). Although the basic features of this three-part periodization are still valid today, it has been refined and further detailed. Even today, a major issue in Caribbean archeology is the conceptualization and terminology of these periods (Wilson 2007: 19f). Irving Rouse (1964) had a major influence on this topic. He developed a system that divided cultural history into series (suffix of -oid) and subseries (suffix of -an). Although this system has been criticized (e.g., Keegan / Rodríguez Ramos 2005) and other approaches have been developed, it is still widely used today.

The Archaic, referred to as Casimiroid by Rouse, is linked to the much-debated question of where the island's first inhabitants originated. Today, it is relatively certain that the occupation took place in several waves and from different locations. The Greater Antilles were settled around 4000 BC, with the oldest settlement vestiges found in Cuba and Hispaniola. While most researchers assume that these originate from the Central American mainland due to stylistic similarities of stone artifacts (Wilson 2007: 27-33), seafaring experiments show the possibility that settlers came from South America (Callaghan 2003; Fitzpatrick 2013: 107f). The Lesser Antilles—except for Tobago, which was still part of the mainland—were settled between 3000 BC and 2000 BC. Archaeological data indicate that colonization did not occur in a stepping-stone fashion, as long assumed, since older vestiges of human settlement are found on the northern islands (Wilson 2007: 46f).

With no further discernible waves of immigration for 1000 to 2000 years, the next period is marked by immigration from a group of farmer-potters from the South American mainland. This period is referred to as Saladoid by Rouse and covers 500 BC to AD 600. It is characterized by the introduction of ceramics (defined by white on red painting), the beginning of agriculture, and the installation of larger settlements. The Saladoid phenomenon stretches across the Lesser Antilles to the Dominican Republic and is expressed in several subseries.

Around AD 500, several changes are visible in the material culture and sociopolitical organization. The population grew and, at around AD 600, Jamaica and the Bahamas were populated for the first time. Sociopolitical hierarchy is discernible and reflected in changes to burial customs (Wilson 2007: 133). These changes are especially visible on Hispaniola and Puerto Rico, where large ceremonial centers emerged, such as Tibes and Caguana (Puerto Rico) or Atajizado and Chacuey (Hispaniola). Central plazas were an important feature of these settlements; they were used to hold ball games (batey) and ceremonies (areytos) (Oliver 2005). The new period heralded by these changes is called the Ostinoid series by Rouse. Some of the ceramic styles are characterized by the absence of painting, while appliqués and incised ornaments are common. Other important objects in material culture are cohoba idols, which were associated with the eponymous ritual in which hallucinogenic drugs were consumed. Another object category is represented by items considered to have supernatural powers, such as Cemís (also zemíes) or deity icons (Oliver 2009). These changes, which began around AD 600, continued and culminated in the Taíno culture encountered by the Spaniards. Reports by the Spaniards describe a distinctly hierarchical society with chiefs and polities that included several thousand people (Oliver 2005; Wilson 2007: 110).

Presumably due to the extensive nature of Spanish sources regarding the Caribbean Islands, the Ostinoid period has received less attention from archaeologists. In contrast, research has been focused on the early periods and questions regarding the islands' population. The Saladoid phenomenon has also received much attention. The main questions that require more research are: 1) what caused the emergence of social hierarchy, 2) what were the consequences of the clashes between different cultural groups (such as Archaic and Saladoid), and 3) what was the nature of the relationships between the inhabitants of different islands and their interisland networks. Questions of mobility and exchange in pre-Hispanic history are also related to this. Another big question relates to the long-distance interaction or connections between islands and the mainland. While evidence of contact, at least for the Lesser Antilles with South America, is quite clear, the issue of contact with the Central American mainland has only been given prominence in recent years (Rodríguez Ramos 2013).

2.4 AD 900–1525 in Middle America

After considering the different culture areas, their definitions, and a brief insight into their cultural histories, this section looks closer at the events and developments that took place from AD 900 to 1525. In northeast Honduras, this period is referred to as the Cocal period. It is usually defined as starting around AD 1000 (e.g., Healy 1984a). The period between AD 800 and 1000 is commonly referred to as the Transitional Selin period. During our research, however, it became clear that this phase of transition is very important for understanding the Cocal period and that the phenomena and characteristics of the Cocal period have their roots here. Thus, the events in these periods should not be considered separately. In the following, AD 900–1525 is defined as the period of study.

This 600 plus year period was very active, and the events at its beginning laid the foundation for later developments. It is noteworthy that we have ethnohistorical accounts available for this phase, which give us insights into aspects of the pre-Hispanic way of life that are not available to us from archaeological research alone. Ethnohistorical reports provide information about political relations, everyday life, customs, cosmovision, and individual stories. Tribute lists inform us about exchanged objects that cannot be proven in the archaeological context. Nevertheless, the interpretation of these sources is also a challenge, as we always have to consider the intentions, interests, and cultural background of the authors. The writings of the conquistadores are motivated by religious and political reasons. Their observations cannot be taken at face value but must be interpreted against the cultural background of medieval Spain (Keegan 2013: 70). Thus, it is often difficult to reconcile archaeological data and ethnohistorical observations. Paradoxically, as in the case of the Caribbean, due to the existence of written sources about the circumstances at the arrival of the Spanish, archaeological investigation has paid less attention to the late periods in many regions of the Americas. This is apparently because it was assumed that the sources already provided the necessary information.

Generally speaking, most regions of Middle America experienced population growth and increasing social hierarchy from AD 900 to 1525. Both ethnohistorical and archaeological sources indicate this. Especially in Southern Central America and in the Caribbean, settlements and centers of unprecedented size emerged. Raw materials and manufactured objects circulated in far-reaching exchange networks, and migrations took place, which can be traced especially well in Mesoamerica. These tendencies existed in previous periods, but they seem to have intensified during the late period. In the following, the principle cultural developments during the last 600 years before the arrival of the Spanish will be covered for the respective culture areas.

The strongest and most extensive data come from Mesoamerica. Here, the late pre-Hispanic period is heralded by the decline of the Classic centers such as Teotihuacán and the city-states in the Maya lowlands. These events had important effects on the existing sociopolitical system. The disappearance of signs of divine kingship and the centralization of power (e.g., palaces and stone monuments with portraits and inscriptions), especially in the Maya region, are clear signs of a change in the sociopolitical structure and of the fact that the institution of the divine kingship ceased to exist (Sharer / Traxler 2006: 499ff). These processes were accompanied by the decentralization of political power and economic structures, which had previously been strongly controlled by the elite. Michael Smith and Frances Berdan (2003b) provide a good overview of how conditions changed during the Postclassic period compared to the preceding Classic period. In contrast to the large, powerful Classic centers, many small polities now compete with each other. This is especially true for the period after the fall of Chichen Itza around AD 1200, which was an important center on the Yucatán Peninsula during the Early Postclassic period. In contrast to the Classic period's city-states, Chichen Itza is characterized as an international center, possibly governed by a supreme council (Sharer / Traxler 2006: 580). The decentralization of political power also impacted economic structures, which were also undergoing a process of decentralization. Whereas exchange had mainly been under the control of the elite until this point, luxury goods were now available to larger population groups and could be purchased at markets. Long-distance exchange increased, and larger quantities of goods began to be exchanged. In particular, this can be observed in obsidian, whose production and exchange grew rapidly during the Postclassic. Metal objects were also becoming increasingly popular and were exchanged over long distances as highly prized luxury items (Sharer / Traxler 2006: 576). At the same time, increasing standardization in exchanged goods can be observed, which facilitated transport, among other things. Ceramic styles, such as Tohil Plumbate or Fine Orange, were widely distributed during the Early Postclassic (Sharer / Traxler 2006: 590). In the Mexican highlands, markets gained importance, and the *pochteca* formed a group of professional traders. The use of currencies in the form of cocoa beans, axe-monies, and copper bells is interpreted as an indication of the increasing commercialization of the economy (Berdan 2003: 94). Maritime exchange routes seemed to play a particularly important role in this respect. A population shift to the coast can also be observed. Between AD 900 and 1500, about 80% of the Yucatán's population lived within a 50 km distance from the coast (Rathje / Sabloff 1973: 222).

Intensification of interaction between people is also evident in the spread of an "international" style and symbolism that can be found in large parts of Mesoamerica. This includes, for example, calendrical information, the spread of the feathered serpent motif, and new styles of sculpture and architecture (Boone / Smith 2003; Evans 2008: 350). The presence of this iconography in distant regions (e.g., Greater Nicoya) is linked to migratory movements that are believed to have occurred during the Postclassic period. The information about these migrations mainly comes from ethnohistorical sources but is often difficult to prove in an archaeological context—a clear example of compatibility issues between ethnohistorical and archaeological data (Evans 2008: 352).

For western and central Honduras, little data is available. However, it seems that the processes in the

Maya area by the end of the Classic period had a significant impact on the societies in Honduras that had connections with Maya centers during this period. Many of the centers in western Honduras were being abandoned, and it seems that some regions were experiencing a significant population decline. This has been noted for Santa Bárbara (Ashmore 1987), the Sula Valley (Robinson 1989), the El Cajón region (Hirth 2010), and the Jamastrán Valley (Hasemann / Lara Pinto / Sandoval Cruz 2017: 146). The site of Naco in western Honduras is one of the few known Period VI settlements. In contrast to these developments, around AD 1000, regions of northeast Honduras experienced a population increase, which is especially clear on the Bay Islands and adjacent mainland. The settlements grew, and a more formal site plan developed. Healy (1984a: 233) assumes an increasingly stratified site hierarchy and summarizes: "it seems, then, that the Northeast region was becoming more receptive by Period VI to contacts and influences from both its southern and its northern neighbors" (Healy 1984b: 156). George Hasemann and Gloria Lara Pinto (1993) draw a similar conclusion for the Mosquitia, where large centers were established during the Period VI. In a later publication, they state: "indeed, the scale of architecture and labor investment is unparalleled in the Central and Northern Zone in the century after the fall of Chichen Itza, around 1200 AD"[3] (Hasemann / Lara Pinto / Sandoval Cruz 2017: 154). Together, these reports paint a general picture of a society unaffected by the problems that influenced the west. Rather, eastern Honduras seems to have experienced an upsurge, while the west was in a state of decline[4].

Period VI also represents an increase in population and social stratification for many Southern Central America regions. At that time, the population was organized into chiefdoms, although the size and political organization of these entities are not entirely understood today (Hoopes 2001; Ranere 2008). In general, it appears that connections to Mesoamerica characterized the Pacific coast, while the Atlantic coast tended to have connections to the south (Willey 1984: 343). Greater Nicoya has long been regarded as a cultural subarea of Mesoamerica beginning in AD 800 at the latest (Lange 1984b). Similarities in the polychrome pottery, such as the feathered serpent motif or Tlaloc imagery, have been attributed to migratory movements from Mesoamerica. However, studies by Geoffrey McCafferty (McCafferty et al. 2012; McCafferty 2015) have shown that no direct migration movement can be identified in the archaeo-

logical evidence. They also demonstrate that ceramics are local productions, and only some elements were adopted from the Central Mexican highlands. At the same time, some researchers see a connection to central Honduras in ceramic styles from Nicoya (Lange 1984b: 179; Willey 1984: 351). While the Pacific coast of Nicaragua is relatively well explored, little is known about the developments on the Atlantic coast. Exceptions are the publications of Magnus (1974) and the research under the direction of Ermengol Gassiot Ballbé (e.g., Clemente-Conte / Gassiot Ballbé / Lechado Ríos 2009; Gassiot Ballbé 2006). This lack of research also contributes to the lack of clarity regarding the situation during Period VI. However, it is interesting to note that pottery apparently developed from painted vessels to unpainted vessels with incised decorations and appliqués.

On the other hand, the Atlantic coast of Costa Rica flourished during Period VI. Many large settlements emerged, which surpassed contemporaneous settlements in Greater Nicoya and those that previously existed. A distinct site hierarchy can be recognized (Snarskis 2003: 184f). These include Guayabo de Turrialba with a sophisticated aqueduct system, Las Mercedes, and La Zoila. Cobble-lined platforms and paved walkways are typical. In the architectural layout and the predominantly round buildings, Snarskis (2003: 188) sees a connection to South America. The presence of large stone statues portraying persons in the paramount centers may testify to the veneration of individual leaders. The depiction of trophy heads and war themes indicate conflicts (Hoopes 2007; Snarskis 2003: 192). Compared to earlier periods, the pottery is crude, and tripod supports with zoomorphic appliqués are typical (Snarskis 1984: 226). Evidence of vessels traded from Greater Nicoya are also present (Snarskis 2003: 190). For Greater Chiriquí in southwestern and western Panama, ethnohistorical sources testify to the geopolitical organization of the area, which was divided into several chiefdoms and whose borders were defended through conflict (Corrales / Badilla 2018). "From AD 600 onward, the Greater Chiriquí thrived as a region with a diverse settlement pattern, connected to regional trade routes linking Greater Nicoya and central Panama" (Geurds 2018: 14).

In Southern Central America, exchange of goods took place primarily between neighboring regions that were located in different ecological niches and had access to different resources. In Panama, some chiefs controlled coastal ports in order to secure access to marine resources. In addition, ethnohistorical sources report on

---

3 Translation from Spanish by the author.
4 The observations regarding the Mosquitia, including the statements by Hasemann and Lara Pinto, are largely based on unpublished reports, which makes their assessment difficult. Data from other regions (Olancho and Culmí) show that large settlements already existed here in the Selin phase and possibly represented the peak of settlement activities (Begley 1999: 190-196; Reyes Mazzoni 1976: 396).

markets where local and regional goods were exchanged (Cooke 2005: 155). Metal objects were among those that were exchanged over long distances. Elaborately crafted metal objects found in the Sacred Cenote in Chichen Itza were produced in Costa Rica and Panama. This clearly indicates that the inhabitants of these regions were in contact with each other.

In contrast to other regions, no significant change around AD 900/1000 has been observed concerning the cultural history of the Caribbean. The emergence of social complexity and thus, the last period before the arrival of the Spaniards is determined to be around AD 600. From this point on, the number of settlements in the Greater and Lesser Antilles increased significantly, and the exchange relations between the islands intensified (Fitzpatrick 2015: 324). While "there was little or any political organization that was above the village level" before this time (Wilson 2007: 110), in the Greater Antilles, the Spanish encountered a dense population and political units that included several thousand people. This society was later referred to as the Taíno culture. According to ethnohistorical reports, Hispaniola was divided into five provinces upon the arrival of the Spaniards, each of which covered more than 1000 km² and was governed by a paramount chief (Curet 2014). Besides the chiefs, or *caciques*, shamans played an important role in society (Keegan 2013: 73). The emergence of large ceremonial centers on Puerto Rico and Hispaniola also occurs in this period. The growing importance of central places, which can be observed between AD 900 and 1500, has been given extensive attention in the literature. Considerable work was invested in their construction; they were used for ceremonial purposes, which probably included ball games (*batey*) and public celebrations (*areytos*). The importance of these plazas is interpreted as a shift towards an increasing social hierarchy and the emergence of a centralized authority (Torres / Wilson 2014; Wilson 2007: 127f). Burials that were previously interred in central plazas were now placed in houses. This change is interpreted as a shift to a linearly-based social organization as opposed to a community-based or egalitarian organization, which is assumed to have previously existed. At the center of these events are the Greater Antilles, especially Puerto Rico and Hispaniola. "It is suggested that these Hispaniolan and Puerto Rican polities were expanding their network through exchange or perhaps even actively colonizing other areas of the Antilles around AD 1300/1400" (Mol / Mans 2013: 320).

For the Lesser Antilles, we also see an increase in social complexity and the number of settlements at the beginning of Period VI. Changes in different aspects of life are also noticeable. The sociopolitical form of organization is seen as "oscillating between extremes in the range of tribal and chiefdom organization" (Hofman 2013: 206). Above all, the increase in social complexity is seen in the existence and expansion of networks linking various political units on and between islands, which were based on controlling material goods and kinship ties (Hofman et al. 2007; Hofman 2013). From about AD 1200 onwards, the northern Lesser Antilles appear to be under the influence of the inhabitants of the Greater Antilles, and developments on Hispaniola and Puerto Rico were accompanied by a decline in population, possibly caused by migration to the south. On the other hand, the southern Lesser Antilles were densely populated until the arrival of the Spanish and were in close contact with the South American mainland, a fact that can be proven archaeologically, ethnohistorically, and linguistically (Hofman 2013).

2.5 The Northeast Honduras Region

Amid the large culture areas presented above lies the northeast Honduras region, in which our study area exists. Some authors see northeast Honduras as an distinct culture area, but its boundaries have been inconsistently defined throughout history. According to current knowledge, it roughly covers the following area (Begley 2000; Cuddy 2007: 6; Dennett 2007:14): The department of the Bay Islands, the department of Colón, the department of Olancho, and the western portion of the department of Gracias a Dios. The western border is drawn at La Ceiba. The eastern border is uncertain due to the state of research but is probably located somewhere east of the Patuca River. In the south, the region reaches approximately as far as Juticalpa or Catacamas in Olancho, while in the north, it includes the Bay Islands (Figure 3).

Since the state of research in the adjacent regions is relatively poor, it is to be expected that the definition will change with future research. The definition of the northeast Honduras area is firmly based on similarities in the material culture, especially during the Cocal period. The pottery is very similar and, at the same time, clearly distinguishes itself from the pottery in surrounding regions. There is also a lapidary tradition of working large quantities of greenstone and producing elaborately decorated metates. Ethnohistorical sources indicate that the region was politically united during the period before Spanish arrival and was organized in a kind of province. However, these sources provide incongruent information regarding this point (see chapter 2.5.4).

The following chapters serve to introduce the concept of the northeast Honduras region. The region's geography is described, and a summary of the research

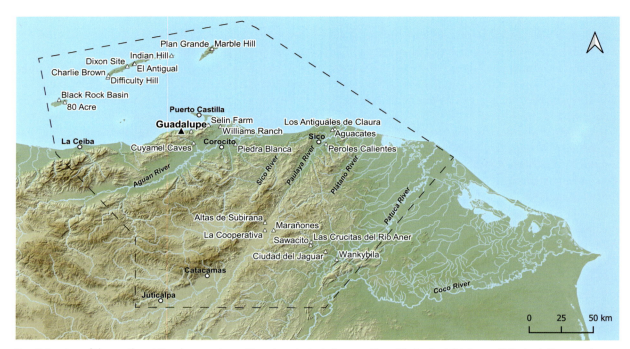

3 Extension of the northeast Honduras region with archaeological sites mentioned in the text (M. Lyons, F. Fecher). Topography derived from ASTER GDEM v3 elevation data (NASA 2019).

history provides an overview of the realized projects and the research strategies that have been applied. This is followed by an overview of the existing data from linguistics and ethnohistory, which, apart from archaeological data, constitute additional sources of information for understanding pre-Hispanic society and reconstructing possible networks during the Cocal period. The section concludes with an outline of traditional views of the region, looking at how it has been conceptualized and the models that were used to explain the unique situation of northeast Honduras.

2.5.1 Geography

With an area of about 112,000 km^2, Honduras is one of the larger countries on the Central American land bridge. In the north, the 735 km long Atlantic coast extends from the mouth of the Motagua River in the west to the Coco River in the east (Figure 4). Several islands are located off the coast. The Caribbean Bay Islands consist of three main islands, Utila, Roatán, and Guanaja, and several smaller islands and cays. In the southeast, Honduras borders Nicaragua, and in the south, it is limited by the narrow Pacific coast, which forms the Gulf of Fonseca. This zone is part of the Central American Volcanic Arc and includes several volcanic islands that belong to the Honduran territory. In the west, Honduras borders El Salvador and Guatemala.

Topographically, the country can be divided into three broad zones. Flat coastal plains run along the north and south, while the center of the country is characterized by mountain ranges that form part of the Central American Cordillera. The Pacific coast is the smallest geographical unit, with the coastal strip only extending about 25 km. The terrain becomes increasingly marshy near the coast, where mangrove forests are the predominant vegetation. The climate is tropical but somewhat drier compared to the north. The center of the country is characterized by two cordilleras that run roughly parallel to the coasts. Covering about 80% of the terrain, they constitute the most prominent topographic feature. The alternation between steep mountain ranges and plateaus results in a rugged landscape. Near La Esperanza and the capital Tegucigalpa, the mountains reach an altitude of 2700 m. While several rivers intersect the mountains, there is only a single large natural lake, the Lago de Yojoa, found in the western part of the country. In 1984, an artificial lake was created in the El Cajón region. Another interesting feature is the Comayagua Graben, a depression that extends from the north coast through the Comayagua Valley to the Pacific coast. The climate in the center of the country is also tropical but more moderate compared to the coasts. The vegetation is highly dependent on altitude and the types of available soil. In the western and southern part of the highlands, where thin, acidic soils predominate, oak and pine forests are common,

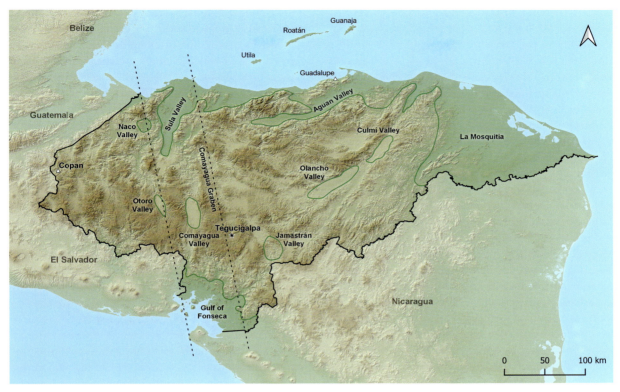

4   Geography of Honduras (M. Lyons, F. Fecher). Topography derived from ASTER GDEM v3 elevation data (NASA 2019).

while the east is dominated by tropical rainforests (Hasemann / Lara Pinto 1993: 151).

Today, the north coast forms the economic center of Honduras. The coastal strip is wide, and several large rivers form fertile alluvial plains. The widest of these plains is the Sula Valley, formed by the Chamelecón and Ulúa Rivers. San Pedro Sula, the industrial capital of the country, is also located here. Further east, the Aguán Valley runs parallel to the coast and is bordered by the Cordillera Nombre de Dios to the north. While the United Fruit Company used this fertile valley for extensive banana plantations until the 1930s, it is now an important location for the palm oil industry. To the east, the valley widens into the Mosquitia, the largest uninterrupted rainforest region in Central America today. In terms of infrastructure, the Mosquitia is scarcely developed; today, it can only be reached by boat or helicopter. The dense vegetation ranges from tropical savannahs and tropical rainforests to pine forests in the more elevated regions. Several brackish water lagoons dot the coast of the Mosquitia and are often associated with mangrove woodlands. The interior is characterized by large rivers that drain into the Atlantic, such as the Paulaya, the Plátano, or the Patuca. A tropical climate dominates the entire north coast, which is characterized by distinct dry and rainy seasons. The rainy season is often accompanied by the occurrence of hurricanes, which mostly affect the

Atlantic coast. The last major hurricane that hit Honduras was hurricane Mitch in 1998. It had catastrophic consequences for the country and its inhabitants.

The northeast Honduras region, as defined above, covers different environmental settings, with varied topographies, climates, vegetation, fauna, and natural resources. The Bay Islands and the Atlantic coast between La Ceiba and the Patuca River are characterized by their proximity to the Atlantic Ocean and the availability of marine resources. The ocean has served as an important route for communication and transportation. The coastal area with the fertile Aguán Valley offers excellent conditions for agricultural activities. In contrast, the dense forests of the Mosquitia are home to tropical hardwoods such as ceiba and mahogany, which could be used as construction material for architecture and canoes. Canoes were likely the most important means of transport, enabling movement and communication along the rivers. The various ecological niches with their diverse flora and fauna create a species-rich environment with a wide-ranging variety of food, while the rivers and their numerous tributaries provide freshwater. In addition to these resources, greenstone sources, which played an important role in the production of jewelry, have been identified both in the Bay Islands and in the Mosquitia (Begley 1999: 175ff; Harlow 1993: 15). Precious metals are also found in small concentrations in the rivers of the Mosquitia.

2.5.2 History of Research

Knowledge of pre-Hispanic developments in northeast Honduras is based on only a few research projects. Research began in the first half of the 20th century and was shaped by explorers who undertook expeditions, often commissioned by US museums. One of the purposes of these expeditions was to collect artifacts for the museum archives, which in turn affected the research strategy. At the beginning of the 20th century, Herbert Spinden was one of the first to travel to northeast Honduras on behalf of the Peabody Museum (Spinden 1925). In his investigations, he concentrated on searching for stylistic elements of Maya culture in the local artifacts. In his opinion, the local cultures were strongly influenced by the Maya culture and, after its decline, were driven out by groups from the south. However, Spinden based this hypothesis on linguistic and ethnohistorical data. At the same time, Eduard Conzemius, born in Luxembourg, was researching in northeast Honduras. He mainly collected information on the colonial period and ethnography but also made some observations regarding archaeological finds (Conzemius 1927, 1928).

In the 1930s, research interest in the Bay Islands and the region around Trujillo increased. This was directly linked to the expansion of the banana industry and the infrastructure that accompanied it. In 1930, Frederick Mitchell-Hedges went to the Bay Islands, where he carried out surveys and test excavations. In the following year, the Boekelman Shell Heap Expedition visited northeast Honduras, in which the young Junius Bird participated as an archaeologist. Besides excavations on Utila, the expedition also explored the mainland, concentrating on the region around Puerto Castilla and the Aguán Valley. The results of the two expeditions were not published, but researchers later had access to their accounts and partly summarized the results in their publications (see Epstein 1957; Strong 1935).

Also, in the 1930s, William Duncan Strong came to Honduras on behalf of the Smithsonian Institution. He also chose the area around Trujillo as the starting point for his research and explored the coast towards the east. Along the Patuca River, he documented several archaeological sites and conducted some excavations (Strong 1934). In the same year, he undertook an expedition to the Bay Islands, where he described numerous sites and carried out excavations (Strong 1935). Strong's work has been well-published and is still an important basis for understanding the archaeology of these areas.

Doris Stone documented additional sites. As the daughter of the then-president of the United Fruit Company, Samuel Zemurray, she had access to many archaeological sites discovered during the clearing activities for banana plantations. Her research area was concen-

trated along the Aguán, Sico, and Paulaya Rivers (Stone 1934a, 1941). In most cases, her observations were limited to surface finds. She also tended to relate the archaeological remains directly to ethnographic and linguistic data, which was sometimes considered critical by her colleagues (see Andrews V / Lange 1995: 96; Joyce 2001: 1212). Her monograph with numerous illustrations still serves as an important reference today. In 1950, Alfred Kidder II, Gordon Ekholm, and Gustav Stromsvik carried out research on Utila, where they conducted excavations in the 80 Acres site. The expedition later documented several sites on the mainland. In 1953, the German geographer Karl Helbig undertook a reconnaissance survey to the Mosquitia, during which he made insightful observations on archaeological and cultural elements (Helbig 1956).

Most researchers only had a vague idea of the chronological depth of their finds until the first chronology was created in 1957 by Jeremiah Epstein. He tried to cross-date the material from northeast Honduras with the ceramics from the better-known Maya area (Epstein 1957, 1959). Since he did not visit Honduras himself, he mainly used material from Kidder, Ekholm, and Stromsvik and supplemented it with Bird and Strong's excavation reports. He defined the two successive phases Selin and Cocal, which he divided into an early and a late phase, respectively. This chronology was now used as the basis for the entire northeast region.

In the 1970s, the chronology was extended by Paul Healy and confirmed by the first application of ^{14}C analyses. Healy carried out surveys and excavations at five sites southeast of Trujillo (Healy 1984a). His work was the first and only multi-year project to carry out excavations at several sites on the northeast coast. The discovery of Formative period pottery, which had been deposited in the so-called Cuyamel Caves and displayed Olmec elements, enabled Healy to expand Epstein's chronology to include an early period. According to his definition, the Cuyamel phase extends from 1350 to 400 BC. Consequently, Healy's chronology has a gap of about 700 years, which has still not been successfully filled by subsequent investigations (see Figure 2). To this day, finds from caves (Talgua and Cuyamel) remain the only evidence of Formative occupation in northeast Honduras. No remains of settlements have been identified so far. Based on his observations, Healy revised Epstein's statement that there had been strong connections to the western Sula valley and the Maya area during the Selin phase. In this phase, he sees mostly local developments and only limited external influences. For the first time, he also made observations about subsistence during the Selin phase. Later, Carrie Dennett (2007) worked on a portion of the material recovered by Healy at Río Claro and helped to refine the ceramic typology of the Cocal phase.

Later on in the 1970s, the Honduran Institute of Anthropology and History (IHAH) undertook several expeditions to the Bay Islands (Epstein / Véliz 1977; Hasemann 1977; Véliz / Willey / Healy 1977). These investigations were mainly limited to surveys. Vito Véliz, an employee of the IHAH at that time, published an analysis of the pottery from the Piedra Blanca site (Véliz 1978). In the 1980s, the "Proyecto de la Costa Norte", initiated by Robert Sharer, carried out a surface survey in the departments of Colón and Atlántida in order to prove whether there were any Formative period sites in this region (Sharer / Sedat / Pezzati 2009). However, no Formative sites could be identified. Another survey project took place as part of Operation Raleigh in the Mosquitia. The team explored pre-Hispanic and colonial settlements along the Rio Tinto (Clark / Dawson / Drake 1982). A second expedition followed in 1985 under the leadership of Mark Horton (Oxford University) and Fiona Wilmot (Cambridge University). It mainly identified settlements on the Islands, but the results were not published.

A large-scale settlement study took place in the 1990s under the direction of Christopher Begley in the Culmí Valley in Olancho. Through a combination of surveys and test excavations, Begley successfully reconstructed the cultural developments in the valley (Begley 1999). Thomas Cuddy did not carry out any excavations of his own but published previously unpublished data from Strong and summarized the available research results on northeast Honduras (Cuddy 2007). He developed the theory that northeast Honduras formed an overarching political organization that led to the region's cultural independence. Consequently, from about AD 300, a common material culture prevailed throughout the entire area, while regional differences also developed due to geographical conditions.

In 2008, the Roatán Project, directed by Christian Wells, was initiated to explore the Caribbean island (Figueroa 2011; Goodwin 2011). The project had to be canceled prematurely, however, because of the 2009 coup. Due to the political upheaval that followed, and the precarious security situation, foreign archaeologists' activities in Honduras sharply declined. The IHAH initiated the still-ongoing Proyecto Sitios Clave during this period. Its objective is to document as many sites as possible on the north coast and in other less explored regions and to prevent their destruction. Recently, LIDAR flights in the Mosquitia drew attention to Honduran archaeology (Fisher et al. 2016). Apart from the activities

in the Mosquitia, excavations are also being conducted in Selin Farm under the direction of Whitney Goodwin (Goodwin 2019).

2.5.3 Linguistics

At the time of Spanish arrival, the territory of present-day Honduras was inhabited by many different linguistic and ethnic groups. The reconstruction of these groups is somewhat difficult since we lack early sources for many regions. The period of the Conquista was very dynamic, resulting in the displacement, decimation, and disappearance of indigenous groups. Nevertheless, some researchers (e.g., Campbell 1976; Holt / Bright 1976; Kirchhoff 1943; Lothrop 1939; Thompson 1970) have used the limited available data to reconstruct the linguistic mosaic that existed at the arrival of the Spanish. Today, there is general agreement that the following groups were present (Healy 1984b):

1. Maya (Chortí and Chontal), Mesoamerican-affiliated language, western Honduras
2. Jicaque (also Tolupan), Mesoamerican-affiliated language, northern Honduras
3. Lenca, Mesoamerican-affiliated language, southern and central Honduras
4. Nahua (Pipil), Mesoamerican-affiliated language, enclaves
5. Mangue, Mesoamerican-affiliated language, southern Honduras
6. Pesh/Pech[5] (formerly known as Paya), Chibchan-language, northeast Honduras
7. Ulva, Matagalpa linguistic group, southern Honduras
8. Tawahka (Sumu), Chibchan-language, eastern Honduras

The Miskito that now reside in eastern Honduras are a group that only formed after the Conquista (Potthast 1988: 59-69). The Garifuna, which today inhabit parts of the north coast, first came to Honduras in the 18th century. The diversity and variety of languages exemplify Honduras's character as an active, transitional region with links to many other areas.

It is assumed that the northeast was mostly inhabited by Paya-speaking groups (known today as Pesh). However, some researchers mention the possibility of the presence of Jicaque, Nahua, and Tawahka in parts of the area (Conzemius 1932:14; Fowler 1983; Stone 1941: 8).

---

5 The two spellings represent phonetic differences which correspond to variations in dialect. Traditionally, Pech is written with "ch" (spoken [tʃ]). However, many people today pronounce it "Pesh" [ʃ]. Since in most regions the variety with "sh" is used, it is preferred in the following text.

Pesh is currently considered as belonging to the Chibcha languages. This language family was first defined by Max Uhle (1890). Although the Muisca culture in Colombia underlies the definition of the Chibcha language family, the origin of the Chibcha languages today is assumed to be in Costa Rica and Panama, not Colombia. A proto-Chibcha language was also identified there. This means that it is an autochthonous, local development and that the speakers of the Chibcha languages originated there and did not, as previously assumed, immigrate from South America (Hoopes 2005: 12; Hoopes / Fonseca 2003: 55f; Fonseca / Cooke 1993: 219). Chibcha languages can be found throughout Southern Central America to northern South America and include languages such as Bribri, Cabécar, Teribe, Kuna, Kogi, and Muisca (Constenla Umaña 1991, 1995; Quesada Pacheco 2008). The widespread distribution and the formation of the largest language group in this area led to the designation of Southern Central America as the Chibcha region by Fonseca (1992). The relationship between the Pesh language and other Chibchan languages is not clear. It is uncertain whether the Pesh language corresponds to a group that migrated north from the core area or whether it is possibly a "remnant" of a formerly larger area (Hoopes / Fonseca 2003: 55). In any case, Constenla Umaña (1995) points out that Pesh is the most isolated of the Chibchan languages and assumes, based on glottochronological data, that it must have split off by 4000 BC from the core language.

2.5.4 Ethnohistory

Ethnohistorical data give us an insight into aspects that archaeological data alone cannot reveal. Therefore, they are an important additional source of information to reconstruct possible networks. At the same time, it is often problematic to reconcile archaeological and ethnohistorical data. Moreover, we see that data from ethnohistorical reports are sometimes adopted uncritically and influence archaeological research.

In the following, a short overview of the existing sources from the early colonial period is given, and the information they can provide us about the societies of the time is summarized. Although the ethnohistorical reports for Honduras are not as extensive as those available for Mesoamerica or the Andes, the region around Trujillo in particular plays a central role in early colonial history. Columbus first encountered the American

mainland here during his 4th voyage in 1502. Before that, the crew had stopped on the island of Guanaja. Columbus himself did not recount much about his stay in Honduran waters. The records of his son Ferdinand, who accompanied his father when he was 13 years old, are an important source. He wrote his report "The Life of the Admiral Christopher Columbus (Historia del Almirante Don Cristóbal Colón)" (1959 [1571]) many years later back in Spain[6]. Another eyewitness report comes from Diego de Porras, who accompanied the 4th journey as a scribe (Porras 1825-37). Bartolomé de las Casas (1986) also gives information about the 4th voyage. He most likely had access to one of Ferdinand's manuscripts. He did not accompany the journey.

After the first landing of Columbus in 1502, the Honduran mainland remained unaffected for the next 20 years, and the Conquista did not begin until around 1524. However, by this time, the Bay Islands were already almost depopulated, as, from 1516 onwards, the indigenous population was shipped to Cuba as slaves (Cortés 1866: 477). The first years of the Conquista were turbulent, and most Spanish settlements were abandoned before long. Various conquistadors competed for the territory. Due to the great distance from the colonial centers in Mexico and Peru, the conquistadors were hardly subject to any control and took advantage of the lack of regulations. It was not until 1536 that the Spanish were able to consolidate their power (Lara Pinto 1980: 10). In these first years, the Spaniards' activity was limited to the northwest and northeast. Thus, today, the available written sources are as well[7]. The sources offer information about some aspects of pre-Hispanic life. Of particular importance here is information on the identity of the inhabitants of that time, their sociopolitical organization, and aspects of mobility and existing networks.

The most often quoted passage from the reports of the 4th voyage is the encounter of the Spanish with a canoe in Guanaja. The canoe carried several people and numerous commodities, which were interpreted as trade goods. The event is repeatedly cited as evidence of trade between northeast Honduras and Yucatán (e.g., Smith / Berdan 2003a: 3), but this information is not apparent from primary sources (Edwards 1978: 203; Lara Pinto 1980: 34-37). Instead, the primary sources indicate that the canoe passengers came from Guanaja and that the exchange took place with inhabitants of the Honduran mainland. The fact that the canoe originated in Yucatán is actually a conjecture of Las Casas, who relied on Fer-

---

6 The work was first published in 1571. However, Ferdinand died in 1539, so he must have written it before then (Lara Pinto 1980: 33).

7 For a detailed description of the existing sources and the events in the early colonial period see Lara Pinto (1980) and Stone (1941).

dinand's records. Ferdinand suspected that the boat came from New Spain, that is, from the north (New Spain is a political entity established by the colonial rulers that did not yet exist at the time of the event), and Las Casas further narrowed this information down by assuming that Yucatán was its origin. Nevertheless, this passage is repeatedly quoted to refer to far-reaching exchange relationships during the Postclassic period. However, apart from the question of the canoe's origin, the story provides important information: 1) the inhabitants of the Bay Islands maintained exchange relations, and 2) goods were transported by sea.

A central aspect that the sources can provide is the ethnic identity of the inhabitants of northeast Honduras. The sources construct a dichotomy that has influenced the conceptualization of the area in archaeology. The dichotomous view has its origins in a story about an interpreter that the Spaniards took with them from Guanaja in order to communicate on the mainland. According to Ferdinand (1959: 232f), this interpreter was sent home at Cape Gracias a Dios because he was no longer able to understand the region's inhabitants. This report suggests that 1) the same or a similar language was spoken on the islands and the mainland until Cape Gracias a Dios, and 2) the language east of the cape was so different from this language that the interpreter was unable to communicate. Unfortunately, the sources do not clarify which languages are meant, partly because the interpreter's origin cannot be clearly determined (Lara Pinto 1980: 34).

As shown above, linguists today assume that the Chibcha languages were spoken here, and it is widely accepted that the ancestors of today's Pesh settled northeast Honduras. Nevertheless, the question of ethnic identity has not been fully resolved, and other possible groups need to be considered in the reconstruction of the region's prehistory. Some researchers are convinced that during the Cocal period, there were enclaves of Nahua-speaking Pipiles in the northeast of Honduras (Fowler 1983; Lara Pinto 1991), which came there through migration from the Mexican highlands. Their postulations are based on ethnohistorical and linguistic data. These include, for example, information from Cortés, who came to Honduras in 1525, stating that his interpreter, who in all probability was capable of speaking Nahuatl, was able to communicate in the region around Trujillo (Cortés 1866: 465). Further arguments are word lists and the numerous Nahua place names that appear in the region. In the archaeological context, however, such a presence has not yet been proven (for a contrary opinion, see Lara Pinto 1991). Another more moderate opinion is that Nahua may have acted as a kind of lingua franca, which was connected to the expansion of the trade network from the Mexican highlands (Lara Pinto 1980: 60f).

Finally, the sources also provide information about the sociopolitical organization in the area before Spanish arrival. In 1525, the first Spanish city of Honduras was founded in Trujillo. This place was not chosen by chance. The Spanish foundation was established on the site of a former indigenous settlement. The region had a high population density, which guaranteed the Spaniards' supply of workforce, foodstuffs, and goods. Cortés commissioned the islanders to supply the Spanish with fish, which indicates that a network already existed between the islands and the mainland (Lara Pinto 1980: 78). Finally, Trujillo also offered an infrastructurally well-connected point of operations. The settlement was equipped with a well-controllable port and a connection to the hinterland via the Aguán River.

Apparently, the region around Trujillo was structured into some form of geopolitical units. Sources refer to "provinces", although the exact organization or function of these units is not clear (Lara Pinto 1980: 70-76). Cortés (1866: 465) mentions two provinces in Trujillo's vicinity: Chapagua (Champagua) and Papayeca. The latter is mentioned in connection with the rebellious behavior of its inhabitants. Peicacura was probably part of the province of Papayeca, which is located in today's Aguán Valley (Lara Pinto 1980: 101f). Also, the term Taguzgalpa is often mentioned in the sources. However, there seems to be some confusion among the authors. Based on the writings of Francisco Vázques, Stone (1941: 8; also adopted by Cuddy 2007) understands the area between Trujillo and the Rio Sico as Taguzgalpa, while Lara Pinto and Hasemann (1988: 11) state that Taguzgalpa was understood to mean the region along the Rio Sico. Conzemius (1927: 267) writes that the entire Atlantic coast from the Aguán River in Honduras to the Rio San Juan in Nicaragua initially belonged to this geopolitical formation, while later it only included the Honduran Mosquitia.

All in all, the ethnohistorical sources of Honduras are an interesting field that can provide important insights into the situation upon Spanish arrival. At the same time, however, the sources concerning our area of investigation have not been sufficiently analyzed. A great deal of work and research will be needed, especially regarding the primary sources, to better assess the reliability and informative value of these sources.

2.5.5 Traditional Views on the Region

Throughout archaeological, linguistic, and ethnohistoric research, our understanding of northeast Honduras has grown, and research projects have made significant contributions to reconstruct key aspects of pre-Hispanic history. However, to this day, the way in which the region is perceived is strongly impacted by the influences received from adjacent culture areas. This view has its origins in the very beginning of research in the area when it was an important focus to define the culture area's boundaries (e.g., Lothrop 1939; Spinden 1917; Stone 1934b, 1939). Northeast Honduras' distinct location at the intersection of several culture areas resulted in archaeological investigation focusing on the relationship and attribution of the area to the surrounding regions. In the early stages of research, attempts were made to assign the region to one of the culture areas. It was interpreted as either the southern part of Mesoamerica or the northern part of Southern Central America. Connections to the Caribbean are only considered in a few exceptional cases. Similarities were explained with the vague notion of "influences" from various directions, which the inhabitants of northeast Honduras received as passive recipients. It was only with more recent research that new approaches were found that also emphasize local developments and characterize these interregional interactions more precisely. The way in which northeast Honduras has been conceptualized in terms of interaction and the theoretical models that have been applied will be shown in the following. These developments are to be seen in the broader context of the conceptualization of Southern Central America and the southern frontier of Mesoamerica.

The first research publications show clear signs of the culture-historical approach and diffusionism as an explanation for culture change. Spinden, for example, assumes that the culture of the Chorotegan Culture Area, to which he considers northeast Honduras a part, is "built historically on Mayan ideas" (Spinden 1925: 34). In the region's artifacts, he sees an adoption of stylistic motifs from the Maya region. The present-day "barbarian" tribes had immigrated from South America and drove out the local population after the collapse of the powerful empires in the north. On the one hand, it becomes clear that the Maya culture is seen as a civilized center whose influences extend into the surrounding areas. On the other hand, the importance of migration as an explanation for cultural change becomes apparent. This is also evident in the writings of Stone. In her monograph on the Honduran north coast (Stone 1941), she addresses settlement areas of various ethnic groups in pre-Hispanic times. In particular, she reconstructs them with ethnohistorical and linguistic data. Concerning the expansion of the Maya region, she notes:

"From here [the Ulúa River] eastward, there is no evidence of the spoken [Maya] language. However,

based on archaeological evidence, artifacts bearing a definite Maya relationship have been found as far east as Trujillo. This bears out the historical references to a Maya region continuing to Caxinas[8]. The Jicaque [...] may have been pushed back by the Maya or may have been intermixed with them" (Stone 1941: 15).

She continues on to cite reasons for the Maya's presence in the Ulúa Valley, Lake Yojoa, and the Comayagua Valley. Strikingly, she equates the presence of elements attributed to Maya culture (dressed stone, glyph inscriptions, etc.) with linguistic data and the presence of Maya ethnic groups. Northeast Honduras, in turn, is considered the settlement area of the Paya. Especially in ceramics, Stone sees a strong stylistic link to the south, such as Costa Rica, Panama, and South America (Stone 1941: 95).

William D. Strong initially directed his research toward defining the southern extension of Maya settlement as well (Strong 1934). During his expeditions to the Bay Islands and the northeast mainland, he made detailed observations of the material culture. In contrast to Spinden, however, he did not observe any signs of Maya presence. Instead, he saw a strong resemblance to finds in Costa Rica and certain "Antillean resemblances" (Strong 1934: 52; Strong 1948c: 77). His detailed observations and the consideration of interactions in all possible directions are exceptional. Like his predecessors, however, he does not go beyond the definition of "influences."

Epstein (1957) also attempts to clarify the various cultural influences in his analysis of ceramics. He is the first to give them a temporal depth. In the Selin phase's mainly bichrome and polychrome painted vessels, he sees strong connections to the western Sula Valley and the Maya culture. He notes that, in the early Selin phase,

"The culture of the Bay Islands and the Olancho valley is considered to be largely an eastern extension of Ulua valley culture [...]. A number of similarities between Selin and Maya shapes and designs suggest that the Selin horizon culture was strongly influenced by Lowland Maya culture [...]" (Epstein 1959: 126).

In the Cocal phase, this influence disappeared, and monochrome vessels with incised decoration and appliqué style prevailed. Epstein also sees a strong connection here to the cultures in Nicaragua and Costa Rica. The most critical element on which these observations

---

8 "Caxinas" refers to the headland near Trujillo, today called Puerto Castilla.

are based is the similarity of the vessel supports and handles, which make up a large percentage of the ceramic material in the entirety of Southern Central America. He also sees apparent similarities in the lithic inventory. Apart from this, he identifies forms that he considers local developments present throughout the entire chronological sequence.

In the 1970s, trade studies emerged as a new approach, and aspects of economic anthropology became a focus. Trade relations now served as the new most important approach to the study of interaction and cultural change. This approach is also evident in the theoretical orientation of the projects in Honduras at that time. Research began focusing on the Bay Islands specifically, which were assumed to have played an important role in pre-Hispanic trade. The projects initiated in the Bay Islands in the 1970s were aimed at studying trade between the islands and the mainland and possibly identifying a port of trade (Epstein / Véliz 1977: 28), as defined by Anne Chapman (1957) for Mesoamerica. However, the investigations, which mainly concentrated on surveys, found only a few small settlements on the coast, which to a certain extent contradicted the theory (Epstein 1978: 156).

With his research near Trujillo in the 1970s, Healy initially pursued the traditional question regarding the definition of the southern border of Mesoamerica as well (Healy 1974, 1974b). His excavations at several sites represent the most extensive excavation work to date and make an important contribution to the characterization of the local material culture. For the first time, observations on settlement structure and the differences between the Selin and Cocal phases are possible. Healy (1983) was also the first to carry out investigations on subsistence. These extensive data allow him to draw a more refined picture of pre-Hispanic cultural history and emphasize local developments. He takes a different position than his predecessors regarding the influences of neighboring culture areas. For the Selin phase, he writes,

"Our picture, then, contrasts considerably with that of Epstein's (1957) view, and most others who preceded him. Maya contacts with the northeast region seem virtually nonexistent. At best there was limited and probably sporadic trade with the Ulua Valley [...]. Neither does the south appear to contribute much to Early and Basic Selin cultural patterns. By and large, our picture of the region is one of local developments" (Healy 1984a: 232).

For the Transitional Selin period (AD 800–1000), Healy sees the onset of influences from Southern Central America in the material culture but, based on the current data, he deliberately omits further statements regarding the motives for or nature of this stronger influence. He also views Cocal-period material culture as very close to that of Southern Central America. However, he points to individual objects that indicate contact (possibly trade) with Mesoamerica, such as copper bells, plumbate pottery, Naco polychrome, and an increased amount of obsidian. In summary, he characterizes northeast Honduras as a frontier zone that was more affiliated with Mesoamerica during the early phases, especially during the Cuyamel period, and in later phases, was "stimulated more by Lower Central America" (Healy 1984a: 236).

The frontier concept was related to the emerging interest in the interaction between state and non-state organized societies. This, in turn, goes back to the introduction of world-systems theory, originally formulated by Immanuel Wallerstein in 1974. It still serves as one of the most popular theories for the study of interregional interaction. World-systems theory was widely used for the study of Mesoamerica (Blanton / Feinman 1984; Carmack / Salgado González 2006; Pailes / Whitecotton 1979; Smith / Berdan 2003b). This was accompanied by the increased use and discussion of the terms frontier, boundary, and periphery (e.g., Hirth 1988; Pahl 1987; Robinson 1987; Schortman / Urban 1986, 1991, 1994) and the conceptualization of Honduras as a peripheral area of the adjacent culture areas. Hasemann and Lara Pinto (1993) create an alternative concept called the *Zona Central* (central zone). The zone encompasses the modern territory of Honduras and El Salvador and the Pacific region of Nicaragua. The *Zona Central* attempts to end the perspective that the area is just an extension or annex of the larger culture regions and places less emphasis on borders. The *Zona Central* is instead understood as a space of interaction where independent cultural developments are emphasized.

Begley (1999), during his research in the Culmí Valley, discovered structures that he interprets as ballcourts as well as settlements that have a rectangular arrangement around a central plaza. He sees both architectural elements as influences from Mesoamerica. He was the first to reflect on the motives for these influences in detail, looking for internal explanations within the society. Begley assumes that, during Period V, an increasingly stratified social hierarchy developed in the Culmí Valley, and an elite emerged that "emulated or copied the models of the great societies in the North, possibly the only example available"[9] (Begley 2002: 42). According to Begley, the newly emerging elite, with its affiliation to the more

---

9 Translation from Spanish by the author.

"complex" societies to the west, pursued an increase in prestige and an expansion of power through the expression of cosmology and the "esoteric knowledge" that is associated with architectural features. With this, Begley follows Mary Helms theory of esoteric knowledge (Helms 1979). In my opinion, the application of this theoretical approach has weak points. The theoretical assumptions are based on very limited data[10]. Although internal factors are considered, the persistence of complexity is nevertheless attributed to external influences, and the complex societies of Mesoamerica are stylized as models. However, what the interaction between the two areas is supposed to have looked like is ultimately not clarified. Lara Pinto (1991) takes an even more extreme view, attributing the presence of monumental architecture in northeast Honduras to Nahua groups that immigrated from Mesoamerica. In doing so, she relies on ethnohistorical and some linguistic data, which, in my opinion, are insufficient to support such a theory. Internal factors for the development of social complexity are wholly denied to the inhabitants of the region.

In marked contrast to these theories that search for the origin of phenomena of social complexity in neighboring regions is the research led by John Hoopes, who attempts to characterize Southern Central America based on local characteristics and internal developments. He and his colleagues show that the population of Southern Central America is not, as previously assumed, characterized by migratory movements but that long-established local, autochthonous traditions characterize the region. They also emphasize indigenous developments on the isthmus. Dennett (2007: 81) relies on these new research results for her interpretative approach. Whereas research was previously focused on connections to Mesoamerica, she is the first to closely look at the relationships to Southern Central America. Her studies focus on the Cocal phase. Dennett develops a frontier model that conceptualizes northeast Honduras as a northern frontier of Southern Central America. She defines a frontier as "populations residing at the geographical extent (or hinterland beyond the 'core') of a culture area whose physical boundaries fluctuate both spatially and temporally" (Dennett 2007: 82). She considers the origin region

of the Chibcha languages in Costa Rica and western Panama as a possible core. Furthermore, she speculates that the population of northeast Honduras corresponds to a group from the core that had split off due to migration and continued to maintain cultural ties with the area of origin. She tries to demonstrate these connections with similarities in the cultural material. In Dennett's work, the relationship between core and frontier is characterized primarily by a spatial relationship, whereby the frontier has a connection to the core that is rooted in a common ancestry and is visible in various areas of life. Due to the distance and the area of origin's lack of control, cultural transformations take place, which form the basis of the unique cultural repertoire in northeast Honduras. Nevertheless, this approach creates a static picture of cultural relationships and does not offer any tools to examine interaction as a process.

In contrast to Dennett, Cuddy (2007) describes northeast Honduras during the Cocal phase as developing a strong identity vis-à-vis the surrounding regions. Cuddy sees this identity as conscious political action, as a power strategy, and thus agrees with Begley.

"[...] the polities of northeast Honduras successfully engaged in corporate strategies of inclusion, promoting a national or political identity constructed from both local and distant cultural traditions that allowed them to maintain political and social cohesion for an extended duration within a setting of political competition" (Cuddy 2007: 11).

Like Begley, he focuses on local processes, concentrating on the political level. He concludes that the elite tried to strengthen their power ideologically through long-distance interaction but that it was ineffective. The population did not adopt the exotic ideology, but the local belief systems, expressed in material culture, especially ceramics, persisted (Cuddy 2007: 136).

In her master's thesis, Goodwin (2011) summarizes research at the Cocal-period site of El Antigual on Roatán. She investigates the relationship between the inhabitants of the Bay Islands and the mainland. In doing so, she uses an approach similar to Cuddy's by exam-

---

10 The only arguments that Begley presents as a connection to Mesoamerica are the presence of parallel structures in two settlements, which are defined as ballcourts without further verification, and monumental architecture arranged around central plazas. Regarding the material culture, he writes (2004: 291): "Hay algunos artefactos portátiles en el Oriente de Honduras, que claramente muestran una conexión con Mesoamérica, como la obsidiana. Hay una cantidad impresionante de piedra verde también, pero casi toda proviene de fuentes de piedra verde blanda y no de jadeíta. Estas están ubicadas en La Mosquitia y posiblemente en las Islas de la Bahía. Estos artefactos son evidencia de una interacción

o una influencia mesoamericana, pero no indican presencia de población mesoamericana." Here, objects are interpreted as a connection to Mesoamerica, where none exists, which Begley himself emphasizes regarding greenstone. Concerning the obsidian, he states in his dissertation (1999: 157) that, in the entire Culmí Valley, only nine obsidian fragments were found, seven flakes and two prismatic blades. He states that the source of the obsidian is unknown (1999: 157). So, obviously, no provenience analyses were carried out. The statement that the material culture shows a connection to Mesoamerica lacks any foundation here.

ining the social identity of the inhabitants. She also assumes that ceramics express a common social identity, which strengthens the inclusive group identity. She suspects a conscious political strategy behind this. "[...] indigenous populations of this region appropriated symbols and designs in an emblematic manner to express a common identity and reinforce a cultural practice of inclusiveness" (Goodwin 2011: intro). The fact that the objects also have a certain similarity with the material culture of neighboring regions is explained by the fact that "they sought to define themselves in relation to groups but not as part of them" (Goodwin 2011: 23). Goodwin goes on to argue that the aim of the elite, in contrast to centralized societies such as the Maya, is not so much to enrich themselves with luxury goods but rather to create a communal identity. In doing so, she follows the ideas of Karl Polanyi (Polanyi et al. 1957), who emphasizes the social component of trade studies. She also refers to theories that consider a heterarchical organization of societies to be more stable due to its greater flexibility (McAnany 2004; Parkinson / Galaty 2007). "Extreme exploitation and the accumulation of resources were not necessarily central goals in an environmentally self-sustaining region, and the practice appears to have contributed ultimately to long-term cultural stability in the region" (Goodwin 2011: intro). In her study, Goodwin closely looks at several levels of interaction. By considering the relationship between islanders and mainlanders, her focus on the regional level is new and adds an important level of observation to the previous studies. However, compared to the archaeological data on which these assumptions are based, the theoretical implications seem very detailed, an issue that Goodwin addresses by stating: "While many brilliant minds have theorized about the endless possibilities for the prehispanic settlements in northeast Honduras, considerably little work has actually been done on the ground" (Goodwin 2011: 139). In her study on Selin Farm (Goodwin 2019), Goodwin uses the communities of consumption approach to examine the extent to which social identity is expressed in ceramic styles and foodways. By using this approach, she is the first to concentrate on understanding local interaction strategies and thus makes a valuable contribution to the understanding of local society.

In summary, early research in northeast Honduras primarily served to investigate the extension of the southern Mesoamerican border. Subsequently, researchers tried to assign the region to different culture areas. In recent years, the area is increasingly perceived as something of its own, and the research focus has shifted to autochthonous developments. Despite these important contributions dedicated to understanding local society, northeast Honduras is still understood as an intermediate region between the major culture regions in many publications. Interaction is studied at the level of culture regions, and it is assumed that these interregional interactions create identity. Mesoamerica, in particular, is regarded as an important area of influence for innovation, while interaction with inhabitants of the Caribbean is hardly considered. Finally, many publications devote a great deal of effort to theory-building, even though it is not always appropriate given the availability (or lack thereof) of underlying data.

A new perspective is needed to understand the complex situation in which the inhabitants of northeast Honduras were embedded. This new perspective should do it justice, overcome the shortcomings of traditional views, and offer an alternative to the inflexible system of culture areas, which focuses on boundaries and differences and views interaction from an inappropriate bird's-eye view. Northeast Honduras and its inhabitants must be placed at the center of observations; inhabitants should be understood as active agents in this constellation. Social interaction at a local, everyday level, is understood as the basis for reconstructing cultural history, following a bottom-up approach. Thus, in the following, the archaeological landscape of Middle America is understood as an assemblage of interconnected networks and subnetworks spanning different geographical levels. The basic theoretical assumptions and their application to our study region are covered in the following chapter.

3 Networks in Middle America: The Conceptual Framework

3.1 Research Questions and Aims

The currently available observations and data that allow for the reconstruction of the pre-Hispanic history of northeast Honduras reveal the complex situation that our area of interest occupies, the understanding and conceptualization of which has challenged researchers from the beginning. At the same time, it is clear that it also occupies a very unique and interesting situation, and its study promises important insights into an area located at the intersection of various cultural traditions. The period before Spanish arrival represents an especially dynamic time for many regions of Middle America, characterized by increasing social hierarchy and the rise of long-distance exchange.

So far, northeast Honduras has mainly been studied in consideration of its unique location between different cultural spaces. It has been characterized as a frontier region, and research has focused on the influences from and interactions with the adjacent culture areas, which has also involved trying to assign northeast Honduras to one of them. Although studies have helped counteract this, the area is still perceived as peripheral compared to the "complex" societies of neighboring Mesoamerica. This paper aims to change this perspective, to focus attention on the events in northeast Honduras, and to focus on the reconstruction of existing connections between regions from the perspective of the inhabitants of northeast Honduras. The inhabitants are perceived as agents who actively arrange and shape their own contacts and networks. Furthermore, the problematic dichotomy between "complex" and "non-complex" societies that still shapes archaeological research will be addressed, and a new perspective on "complexity" and the concept of culture areas will be developed based on network theory.

The Archaeological Project Guadalupe began research in northeast Honduras with the initial aim of investigating the intercultural dynamics and clarifying the various cultural influences from adjacent regions, as other projects have done before. However, throughout the investigations, it became clear that its characterization as a mere frontier region does not do justice to its actual situation. Although it is possible to determine the relationships that extend out in different directions, it is not sufficient to reduce the definition of the region to these observations. Instead, a new approach is needed that recognizes northeast Honduras as an area of investigation in its own right and focuses research on the events in northeast Honduras to counteract the region's conceptualization as periphery. Therefore, it is necessary to first investigate local society with its autochthonous and local processes and developments while understanding local, everyday activities and interactions as important elements that shape and define the local society. The following research questions are to be addressed: How can the region's material culture be characterized? Which observations can be made about the local economy, which raw materials were used, and which products were manufactured? What information is available about subsistence? What cultural aspects can we observe, for example, concerning burial customs? And how was the society organized in sociopolitical terms? Based on these considerations, observations on regional as well as interregional relations can be made. These include the following questions: What relations did the inhabitants have with the surrounding regions, and can we reconstruct the nature of these relations? Can we identify differences in the intensity of these relations? What were the effects of events in the neighboring areas, for example, the decline of the Maya centers at the end of the Classic period? And what position did Guadalupe have in these networks of interaction? To answer these questions, it is vital to not only look at influences but to understand connections as mutual relations and interaction and to examine them in detail. In order to comprehend this complex situation, which involves several levels of interaction, network theory is applied. Since network theory focuses on the connections between agents, and thus links and interaction become the object of investigation, this theoretical approach is well-suited to northeast Honduras' situation. Looking at the settlements of northeast Honduras as part of a network with connections reaching in different directions and having various natures will bring us closer to the reality of pre-Hispanic societies in northeast Honduras and provide a better understanding of the relationships with the surrounding regions.

As a case study to answer these questions, a settlement was selected that forms the central node or agent to

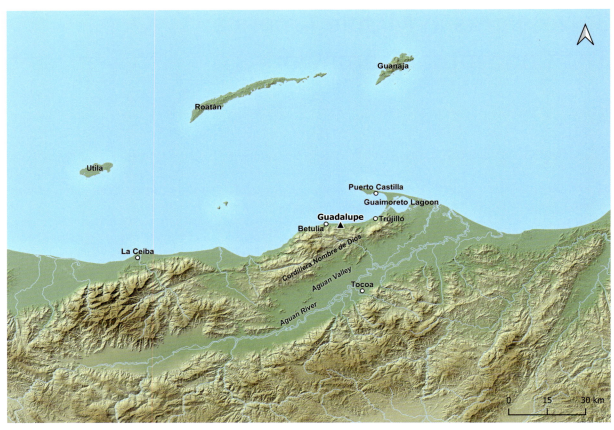

5   Location of Guadalupe on the Honduran north coast (M. Lyons). Topography derived from ASTER GDEM v3 elevation data (NASA 2019).

be studied. Based on its features and material culture, the existing connections to other settlements and societies were reconstructed, thus exploring the structure of existing networks. A suitable settlement for this analysis was found in the Cocal-period (AD 900–1525) coastal settlement of Guadalupe (Figure 5, Figure 6). The results of the investigations in this settlement and its surroundings contribute to our understanding of how a Cocal-period settlement can be characterized, what function it had, how we can describe its material culture, and which conclusions can be drawn about the organization of activities and social interaction. Based on these observations, we investigate the extent to which Guadalupe was integrated into a network of settlements on a regional level, what place it occupied in this system, and what connections existed to the surrounding settlements while also addressing the question of how the regional settlement system can be characterized. Next, the identification of connections to more distant regions is addressed. While earlier studies mainly focused on interaction with Mesoamerica and to a lesser extent with Southern Central America, all potential directions of interaction are considered here, including links to the Caribbean. Just as various spatial levels are considered, different types of relationships are taken into account as

well. To reconstruct the most comprehensive picture possible, cultural, economic, and sociopolitical interrelationships are examined.

Since objects are one of the most important sources of information in archaeology, networks are mainly reconstructed based on material culture. Social practices and ethnohistorical and linguistic data are additional sources of information that serve to reconstruct the situation during the Cocal phase in the best possible way. Because the area is under-researched, the work also aims to distinctly focus on the systematic analysis and, above all, presentation of the primary data obtained, thus creating a solid basis for future research in the field. Particular attention is given to ceramics. The excavations revealed a large number of well-preserved specimens that represent a particularly diagnostic find category, which offers a suitable starting point for reconstructing interactions.

3.2 Theoretical Framework

Northeast Honduras represents a unique and interesting case from an archaeological perspective. The confluence

6   Aerial photo of the modern village of Guadalupe (M. Reindel).

and overlapping of different culture areas and cultural influences make it a key region, the study of which can shed light on the dynamics between the various culture areas. At the same time, however, the area also represents something of its own, and autochthonous developments must be brought into focus. To examine and conceptualize this distinct situation of northeast Honduras, an appropriate model is needed that considers the limited available data. It became clear during our research that the theoretical approaches used to study northeast Honduras so far are not satisfactory. This is primarily due to many of them using a top-down approach while looking at the region from an external, passive perspective and characterizing pre-Hispanic societies in northeast Honduras mainly based on influences from and relationships to the surrounding culture regions. To circumvent this problem and develop an active perspective that focuses on the autochthonous developments in our research area, a new approach is needed. Network theory is a suitable approach and is applied to northeast Honduras for the first time here. Network theory is based on mathematical graph theory. The subjects of study in this theory are graphs that consist of nodes and edges. With the help of these graphs, net-like structures in the real world are visualized schematically with nodes and edges representing objects or agents and their relationships to one another. Graph theory aims to investigate the structures of the formal networks that are created in this way.

By considering northeast Honduras and the adjacent regions as an arrangement of interconnected networks, the focus of research shifts to mutual connections. This view does not presuppose any existing borders; thus, it is far more flexible than the concept of culture areas, and investigations can take place at different geographical levels. It is possible to investigate connections on local, regional, and interregional levels and to consider all existing interactions equally. Furthermore, this approach considers the Cocal-period settlement of Guadalupe and its inhabitants as active agents and brings them to the center of our studies. To understand why network analysis is used here and why it is a preferable approach, an overview of other approaches that were previously used in the investigation of frontier regions and intercultural interaction is given. The strengths and weaknesses of the respective theoretical approaches are discussed, and the extent to which they are suitable for our research is highlighted. Subsequently, the basics of network analysis are presented, and how this approach is applied to our research area is outlined.

3.2.1 EXISTING MODELS OF INTERACTION

One of the first approaches to studying interaction and cultural change was diffusionism, which has its origins at the end of the 19th century. Diffusionism equated culture to language, race, and material culture. It was furthermore understood as a complex consisting of various isolatable cultural traits. It was assumed that innovations were only ever invented once and that this was done in innovative centers. From there, innovations reached the surrounding, peripheral areas through migration (Bauer / Agbe-Davies 2010: 30). This theory dominated archaeological research until the 1920s and 30s. In Central America, it was the predominant theory used to explain culture change and cultural interaction until the 1950s and, in some cases, later (Schortman / Urban 2012: 471). Over time, however, this approach has been criticized because it represents a very simplified model. It does not account for the reasons that diffusion occurs. Moreover, it understands cultural change as something external. Although this model is presently considered outdated, it still influences current research. The conceptualization and definition of culture areas, which reflect the spatial distribution of specific cultural traits, have their origins in this theoretical model. And although the concept of culture areas is also considered outdated, it is still used for practical reasons and thus continues to structure and influence modern research (Schortman / Urban 2012: 472).

While the use of diffusionist approaches declined, evolutionist theories gained importance in connection with the developments of New Archaeology. Evolutionist theory understood culture as a human extrasomatic means of adaptation (White 1959). Just like the body, culture adapts to the environment. Environmental factors cause cultural change, which usually develops from simple to complex. It was assumed that there are laws for these evolutionary developments that must be identified (Schortman 1989). Since the relationship between humans and the environment was seen as an explanation for cultural change in this theoretical model, the significance of the relationship between different societies faded into the background, which is why the approach is not suitable for examining the effects of the interaction of cultures. Both diffusionist and evolutionist theories are extremes and were designed as opposites of each other (Schortman / Urban 1987: 48). However, as Alexander Bauer and Anna Agbe-Davies (2010: 33) show, some approaches tried to combine aspects of both theories. Caldwell's (1964) interaction sphere is an example of this. The concept was originally developed for the study of the Hopewell culture. Caldwell understands an interaction sphere as a system in which culturally different autonomous groups were integrated into a supra-regional network through the exchange of particular objects associated with religious ideology. In doing so, they shared a common code of beliefs and values. Caldwell also sees this exchange as a driver for the emergence of elites. At the same time, he acknowledges that societies can be integrated into several networks that affect different levels or areas of everyday life.

A model that partly draws on Caldwell's considerations is peer-polity interaction developed by Collin Renfrew and John Cherry (1986). Originally developed for the Greek city-states, this model pursues the question of culture change and the emergence of social complexity.

"Peer polity interaction designates the full range of interchanges taking place (including imitation and emulation, competition, warfare, and the exchange of material goods and of information) between autonomous (i.e. self-governing and in that sense politically independent) socio-political units which are situated beside or close to each other within a single geographical region, or in some cases more widely" (Renfrew 1986: 1).

Thus, sociopolitical units are not considered in isolation, but the focus is on the interaction between these units and how it affects cultural change and the emergence of social hierarchy. It is important to note that no subordinance or domination of an interaction partner is assumed in this approach. Although this concept was initially developed to investigate early states, it can also be applied to chiefdoms, according to Renfrew (1986). However, the identification of autonomous units is a prerequisite.

With the emergence of trade studies in the 1960s and 70s, diffusion theory was finally replaced as the primary explanatory approach for interaction and cultural change (Bauer / Agbe-Davies 2010). Concentration on the exchange of goods allowed the examination of interaction based on tangible criteria. The development of the formalist and substantivist approaches can be seen in the context of trade studies. The formalist approach assumes that data is quantifiable and that predefined concepts can be applied to specific situations, including concepts and theories developed for modern capitalist society. The substantivist approach, which has its origin in Karl Polanyi's writings (et al. 1957), does not share this view. Polanyi stresses that pre-capitalist societies did not act according to the same economic laws as today but that the social aspect played an important role in economic interactions. Furthermore, the substantivist approach follows inductive reasoning (i.e., from the specific to the general) (Rössler 1999).

One theory that is still very popular today and has been applied to many regions throughout the world is world-systems theory. It was originally developed by the social historian Immanuel Wallerstein (1974) and served to explain the emergence of capitalism in Europe and North America. The initial example was the relationship that had developed between the West Indies and Europe during the 16th century. The model's core is based on the assumption that capitalism is rooted in the difference between center and periphery. While the periphery is weakly developed and provides raw materials, these raw materials are processed in the center by specialists where the end product is consumed. Production was no longer seen as organized within societies but instead across social boundaries. "[…] world systems are composed of multiple sociocultural systems bound through a single division of labor that transcends cultural and political boundaries" (Kepecs / Kohl 2003: 14).

This approach was quickly applied to the study of pre-capitalist societies (e.g., Blanton / Feinman 1984; Pailes / Whitecotton 1979; Schneider 1977). Stein (2002: 904) states that world-systems theories and the related acculturation models are the "most widely used frameworks for the analysis of culture contact or interregional interaction." It is particularly popular because it is a new tool to capture dynamics that reach beyond migration and trade, which had previously served as the main explanatory approaches. Just as quickly, however, the question was raised as to what extent Wallerstein's theoretical approach can be applied to pre-capitalist societies at all, and criticism arose (e.g., Hall / Kardulias / Chase-Dunn 2011; Harding 2013; Hudson / Henderson 2014; Stein 1998, 1999, 2002). A major criticism is that a hierarchical relationship between center and periphery is hypothesized even before data is generated. In addition, a unidirectionality of interaction is often assumed where the center is characterized as active and the periphery as passive (e.g., Stein 2002). The second problem in Wallerstein's model is that the focus is on the production and exchange of key commodities, while luxury goods are hardly considered. However, in pre-capitalist societies, especially in Central America, luxury goods played an essential role in exchange. Edward Schortman and Patricia Urban (1987: 58) also criticize the model's economic focus, while social systems are not considered. Thus, to apply the theoretical model to pre-capitalist societies, it is often modified and adapted to the extent that it loses many of its defining elements.

The world-systems approach has had a significant influence on the perception of frontier regions. It has led to them being analyzed in a core-periphery relationship, with research focusing on cores and frontiers being seen as passive recipients of core innovations. In the 1990s, dissatisfaction with this approach grew and, inspired by postcolonial theories (e.g., Bhabha 1996), among others, new ideas emerged that called for an approach from the perspective of frontiers and regarded frontiers as active and even innovative places (Feuer 2016: 31; Schortman / Urban 2012). Kent Lightfoot and Antoinette Martinez (1995), for example, present such an approach, and in addition to the hierarchical view, they criticize the macro-scale analysis employed in frontier studies. The authors argue "for the reconceptualization of frontiers as socially charged places where innovative cultural constructs are created and transformed" (Lightfoot / Martinez 1995: 472).

The overview shows that there were and still are many different approaches to investigate and conceptualize the interaction of societies. Although some models provide some useful insights, none are particularly well-suited to meaningfully capture the complex situation in Honduras, considering the limited state of research. For our analysis, many different interaction partners and types of interaction must be considered. Furthermore, not only is intercultural interaction investigated, but local and regional systems are also characterized. However, the weakness of the above theories is that some are limited to the observation of certain types of interaction (e.g., trade or religion). Others assume a unidirectionality of action or inequality of the interaction partners and define center and periphery in anticipation of this (diffusionism and world-systems theory). The peer-polity interaction model does not have these disadvantages, but it is currently difficult to make statements about the political structure and to identify autonomous polities in northeast Honduras. The approaches that consider frontiers as active places change the previously existing picture and provide important arguments for the importance of studying frontier regions. However, they do not provide tools to systematically evaluate the data, which is true for most of the theories presented above.

3.2.2 Network Theory

In light of the overview of existing theoretical models, none appear to be especially suitable for studying the situation in pre-Hispanic northeast Honduras. The unique, entangled situation requires new ways of thinking. For our project, we need an approach that:

1. allows for the consideration of different geographical levels (local, regional, and interregional)
2. enables the consideration of different types of exchange (economic, social, cultural, political, etc.)
3. can consider interaction in both directions, i.e., does not imply unidirectionality,
4. does not presuppose any assumptions of hierarchies
5. can be effectively used and applied despite the fragmentary character of available data

Network theory was found to be a suitable approach, as it enables a neutral view that does not establish dichotomies but instead creates a basis for a differentiated analysis. It further provides a relational approach that focuses on connections instead of delimitations. The idea of Guadalupe as part of a network approximates reality and gives a better understanding of Guadalupe and the neighboring regions than previous approaches. At the same time, network theory can be applied—although with restrictions—despite the limited available data for northeast Honduras. The following chapters highlight the basics of network theory and discuss the elements that have to be considered when applying it to our research area.

3.2.2.1 Basics of Network Theory

Network theory is based on mathematical graph theory, which has its roots in the 1930s (Müller 2009). The basic principle of graph theory is relatively simple. Graphs consist of only two elements: nodes (also called "vertices") and links (also called "edges") (Figure 7). Network theory understands nodes as agents and links as connections or interactions between these agents. The structure and topography of the graph or network are based on the arrangement of the nodes and links, which in turn provide different properties. These basic elements of graph theory have meanwhile been adopted in various sciences. In sociology, it has been firmly in place since the 1970s and is used in the form of social network analysis, which archaeology also largely draws on. In social network theory, nodes are primarily understood as individual persons or other entities of social life. Network theory is applied here, for example, in order to investigate the circulation of information, social media networks, knowledge networks, or business relations. Network theory also became very popular in other sciences, such as geography, physics, and biology (Knappett 2013a). It has only become more common in archaeology in the last 15 years with few exceptions (e.g., Collar et al. 2015; Jenkins 2001; Knappett 2013b; Peregrine 1991; Sindbaek 2007). It has been applied, for example, to study obsidian distribution networks (e.g., Freund / Batist 2014; Golitko et al. 2012; Golitko / Feinman 2015) and interisland networks in the Caribbean (Hofman et al. 2014; Mol 2014; Mol / Mans 2013), and to map political affiliations (Scholnik / Munson / Macri 2013).

This method of analysis has been widely accepted because it offers a relational approach and focuses on the connections between entities. Relationships and structures between agents become the unit of analysis (Mills 2017). The simplified and systematic depiction of networks opens up different analytical possibilities concerning the position of specific nodes in the network and the overall network topography. First, it is essential to define both the type of network to be investigated and the nodes and links that make up the overall network structure. These elements strongly depend on the available data and the underlying research question. A distinction is made, for example, between an ego network, in which all connections of a single node are considered, and a whole network, in which all nodes in a network and their links to each other are considered. The nodes are subject independent, i.e., one is free to define what is understood as a node (Collar et al. 2015). In a one-mode network, all nodes have the same quality or are of the same kind, for instance, connections between archaeological settlements. In a two-mode network, links between nodes of different types are investigated within a

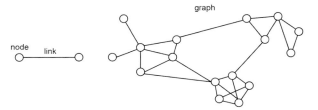

7   Example of a network graph consisting of links and nodes (F. Fecher).

network, such as archaeological settlements and raw material sources.

Similarly, the meaning of a "link," or the connection between nodes, must be defined. In archaeology, links are often reconstructed based on objects, so the studied networks are usually material networks, which reconstruct links based on the distribution and similarity of material culture such as raw materials, artifacts, and architecture. Historical networks based on written sources and spatial networks, which often go hand in hand with GIS analysis, can also play a role (Mills 2017). If the focus is on material networks, they can be reconstructed based on material culture, but the processes that led to the distribution of objects should also be investigated. For example, these processes can concern the flow of goods, information, or people. It is important to define these elements in the best possible way and to consider what the different types of links can tell us about the interaction between nodes (Peeples et al. 2016). The intensity and direction of links can also be considered. Does a link between two nodes consist of frequent, intensive interaction (strong ties) or less frequent interaction (weak ties) (Granovetter 1973)? Is a link undirected, as in the case of political alliances or marriage links, both of which constitute mutual relationships, or directed, as is the case of raw materials, which usually move from a geological source to a settlement?

Once the basic aspects of a network have been defined and the elements under investigation are determined, the network structure can be analyzed. There are two basic approaches: the analysis of node position or the analysis of overall network topography. Suppose the position of a single node in a network is examined more closely. In that case, questions of the degree of connectivity (determining the centrality of a node in a network based on the number of links to other nodes), closeness centrality (how central a node is concerning its proximity to other nodes, i.e., how quickly other nodes can be reached, and also how long it takes to spread information from A to B), or betweenness centrality are to be addressed. Betweenness centrality refers to the fact that certain nodes connect otherwise separate networks with each other and thus take on a bridge function between the networks, acting as so-called brokers (Burt 1992). The theory of weak ties by Granovetter (1973) also deals with this phenomenon. Weak ties are defined as weak or infrequent relationships between nodes. However, these weak ties can establish connections between networks and present the only connection for the flow of information or resources and thus fulfill an important function.

The analysis of the network topography looks at the overall architecture of the network, i.e., how different elements are arranged and interconnected. It is essential to understand that different arrangements have different properties. Decisive factors are, for example, connectivity (density or determination of the number of relationships concerning the largest possible number of relationships), scale (size of a network), clustering (the presence of subnetworks), or questions of centrality. Examples of special network topographies are scale-free networks, where a few nodes have a high connectivity (i.e., many connections to other nodes) and many nodes have a low connectivity. The number of these nodes corresponds to the power-law distribution. This distribution results in a highly centralized network, in which information or resources flow from one central node to less central nodes (or vice versa), but the surrounding nodes have few connections to each other (Figure 8). In contrast, decentralized networks have a more egalitarian degree of connectivity, i.e., each node has a similar number of connections.

3.2.2.2 Social Network Analysis in Archaeology

The points above have shown the various possibilities of social network analysis and have given a brief insight into the different network types and topographies. However, in archaeological research, we are usually confronted with the limitations of these analyses. While social research can request information directly from individuals, in archaeology, we depend on the interpretation of material remains, which can only ever provide an incomplete picture of a past situation (Coward 2013). While sociologists at the beginning of the analysis already have a network at their disposal of which various questions can be asked, Sindbaek (2013) observes that in archaeological research, we often find ourselves at the stage of reconstructing networks rather than being able to deal with their analysis.

To examine connections and identify interactions, archaeology often relies on the principle of similarity, which can be reconstructed based on archaeological evidence. The strength of interaction between nodes coincides with the strength of similarities in archaeological evidence and the number of similarities between nodes (e.g., settlements). In addition to this "shared underlying general hypothesis" of the relationship between similar-

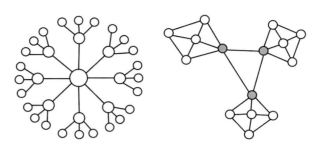

8   Example of centralized (left) and decentralized (right) networks. Note that the flow of information in the centralized network only needs two steps to reach every single node, whereas several steps are required to reach each node in the decentralized network. In turn, the nodes in the decentralized network are connected and can exchange information without passing through a center. The grey nodes in the decentralized network function as brokers, as they connect different subnetworks (F. Fecher).

ity and interaction (Prignano / Morer / Diaz-Guilera 2017: 4), scientific analyses are also used to determine interactions with a higher degree of certainty. For instance, isotope analyses allow for the reconstruction of human and animal life trajectories, and chemical analyses enable the attribution of raw materials to geological sources. Obsidian is an ideal candidate for such an analysis because it can be assigned to a specific source with a high degree of certainty (see, e.g., Golitko et al. 2012). A link can thus be established between geological sources and settlements where objects from a specific source have been found. However, such an analysis does not clarify if this represents a direct connection or, as in most cases, if there were other agents in between that cannot be reconstructed today.

This example of the connection between settlements and geological sources shows that archaeology often deals with two-mode or even multimodal networks, i.e., networks in which the connection between nodes of different types is examined (Mills 2017). This is mainly because it is not always possible to identify settlements that were responsible for extracting and processing the raw materials. We may not even be able to pinpoint similarities between individual settlements but have to extend them to regions, for example, when no exact origin is known for looted finds or those in museum collections. Therefore, it is always important to consider and define what is understood as a node in a network. Another aspect to consider is the definition of the links, i.e., what actually constitutes the connection between our nodes. Since we rely primarily on material remains in archaeology, connections are often determined by the presence, absence, or similarity of objects. However, which mechanisms have led to this? Does it pertain to the flow of goods, persons, ideas, techniques, etc.?

Another interesting aspect regarding the application of network analysis in archaeology is the issue of chronology. Usually, networks represent a snapshot of the arrangement of links between agents, which implies simultaneity. In archaeology, finds and features can rarely be dated so precisely that they can be regarded as simultaneous in the term's original definition. This is especially true of a study area such as northeast Honduras, where the chronology is poorly defined. We can, therefore, only point out tendencies or pursue a long-term perspective by comparing archaeological phases that can be identified and distinguished from each other in the archaeological evidence (Peeples et al. 2016: 67). Lastly, we can assume that networks and their graphs have always been much more complex than we can currently reconstruct based on archaeological information and that we tend to underestimate the network size, number of links and nodes, and their flexibility.

3.2.2.3 Reconstruction and Analysis of Networks in Northeast Honduras

In the following, the elements relevant to applying the network approach in northeast Honduras are defined. In the subsequent analysis, the investigation of an ego network will be pursued. The Cocal-period settlement of Guadalupe and its inhabitants are the focus of the observations; Guadalupe is defined as the network's central node. Based on the finds and features discovered during our investigations, Guadalupe's connections to other nodes will be reconstructed, which are mainly understood as archaeological settlements. The links to geological sources are also considered, and thus it constitutes a two-mode network. This study is to be understood as an exemplary approach and approximation to the reconstruction of the overall network of pre-Hispanic northeast Honduras during the Cocal period.

To reconstruct these links, we rely in particular on material remains such as artifacts and architecture that correspond to material networks, but social practices such as burial rites are also considered. Because northeast Honduras is a little-explored area and each source can provide valuable information, ethnohistorical and linguistic data are also considered. The excavations in Guadalupe provided numerous data that lend themselves to such analysis. The find groups include ceramics, animal bones, mollusks, obsidian, stone tools, greenstone, metal objects, and human remains. The careful and detailed documentation of our investigations' finds and contexts serve as a basis for subsequent analysis of networks. The principle of similarity is applied to reconstruct links, which assumes that increased similarity in a find inventory indicates more intense interaction between two nodes. This principle is mainly applied to the

study of the distribution of ceramics. Obsidian, greenstone, and metal are particularly suitable for scientific provenance analysis since they can be assigned to specific geological sources and help us identify links and nodes scientifically. The methods applied to each category are presented in detail in the respective chapters on the excavation and find analysis below. Whenever possible, observations are made on the nature of the connections, i.e., whether they are primarily economic, social, political, etc.

First, Guadalupe, as the central node of the network, is presented and characterized. Based on this, connections and networks are reconstructed on different spatial levels, from small to large, i.e., regional and interregional, and in all possible geographic directions using the criteria described above. In each case, Guadalupe's position within these networks is considered, and to a certain extent, the entire network structure and the relationships between the networks are discussed. This approach allows the consideration of different networks on different spatial levels, such as subnetworks and their interconnection. This flexibility is critical since the body of research has primarily focused on interregional interactions thus far. Furthermore, the network approach allows for consideration without the predefinition of a hierarchy or a (artificial) delimitation between culture areas or between center and periphery.

Network theory has been criticized for being a method rather than a theoretical approach and for requiring additional theory building to contextualize results (Mills 2017). However, I believe that, despite this critique, the network approach involves three very important aspects: 1) In northeast Honduras, considerable emphasis has been placed on theory building but little on systematization of data. Here, the network approach can function as a tool to structure and systematize the existing data and allow us to make a clear distinction between data and interpretation in the first step. In this way, the influence that an existing model has on the interpretation of the data based on a predefined idea is avoided. 2) The network approach focuses on the investigation of connections. Connections between entities are the focal point. Thus, this approach *does* contain a theoretical assumption, namely that—on whatever geographical level—connections and interaction played an important role for pre-Hispanic societies and were a central part of everyday life. This aspect is vital to approach an understanding of pre-Hispanic society. 3) The network approach offers an alternative perspective to the concepts of culture areas and complexity. These concepts have been identified as problematic but continue to be used and still affect archaeological research. This argument will be detailed in the following chapter.

3.2.2.4 Towards a New Perspective of Complexity and Culture Areas

In the archaeological discourse of Middle America, the concepts of "complexity" and "culture areas" are omnipresent. They are primarily relics from the history of archaeological research but continue to be used and thus continue to strongly influence archaeological practice. The ongoing use of these concepts can largely be explained by the fact that they provide categories and designations for phenomena that are otherwise difficult to grasp. Thinking in terms of categories and delimitable concepts is consistent with human thinking in that it helps us structure and understand our environment. However, applying such categories to the archaeological record is highly simplistic and should be questioned for several reasons. Concerning these concepts in Middle American archaeology, a dichotomy is built between supposed "complex societies" in Mesoamerica and less complex societies outside of this culture area (Sheets 1992). Regarding complexity in the archaeology of Southern Central America, the question is often raised as to why complex societies did not develop there. This view originates from the history of research but has become firmly established over time. Complex societies are characterized by visible archaeological remains, such as large settlements with stone buildings, palaces, and temples, and high-quality material culture. They are considered different from less complex societies by the degree of organization and achievements of civilization, such as elaborate art or writing systems. At the same time, the term "complex society" still carries the underlying notion of a more developed or progressive society, which, in the end, is more similar to modern western societies and thus perceived as more positive. This view originates from an evolutionary model that proposes a linear development of socio-political organization from simple (band) to complex (state) (Oberg 1955; Service 1962). In effect, complexity here refers to a hierarchy in the sociopolitical structure, namely a vertical hierarchy. According to the traditional view, this form of organization with its hierarchical structure enables the formation of specialists and the mobilization of labor.

This dichotomic perspective is considered to be in need of reform for several reasons. The view that societies follow a linear development and that the state can be seen as the end of a "development ladder" has long been recognized as obsolete (see, e.g., Blanton et al. 1996). The dichotomy resulting from the term's use represents a simplification that divides the types of social organization into two categories, complex or non-complex. However, this does not cover the multitude of possible organizational forms that exist between these models. Therefore, the added value as an analytical tool is questionable; the application of the term actually prevents a

detailed study (Campbell 2009). Moreover, with increasing research, it has become clear that the elements mentioned above, which are seen as characteristics of "complex societies," are not necessarily dependent on each other but can occur separately. High-quality artifacts, for instance, are also produced by societies without a distinct social hierarchy. A final point of criticism is that the concept of complexity is often not precisely defined when used in archaeological publications, which makes a standardized definition or comparison difficult. Even though many archaeologists are indeed aware of these inherent problems, the continued use of this term in archaeology leads to the conclusion that there is a desideratum to make comparative analyses and to name differences but that there is no satisfactory alternative yet.

In systems theory, closely related to network theory, we find an alternative approach to complexity. Complexity here is related to the number of connections between elements and their possible arrangements. Furthermore, a complex system's behavior cannot be predicted due to numerous influences and interdependencies (Bar-Yam 2003; Ziemann 2009). This approach allows us to consider different types and especially degrees of complexity that result from the topography of the systems or networks in question. The traditional understanding of a complex society in a socio-political sense corresponds, for example, to a centralized network where a few nodes have a high degree of connectivity, and many nodes have a low degree of connectivity. This can be contrasted with other network topographies, such as linear networks or decentralized networks. At this level of observation, the units of analysis are comparable. Differences and similarities can be defined, and even a degree of complexity can be measured. The analyses of networks of past societies are limited by the elements discussed above, but I still consider this approach a step in the right direction.

A similar problem exists with the concept of culture areas. This concept, too, is essentially a relic of research history and originates from the culture-historical approach. Here, culture areas are defined based on similar cultural traits, and the boundaries of culture areas are drawn based on the distribution of these cultural elements. This view is outdated for several reasons, and the concept of networks can provide a new approach (Coward 2013). Similar to the concept of complexity, the monolithic concept of culture areas is highly simplifying and prevents the analysis of regional differences. Again, a dichotomy emerges that leads to regions outside of the Mesoamerican culture area appearing less interesting for research. Concerning frontier regions, it becomes evident that this concept lacks a dynamic nature, which, for example, would consider the variation of a frontiers'

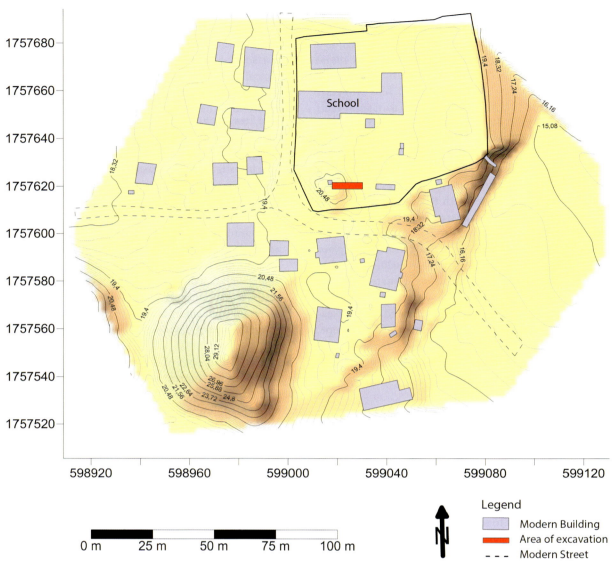

9   Topographic map of Guadalupe (M. Lyons, M. Reindel, F. Fecher).

10   Surface ceramic concentration in Guadalupe (M. Reindel).

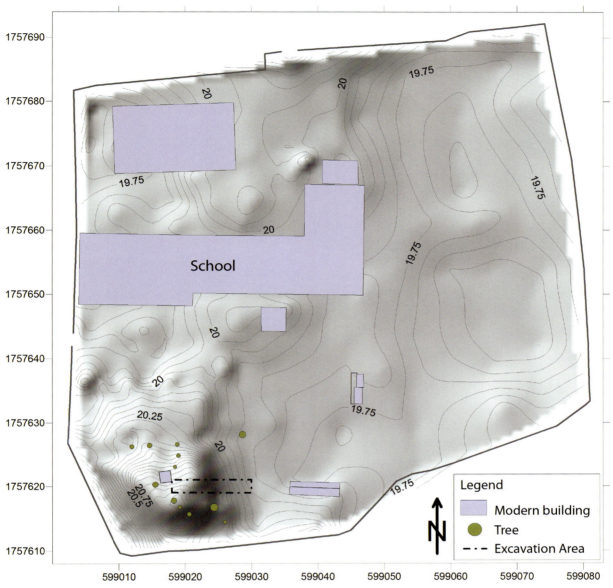

11   Topographic map of the school terrain. The mound is clearly visible in the southwestern corner (M. Reindel, F. Fecher, M. Lyons).

12   Pre-Hispanic mound in Guadalupe (M. Reindel).

4.2 Excavations in Guadalupe

The first step in the investigation of Guadalupe consisted of careful mapping of the topographic situation of the school property and the surrounding area (see Figure 9 and Figure 11). A total area of approx. 3.2 ha was surveyed with a total station. A local coordinate system, which was set up by defining three fixed points, served as a reference. The coordinates of these fixed points were determined with a hand-held GPS.

– FP1: 0599004 E / 1757634 N, 20 masl
– FP2: 0599004 E / 1757681 N, 19,822 masl
– FP3: 0599076 E / 1757634 N, 19,779 masl

In order to investigate the function, stratigraphic structure, and chronology of the mound, a 2 x 12 m profile section was placed in the mound (Figure 13). The section extends from the center of the mound to its periphery and follows an east-west direction. It is delimited by the following coordinates: 599018 E / 1757621 N (northwest corner) and 599030 E / 1757619 N (southeast corner). The excavation section was divided into four units of 3 x 2 m each, with increasing numbering from west to east.

Depending on the nature of the earth and the finds, picks, trowels, sharpened bamboo sticks, and brushes were used for the excavation. First, excavations followed the slope of the mound to identify possible natural layers. However, as the nature of the sediments didn't allow for the clear identification of separate layers, the strategy was changed to excavate artificial layers from the 2017 field campaign onwards. Whenever natural layers became visible, they were excavated as such. If this was not the case, artificial strata 10 cm in thickness were excavated. In order to have better control, an additional intermediate level was created at 5 cm, but this was only documented if there were any irregularities. Plana were photographed and drawn at a 1:20 scale. The profiles were photogrammetrically documented and drawn at a 1:10 scale. Special finds and features were additionally documented with photography, drawing, or photogrammetry. The coordinate positions of the respective features were recorded. An inventory number was assigned to each layer and to each feature. The supervision of the excavation was handled by Markus Reindel and the author. A database (Filemaker) was used to collect and manage excavation results, finds, and results of analyses (Figure 14).

The excavations of Guadalupe's mound yielded information on its chronology, the characterization of the material culture during the Cocal period, the understanding of local production techniques, subsistence, architecture, burial customs, and integration into exchange networks. The results of the excavations are presented in detail in the following chapters.

4.2.1 STRATIGRAPHY

The stratigraphy of the Guadalupe profile section can be observed particularly well on the 12 m long north and south profiles (Figure 15, Figure 16). The stratigraphy is described from top to bottom, following the course of

13   Excavation in 2018 (M. Reindel).

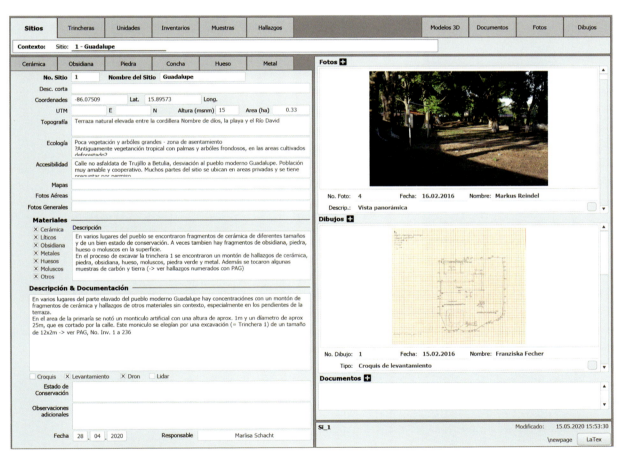

14   FileMaker Pro database user interface (F. Fecher).

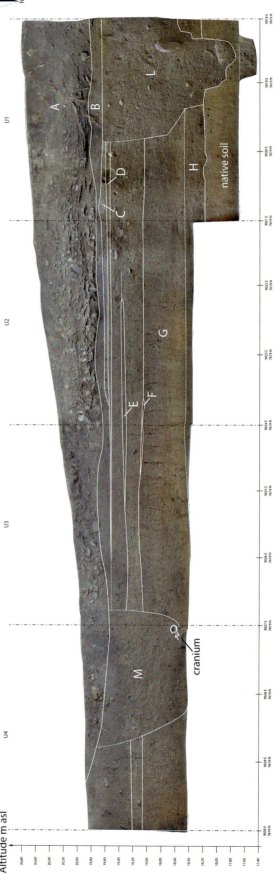

Altitude m asl

15   North profile (M. Lyons, F. Fecher).

Altitude m asl

16   South profile (M. Lyons, F. Fecher).

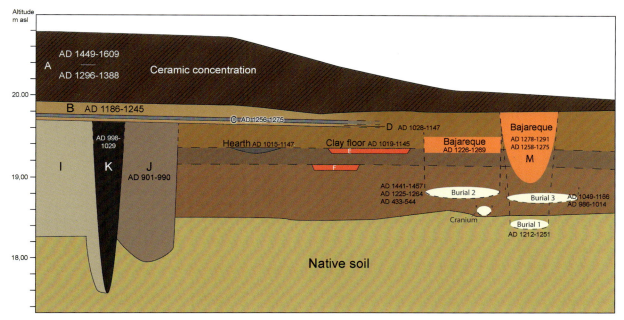

17   Schematic representation of the stratigraphy showing the most important features. Dashed lines indicate uncertain boundaries (F. Fecher).

excavations. For orientation, the layers are labeled with capital letters on the profile drawings. A schematic representation of the stratigraphy with the most important features is provided in Figure 17.

The upper layer (A) consists of densely packed ceramic broken into large fragments and surrounded by dark brown, humic earth. The thickness of the layer decreases significantly from west (center of the hill) to east (periphery). While in the western-most part of the excavation of Unit 1, it measures approx. 1 m thick (ca. 20.80 to 19.85 masl), in the western section of Unit 4, it is only a few centimeters thick and disappears in the eastern part. In addition, the layer slopes slightly downward to the east of Unit 2's midline. Associated materials include charcoal, stone implements, shells, animal bones, obsidian, metal, and greenstone objects. No clear internal stratigraphy can be detected within the layer, although the earth shows differences in color. It is notable that the ceramic fragments are mainly concentrated in the lower part of the layer where they more often lie in conjunction with one another (Figure 18). It is also important to mention that the surface of the layer is partly disturbed by modern activities (horticulture, earth removal, etc.).

Below the ceramic layer, in Units 1 and 2, there is a sandy, light brown earth (Inv. 62 and 74) (B). It is clearly separated from the dark earth above. It is associated with considerably fewer ceramic sherds that are heavily fragmented. Other associated materials are charcoal, few bones, shells, and small stones. Only one obsidian fragment was found in Unit 1. Some fragments of *bajareque* were also recovered. The term *bajareque* is used in

the following to refer to burnt clay fragments from wattle and daub constructions. The layer is about 10 cm thick and is located between 19.74 and 19.85 masl. Towards the east, it becomes thinner and ends in Unit 2.

Below this layer is a thin layer of light brown-grey earth that is mainly composed of gravel (Inv. 70, 89, and 90) (C). It is clearly visible in the profiles of Units 1 and 2. It is about 10 cm thick and shows a slight inclination from the center of Unit 2 eastwards. In Units 3 and 4, the layer is no longer visible in the profiles and was also not evident in the plana during the excavation.

Just below this layer, there is a very hard and compact light brown earth (Inv. 82, and 91) (D). In Unit 1, it runs from about 19.59 to 19.66 masl. This layer also seems to end in Unit 2, while it is still slightly visible in the southern profile of Unit 3. While this layer is not very clearly visible in the profiles, it was noticed during the excavation due to the increasing hardness of the earth. Due to the compactness of the earth, it can be assumed that this is an occupation layer. This layer is associated with pieces of charcoal, few stones, small fragments of pottery, animal bones, shells, and *bajareque*. In Units 3 and 4, the situation of the layers below the ceramic layer is not clear. Here, too, a light-colored earth contrasts with the dark, humic earth. Almost directly below the ceramic accumulation, *bajareque* concentrations appear in Unit 4.

In Unit 1 and Unit 2, there are more layers below layer D, but their boundaries are not well defined. Presumably, these are additional settlement horizons that accumulated over time. The next distinct layer can be identified at an elevation of about 19.30 masl (E). In Unit

18   Ceramic concentration in the lower layers of Unit 2 (M. Reindel).

3's northern profile, this is marked by a red clay floor, hardened from burning (Inv. 111, 121, and 135); in the southern profile, the horizon is indicated by a dark grey layer, possibly a burnt layer. At the same level in Unit 2, we also found a hearth (Inv. 109), which is not visible in the profile. In the northern profile, it is difficult to identify more layers below the clay floor. In the southern profile, another distinct layer is visible at 19.10 masl (F). It is also marked by a red, hardened clay floor in Unit 3. This feature (F) is located in the planum slightly below the above-mentioned floor (E) that reaches into the northern profile. It remains unclear to what extent the two floors and, consequently, the two layers are associated. Additional layers run below this feature in the southern profile, but these cannot be clearly distinguished from each other (G and H). In the northern profile, such layers are no longer discernible.

Apart from the mentioned layers, it should be noted that several pits can be observed in the profiles. In the northern profile of Unit 1, there are at least three pits that partially overlap and whose boundaries are difficult to reconstruct. In the profile, it appears that a pit was first dug in the west (I), followed by a pit in the east (J), which cuts through the west pit. Finally, a narrow, elongated pit was dug that contains large stones, burnt clay, and very large charcoal fragments (K). In the southern profile of the same unit, another large pit is visible (L). Unfortunately, the contours and especially the starting points of these pits are not clear either in the profile or in the plana, which makes it difficult to interpret their chronological sequence. In addition, concentrations of *bajareque* are visible in the north and south profiles of Unit 4 (M). These were already clearly identified in the plana at a higher elevation. Below these concentrations, we found burials. In the northern profile, it is clear that

the *bajareque* and the burial are related and are part of the same pit.

Central to the interpretation of the site is the relationship between these burial pits, the various identified occupation layers, and the ceramic accumulation. However, the relationship cannot be clearly identified based on the profiles, as the situation is unclear, especially in the area between the burnt layer and the *bajareque* concentrations. Based on the stratigraphic situation, there are two possible theories.

–   Hypothesis 1: The burial pits were excavated from the level that is marked by the hearth and the red clay floor. The *bajareque* in the pit could be related to the fire that also hardened the clay floor.
–   Hypothesis 2: The burial pits were excavated from the layer beneath the ceramic concentration. This would mean that the lower layers of the pottery accumulation could be related to the burials.

Since these questions cannot be answered from the information that the profiles provide, we need to draw on information from the plana. It becomes clear that the clay floor (E) and the hearth lie at an elevation of approx. 19.30 masl and measure approx. 15 cm in thickness. The stratigraphic circumstances indicate the possibility that both features belong to the same occupation layer and may be contemporaneous. For the pits in Units 3 and 4, which include *bajareque* and burials (M), the situation is somewhat different.

The concentrations of *bajareque* were defined on the plana for the first time at an elevation of 19.52 masl (Inv. 104; Unit 3; feature does not reach into the profile), 19.50 masl (Inv. 61 and 79; Unit 4), and 19.40 masl (Inv. 80; Unit 4), with the northern profile clearly showing that Inv. 61/79 already starts further above and thus lies just beneath the pottery concentration (see Figure 15; Figure 19). Below these concentrations of *bajareque*, dark discolorations are visible, which include the burials at their bottom (Figure 20, Figure 21, Figure 22). It can be assumed that the *bajareque* and the burial pits below are connected with each other. This becomes particularly clear in the case of Inv. 61/79, where the distribution of the *bajareque* corresponds almost exactly to the location of the burial pit and where it is also clearly visible in the profile that the discoloration of the burial pit continues below the *bajareque* concentration. The fact that the *bajareque* concentrations are elevated in comparison to the hearth and lie closely below the pottery layer suggests that they are associated with later horizons and thus support Hypothesis 2. Further evidence for the verification of this hypothesis and for the examination of the stratigraphy, in general, is provided by radiocarbon dating.

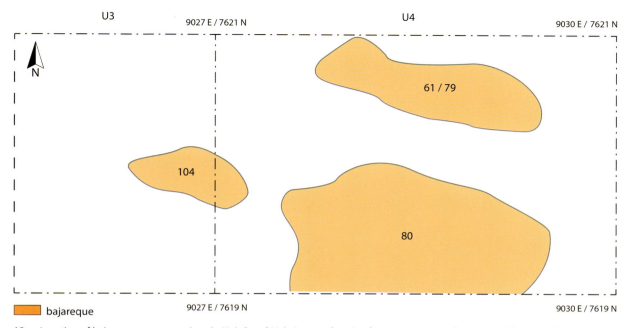

19   Location of bajareque concentrations in Unit 3 and Unit 4 at an elevation between 19.50 and 19.40 masl (F. Fecher).

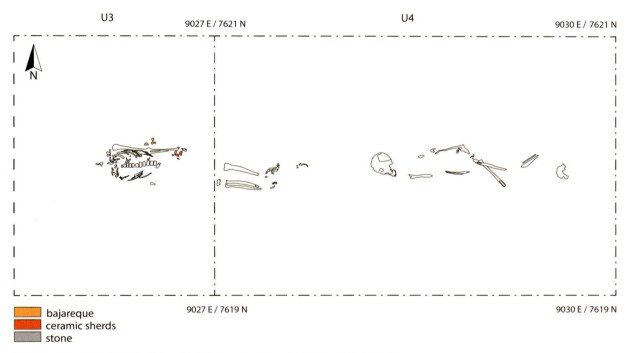

20   Location of burials in Unit 3 and Unit 4 at an elevation of 18.75 masl (F. Fecher).

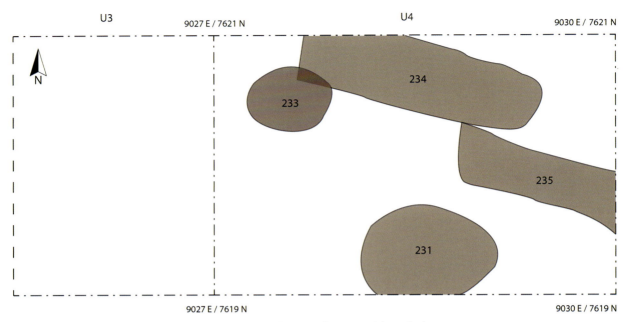

21   Location of discolorations in Unit 3 and Unit 4 at an elevation of 18.45 masl (F. Fecher).

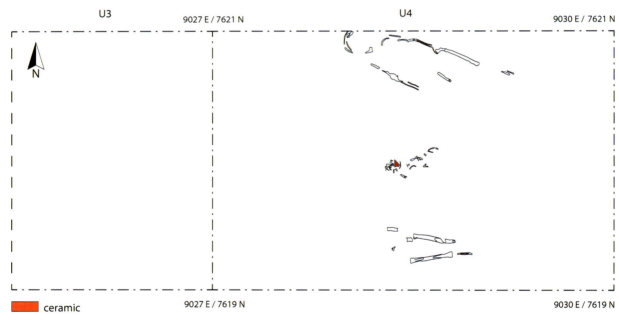

22   Location of burials in Unit 3 and Unit 4 at an elevation of 18.40 masl (F. Fecher).

4.2.2 RADIOCARBON DATING

The analysis of carbon samples is essential to temporally map the activities and relationships that we want to reconstruct for Guadalupe and to enhance the existing chronological picture for northeast Honduras. A total of 35 samples, all consisting of charcoal, were submitted for radiocarbon dating. Care was taken to ensure that each sample came from a context that could be interpreted in an archaeologically meaningful way. The analyses were carried out by the Klaus Tschira Archaeometry Centre at the University of Heidelberg under the direction of Ronny Friedrich. All dates were determined using a MICADAS accelerator (AMS dating). The ^{14}C ages are normalized to δ^{13}C=-25‰ and calibrated to calendar ages using the data set INTCAL13 and the software SwissCal (L. Wacker, ETH-Zurich). Most samples cover a period between AD 900–987 cal 1 sigma and 1471–1622 cal 1 sigma (Figure 23, Table 1) and thus correspond to the Transitional Selin, Early Cocal, and Late Cocal periods of the existing chronology. Three samples date to the Early and Basic Selin phases but are currently difficult to interpret. In the following, the dates obtained from the analyses are used in combination with stratigraphic observations to reconstruct the chronology of the occupation of Guadalupe (see also Figure 17).

Sample No.	Inventory No.	Context	Age BP	Age cal 1 σ	Age cal 2 σ
5	28	Ceramic layers	391 +/- 22	1449 - 1609 AD	1443 - 1619 AD
8	29	Ceramic layers	409 +/- 22	1444 - 1473 AD	1438 - 1615 AD
2	10	Ceramic layers	470 +/- 23	1427 - 1443 AD	1416 - 1449 AD
11	15	Ceramic layers	477 +/- 22	1425 - 1441 AD	1415 - 1447 AD
7	12	Ceramic layers	508 +/- 23	1414 - 1432 AD	1404 - 1442 AD
12	15	Ceramic layers	611 +/- 23	1303 - 1394 AD	1297 - 1400 AD
13	53	Ceramic layers	635 +/- 25	1296 - 1388 AD	1287 - 1011 AD
32	84	Pit U1	357 +/- 24	1471 - 1622 AD	1454 - 1633 AD
25	68	Posthole	476 +/- 23	1426 - 1442 AD	1415 - 1448 AD
29	54	Natural layer	738 +/- 18	1267 - 1279 AD	1260 - 1285 AD
19	62	Natural layer (B)	833 +/- 23	1186 - 1245 AD	1166 - 1256 AD
22	55	Natural layer	883 +/- 23	1059 - 1207 AD	1046 - 1217 AD
23	70	Natural layer (C)	765 +/- 18	1256 - 1275 AD	1225 - 1278 AD
46	79	Bajareque concentration	698 +/- 19	1278 - 1291 AD	1271 - 1379 AD
34	61	Bajareque concentration	760 +/- 18	1258 - 1275 AD	1225 - 1280 AD
98	234	Burial 1	823 +/- 19	1212 - 1251 AD	1170 - 1260 AD
88	176	Burial 2	425 +/- 18	1441 - 1457 AD	1436 - 1477 AD
38	104	Bajareque concentration	778 +/- 18	1226 - 1269 AD	1223 - 1273 AD
80	185	Burial 2	786 +/- 18	1225 - 1264 AD	1220 - 1270 AD
104	185	Burial 2	1551 +/- 19	433 - 544 AD	428 - 557 AD
87	192	Burial 3	900 +/- 19	1049 - 1166 AD	1043 - 1205 AD
101	201	Burial 3	1056 +/- 18	986 - 1014 AD	907 - 1021 AD
48	80	Bajareque concentration	768 +/- 19	1251 - 1274 AD	1224 - 1277 AD
96	231	Bone concentration	1371 +/- 23	648 - 664 AD	625 - 679 AD
56	100	Pit	877 +/- 19	1158 - 1205 AD	1051 - 1217 AD
69	191	Pit	946 +/- 19	1033 - 1149 AD	1027 - 1153 AD
67	183	Pit (K)	1008 +/- 19	998 - 1029 AD	988 - 1037 AD
36	144	Pit (J)	1086 +/- 22	901 - 990 AD	895 - 1013 AD
42	82	Stone row	957 +/- 19	1028 - 1147 AD	1023 - 1153 AD
50	121	Clay floor (E)	981 +/- 22	1019 - 1145 AD	1000 - 1151 AD
35	128	Charcoal concentration	984 +/- 20	1018 - 1117 AD	998 - 1150 AD
53	109	Hearth	987 +/- 32	1015 - 1147 AD	989 - 1153 AD
17	57	Natural Layer	1093 +/- 26	900 - 987 AD	892 - 1011 AD
51	142	Posthole	1089 +/- 19	902 - 988 AD	894 - 1011 AD

Table 1   [14]C dates and their contexts in stratigraphical order (F. Fecher).

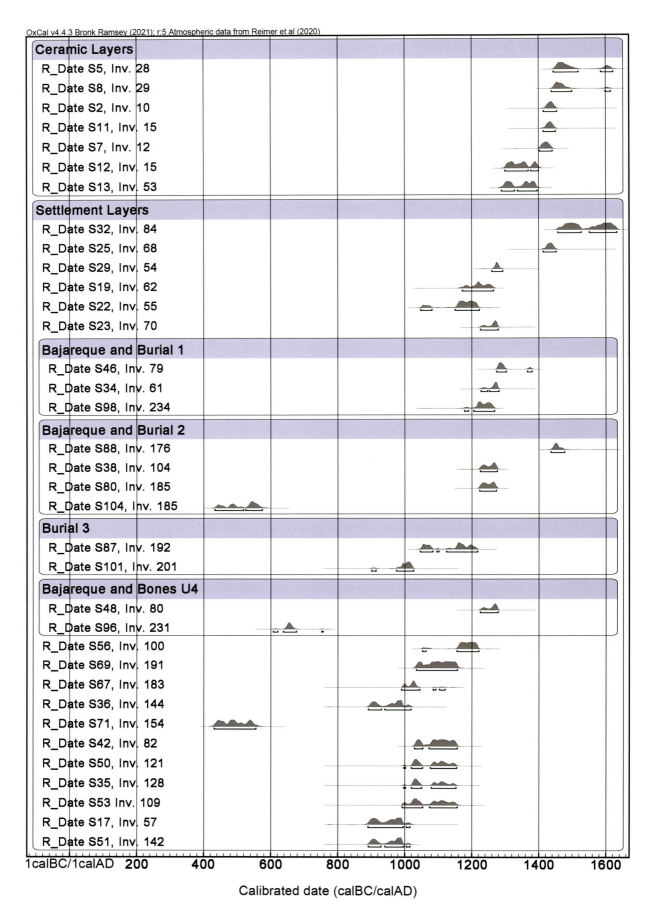

OxCal v4.4.3 Bronk Ramsey (2021); r:5 Atmospheric data from Reimer et al (2020)

Ceramic Layers
R_Date S5, Inv. 28
R_Date S8, Inv. 29
R_Date S2, Inv. 10
R_Date S11, Inv. 15
R_Date S7, Inv. 12
R_Date S12, Inv. 15
R_Date S13, Inv. 53

Settlement Layers
R_Date S32, Inv. 84
R_Date S25, Inv. 68
R_Date S29, Inv. 54
R_Date S19, Inv. 62
R_Date S22, Inv. 55
R_Date S23, Inv. 70

Bajareque and Burial 1
R_Date S46, Inv. 79
R_Date S34, Inv. 61
R_Date S98, Inv. 234

Bajareque and Burial 2
R_Date S88, Inv. 176
R_Date S38, Inv. 104
R_Date S80, Inv. 185
R_Date S104, Inv. 185

Burial 3
R_Date S87, Inv. 192
R_Date S101, Inv. 201

Bajareque and Bones U4
R_Date S48, Inv. 80
R_Date S96, Inv. 231
R_Date S56, Inv. 100
R_Date S69, Inv. 191
R_Date S67, Inv. 183
R_Date S36, Inv. 144
R_Date S71, Inv. 154
R_Date S42, Inv. 82
R_Date S50, Inv. 121
R_Date S35, Inv. 128
R_Date S53 Inv. 109
R_Date S17, Inv. 57
R_Date S51, Inv. 142

1calBC/1calAD 200 400 600 800 1000 1200 1400 1600

Calibrated date (calBC/calAD)

23   Plotted diagram of radiocarbon dates in stratigraphic order, created with Oxcal (F. Fecher).

The following samples were taken from the ceramic layer (A): 2, 5, 7, 8, 11, 12, and 13. All samples were associated with ceramic concentrations. However, as these are not whole vessels but broken vessels, it cannot be assumed that the samples date the contents of the respective vessels. The data must be interpreted with caution and can only be used for orientation here. They date from AD 1296–1388 cal 1 sigma to AD 1449–1609 cal 1 sigma. We can therefore assume that the ceramic layer accumulated between AD 1300 and 1450. The ^{14}C dates further suggest that the deposit is not the result of a single event but that it accumulated over several years. One sample (Sample 19) was taken from the light-colored earth directly below the pottery (B) and dates to AD 1186–1245. One sample from the gravel layer (C) (Sample 23) dates to AD 1256–1275. Since both samples were taken from the layer without having any particular context, caution should be taken when interpreting them. However, the upper occupation layers tend to have a similar dating to the *bajareque* concentrations and the burials.

Hearth and burnt layer (E): For both the hearth and burn feature, we were able to recover a single carbon sample each. Sample 53 comes from the hearth and dates to AD 1015–1147. Sample 50 is from the red clay floor and dates to AD 1019–1145. The dates support the stratigraphic observations that both features belong to the same occupation layer and are approximately contemporaneous.

Pits in Unit 1: Only three dates can be assigned with certainty to the pits in Unit 1. The problem here is that the pits were not clearly defined in the plana and only became partly visible in the profile. The extension in the plana cannot be definitively reconstructed. Nevertheless, Sample 36 can be assigned to Inv. 144 (J) (AD 901-990). Sample 67 can be assigned to Inv. 183 (K) (AD 998–1029). Sample 69 can be assigned to the pit in the south profile (L) (Inv. 191) (AD 1027–1153). The dating suggests that the pits were dug during the period of one of the older occupation layers, but even here, the dating is uncertain, especially since the samples come from the pit fill.

Bajareque: Four samples were taken from the *bajareque* concentrations (M). Sample 34, 38, 46, and 48 belong to these features (see Table 1). They all date to the period between AD 1228 and 1291 and make it seem very plausible that the accumulations were formed at about the same time or within a few years. The stratigraphic situation also supports this assumption. Furthermore, the dating shows that the *bajareque* concentrations tend to date to a later time than the hearth and the clay floor.

Burials: The radiocarbon dates of the burials do not provide a clear picture. The following samples can be assigned to the burials: 80, 87, 88, 96, 98, 101, and 104.

Note, again, that these samples are not bones but charcoal found in close proximity to the bones; thus, the interpretation is uncertain. The samples date to very different periods. The oldest sample dates to AD 433–544 1 sigma cal, while the youngest to AD 1441–1457 1 sigma cal. Only two dates overlap in time, Samples 80 and 98. These correspond to the burials found below the *bajareque* concentrations (Burials 1 and 2). Interestingly, their dating coincides with the dating of the *bajareque*, which suggests an association between the *bajareque* and burials is likely. Concerning the other samples, an interpretation is difficult. They may indicate that the burials were interred over a longer period of time.

We can conclude the following: The data from stratigraphy and radiocarbon dating identify Hypothesis 2 as the more likely hypothesis. This hypothesis states that the *bajareque* is associated with the burials and that these pits were deepened by the youngest occupation layer below the pottery layer. This is suggested by the following facts:

1. The *bajareque* in Units 3 and 4 is located directly below the ceramic layer.
2. The concentrations of *bajareque* are located on a similar level but higher than the clay floor and the hearth.
3. The radiocarbon dating indicates that the concentrations of *bajareque* and the burials below it date to the same period.
4. The dating of the occupation layer below the ceramic layer (B) coincides with the dating of the burials.
5. The hearth and the clay floor (E) tend to date earlier.

In addition, a second occupation layer is identified at the level of the clay floor and the hearth (E), which can also be seen in the profile and was probably related to a fire. To what extent the second clay floor in Unit 3 (F) is associated with this horizon remains unclear; based on the stratigraphic conditions, it is probably older. Unfortunately, there are no radiocarbon dates from this feature. Furthermore, it remains unclear from which level the pits in Unit 1 were excavated. From a purely stratigraphic point of view, their sequence is difficult to reconstruct. At least for Pit 1 (I) and Pit 2 (J), it seems as if they are more associated with the older occupation layer. The ^{14}C dates tend to support this hypothesis.

When interpreting the situation, we have to keep in mind that the excavation only gives us insight into a small portion of the mound, which makes it difficult to recognize and assess stratigraphic relationships. A large-scale excavation would certainly contribute to a better understanding of the situation and further clarify the connection between the features, especially with regard to the sequence of the pits in Unit 1.

4.2.3 Features

Now that the stratigraphic sequence and dating of the features have been discussed in the sections above, the most important features will be presented again and described in more detail here. If the features are visible in the profile, the corresponding capital letter that identifies the feature in the profile drawing is indicated.

4.2.3.1 Ceramic Layers

Inv.: 5-17, 21-33 43, 44, 46, 47, 52, 53, 58, 59, and 71 (A): The ceramic concentration is addressed here as a single feature, even though we assume that it is not the result of a single event. The concentration almost covers the entire profile section. It is about 1 m thick in the center of the mound and becomes thinner towards the east. It mostly consists of ceramic sherds broken into large fragments. Due to their state of preservation, we must assume that the fragments were intentionally deposited. Especially in the lower layers, the fragments often lie in conjunction with one another (see Figure 18). This deposit may have been related to the consumption of food and drinks, which is suggested by the high number of animal bones and mollusks associated with the sherds. It is possible that these acts were accompanied by ritual activities, which are indicated by the presence of musical instruments.

Although no internal stratigraphy is evident within the ceramic accumulation, we assume that it is not the result of a one-time event but that the accumulation formed over several years or decades. We, therefore, believe that the ceramic accumulation represents the remains of periodically performed ritual activities, more precisely the remnants of feasts (see below). This is corroborated by the following facts:

1. The accumulation consists of a very large number of ceramic fragments that were not deposited simultaneously or within a short period.
2. The radiocarbon dating suggests a time span from AD 1296–1388 to AD 1449–1609 for its formation.
3. The stylistic analysis of ceramics indicates that there is a stylistic development within the deposited ceramics (see below).

4.2.3.2 Hearth

Inv. 109 (Figure 24): The hearth feature is located in Unit 2 and is delimited by the following coordinates: 9023.40 E / 7620.35 N and 9024 E / 7619.20 N. It was first defined at an elevation of 19.35 masl and has its lower limit at 19.20 masl. The feature is clearly delimited, and it is characterized by its oval shape. It consists of a grey-brown, dark, loose earth with numerous pieces of charcoal. Additionally, medium-sized stones (about 10 cm) and a few ceramic fragments were associated with it.

4.2.3.3 Stone Rows

Inv. 97 (Figure 25): In Unit 1, at an elevation of about 19.40 masl, we encountered a cluster of medium-sized stones (5–12 cm). The stones are especially concentrated in the eastern part of Unit 1, where they are arranged in two rows with a north-south orientation. In the north as well as in the south, the rows extend into the profile. Most of the stones are unworked, whereas one of the stones has a strikingly rectangular shape and may have been worked. This is possibly the demarcation of an area (pit?) or the base of a house wall. The earth surrounding the stones is very hard and associated with charcoal fragments and small ceramic fragments. It might belong to the same occupation layer that is marked by the hearth and the clay floor.

4.2.3.4 Clay Floors

Inv. 111, 121, and 135 (E) (Figure 26): The feature is a red clay floor, hardened from either accidental or intentional burning. Three different inventory numbers were assigned to the feature. In this case, a new inventory number was assigned for each artificial layer where the floor was identified. It is located in the north-western part of Unit 3 and is delimited by the following coordinates: 9024 E / 7619.64 N and 9025.70 E / 7621 N. The feature was first identified at 19.30 masl and ends at about 19.15 masl. It is composed of a reddish, hard-packed earth in which small gravel inclusions are found. The feature contained small pieces of charcoal, small ceramic fragments, and a burnt animal bone. In the north, the feature extends into the profile. In the west (Unit 2), the strong reddish color is no longer visible, but at about the same level or slightly elevated, there is a very hard earth that can be interpreted as the continuation of the floor (Inv. 113). The hearth (Inv. 109) is associated with this feature.

Inv. 148 and 151 (F) (Figure 27): The feature is another reddish clay floor hardened by fire. It is located on the southern border of Units 2 and 3 and is delimited by the following coordinates: 9023.50 E / 7619 N and 9025.05 / 7620.30 N. It was first defined at an elevation of 19.19 masl and ends at about 19.10 masl. The feature has an amorphous shape and extends into the south profile. It is characterized by a very hard, reddish earth. Small pieces of charcoal and small ceramic fragments were found associated with it.

4.2.3.5 Postholes and Ditches

Several small round discolorations were identified that likely represent postholes. The interpretation of these features is complicated by the fact that they were often not clearly visible during excavation, and their upper portion was not recognized in all cases. However, some patterns can be observed.

Several postholes are located in Unit 3. Some of them (Inv. 63, 65, 67, 68, 69, 76, 95, and 96) were first observed at an elevation between 19.56 masl and 19.50 masl (Figure 28, Figure 29). They have different depths ranging from 5 to 36 cm. They may represent the traces of one or more buildings. However, a building layout cannot be reconstructed due to the small section revealed by the excavation. At the same level, there is another discoloration (Inv. 66) in Unit 3 (see Figure 28). It lies in the southern part and extends into the southern profile. The discoloration is T-shaped, about 20 cm wide, and 5 cm deep. It is possibly a kind of ditch associated with the architecture.

Three round discolorations are located in Unit 2 and were first defined at an elevation between 19.21 masl and 19.18 masl (Inv. 140–142) (Figure 30). Inv. 140 and 141 represent possible postholes, with diameters of 25 cm. They are about 6 cm deep. The third discoloration (Inv. 142) is more likely to be a small pit with a diameter of 47 cm. It is 61 cm deep and tapers towards the bottom. It is possible that these depressions are related to the occupation layer indicated by the older clay floor.

4.2.3.6 Concentrations of Bajareque Fragments and Burials

During excavations, the remains of at least five individuals were found. The remains of two individuals (Burials 2 and 3) were recovered by block excavations to allow osteological analysis in a laboratory. Since the bones were in a very fragile condition, consolidation and conservation were also part of the analysis. The latter were carried out under the direction of Dr. Luisa Mainou (Instituto Nacional de Antropología e Historia). Preliminary osteological studies were conducted by Dr. Julio Chi Keb (Universidad Autónoma de Yucatán). Like the analysis of vertebrate fauna, the analysis of human remains was planned for the 2020 spring campaign. Due to the early termination of the campaign, only preliminary studies could be carried out. The conservation work was therefore limited to an initial inventory and the development of a strategy for future consolidation and conservation. The osteological studies did not go beyond initial visual analyses and served to identify the bones present and to draw conclusions about the burial types. Due to the poor preservation of the bones and the limited time available, no observations on age, sex, or pathology could be made. These studies are to be complemented by more detailed analyses in the future. As we assume that concentrations of *bajareque* and the burials are related, these features are considered together from here on.

Unit 4 North: Inv. 61, 79, 157, and 234 (M; Burial 1). This feature is located in the northern section of Unit 4 and extends into the northern profile. It is marked by a concentration of *bajareque* on its top (Figure 31). The concentration was defined as a feature for the first time at 19.50 masl (Inv. 61, later continued as Inv. 79), although it is clear from the northern profile that the *bajareque* already appeared above this level. At an elevation of 19.50 m, the concentration has a distribution of 9027.74 E / 7620.26 N to 9029.44 E / 7621 N and displays an elongated-oval shape. The state of preservation indicates that the *bajareque* fragments were exposed to fire. They are reddish-brown in color and range in size from 1 to 8 cm. Impressions on the fragments indicate the construction technique and the material the walls were constructed with, which seems to have been cane or some other straight material (Figure 32). Beside the *bajareque*, small pieces of charcoal, stones, two obsidian fragments, and small ceramic fragments were found. The concentration decreases more and more towards the bottom and ends at about 19.10 masl.

Below the concentration of *bajareque*, a discoloration is very clearly defined (Inv. 157) (Figure 33) that has approximately the same distribution as the *bajareque*: 9027.58 E / 7620.5 N to 9028.5 E / 7621 N. It is elongated-oval and also extends into the north profile. The earth is light brown and hard, interspersed with gravel, single pieces of *bajareque*, small ceramic fragments, and pieces of charcoal. The discoloration extends over several layers. At an elevation of 18.45 masl, it takes on a very distinct rectangular shape with a length of 185 cm and is assigned a new inventory number (Inv. 234) (Figure 34). It now stands out clearly from the surrounding earth due to its dark color. The excavation of this feature revealed an inhumation in a poor state of preservation (Burial 1, Figure 35). Not all bones were clearly visible as the upper part of the burial extends into the north profile. After careful documentation, no further studies were conducted, and the burial was buried again for future research. Due to the continuity of the *bajareque*, the discoloration, and the burial pit, it is assumed that the respective features represent a single feature and belong together.

Unit 4 South: Inv. 80, 202, and 231 (M): The feature is located to the south of Unit 4 and extends into the south profile. It was observed for the first time at an elevation of 19.40 masl (Inv. 80) (see Figure 31). It is limited by the following coordinates: 9027.50 E / 7619 N and 9029.52 E / 7620.02 N. The feature consists of a concentration of *bajareque* fragments, which range up to 6 cm in diameter. Furthermore, ceramic fragments, obsidian fragments, and pieces of charcoal were found. The concentration decreases towards the bottom and ends at about 19.10 masl. Below the *bajareque* concentration, a dark discoloration was noted at an elevation of 18.80 masl (Inv. 202). It is round and measures about 36 cm in diameter. The discoloration consists of dark, sandy earth with pieces of charcoal and small ceramic fragments. At 18.70 masl, the discoloration was no longer present. It remains unclear if the discoloration is stratigraphically related to the *bajareque* concentration (Inv. 80).

At an elevation of 18.45 masl, a concentration of human bones was discovered at the same position (Inv. 231) (see Figure 34; Figure 36). The bones were surrounded by a round, dark discoloration measuring 102 cm in diameter. The bones were in a very poor state of preservation and were not extracted. The extent to which the three features are associated remains unclear at this point since the stratigraphic continuity is not as clear as in Inv. 61. It cannot be reconstructed in the south profile either. Here it rather looks as if the *bajareque* concentration (Inv. 80) is associated with a cranium located on the border between Unit 3 and Unit 4 in the south profile (Inv. 219).

South Profile: Inv. 219 (Figure 37): This feature is a human cranium. It is located in the lower part of the south profile on the border between Units 3 and 4. It has an elevation between 18.68 and 18.56 masl. It is 20 cm wide and 12 cm tall. The cranium faces east, with only the left half being visible. The right half is embedded in the profile. The cranium was left in its original position at the end of the excavation, and no analyses were realized.

Unit 3/Unit 4 Center: Inv. 104, 123, 138, 173, 174, 176, and 185 (Burial 2): This feature represents a concentration of *bajareque* and is located in the center of the planum between the borders of Unit 3 and Unit 4 (Figure 38). The position between units sometimes makes it difficult to obtain an overview of the features. Initially, the feature was observed in Unit 3 at an elevation of 19.52 masl. The concentration ends at approx. 19.30 masl. Below this concentration, a dark discoloration was noticed (Inv. 123 and 138) (see Figure 26). From an elevation of 18.90 masl, this discoloration takes on a clear rectangular shape (Inv. 173 and 174) (Figure 39) and is also visible in Unit 4 (Inv. 176). It has an east-west orientation. The earth differs clearly due to its dark color and is associated with *bajareque* fragments and small ceram-

ic fragments. In the western part of the feature, there is a large, vertically positioned ceramic sherd.

During the excavation of the feature, an inhumation was uncovered (Inv. 176 and 185) (Burial 2, Figure 40). The human remains were in a very fragile condition and were recovered by a block excavation for subsequent analysis. The analysis of the bones showed that the individual was buried in an extended dorsal position. The anatomical position of the bones further indicates that the deceased was buried in a kind of box or coffin or was wrapped in a cloth. Thus, the shoulders are slightly elevated, and the arms lie close to the body. The position of the articulated bones indicates that this is a primary burial. However, the skeleton is not complete; some bones are missing. Notably, the pelvis, femurs, and right arm were not present. The cranium is also no longer present; only individual fragments were found near the sternum, which may indicate that the head was once supported but fell forward when the organic material perished. Nevertheless, the absence of these bones remains puzzling. One possible explanation may be the preservation conditions, which can have quite different effects on individual bones, depending on their composition and properties. Pathologies can also have negative influences on the preservation of bones. Another possible interpretation would be a secondary use of the burials, where single bones were removed for ritual purposes. There is evidence for secondary burials in other archaeological sites in northeast Honduras, and such practices are mentioned in ethnohistorical reports (see chapter 5.1.3.2). No observations could be made regarding sex or age, and pathologies could not be detected due to the poor state of preservation of the bones.

Unit 4 Center: Inv. 192, 201, and 215 (Burial 3) (Figure 41): This feature is another individual. It is located in Unit 4, just east of the individual in the center of Unit 3/Unit 4. It was first observed at an elevation of 18.80 masl, where it was noticed due to a discoloration (Inv. 201). The earth is soft and associated with small pebbles, ceramic fragments, pieces of *bajareque*, and charcoal. In the eastern part of the feature, we also found a large vertical ceramic fragment, similar to the feature in the center of Unit 3/Unit 4. During excavation of the discoloration, several human bones were exposed. These bones were recovered through block excavation and analyzed. The analysis revealed an individual in a semiflexed lateral position. This is specifically indicated by the cranium that lies on its right side and faces south. However, several bones are missing, such as the pelvis, the thorax region, and parts of the arms. And again, it is not clear whether the absence of bones is related to preservation conditions or indicates secondary use. About 20 cm further to the east, we identified another bone, which is interpreted by Julio Chi Keb as the base of a cranium. This bone cannot be assigned to either of these two individuals and possibly indicates the presence of another individual.

Unit 4 East: Inv. 235: After the extraction of the bones from Inv. 201 and 215, a dark discoloration became visible at an elevation of 18.45 masl (see Figure 34). It clearly stands out from the surrounding earth and has a rectangular shape. It has the same orientation as Inv. 234 and extends into the east profile. This feature has not been excavated, but we suspect that, just as Inv. 234, it represents a burial pit.

In summary, the excavation revealed the remains of at least five individuals (three skeletons, the skull in the profile and the skull base), of which two skeletons were recovered and subjected to preliminary analyses. It is clear from these observations that we are dealing with a burial site with multiple interments and that the concentrations of *bajareque* are clearly connected to them.

4.2.3.7 Other Pits

Unit 1 South: Inv. 191, 156 (L): The pit is located in the southwest corner of Unit 1 and extends into both the western and southern profiles. The feature was first defined at an elevation of 18.60 masl, where it was clearly identified by its dark color. The feature reduces in size towards its bottom and ends at an elevation of 17.44 masl. The pit fill consists of earth, pebbles, pieces of charcoal, stones, small and medium-sized ceramic fragments, and a few animal bones. The purpose of the pit remains unclear, as does its upper limit. At an elevation of 18.60 masl, it became clearly visible for the first time, but even before that, it was noticed during excavation that the earth in this area is darker. A feature was already defined in the same location at an elevation of 19.00 masl. So, it is possible that the pit was excavated from a higher level. The southern profile also suggests this, but the level at which the pit was introduced cannot be clearly determined here either.

Unit 1 North: Inv. 83, 84, 98, 107, 115, 130, 144, 145, 154, 183, 184, 190, 212, and 213 (I, J, and K): In the northern section of Unit 1, several perturbations are visible which are interpreted as likely pits. However, the boundaries of the respective pits are unclear in both the profile and the plana, and so the features were defined differently at different elevations. The sequence and extent of the pits cannot be reconstructed with certainty. We can likely identify three pits here, two of which did not contain any special finds. However, a suspected third pit contains

noticeably large charcoal fragments, as well as burnt clay. It is very narrow and deep and must have taken great effort to create. The purpose of this pit remains a mystery; no comparable features are reported in the region. It is possible that this pit is related to production, perhaps food was prepared here, or even pottery was fired. The interpretation of these pits is further complicated by the fact that the excavation only gives insight into a part of the situation. It is possible that the contents of the respective pits were not revealed by our excavations. It is also conceivable that some of them are additional burial pits, of which the contents are no longer preserved. However, this remains speculation at this point.

4.2.3.8 Summary

The stratigraphy, radiocarbon dating, and features show us that Guadalupe was a site of ritual importance that was occupied during the end of the Transitional Selin period and throughout the Cocal period. The current state of knowledge provides the following picture: During the Transitional Selin at the latest, Guadalupe was used as a settlement site. Postholes and floors indicate the presence of structures. It is possible that the site was already used as a burial ground at this point. In Unit 1, several pits were excavated, the purpose of which remains an open question at the moment. Future excavations may indicate that these pits were also related to burials. Starting at around ca. AD 1260, burials were introduced into the occupation layers, which were covered with earth and *bajareque*. Two individuals were recovered, one in an extended position and one in a flexed position. The discovery of a cranium in the south profile and a cranial base to the east of these two individuals indicates the presence of other burials at this level. Below the recovered individuals, there are at least two more burial pits, one of which was excavated in order to confirm the presence of another individual. Obviously, this is a burial site that was used over an extended period of time. In connection to the burials, ritual activities were performed in which the consumption of food and drinks played a central role. Ceramic vessels were deposited in the vicinity of the burials. These activities were carried out repeatedly, resulting in the accumulation of a dense concentration of ceramics over time. These deposits apparently took place throughout the entire Cocal period and ended sometime in the 16th century, possibly as a consequence of Spanish arrival. It is assumed that these deposits are the remains of feasts that were related to the burials, which will be elaborated on in section 5.1.3.

24   Hearth (Inv. 109) in Unit 2 (T. Remsey).

25   Stone rows in Unit 1 (Inv. 97) (M. Schacht).

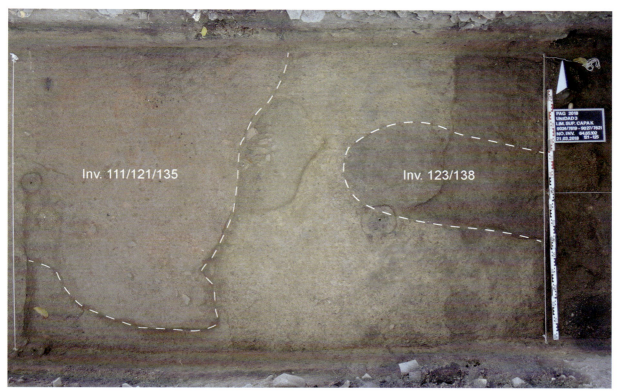

26   Red hardened clay floor (Inv. 111/121/135) and dark discoloration (Inv. 123, 138) in Unit 3 (N. Hoge).

27   Hardened clay floor in Unit 3 (Inv. 148, 151) (M. Schacht).

28   Postholes and discolorations in Unit 3 (N. Mejía).

29   Postholes in Unit 3 (M. Reindel).

30   Postholes and pits in Unit 2 (T. Remsey).

31   Bajareque concentrations in Unit 4 (J. Mattes).

32   Bajareque fragments with imprints (M. Reindel).

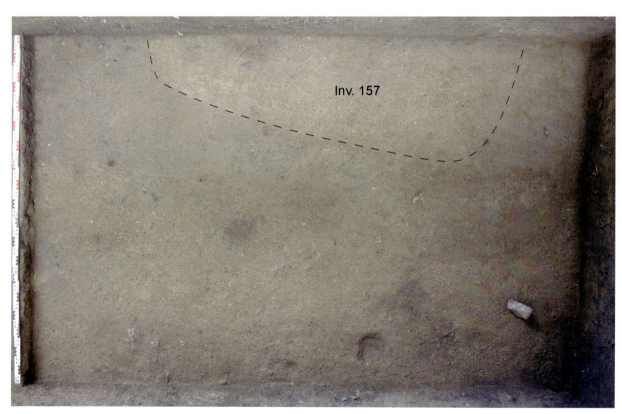

Inv. 157

33   Discoloration in Unit 4 (Inv. 157) (J. Mattes).

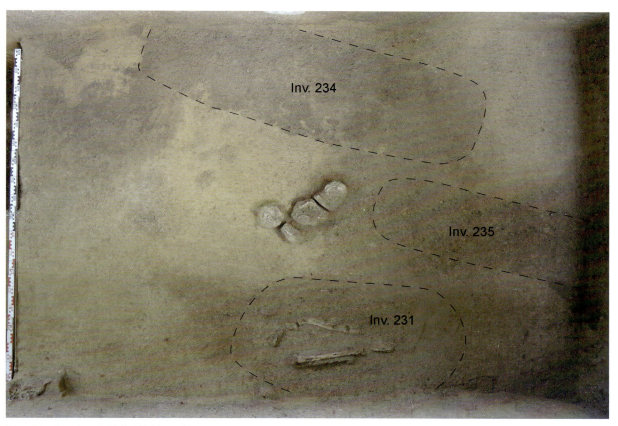

34   Discolorations in Unit 4 (J. Mattes).

35   Burial in poor state of preservation (Inv. 234, Unit 4) (J. Langmann).

36   Long bones in Unit 4 (Inv. 231) (J. Mattes)

37   Cranium in the south profile of Unit 4 (Inv. 219) (K. Engel).

38   Bajareque concentration in Unit 3 and Unit 4 (Inv. 104) (M. Schacht).

39   Discoloration in Unit 3 and Unit 4 (Inv. 173, 174) (K. Engel).

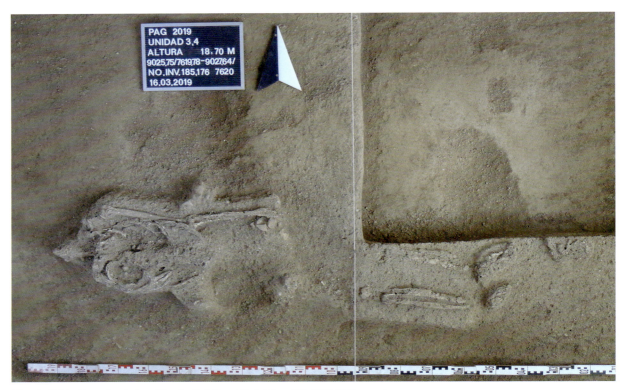

40   Individual in extended position in Unit 3 and Unit 4 (Inv. 176, 185) (T. Remsey).

41   Individual in flexed position in Unit 4. The base of the cranium is in the east, which can likely be attributed to a different individual (J. Mattes).

4.3 Survey

The excavations of the mound in Guadalupe have provided important information on the chronology, structure, and activities in a Cocal-period coastal settlement and have given us insight into local burial customs. Guadalupe is part of a larger network of settlements, the study of which was another objective of our activities. Several surveys were conducted to reconstruct the settlement system on the north coast, identify additional nodes in the network, and understand Guadalupe's function in this system. The first step was the exploration of the modern settlement itself. This was aimed at estimating the extent of the pre-Hispanic settlement (based on the distribution of pottery concentrations and the dark soil) and documenting possible further architectural remains on the surface. Several inspections took place, usually accompanied by a local guide who was familiar with the site. The distribution of the pottery concentrations was recorded with a hand-held GPS, and based on this data, a distribution map was made showing the presumed extent of the pre-Hispanic settlement (Figure 42).

Surveys around Guadalupe served to identify previously unregistered sites. The regional survey concentrated on the coastal strip, including the northern slope of the Cordillera Nombre de Dios in the area between Betulia in the west and Trujillo in the east. Another area of interest was the Guaimoreto Lagoon area and the Aguán Valley to the south. In order to investigate possible contacts to the north and to assess the relationship to the offshore islands, trips were made to the island of Guanaja. The aim was to get an idea of the surrounding settlements and the settlement structure in the area during the Cocal period. What did the settlements look like, what dimensions and layouts did they have, which locations were preferred? During the surveys, we looked for surface material that could provide information about the chronological position of the settlement. A series of test excavations were to provide information about settlement chronology and explain possible diachronic changes in the settlement system. First, we gathered information from local people, which led us to archaeological sites. After we had visited some sites, we analyzed the location of other possible sites by predictive modeling in a GIS. The areas with a high probability for the location of sites were visited together with local guides. The information was recorded in forms and later collected in the database. The survey was documented by sketches and photographs. We also worked closely with the IHAH, which developed a new interest in the region, and conducted surveys between the respective field campaigns. Through the joint activities, 16 sites could be registered on the coast, the coastal cordillera, the Aguán Valley, and the Bay Islands. GPS coordinates were taken from all locations with a hand-held GPS. If there were surface finds, a selection was made and documented. In addition, 3D models of the sites Coraza Alta and Panamá were created with structure from motion via areal images captured with a drone. However, as the main survey work was planned for the 2020 field campaign, only preliminary results can be presented here.

Guadalupe. The survey in Guadalupe itself mainly investigated the distribution of pottery on the surface, as well as the distribution of dark, humic earth. Attention was also paid to the presence of architectural remains. The mapping of the surface ceramic shows that it is concentrated on the terrace and thus corresponds approximately to the modern area of habitation (see Figure 42). No archaeological material was observed east of the terrace. From the edge of the terrace in the east, the archaeological remains extend about 200 m to the west. In the south, they extend approximately to the heights of the modern road connecting Guadalupe to Trujillo. In the north, the ceramic concentrations are also limited to the terrace. Where the terrain slopes down to the beach, there are no more finds, and the earth is clearly different in its light color and sandy consistency. So, we can assume that the pre-Hispanic inhabitants deliberately chose the terrace as a settlement ground. The elevated location certainly relates to protection from flooding, which is common during the rainy season due to the rise of the nearby riverbed. Apart from the earthen mound on the school grounds, there are no other conspicuous elevations, as was proved by the topographic measurements. As an additional architectural feature, however, stone rows were discovered 50 m northwest of the excavation site. They consist of several unworked stones arranged in a linear pattern (Figure 43). They are associated with surface ceramics and possibly represent the foundation of a pre-Hispanic building. Other architectural elements have not been found, so we must assume that they were destroyed by modern settlement activities. Another possibility is that buildings were not erected on platforms but directly on the ground, which would be visible today only through rows of stones as mentioned above.

Coastal Strip and Cordillera Nombre de Dios. The descriptions of this area are based on the results of the survey activities led by Mike Lyons in 2020. The region from Betulia in the west to Trujillo in the east was the focus of the settlement surveys. Initially, the survey was carried out unsystematically, following information from local people. Based on these results, the hypothesis was developed that settlements were mainly located on flat terrain, next to river courses. In our GIS, predictive modeling was used to search for such places. These areas were visited, and, in many cases, sites were actually identified. The description of the sites follows from west to east, with emphasis on the Cocal-period settlements (Figure 44).

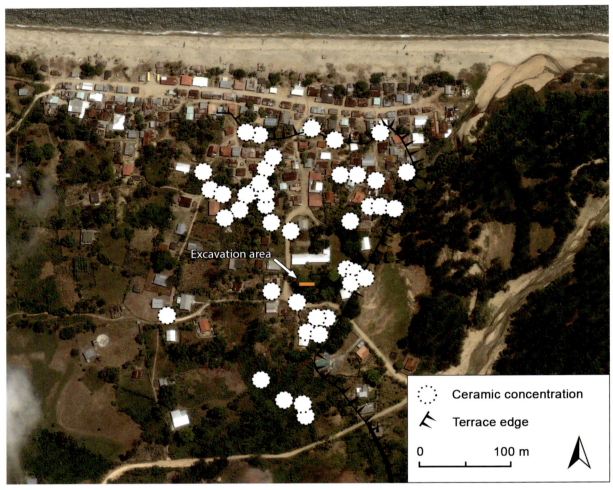

42   Map of ceramic concentrations in Guadalupe. Note that the location of the concentrations coincides with the extension of the river terrace (N. Hoge, P. Bayer).

In Betulia, where the Rio Betulia drains into the Atlantic Ocean, there are several sites whose relationship to each other is not yet clear. Near the eastern river bank (Betulia Bosque), there are several pottery concentrations, and isolated flat, elongated mounds are visible. In addition, paved paths were recorded at several locations (Figure 45). Such paved paths are a typical architectural element for Southern Central America. In northeast Honduras, they were documented in Río Claro (Healy 1978a), in the Culmí Valley (Begley 1999: 213f), on the Bay Islands (Rose 1904, cited in Hasemann 1977), and in the Aguán Valley (see below). The overview of the sites is impeded by dense vegetation. The surface material dates mainly to the Cocal phase. Further mounds and pottery concentrations were found in the modern settlement, which extends along the western river banks (Betulia Pueblo).

Some settlements are located at a higher elevation in the Cordillera. La Esperancita is located in the modern settlement of the same name. Here few surface pottery finds indicate the presence of a pre-Hispanic settlement. Very few artifacts have been found at the site and consist of only small undiagnostic ceramic fragments, which prevents preliminary dating of the site. Colonia Suyapa also lies in an elevated location (190 masl) on flat terrain along the Mármol Ravine, in a modern settlement. Mounds and dense artifact concentrations are found throughout nearly the entire site. Based on the large amount of evidence of intense human activity, we can assume that Colonia Suyapa must have been an important settlement in pre-Hispanic times. Surface finds include ceramic fragments, stone tools, and obsidian. The latter group of finds also includes fragments of prismatic blades. Of particular note are the many manos and metates found throughout the entire site. A zoomorph ocarina in a private collection is also said to have come from this site. The numerous diagnostic pottery fragments allow the occupation of Colonia Suyapa to be dated to the Cocal period and to portions of the Selin period. The site of La Polaca lies about one kilometer to the

43   Pre-Hispanic stone row in Guadalupe (N. Hoge).

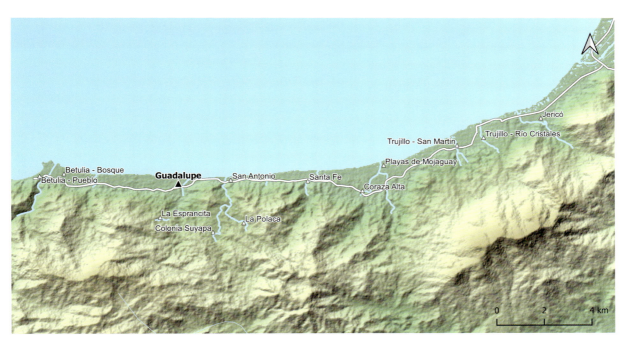

44   Coastal strip between Betulia and Trujillo with archaeological sites visited during the survey (M. Lyons). Topography derived from ASTER GDEM v3 elevation data (NASA 2019).

northeast of Colonia Suyapa and has an elevation of roughly 180 masl. It is located on a flat extension of terrain in the foothills of the cordillera Nombre de Dios and is traversed by the course of the Mármol River. Only a few artifacts have been found during inspection. Sur-face ceramics mainly consist of small, undiagnostic sherds and prevent the preliminary dating of the site.

The site of San Antonio occupies a part of the alluvial plain at the foothills of the Nombre de Dios mountain range, just a few meters from the sea. To the west, the

67

45   Cobble path in Betulia (K. Engel).

settlement is bordered by the Mármol River, which drains into the Atlantic Ocean. No clearly recognizable architectural structures have been observed so far, but ceramic fragments and obsidian on the surface indicate pre-Hispanic activity. Based on the ceramic fragments, the site can be dated to the Cocal phase.

The site of Santa Fe is located on the alluvial plain about 2 km west of San Antonio and is bordered by the Guinea River on its southeastern periphery. The site lies within the modern settlement of Santa Fe and has been largely overbuilt by recent settlement activities. However, a ceramics concentration could be identified near the northern shore of the Guinea River. An exceptionally dense concentration of obsidian fragments was found here, including an exhausted polyhedral core. The ceramics date to the Cocal period.

The site of Coraza Alta was first shown to us by Cruz Castillo. It occupies a part of the alluvial plains on the foothills of the cordillera Nombre de Dios and is crosscut by the modern road that runs along the coast. In the southeast, the site is bordered by the Corozo Alto Ravine. A large area of land was apparently modified in pre-Hispanic times, including the construction of ter-

races. Numerous earthen mounds are clearly visible on the surface. However, some of the features have been disturbed, as the site is now used as a cattle ranch. Several artifacts were found on the surface. These include pottery, greenstone objects (Figure 46), and a notably high number of stone artifacts. The latter include carefully crafted manos and metates of various sizes. The presence of large stones with elongated grooves (Figure 47), which may have been used for the production of other stone artifacts, indicate that that the site is a lithic workshop. Similar stones were already described by Sharer et al. (2009: 87f) along the river and were relocated by the project (Figure 48). Ceramics are abundant throughout the site and can be dated to the Selin period.

The site of Playas de Mojaguay is located on the coast, on the eastern bank of the Mojaguay River. Artifacts are very sparse throughout the site. Based on the few ceramic fragments, that have been found, the site may date to the Cocal period. Several sites have been identified in the settlement area of the town of Trujillo. They consist of ceramic concentrations and are located on the banks of the Cristales River and in the neighborhood of San Martín. In both cases, the pottery is undi-

46   Greenstone objects found at Coraza Alta (M. Reindel).

47   Ground stone with elongated grooves at Coraza Alta (J. Mattes).

48   Stones with engravings along the river course at Coraza Alta (M. Reindel).

agnostic and was not dated. Jericó is located east of the town center. It is located on a naturally raised terrace directly to the north of the Negro River. The site has been known for some time and was investigated by Cruz Castillo (2007). Dense concentrations of ceramic fragments and shell material can be found throughout the site. Other artifacts found include obsidian and a bark beater. The settlement has attracted attention mainly because two large boulders were found along the Negro River that have clear modifications. One of them has elongated grooves, similar to the boulders found at Coraza Alta. However, it was removed a few years ago. The second boulder has numerous round depressions on its surface (Figure 49). It is possible that these stones were also associated with the production of stone tools. The preliminary assessment of the pottery suggests a dating to the Cocal phase.

Surroundings of the Guaimoreto Lagoon. The most famous site in the area around the lagoon is Selin Farm, the "type site" for the Selin phase. The site was investigated by Healy (1978b) and was reexplored by Whitney Goodwin in her dissertation (2019). Since it is discussed in detail in these publications, it will not be addressed here. Additional sites were found in surveys conducted by the IHAH under the direction of Cruz Castillo. They are all located along the road leading south from Trujillo (Figure 50) and were visited together with Cruz Castillo. The Aldea Silin site consists of several small earthen mounds. There were no surface finds. Honduras Aguán consists of a very extensive terrace, which was probably settled at some point. The surface pottery dates the site to the Cocal period. Luz del Valle exhibits both the largest and most numerous architectural structures. A large settlement must have once existed here as there are several mounds about 4 m tall and up to 20 m long. Two elongated mounds are aligned parallel to each other, which is why Cruz Castillo interprets them as a possible ball court (Figure 51). The few surface ceramics are barely diagnostic, but I would tend to assign them to the Selin or early Cocal periods.

Aguán Valley. Three sites were visited in the Aguán Valley: Panamá, Rio Arriba 1 and Rio Arriba 2. While Panamá was also discovered during IHAH's surveys, Rio Arriba 1 and 2 were shown to us by Roby Payes, a local resident near Guadalupe. The Panamá site consists of at least ten earthen elongated mounds (Figure 52). The extension of the site to the south is not visible due to dense vegetation, but there may be more mounds in the area. Four elongated mounds are arranged more or less rectangularly and form a central space in which other mounds are located. This is a pattern that can often be observed in the northeast (Begley 1999; Mattes 2019). Mound B is the longest mound with a length of about 100 m. Mound A reaches a height of 3.5 m, which is rel-

49   Boulder with rounded notches at Jericó (J. Mattes).

atively high for the region. Mike Lyons mapped the site using structure from motion with areal imagery from a drone and created a digital elevation model and site map. Due to the surface ceramics, Panamá can be dated to the Cocal period.

Rio Arriba 1 and 2 are two neighboring sites near Rigores. They were shown to us by Roby Payes in 2018. Due to the surface pottery, Rio Arriba 1 can be assigned to the Selin period (Figure 53). It consists of several mounds up to 5 m in height that extend over a considerable area. Rio Arriba 2 is only a few meters away and dates to the Cocal period. Here, similar to Panamá, mounds extend up to 80 m long and form a large central plaza. The mounds are constructed on a terraced surface, the margins of which are supported by walls. Here, an active shaping of the environment is recognizable with a great deal of work put into structural engineering, which has not been registered in any other site in our study area. A paved path runs through the site, which according to local informants, leads to the coast (Figure 54). Interestingly, Rio Arriba 2 is located directly south of Guadalupe by about 20 km. Thus, the distance between the sites can easily be traversed within a day's

walk. Whether or not the pavement of the path is actually pre-Hispanic cannot be determined with absolute certainty. But one can assume that even if the paving corresponds to a later date, the course of the path goes back to pre-Hispanic times. Other sites in the Aguán Valley that have been registered but not yet investigated are discussed in Sharer et al. (2009).

Guanaja. Guanaja is the easternmost of the Bay Islands, which are located off the Honduran Atlantic coast. There, the already-known sites Plan Grande and Marble Hill were visited. Previously unregistered sites were visited together with local guides. Marble Hill is a hill with a diameter of about 100 m and a height of about 30 m. However, the geological formation does not consist of marble, as the name suggests, but of karst, which has eroded more slowly than the surrounding rock and has remained standing, resulting in a prominent landscape feature (Craig 1977). Due to its elevated position and its particular nature, it was referred to as a "fortress" in the literature (Strong 1935). During the visit, however, it could be noted that it must have been a typical settlement site. In addition, the karst rock is interspersed with smaller and larger caves, which were apparently used for

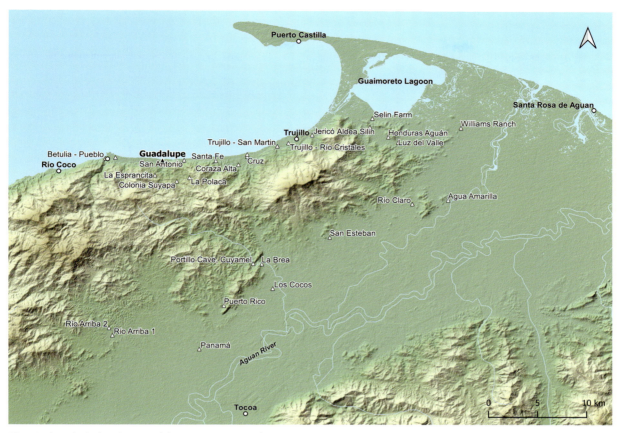

50   Archaeological Project Guadalupe survey area with sites mentioned in the text (M. Lyons). Topography derived from ASTER
GDEM v3 elevation data (NASA 2019).

51   Parallel mounds in Luz del Valle (F. Fecher).

the deposition of offerings. The surface pottery points to occupation during the Cocal phase.

Plan Grande is located about 500 m to the west. As the name suggests, it is located on a wide flat plain, which extends over the northeastern part of the island between Savannah Bight and Mangrove Bight. The site has been described several times, and test excavations were conducted by Mitchell-Hedges (unpublished) and Strong (1935). However, a comprehensive, systematic investigation has not yet taken place. Our interest was sparked by a publication by Feachem (1940), in which he depicted a large stone slab with a geometric design but was uncertain about the meaning of this pattern. I was able to identify this pattern as a *patolli* game board

known from the Mesoamerican culture area (Fecher 2019). The stone could be relocated in 2018, but the pattern was only barely recognizable. Additional flat stones with slight traces of engravings were discovered and photogrammetrically documented (Figure 55). These photographs were used to create 3D models. By applying filters to the models, incisions virtually invisible to the naked eye could be seen: Four further stone slabs show *patolli*-incisions (Figure 56). *Patolli* was a popular game that was often played during feasts and was tied to religious practice and cosmovision. Beans, *patol*, were used as dice, and tokens were set on a scoreboard that consisted of a cross or X-shaped pattern subdivided into quadrangular fields, sometimes accompanied by an additional frame of fields (Mountjoy 2001). Information on the game comes mainly from ethnohistorical sources about the Aztecs (Durán 1971:302f; Sahagún 1938:298, 320), but game boards were also found in the Maya area and West Mexico (Mountjoy 2005; Walden / Voorhies 2017). The presence of *patolli* game boards on Guanaja shows that the inhabitants were in contact with people from Mesoamerica, exchanging not only goods but also ideas. The five or more boards at Plan Grande further suggest that the site must have

52   3D mesh of the Panamá site, created with SfM from drone flight images (M. Lyons).

53   Selin period ceramic fragments from Rio Arriba 1 (F. Fecher).

54   Paved walkway in Rio Arriba 2 (J. Mattes).

been a central place of considerable importance. Interestingly, another *patolli* stone is known from the Mosquitia, which was shown to the author by Christine Woda (Figure 57). The implications regarding cultural contacts that can be drawn from the presence of these stones are addressed in more detail in the discussion section.

In addition to the two known sites, our team was led by the local guides Edgardo Ortega and Hans Weller to different locations where more petroglyphs are present (Figure 58). Another settlement site was identified on a private property in El Bight. The survey activities confirmed that Guanaja features a very similar material culture as our study area on the mainland, so it is assumed that the inhabitants of the respective regions were in close contact. The similarity of the pottery suggests that Guadalupe had contact with the islands as well as with the settlements in the hinterland, thus forming a kind of connection node between the two regions.

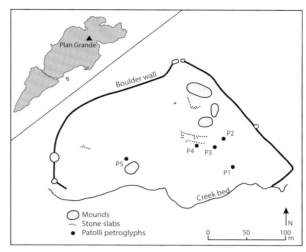

55 Map of Plan Grande with the location of patolli petroglyphs (after Strong 1935). First published in "F. Fecher, Patolli Petroglyphs in Northeast Honduras, Latin American Antiquity 30(3), p. 625", reproduced with permission.

56 Patolli petroglyphs from Plan Grande. a: photograph; b-d: 3D models of petroglyphs, on which the engravings become visible (M. Lyons, F. Fecher). First published in "F. Fecher, Patolli Petroglyphs in Northeast Honduras, Latin American Antiquity 30(3), p. 627", reproduced with permission.

57   Patolli petroglyph in Sawacito (courtesy of C. Woda). First published in "F. Fecher, Patolli Petroglyphs in Northeast Honduras, Latin American Antiquity 30(3), p. 625", reproduced with permission.

58   Petroglyph in Guanaja (M. Lyons).

4.4 Find Analysis

Both the excavations and the surveys have yielded numerous finds. Investigation of the material culture is particularly important because it can give us insight into everyday life, provide information about activities, subsistence, production, but also about existing networks. Because of their portability, finds and their analysis are the most important tools for an archaeologist to reconstruct networks and links, which is why they are given special attention here. The following chapters deal with the detailed presentation and description of the finds. The methods used for their analysis are outlined, and the results of the analyses are presented.

4.4.1 Ceramics

Ceramics represent the most extensive category of find by far. The thorough analysis of the pottery is important because it represents a large percentage of the material found in Guadalupe and thus is crucial for the interpretation of the site. It provides information about chronology and helps us to understand the function of the settlement. It is also present in most other settlements as a diagnostic element. By categorizing the pottery from Guadalupe and comparing it with pottery from other sites, we can reconstruct possible relationships between sites. For the investigation of ceramics, a new classification scheme has been developed, which helps systematize the material and address our research questions. The ceramic material can be divided into two groups: 1) vessels, which represent the majority, and 2) unique forms that include ocarinas, figurines, roller stamps, spindle whorls, and miniature vessels. In this chapter, vessels are addressed first, and a classification system is developed to describe them. The unique forms are then considered separately.

The ceramics of Guadalupe are characterized by incised decorations and plastic appliqués representing handles and supports. They are often shaped in human or animal form (Figure 59). As far as we understand, there are usually three supports and two handles on a vessel. Only a few fragments are painted. Thus, most vessels are the color of the clay, which is influenced by different firing techniques. Colors range from creamy-white to reddish-brown and dark grey. The considerable quantity and good preservation conditions of pottery in Guadalupe are especially suitable for describing and characterizing the pottery of the Cocal period. For this purpose, a classification scheme is developed below.

Material Basis for Classification. Classification of the ceramics is based on sherds from Unit 2 of the excavation (Figure 60). This unit was specifically chosen be-

cause there are many well-preserved fragments, and the stratigraphy is relatively straightforward. A total of 55,435 sherds were recovered in this unit. All ceramic sherds were washed, dried and separated into diagnostic and non-diagnostic objects. In the next step, diagnostic and non-diagnostic sherds were separated. The following sherds were treated as diagnostic sherds: 1) rim sherds, 2) sherds with decoration (incised or painted), 3) sherds with appliqués or individual appliqués, and 4) base fragments. The diagnostic material was labeled with an object number according to the following scheme: PAG (for Proyecto Arqueológico Guadalupe) - inventory number - object number, for example PAG-12-48. A total of 8241 diagnostic sherds were identified in Unit 2 and it is estimated that the enitre excavation yielded about 22,000 diagnostic ceramic fragments.

Only the diagnostic sherds were considered for further analysis, of which 7603 come from the ceramic layer. The amount of material from this layer had to be narrowed down further, to create a meaningful and manageable basis for classification. For this purpose, the fragments with the greatest possible information content were selected. In other words, this included sherds that exhibit as many combinations of attributes as possible (form, incisions, appliqués, paint). At the same time, care was taken to include as many different varieties of attributes as possible. An equal percentage was selected from each inventory number to ensure that the frequency of the attributes in each was reflected in the sample. For the settlement layers, all diagnostic sherds from which information could be obtained were selected. The sample contains a total of 868 fragments, i.e., slightly more than 10% of the total diagnostic sherds from Unit 2. It consists of 437 rim sherds, 133 wall sherds, 24 base sherds, and 273 appliqués. Only a single object could not be assigned to any of these categories (PAG-91-155). Observations of the sample were checked against the remaining diagnostic sherds of Unit 2.

This sampling strategy does not allow for statistical analysis. Instead, the aim is to illustrate and characterize the material in the best possible way, expand the existing range of forms, and create a typology as a basis for cultural comparisons. In the following, the research questions and the resulting methodology will be presented in more detail.

4.4.1.1 State of Research, Problems and Objectives

Research Questions. In order to gain an overview of and to organize a large amount of material, classification is necessary. Only by taxonomically structuring the material can patterns be recognized, regularities and irregularities identified, and comparable units created, or in the words of Manfred Eggert (2012: 125), "something

59 Zoomorph appliqués found in Guadalupe. Figurative appliqués are especially characteristic of the ceramic material from Guadalupe and were found in large numbers (M. Müller).

essentially unstructured can be transformed into something essentially structured"[11]. Classification depends on the research questions, and its methodology must be adapted to the existing material and the questions posed (Dunnell 1971: 115). In the first step, therefore, questions were defined that are to be asked of Guadalupe's material while ensuring that they *can* be asked due to the nature of the material selected for this work.

So far, little is known about the pottery of the Cocal phase in northeast Honduras. Therefore, only the more basic or fundamental questions can be asked about it. The first task is the comprehensive and detailed description of the material. Additionally, questions of the temporal and spatial distribution of the pottery have to be determined. Furthermore, we need to clarify what information the pottery can provide us about the activities that took place in Guadalupe. Finally, the formation of comparable ceramic categories and the comparison with the ceramic material of other regions should help address the extent to which Guadalupe's inhabitants were involved in networks. The specific questions that will be posed based on the ceramic material of Guadalupe are the following:

1. How can the ceramics of Guadalupe be characterized (descriptively)? Which attributes are present?
2. Is there a diachronic development of the material; can temporal differences be determined? Which attributes are relevant here?
3. Which attributes occur frequently and in which combinations? Can types be defined based on these observations?
4. Can the pottery tell us something about the activities that took place in Guadalupe?
5. To what extent does Guadalupe's material show similarities to ceramics from other places (regional and supra-regional), and what does this tell us about possible contacts?

Requirements. The ceramic classification should meet the following listed criteria in order to answer the questions mentioned above. However, it must also be appropriate for Guadalupe's material and provide a firm basis for further research.

1. The Cocal period has experienced little research so far, and it can be assumed that excavations at other sites will extend the pottery complex and that new attributes and forms will be added. The classification should, therefore, be flexible and expandable.
2. So far, only a few complete vessel profiles could be reconstructed. The classification should, therefore, also apply to fragmented material.
3. The parameters of form and decoration should be considered. Since we assume that appliqués, which occur in large quantities and are often detached from the vessels, have significant diagnostic value, they

11 Translation from German by the author.

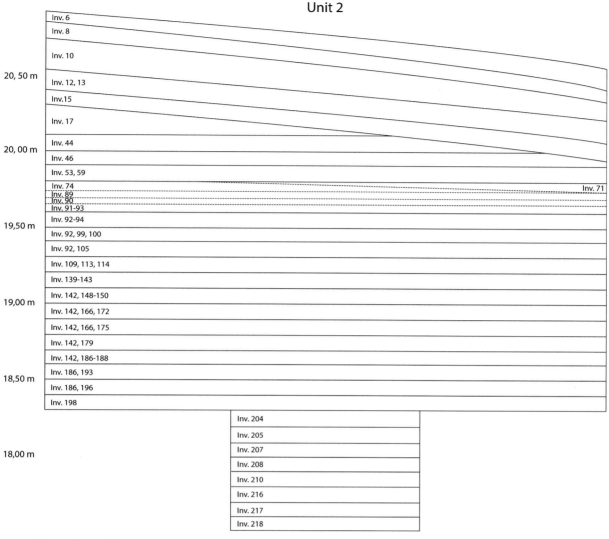

60   Scheme showing the inventory numbers of Unit 2. Dashed lines indicate natural layers, other lines correspond to artificial layers of ca. 10 cm. The ceramic layer ends with Inv. 71 (M Schacht, F. Fecher).

should also be comprehensively included in the analysis.

4. The classification system should be as objective, comprehensible, and reproducible as possible.
5. The classification should be based on clear definitions that are well-described and illustrated so that it can be used as a basis for comparisons in future research.

Previous Research and Existing Typologies. Several attempts have been made to classify the pottery of northeast Honduras. Initially, surface finds from surveys and material from test excavations formed the foundation of these classifications. Later, extensive excavations and radiocarbon dates were able to consolidate and extend the chronology. The authors repeatedly refer to each other and work to extend the existing classification scheme, adapting it to the respective material. The classification scheme currently used is the type-variety system. In the following, the different approaches will be presented and critically reviewed to see whether they meet the requirements defined above.

The first to attempt to classify the pottery of northeast Honduras was Strong, who provides an overview of the pottery he found during his surveys and test excavations on the Bay Islands in his monograph (1935). He arranged the material into four groups based on decoration:

–   Plain Monochrome: plain or poorly decorated types
–   Elaborate Monochrome: elaborately incised type, comprises all monochrome painted, slipped, and unpainted vessels with incised, punctate, appliqué, and/or modeled decoration
–   Polychrome I: thin polychrome ware
–   Polychrome II: high polished vessels painted with linear, curvilinear, and/or geometric motifs

In a later article, Strong (1948c) reviewed and rearranged this classification, which incorporated reference to the material found by Stone (1941) on the mainland. In doing so, he also refers to Lothrop's (1926) ceramic classification for the highlands of Costa Rica, to which he sees a remarkable similarity (Strong 1948c: 77). He now summarizes the monochrome ceramics under the term "North Coast Applique style." Polychrome I is renamed Bay Island Polychrome.

Concerning the chronological sequence of the material, Strong can only make vague observations based on the data available. Epstein (1957) gives the material temporal depth by defining the two phases Selin and Cocal, which in turn are divided into early and late phases. To create his chronology, he evaluated a collection he had come across in the American Museum of Natural History. It was composed of material from the Boekelman Shell Heap Expedition from Selin Farm and Cocal Farm and from excavations by Kidder II, Ekholm, and Stromsvik in 80 Acres on Utila. Epstein himself had not yet conducted any excavations, nor had he even been to Honduras at this point. He orients himself based on the pottery groups defined by Strong, renames them, and assigns them to the defined phases. He places the Elaborate Monochrome and Polychrome I groups in the Cocal phase, although the Late Cocal phase remains less detailed. Elaborate Monochrome becomes Incised Punctate, which he divides into the Abstracted Scroll Type and Simple Incised groups. The Bay Island Polychrome Type is adopted from Strong.

Epstein's chronology remained unmodified for a long time. However, in the 1970s, Healy was able to expand on it. His discovery of the Cuyamel ceramics led to the addition of the Cuyamel phase (1350–400 BC). Epstein's chronology, based on stratigraphic excavations, could be confirmed for the first time with ¹⁴C dates. Regarding the Cocal phase, Healy adopts Epstein's two groups, renames them (Abstracted Scroll Type becomes Dorina Abstract Incised Punctate and corresponds to the Early Cocal phase, and Simple Incised becomes Concha Simple Incised Punctate and corresponds to the Late Cocal phase) and describes them in more detail. Here, too, the Late Cocal phase is based on a very limited set of 100 sherds (Healy 1993: 212). In Begley's (1999) work in the Culmí Valley, this typological scheme was also applied, whereby Begley showed that the material culture in Olancho is similar to that of the coast. He also defined local types. For his definition, Begley concentrated on decoration and fabric, as the encountered sherds were too small for form analysis.

The most recent version of the ceramic typology for the Cocal period can be found in the master's thesis by Dennett (2007), who worked on the material excavated by Healy in the Cocal period settlement of Río Claro in the Aguán Valley. Dennett adopts the types defined by Healy and divides them into several varieties. Her classification is based on 325 sherds. There are additional classification approaches and local typologies, which shall be mentioned here for the sake of completeness: Beaudry-Corbett 1995; Véliz 1978; Véliz / Willey / Healy 1977; Viel / Begley 1992. However, these approaches have not been fully formulated or have not been published, so they are not discussed in detail here.

The existing typology is based on the type-variety system, which has found widespread application in Mesoamerican archaeology and is also used in Honduras mainly as a classification system (Henderson / Beaudry-Corbett 1993). The type-variety system is a taxonomic system based on the grouping of individual specimens into classes or taxa, which are defined in terms of clusters of attributes (as opposed to a modal analysis, which examines individual attributes) (Beaudry-Corbett / Henderson / Joyce 1993: 3). As Michael Vallo (2000: 49) summarizes: "Within the 'type-variety: mode' concept, the archaeological artifacts found at a site are interpreted as the result of the cultural activities of a group of people that can be confined in space and time"¹². A type is defined as "a ceramic unit recognizably distinct in certain visual or tactile characteristics" (Beaudry-Corbett / Henderson / Joyce 1993: 4). Decoration and surface treatment are focused on the definition because it is assumed that these do not follow technical specifications as much as the other categories but are primarily inspired by the culture of the producers (Gifford 1976: 17). Varieties are subunits of types. They present minor technological or stylistic deviations within a type. The respective definition of types and varieties is preceded by the intuitive identification of groups (Vallo 2000: 5). When the system was first introduced, it was common to first define varieties and then group them into broader types. Henderson et al. (1993: 3) show that, over time, it has become more common to first define types and to record differences within the types through varieties. At higher levels, types can be subsumed under groups or ceramic complexes.

Critiques. The type-variety system was originally developed in 1958 by Joe Wheat, James Gifford, and William Wasley to classify ceramics in the southwestern United States (Wheat / Gifford / Wasley 1958). Soon after its introduction into Mesoamerican archaeology in the 1960s (Smith / Willey / Gifford 1960), the shortcomings of the type-variety system were pointed out, and in some cases, vehement critique was expressed (e.g., Dunnell 1971; Smith 1979). Nevertheless, the system is still

---

12 Translation from German by the author.

frequently used today, at times seemingly for lack of an alternative. Vallo (2000) summarizes the main arguments of these critiques. In the following, the points that are particularly relevant to the present study are highlighted.

A significant problem of the type-variety system is that it is based mainly on surface treatment (decoration) and partly on fabric as criteria for defining types and varieties. While the vessel form also plays a role in the theoretical conceptualization of the type-variety system, in practice, it is often disregarded as a criterion for classification. The basis for this methodology is the assumption that decoration is not a necessary step for production, but that the culturally influenced perceptions of the producers find particularly strong expression in it (Gifford 1976: 17; Vallo 2000: 55). However, by concentrating on the decoration, much information is lost. Little attention is paid to the form, which is also based on a decision-making process and can provide important information about the ceramic function and use. This approach also leads to a lack of flexibility or adaptation to different research questions. Furthermore, it allows fragments of the same vessel to be classified in different ways (e.g., if a decoration does not extend over the entire vessel and is not visible on every fragment). A further criticism is that the definitions that underlie classifications are often intuitive and, therefore, not specified. Smith (1979) convincingly demonstrates that the attributes underlying the definition of types and varieties are not sufficiently described and defined. Also, clear criteria for the distinction between types and varieties are often not revealed. So, whether a group is defined as type or variety is a subjective decision of the investigator and usually cannot be verified. Not only are the definitions and considerations underlying the established classifications insufficiently presented, but the data itself is as well. If these are not published, definitions cannot be comprehensive or verifiable, which results in the typologies of the type-variety system being useless for future researchers, as Smith (1979) demonstrates. Also, in the presentation of the results, we can usually see evident deficits. The sherds on which the respective definitions of the classification units are based are rarely depicted adequately. Images, however, are the most important tools for an archaeologist to carry out comparative studies.

Many of these problems can be found in the existing typology for northeast Honduras. The existing typology also considers decoration to be the most crucial factor for defining types and varieties. The form as an analytical category is given little emphasis. As a result, there is still no comprehensive overview of the existing vessel forms. In addition, the focus on decoration results in undecorated sherds receiving little attention in the typolo-

gy, and vessels of very different shapes are grouped in types. In general, the criteria for creating types and varieties are not well explained and are not readily discernible to the reader. Thus, decorations with different patterns and different techniques are grouped together. Also, terms that require a definition, as no generally valid understanding can be assumed, are not defined (e.g., what is meant by bowl, dish, etc.). Overall, few illustrations of the respective defined types are provided, making it difficult for the reader to compare their own data with the described types. Finally, it should be noted that the typology, especially for the Cocal phase, is poorly developed and based on a small amount of material. Dennett (2007) uses only 325 sherds for her analysis. These deficits lead to a low level of comprehensibility and comparability, which are necessary to answer our research questions. This is why I chose to apply a different system in addressing these shortcomings. A new classification scheme is presented in detail below.

4.4.1.2 Development of a New Classification System

Approach. As described in the previous section, the existing system has several shortcomings and, in many respects, does not meet the requirements defined above. Therefore, I have decided not to follow the type-variety system but to design a new system for the description and organization of ceramics from Guadalupe. Since Cocal phase pottery is a little-known ceramic complex, the characteristics relevant for a typology and considerations for the development of a chronology must be identified. Classification based on individual attributes lends itself to answering this question. This approach also allows the classification to be expanded upon as knowledge increases. Iken Paap (2002) described a suitable approach in her dissertation, in which she developed a classification system for the hitherto little-known ceramic complex of Khyinga, Nepal. Her classification system was developed for a similar situation and research question to Guadalupe's case, thus meeting our requirements. The application and further development of the system by Angelika Wetter (2005) for the Paracas pottery from Jauranga, Peru, demonstrates that the system is not culture-specific but can be applied to other ceramic complexes as well.

Paap's approach is based on an inductive method and offers a classification system based on individual attributes. To approach a previously unknown ceramic complex, Paap first defines attributes that she considers important for the analysis. She observes three categories: fabric, form, and decoration. For example, she defines the attributes color, hardness, tempering, surface structure, and fracture structure for the category of fabric. For each fragment, the defined attributes are described, recorded, and displayed in her thesis. For the detailed recording of the attributes, Paap designs a key with which the respective attributes can be documented in detail. Such a procedure allows a clear, exact numerical designation of the individual attributes while guaranteeing the required objectivity and verifiability. Subsequently, the frequency of specific combinations of the respective attributes is examined and, in the case of Paap, statistically analyzed to define groups of attributes and ultimately classify them chronologically.

Adaptations. To apply this approach to the Guadalupe material, it is necessary to make some adjustments to take into account the specific characteristics of the material. First of all, the category of fabric is not considered in the context of this work. A supplementary, detailed study of the fabric and further technological aspects of ceramics is being carried out by Mike Lyons. This present work focuses on the categories of form and decoration. One of the main challenges in applying this approach here was integrating the appliqués, which represent a significant portion of the material and constitute an essential part of the classification. It is, however, difficult to assign the appliqués to the categories of either form or decoration. The following example demonstrates this problem. It cannot be denied that a D-shaped handle fulfills a function. It serves to facilitate the transport of a vessel or to suspend it; thus, it is undoubtedly part of the form. Similarly, the appliqué in Figure 61 (PAG-12-410, left) probably has a function. The perforation near the wall suggests that it was used for hanging the vessel. However, it is zoomorphic in design and thus also serves a decorative purpose. Appliqué PAG-10-342 (Figure 61, right) shows the same motif but is not perforated. Does it, therefore, serve no functional purpose, but only a decorative one? Or was it used as a handle? Furthermore, what about an appliquéd band? Is it still part of the form, or should it only be assigned to the decoration?

These examples demonstrate that the appliqués cannot merely be assigned to the category of either form or decoration. On the one hand, this is because we cannot currently reconstruct the purpose of the appliqués (i.e., decorative or functional) with any certainty. On the other hand, even if we could, this categorization would mean an artificial separation of the appliqués into two different categories, even though there will always be borderline cases where an exact assignment is not possible. It is clear at this point that the categories of form and decoration do not allow for a meaningful analysis that satisfactorily reflects the characteristics of the objects. Rather, it is an artificial categorization, an external perspective that has its roots in archaeological research but has little to do with the vessel's actual production process. Therefore, I have tried to apply the potter's perspective as much as possible to arrive at a meaningful cate

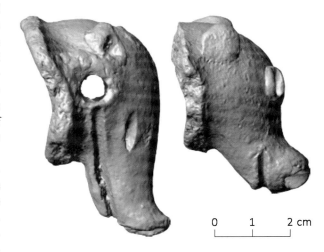

61   Zoomorph appliqués: PAG-12-410 (left) and PAG-10-342 (right) (P. Bayer).

gorization. From ethnohistorical sources, we know that potters do not make a clear distinction between form and decoration (Rye 1981: 89). Rather, both categories represent steps that are carried out after the vessel body has been manufactured. This means that the form of a vessel is first considered and produced before modifications are applied in a second step that complete the vessel and give it its final appearance. Many different modification techniques can be distinguished here, but they can broadly be divided into three main categories: 1) techniques in which clay is removed or displaced from the body of the vessel, creating a sunken relief, 2) techniques in which the clay is shaped or added to create a raised relief, and 3) techniques where paint is applied to the surface. Following this logic of the production process, I define the following categories for the subsequent analysis: "Form" refers to the vessel's basic shape without any modifications. "Modification" summarizes everything that changes or modifies the vessel surface after the production of the vessel body. This category is again subdivided according to the technique used for the respective modification, i.e., "incision" (sunken relief), "appliqué" (raised relief), and "paint" (application of color) (Figure 62).

This separation may seem unfamiliar at first glance. However, in this case, it is appropriate. It allows for a thorough examination of the appliqués—which are often detached from the vessel—as a separate category while simultaneously avoiding the artificial separation of vessel forms based on the presence or absence of appliqués (see Paap 2002: 35). In the analysis of attribute combinations, the possible combinations of basic form and modification are discussed, and the existing spectrum of complete vessel forms is shown.

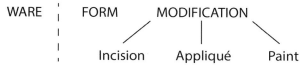

62 Categories of the new classification system (F. Fecher).

In the next step, a scheme is developed for the categories of form and modification, which allows individual attributes to be described and their combinations considered. Paap pursued the idea that the frequent occurrence of combined attributes is the basis for defining a ceramic type. Since the amount of material in the sample considered here is relatively small compared to the actual number of existing sherds, statistical evaluation was intentionally omitted, as such an analysis would present a biased result (Bernbeck 1997: 213). Nevertheless, combinations of specific attributes tend to appear in the sample and can be identified. These serve as a basis for the preliminary definition of types. The results obtained from the sample analysis were also checked against the remaining ceramic material from Unit 2 in order to test their informative value. In the following, the development of the classification system, the selected attributes, and the individual steps taken to create the classification are described in detail.

Classification
Form (Figure 63). Until now, the range of ceramic forms from northeast Honduras had not been described comprehensively and systematically. Because of this, one of the tasks of classification is to describe the spectrum of forms. The material from Guadalupe is fragmented; no complete vessels were recovered. However, some profiles were able to be completely reconstructed. Therefore, the system should be open, easy to use and allow for an exact description of the vessel parts without becoming too complex. It should allow for examining individual aspects of form for chronological relevance and generate an initial idea of the existing forms. The attributes defined for the analysis are: proportion (product of the diameter at the widest point and the height), diameter of the opening, composition (number of breaks), rim position, rim shape, lip shape, base form, minimum wall thickness, and maximum wall thickness.

With regard to vessel forms, there are numerous definitions and systems that depend on the region of interest and the analyzed material, e.g., Karstens (1994), Kunow et al. (1986), or Bauer et al. (1993). In Mesoamerican archaeology, the prevailing classification system categorizes vessels into plate, dish, bowl, jar, and vase, which is based on the definitions by Sabloff (1975) and

Rice (1987). These basic forms result from the ratio of height and diameter and certain characteristics of form. However, upon closer inspection of these definitions and after attempting to apply them to the Guadalupe material, it quickly became apparent that our material could not be easily assigned to these categories. This is partly due to the existing definitions not being clearly defined. In particular, problems arose in the assignment of material to the categories of jars and vases because no congruent definition could be derived from the two publications. Rice (1987) addresses the problem of differentiating between these categories, which is in part due to different cultural conceptions, but she does not offer a concrete solution. I have therefore decided not to include these terms, but to use a neutral formulation instead. The system of forms developed here is firstly based on the relationship between height (H) and diameter (D). This results in the following categories:

- A: $\frac{1}{3} D > H$
- B: $D \geq H \geq \frac{1}{3} D$
- C: $H > D$

The second attribute concerns the composition or the geometric structure of the vessel. For this purpose, the number of vessel breaks is considered. A break is defined here as a point at which the contour of a vessel changes its direction. This allows us to identify the number of "components" that a vessel consists of if defined as a combination of geometric objects (see Paap 2002: 36). Depending on the vessel's structure, these components correspond to rim/neck, upper wall, and lower wall/base. In the next step, the components are described.

Special consideration is given to the rim. The rim is often an important criterion for the description and chronological classification of pottery fragments. Because whole forms are not always preserved, the rim can serve as a point of reference. It is, therefore, surprising that the definitions of what constitutes a rim differ as well. Moreover, it is difficult to distinguish between rim and body if the rim is not clearly set apart (Hecht 2013: 63). In our case, the rim is considered to be the upper part of the vessel, or more precisely, the area before the first break. If there is no break, as in the hemispherical bowls, the rim corresponds to the upper section of the body. Paap's classification scheme is very detailed with regard to the "finishing" of the rim. Rim position, rim finish, lip form, interior details, and exterior details are examined. Such a detailed picture has not proven to be useful for the material from Guadalupe. This is because it would result in too many subdivisions of the material, and more importantly, because the material is hand-formed and the shape of the rim is subject to considerable variations. Consequently, the examined attributes

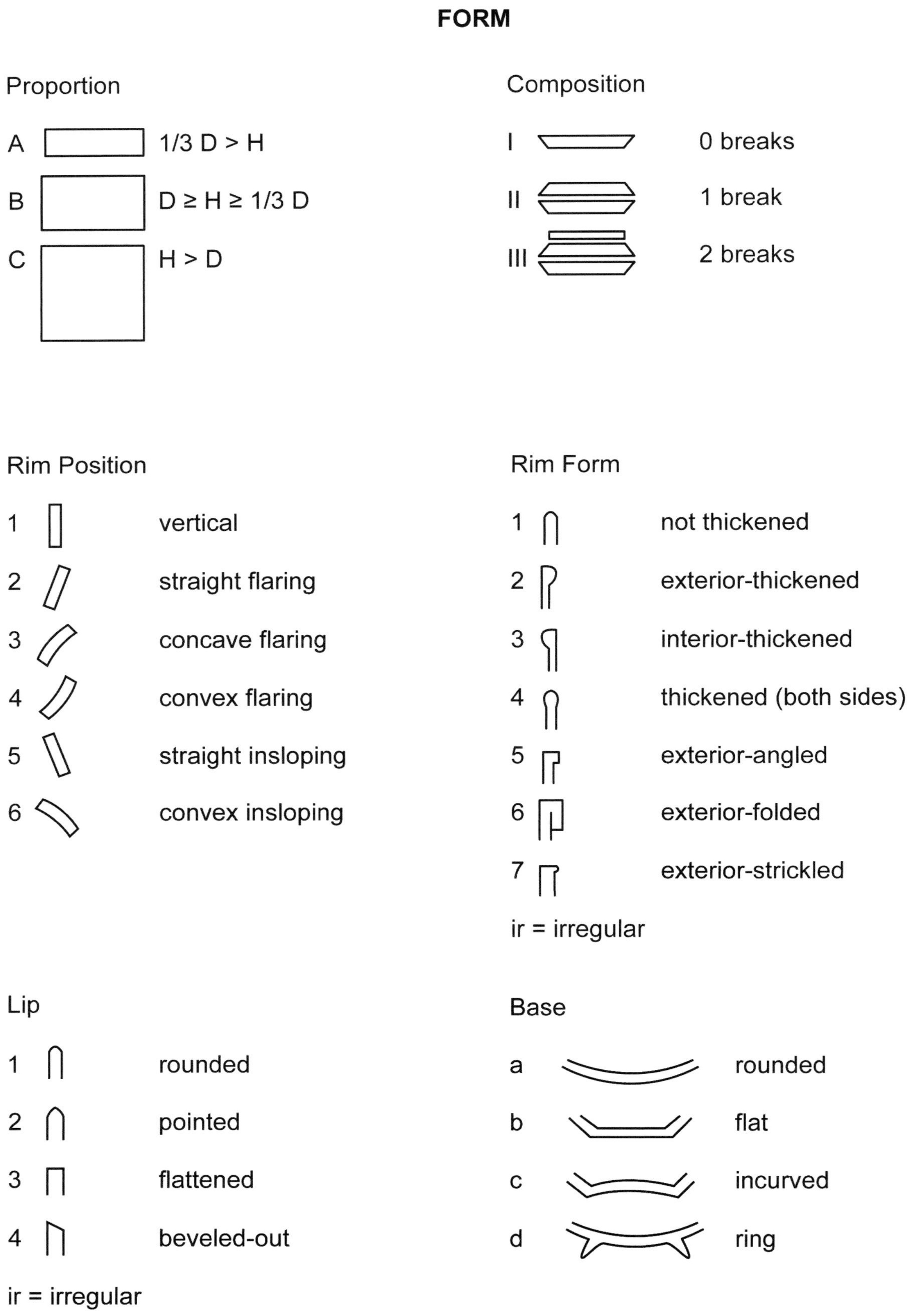

FORM

Proportion

A   1/3 D > H

B   D ≥ H ≥ 1/3 D

C   H > D

Composition

I   0 breaks

II   1 break

III   2 breaks

Rim Position

1   vertical

2   straight flaring

3   concave flaring

4   convex flaring

5   straight insloping

6   convex insloping

Rim Form

1   not thickened

2   exterior-thickened

3   interior-thickened

4   thickened (both sides)

5   exterior-angled

6   exterior-folded

7   exterior-strickled

ir = irregular

Lip

1   rounded

2   pointed

3   flattened

4   beveled-out

ir = irregular

Base

a   rounded

b   flat

c   incurved

d   ring

63   Form classification system.

MODIFICATION - INCISION (In)

Position

I Exterior   **II** Interior   **0** Unknown

Motifs

1

2

3

4

5

6

7

8 |||||

9

10

11

12

13

14

15

16

17

18

19

20

21

64 Incision classification system.

were reduced to rim position, rim shape, and lip shape to ensure a meaningful and significant description. The body's position is not considered in detail, partly because it corresponds to the rim position in some forms. The base shapes are considered separately.

Should our understanding of Guadalupe's material allow or require a description of the other vessel parts in the future (e.g., lower body or type of break), as demonstrated by Wetter (2005), these aspects can be added to the classification without any problems.

Modifications. This category includes all modifications added to the basic form of the vessel during the production process. It is divided into incisions, appliqués, and paint. So far, there is no systematic overview of existing modifications. Therefore, the aim is to create a clear and comprehensible system for the description of the modifications.

For incisions, the position on the vessel is first recorded. These are exterior, interior, and unknown. In the next step, the incision motif is defined (Figure 64). A motif was only defined if it appeared four or more times in the sample. Twenty-one different motifs were identified, some of which show variations. Additionally, a category "single motives" was established, which includes motifs that only occur sporadically.

Regarding the appliqués, their position on the vessel is also determined first. These are lip, rim/body (handles), or base (supports) (Figure 65). In some cases, assignment to a specific category is difficult, especially when the sherd does not retain any wall material. In this case, the examination of use-wear can be helpful. If no clues can be identified regarding the position, it is marked as unknown. In the next step, motifs are defined, some of which show several variations. In total, thirty-four motifs were defined. Also here, the category "single motives" includes motifs that only occur sporadically.

For paint, a distinction is made between polychrome, monochrome, and slip, the latter of which covers the entire surface (Figure 66). Because only a few painted sherds have been found in Guadalupe as of yet, further subdivision does not seem reasonable at the moment. Thus the system remains on this basic level for the time being but can easily be extended in the future to include further finds.

MODIFICATION - APPLIQUÉ (Ap)

Position

I	Lip	III	Base
II	Rim/Body (upper part)	0	Unknown

Motifs

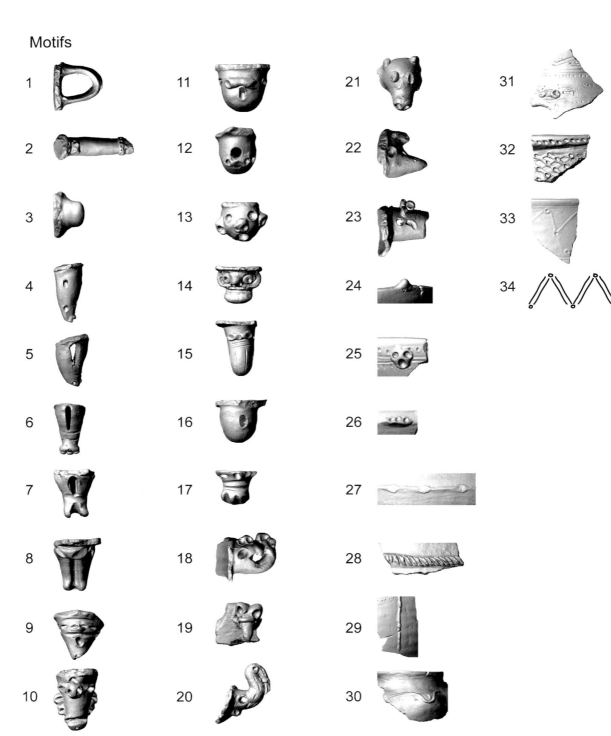

65   Appliqué classification system.

MODIFICATION - PAINT (P)

Technique

I   Polychrome paint

II   Monochrome paint

III   Slip

66   Paint classification system.

Attribute Key. For documenting these attributes, a key was developed based on Paap (2002) and Wetter (2005). It is composed of alphabetical and numerical characters and allows a precise and comparative description of each sherd. Each attribute occupies a single position in the key. Categories are separated by underscores (form_incision_appliqué_paint), while attributes within categories are separated by hyphens. If an attribute is not identifiable or absent, the position is filled with a zero. In this way, the maximum amount of information can be recorded—even when dealing with heavily fragmented material. See Figure 63 for a comprehensive concordance of the key. An example follows for clarification.

FORM		
Proportion	e.g., A	1/3 D > H
Composition	e.g., A-II	one break
Rim Position	e.g., A-II-3	concave flaring
Rim Form	e.g., A-II-3-2	exterior-thickened
Lip	e.g., A-II-3-2-1	rounded
INCISION (In)		
Position	e.g., I	exterior
Motif	e.g., I-3	wave motif
APPLIQUÉ (Ap)		
Position	e.g., III	base
Motif	e.g., III-16	hemispherical plain
e.g., A-II-3-2-1_In-I-3_Ap-III-16		shallow vessel with one break, concave flaring rim, exterior thickened rim, rounded lip, exterior incised wave motif, and hemispherical plain support
e.g., 0-0-3-2-1_In-I-3		proportion and composition are unknown, concave flaring rim, exterior thickened rim, rounded lip, and exterior incised wave motif

Documentation. After this classification system was established and attributes were defined, the Guadalupe sample was documented. Besides the use of traditional hand drawing and photography, structured light scanners were used to create 3D models of the objects. This method provides a precise and time-saving alternative, especially for complex vessel shapes and three-dimensional appliqués. The exact procedure, as well as the advantages and disadvantages of traditional and new digital documentation techniques, are described in detail in Fecher et al. (2020). Either a drawing or a 3D scan was produced of each rim sherd, for which a position could be determined. The 3D model served as a basis for the later production of a profile drawing. A photo was also taken of each sherd in position in order to fit it into the profile drawings. Based on the drawings and scans, the attributes defined earlier were recorded using the key outlined above and entered into the project database. This documentation work served as a basis for the subsequent analysis.

4.4.1.3 Analysis

In this chapter, the results of the analysis are described. The evaluation considers the quantitative distribution and stratigraphical and chronological occurrence of the above-defined attributes within the following groups: form, incision, appliqué, and paint. Based on this, chronological changes and chronological relevance of attributes are noted[13]. Next, combinations of the individual attributes are considered, and the possibility of defining types is examined. Their spatial and temporal distribution is also examined. These observations form the basis for supporting the stratigraphic interpretation of the excavation and can be used in a further step to make comparisons between pottery features of different sites in the region.

4.4.1.3.1 Form

The sample contains 437 rim fragments. For 357 rim fragments, the vessel proportion could be determined; for 298 fragments, both the proportion and composition could be determined, i.e., a basic shape could be reconstructed (Figure 67). The majority of the fragments to which no proportions could be assigned due to their small size originate from the settlement layers. Some of the fragments that could not be assigned to either category represent transitions between categories.

In the case of fragments to which no basic form could be assigned, the other attributes were still determined and documented (rim shape, lip, and wall thickness). The combination of the attributes proportion, composition, and rim position results in a range of vessel forms identified in Guadalupe (modifications are not yet considered here) (Figure 68). See Figure 69 for a sche-

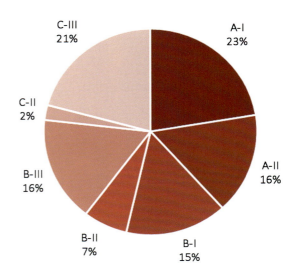

67   Percentages of vessel forms in the sample (F. Fecher).

matic representation of possible combinations of vessel forms and modifications from Guadalupe.

It must be noted that there are transitional forms that do not strictly adhere to the basic forms; the boundaries are fluid. This is because the ceramics in Guadalupe do not appear to be completely standardized productions. The pottery is handmade; the use of a potter's wheel has not been proven for pre-Hispanic America, which is why the shape of the vessels is subject to variation.

13 As shown above, no clear stratigraphy can be determined within the ceramic layer. For this reason, only tendencies of the spatial distribution can be observed at this point.

Basic Forms

A I 2

4

II 1/2

3

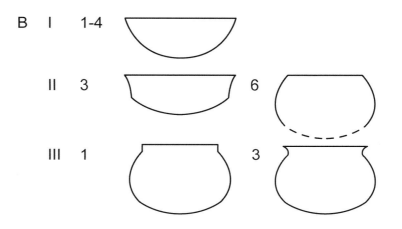

B I 1-4

II 3

6

III 1

3

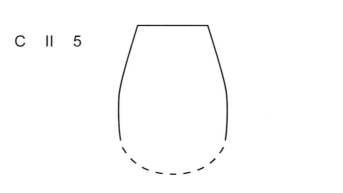

C II 5

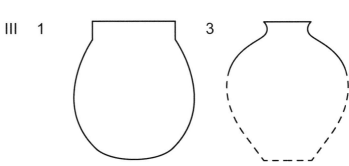

III 1

3

68   Basic forms present in the Guadalupe sample.

sels of lower quality remarkably often, while Lip 1 occurs with finer, decorated vessels. The minimum wall thickness ranges from 1 mm to 8 mm and averages 5 mm. The maximum wall thickness ranges from 2 mm to 10 mm and averages 6 mm. As Form B-I is an unrestricted form, the diameter corresponds to the vessel's widest part and ranges from 8 cm to 42 cm and averages 24 cm.

B-II – Medium-Deep Vessels with one Break
Twenty sherds were assigned to the B-II basic form (Figures 84-86). Medium-deep vessels with one break occur with two different rim positions: 3 (10 fragments) and 6 (10 fragments). The vessels with Rim Position 3 usually have a pointed break. They are similar to Form A-I-3 but differ in their greater depth. All but one (Inv. 17) of the specimens of this variety originate from Inv. 46 and 53. It is possibly a temporally limited phenomenon. The associated rim forms are 1, 2, 3, and in a single case, 5. Most lips are rounded. The minimum wall thickness ranges from 5 mm to 7 mm and averages 6 mm. The maximum wall thickness ranges from 6 mm to 10 mm and averages 9 mm. The diameters of these unrestricted vessels range from 28 cm to 48 cm and average 38 cm. These are, therefore, relatively large vessels.

The version with Rim Position 6 has a round break, resulting in an almost spherical shape. The upper wall is strongly insloping, which results in a restricted vessel. In other typologies, this shape is also known as *tecomate*. This version is found throughout the entire ceramic layer. One example was identified below the ceramic layer in Inv. 91. Form B-II-6 is found with Rim Forms 1 to 3, although the differences between the forms are small. The lip is rounded in 9 of 10 cases (Lip 1). The minimum wall thickness ranges from 3 mm to 6 mm and averages 5 mm. The maximum wall thickness ranges from 4 mm to 10 mm and averages 7 mm. On average, the vessels are about 30 cm wide at their widest point and thus represent relatively large vessels.

Nothing concrete can be said about the associated base form because no preserved bases were identified on any of the fragments. However, I suspect that they are round, judging from their similarity to A-II vessels, which have been identified with round bases.

B-III – Medium-Deep Vessels with two Breaks
Forty-nine fragments were assigned to the B-III category (Figures 87-92). They occur with Rim Positions 1 and 3. Twelve fragments have a vertical rim (Rim Position 1). These vessels tend to be rather restricted and undecorated. Most of the rim forms are not thickened, but forms 2, 4, and 5 also occur sporadically. Associated lip forms are 1, 2, 3, and irregular. The minimum wall thickness ranges from 3 mm to 7 mm and averages 5 mm. The maximum wall thickness ranges from 5 mm to 11 mm

and averages 7 mm. The diameter at the opening ranges from 6 cm to 40 cm and averages 20 cm. These are, therefore, medium-sized vessels. Two vessels are relatively small, with a diameter of 6 cm and 8 cm, respectively. Variant B-III-1 is concentrated in the lower portions of the ceramic layer (Inv. 15–71).

Thirty-three fragments have a concave or straight flaring rim. Four fragments are wall fragments for which the rim position could not be determined. Transition forms between concave and straight flaring are fluid, and the value of a subdivision is questionable. For this reason, the variants were all categorized under Rim Position 3.

This variant tends to be relatively unrestricted. Associated rim forms are 1 to 5, with Rim Forms 1 and 2 being particularly common. One specimen has a strikingly angular rim (Figure 92f). Most lips are rounded, while a few are pointed. However, no specific combinations can be recognized. Concerning stratigraphy, this variant occurs mainly in the upper portion of the ceramic layer. One fragment was identified in the settlement level; however, assigning it to this form is not certain due to its poor preservation. Two vessels have a round base (Base a). I assume that a large portion of this form has round bases, but this cannot yet be verified. The minimum wall thickness ranges from 2 mm to 8 mm and averages 4 mm. The maximum wall thickness ranges from 4 mm to 11 mm and averages 7 mm. The orifice diameter ranges from 4 cm to 30 cm. The average is 19 cm.

C-II – Deep Vessels with one Break
Seven fragments can be assigned to the C-II vessel type (Figure 93, Figure 94). All fragments have a straight insloping rim (Rim Position 5), creating a restricted vessel. In other classification systems, such deep vessels are called vases or jars. The rim forms include 1, 3, 5, and 7, and lip forms are rounded, pointed, flattened, or irregular. As it is not possible to reconstruct a complete profile for any of these vessels, it is not clear which base forms are associated with them. However, it is possible that they have round bases with supports. In one case, a round base with a well-preserved profile (see Figure 105d) can definitely be assigned to a deep vessel (C). Unfortunately, the rim was not preserved, so it is not clear whether it belongs to Form C-II or C-III. With only a single exception (Inv. 53), the vessels are large and rather coarse. The orifice diameter of the restricted vessels ranges from 14 cm to 38 cm and averages 28 cm. The minimum wall thickness ranges from 4 mm to 8 mm and averages 6 mm, while the maximum wall thickness ranges from 6 mm to 9 mm and averages 8 mm. Vessels with these basic forms occur throughout the entire ceramic layer but are concentrated in the upper area. The small number of fragments, however, does not allow for any firm conclusions regarding stratigraphic distribution.

C-III – Deep Vessels with two Breaks

Sixty-two fragments were assigned to the C-III basic form (Figures 95-102). These are deep vessels with two breaks, creating a collar or neck. Depending on the classification scheme used, these vessels can also be called vases or jars. They occur with Rim Positions 1 and 3. Thirty-two fragments have a vertical rim (Rim Position 1) and are slightly restricted. For some vessels, the break that separates the rim from the wall is very distinct. In other examples, it is only slightly separated from the wall, resulting in transitional forms that tend toward C-II-5. The rim forms associated with the basic Form C-III-1 are 1, 2, 3, 4, 5, 7, and irregular. Rim Forms 1 and 2 are particularly common. Fragments with Rim Form 7 are large, coarse, undecorated vessels—just as the B forms associated with this rim form are. The lips are rounded or pointed. For one vessel, the profile could be completely reconstructed. This vessel has a round base and serves as the general reasoning behind the assumption that other vessels of this basic form also have a round base. There are some Bay Island Polychrome vessels in the Fortaleza de Santa Bárbara museum and the National Museum of Natural History collections that are completely preserved and also have this form, which includes three supports attached to the round base. Strong (1935: frontispiece, Fig. 37) also shows such forms associated with round bases and supports. The diameter of the vessels ranges from 9 cm to 40 cm and averages 22 cm. The minimum wall thickness ranges from 2 mm to 9 mm and averages 5 mm. The maximum wall thickness ranges from 4 mm to 13 mm and averages 8 mm. This form occurs in all inventory numbers of the ceramic layer but is concentrated in the lower layers. Two specimens come from the settlement layers. It is noticeable that the vessels of the upper layers are undecorated, while those of the lower layers mostly have incisions.

The combination of this form with Rim Position 3 occurs 24 times. These are deep, restricted vessels with upper walls that are strongly insloping, creating a narrow orifice. The rim is almost always not thickened (Rim Form 1); only a single vessel has Rim Form 4. The lip is rounded in all cases. The minimum wall thickness ranges from 2 mm to 10 mm and averages 5 mm. The maximum wall thickness ranges from 3 mm to 10 mm and averages 6 mm. The diameter of the orifice ranges from 6 cm to 16.5 cm and averages 9 cm. Since the orifice diameter of these vessels differs significantly from the diameter of the widest point, it does not provide any vital information about the overall size of the vessel.

Apart from the two basic forms described, some other vessels also likely have the deep form (C). At the moment, however, they cannot be assigned to any of the categories described above because they are not preserved well enough to describe the number of breaks and overall shape. These objects can be grouped into two categories (Figure 103).

The first group, C-0 (a), comprises vessels with various rim positions (straight, straight insloping, or convex flaring). What they have in common, however, is that they are almost cylindrical, relatively coarse, and have simple D-handles as appliqués. With an average diameter of 19 cm, they are relatively large vessels.

The second group C-0 (b) comprises vessels with a strongly concave flaring rim (Rim Position 3). In contrast to the defined Form C-III-3, however, the upper wall is only slightly insloping. They seem to be relatively unrestricted or only slightly restricted vessels. However, because they have only been found with a small piece of preserved rim and sometimes a portion of the upper wall, little can be said about the vessels' remaining shape. It is notable that this form only occurs in the settlement layers and thus seems to be an early phenomenon.

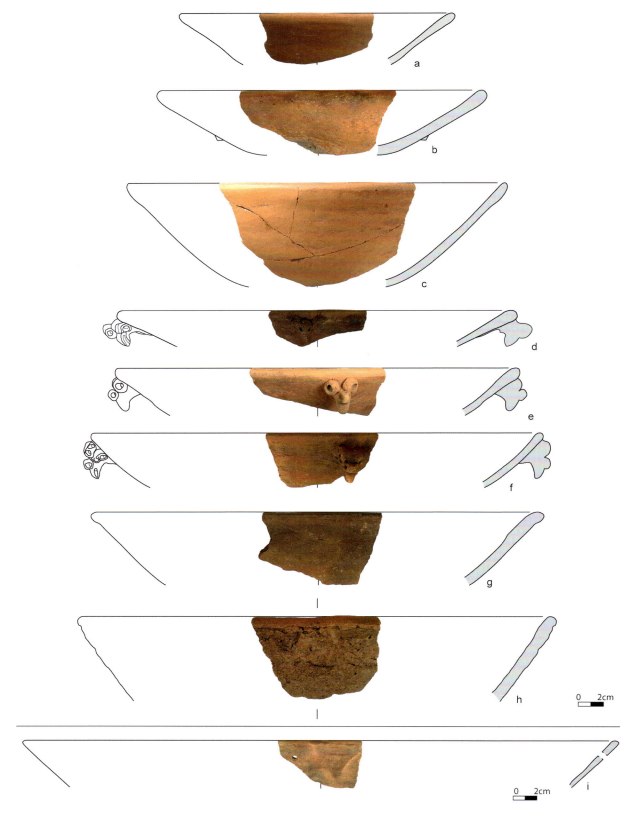

70   A-I-2 with variable rim form and lip. a PAG-53-114; b PAG-71-11; c PAG-53-98; d PAG-53-92; e PAG-44-24; f PAG-53-90; g PAG-53-73; h PAG-53-95; i PAG-46-61.

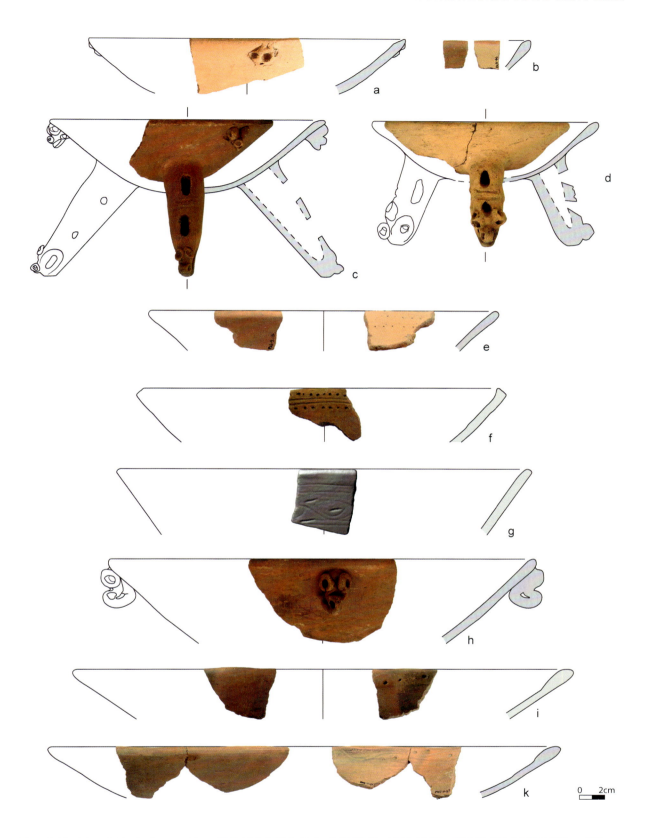

71   A-I-2 with variable rim form and lip. a PAG-44-9; b PAG-46-4; c PAG-53-65; d PAG-46-70; e PAG-91-134; f PAG-8-595; ; g PAG-114-25; h PAG-53-88; i PAG-44-686; k PAG-17-29.

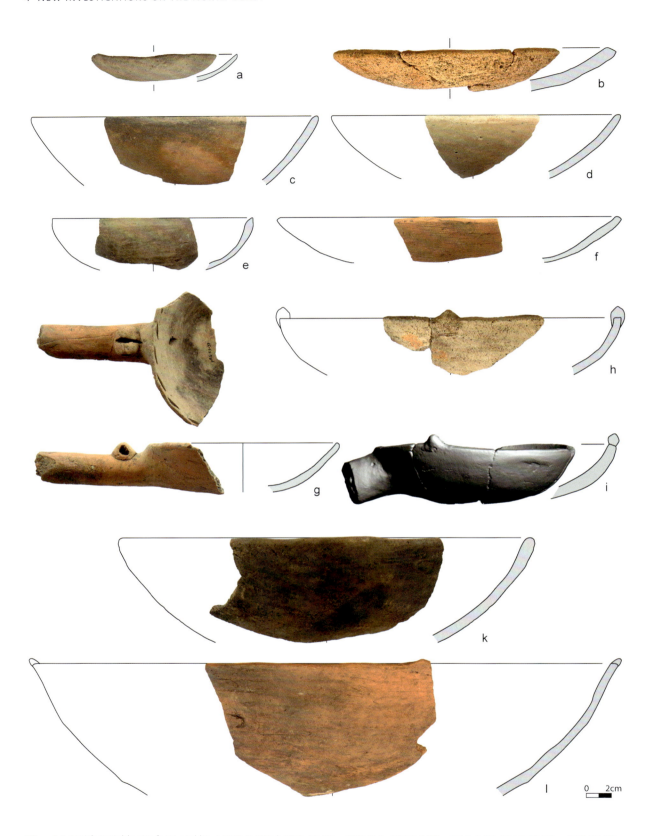

72   A-I-4 with variable rim form and lip. a PAG-8-207; b PAG-46-80; c PAG-8-2; d PAG-8-23; e PAG-8-59; f PAG-53-25; g PAG-53-37; h PAG-46-76; i PAG-44-17; k PAG-13-2; l PAG-46-62.

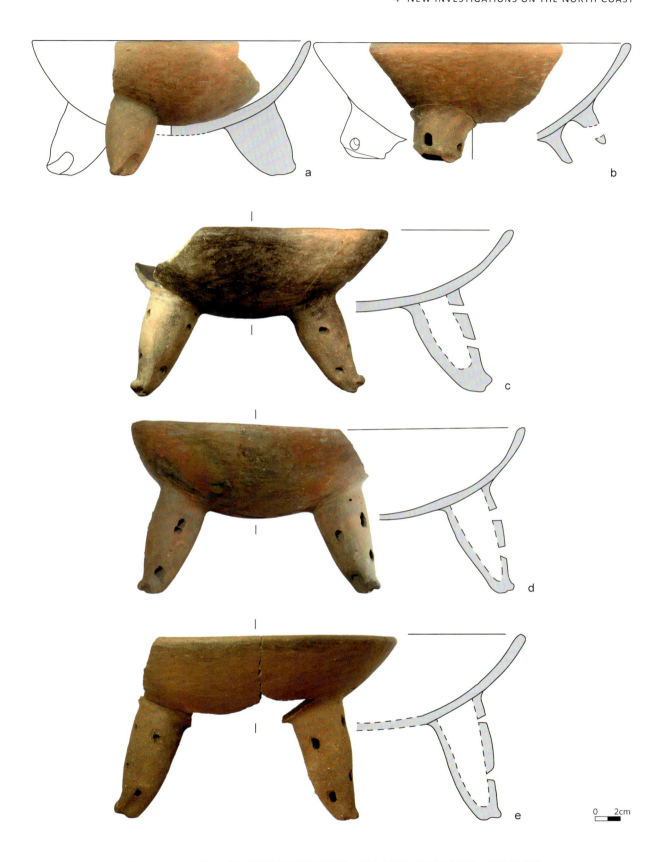

73   A-I-4 with variable rim form and lip. a PAG-12-114; b PAG-12-308; c PAG-8-205; d PAG-15-682; e PAG-15-288.

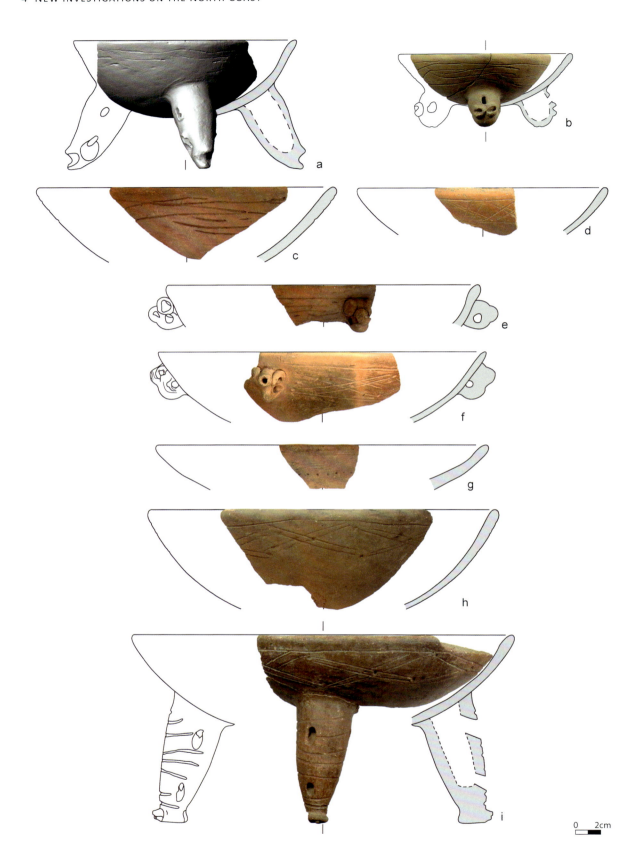

74   A-I-4 with variable rim form and lip. a PAG-6-98; b PAG-8-526; c PAG-6-63; d PAG-8-551; e PAG-8-558; f PAG-10-151; g PAG-46-74; h PAG-44-31; i PAG-15-10.

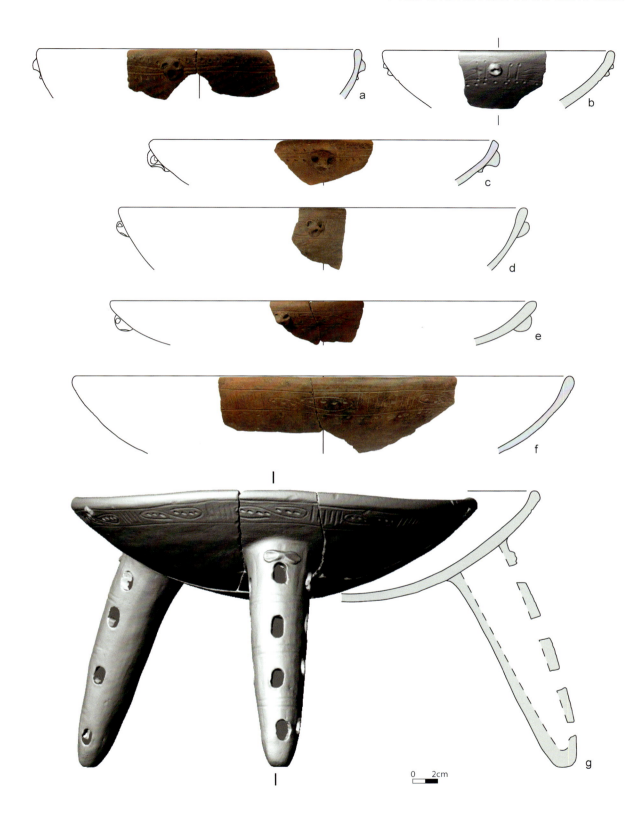

75   A-I-4 with variable rim form and lip. a PAG-53-23; b PAG-46-22; c PAG-53-107; d PAG-44-674; e PAG-44-269; f PAG-17-23; g PAG-46-57.

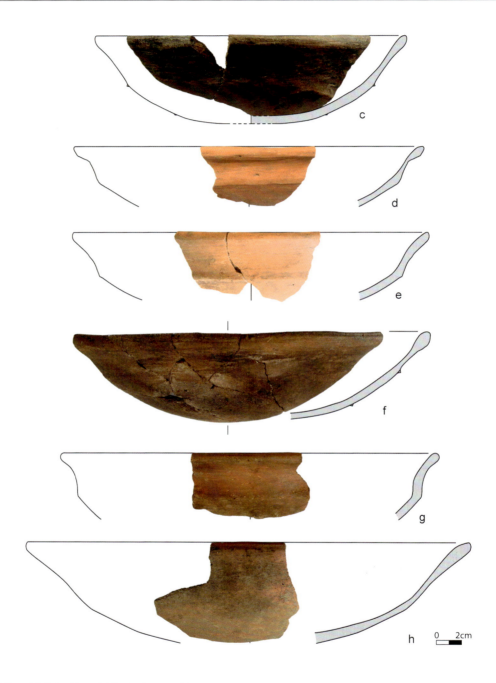

76   A-II-1/2 and A-II-3 with variable rim form and lip. a PAG-99-18; b PAG-94-28; c PAG-17-14; d PAG-17-21; e PAG-44-38b; f PAG-44-13; g PAG-53-71; h PAG-44-27.

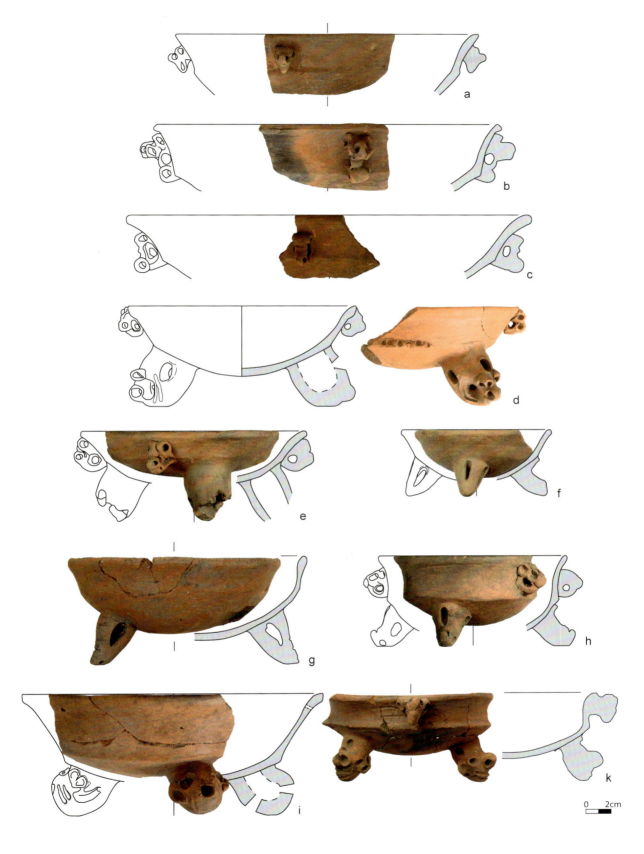

77   A-II-3 with variable rim form and lip. a PAG-46-60; b PAG-46-59; c PAG-71-7; d PAG-44-15; e PAG-44-26; f PAG-17-19; g PAG-44-1; h PAG-44-25; i PAG-44-11; k PAG-53-29.

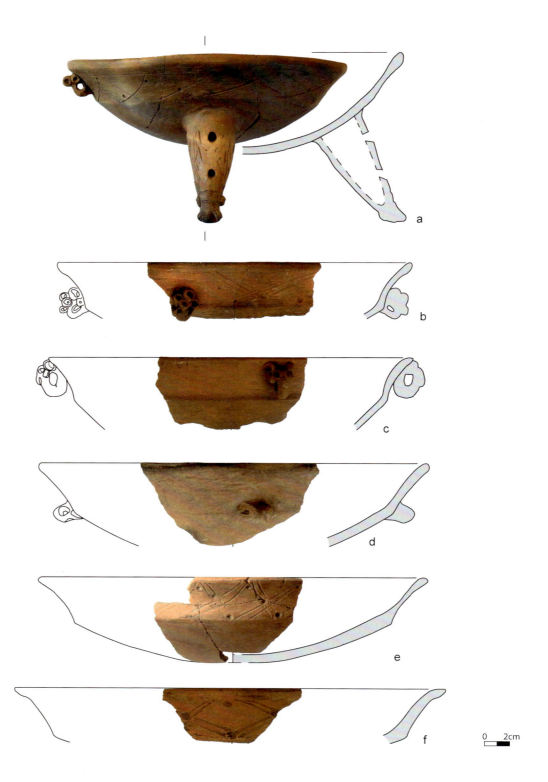

78   A-II-3 with variable rim form and lip. a PAG-15-683; b PAG-71-6; c PAG-53-64; d PAG-46-66; e PAG-44-34; f PAG-53-106.

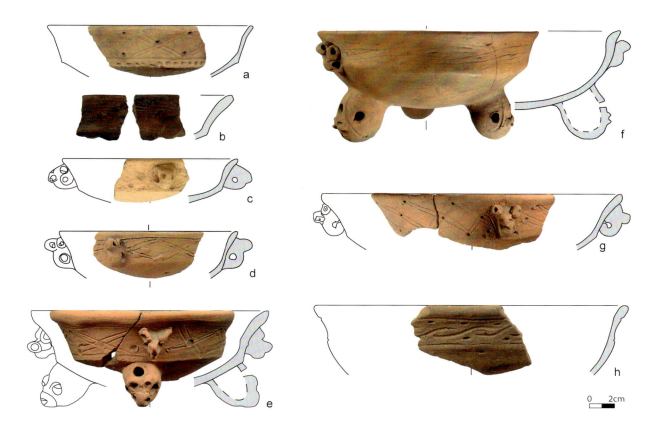

79   A-II-3 with variable rim form and lip. a PAG-17-30; b PAG-6-301; c PAG-46-75; d PAG-15-13; e PAG-46-20; f PAG-10-487; g PAG-44-28; h PAG-105-25.

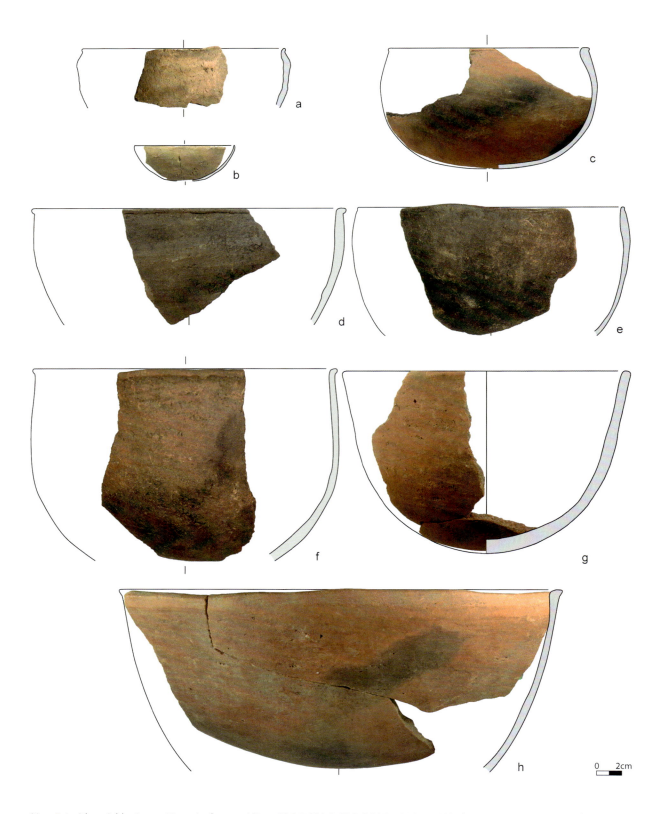

80   B-I with variable rim position, rim form and lip. a PAG-8-201; b PAG-6-585; c PAG-15-692; d PAG-6-215; e PAG-17-17; f PAG-6-202; g PAG-13-21; h PAG-15-130.

81   B-I with variable rim position, rim form and lip. a PAG-10-3; b PAG-10-321; c PAG-8-382; d PAG-12-339; e PAG-17-33; f PAG-6-503; g PAG-17-22.

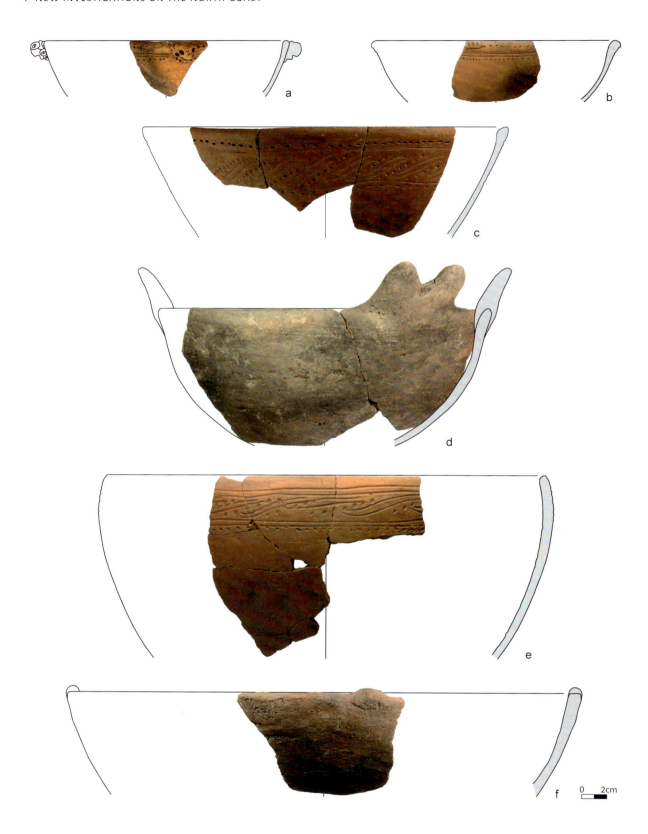

82   B-I with variable rim position, rim form and lip. a PAG-71-10; b PAG-53-22; c PAG-46-17; d PAG-10-24; e PAG-17-41; f PAG-8-177.

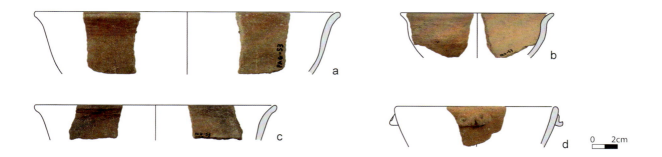

83   B-I with variable rim position, rim form and lip. a PAG-53-6; b PAG-53-4; c PAG-53-8; d PAG-90-85.

84   B-II-3 with variable rim position, rim form and lip. a PAG-53-94; b PAG-17-1; c PAG-46-72; d PAG-53-100.

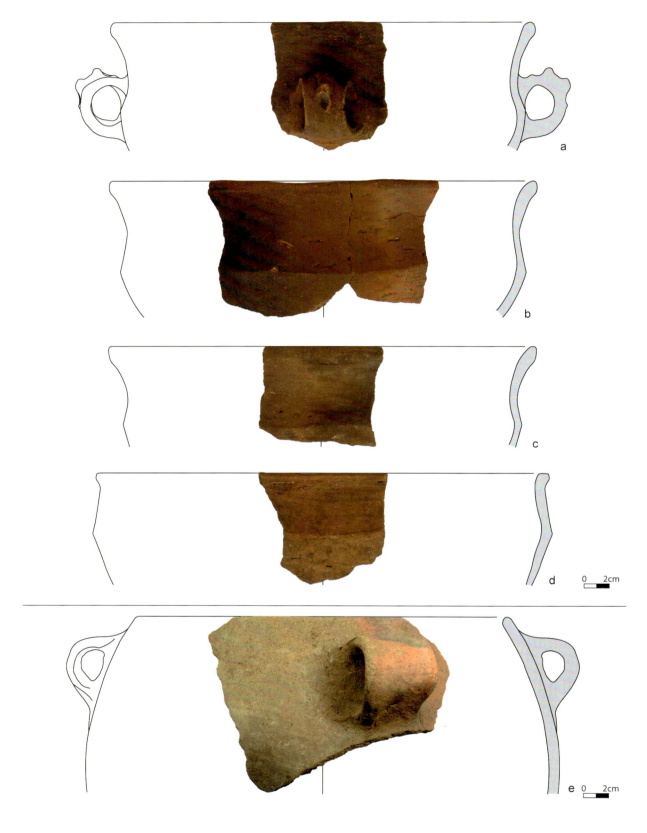

85   B-II-3 with variable rim form and lip and B-II-6 with variable rim form and lip. a PAG-53-82; b PAG-53-68; c PAG-53-89; d PAG-53-70; e PAG-12-139.

86   B-II-6 with variable rim form and lip. a PAG-53-562; b PAG-13-8; c PAG-6-18; d PAG-53-42; e PAG-53-104; f PAG-46-26.

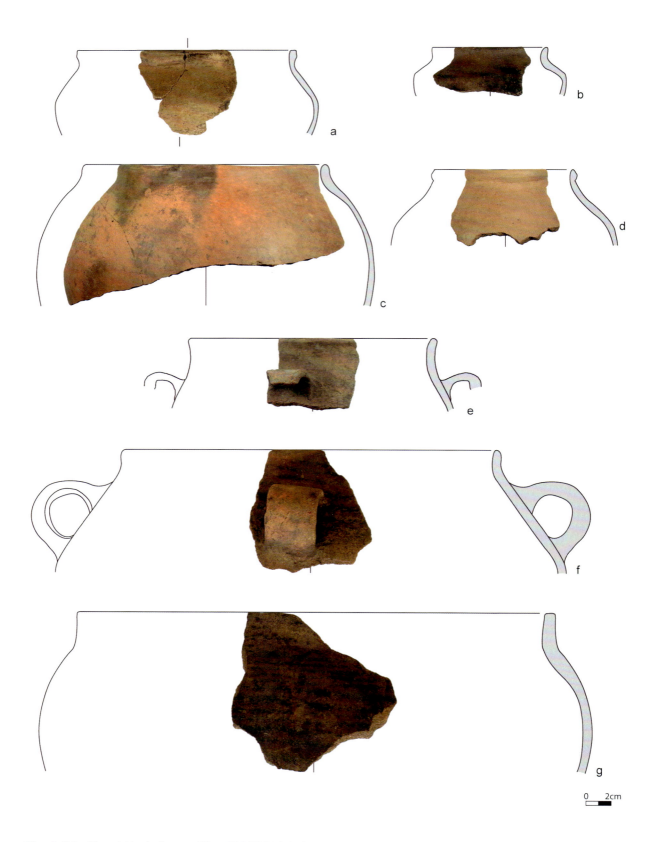

87 B-III-1 with variable rim form and lip. a PAG-53-76; b PAG-46-69; c PAG-15-244; d PAG-44-20; e PAG-71-32; f PAG-71-14; g PAG-71-18.

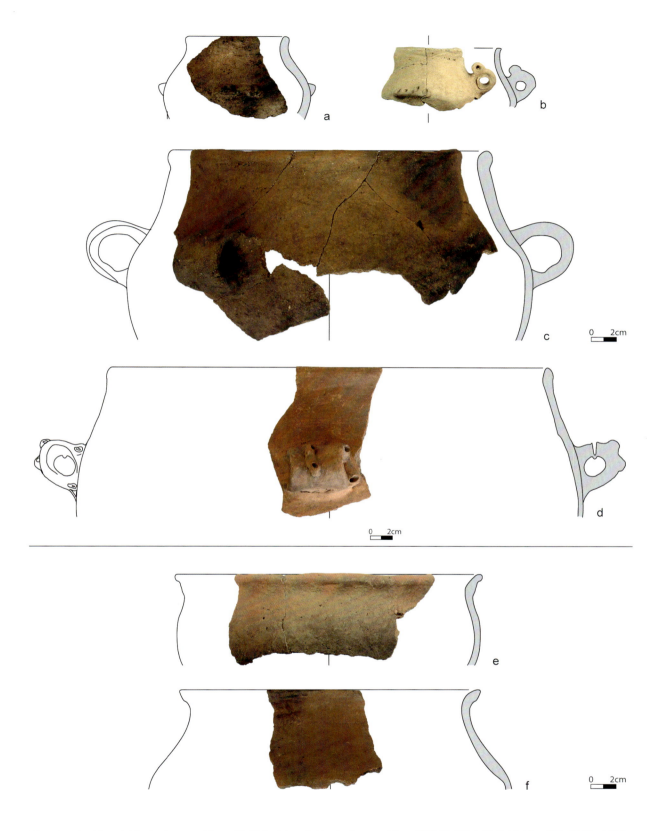

88   B-III-1 with variable rim form and lip and B-III-3 with variable rim form and lip. a PAG-53-102; b PAG-44-40; c PAG-46-78; d PAG-44-18; e PAG-17-5; ; f PAG-71-37.

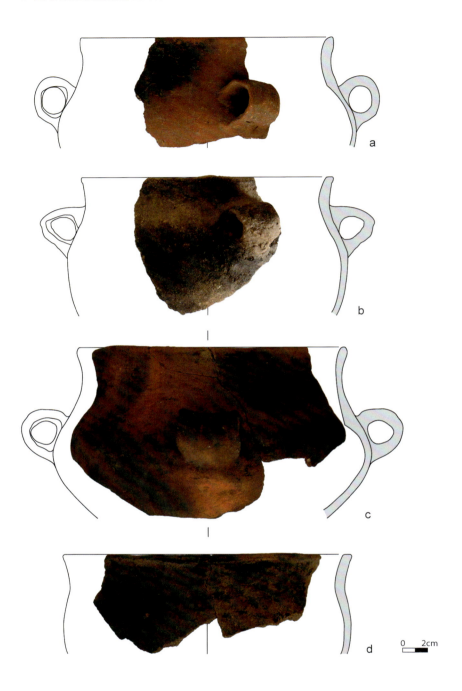

89   B-III-3 with variable rim form and lip. a PAG-53-80; b PAG-44-36; c PAG-53-109; d PAG-53-75.

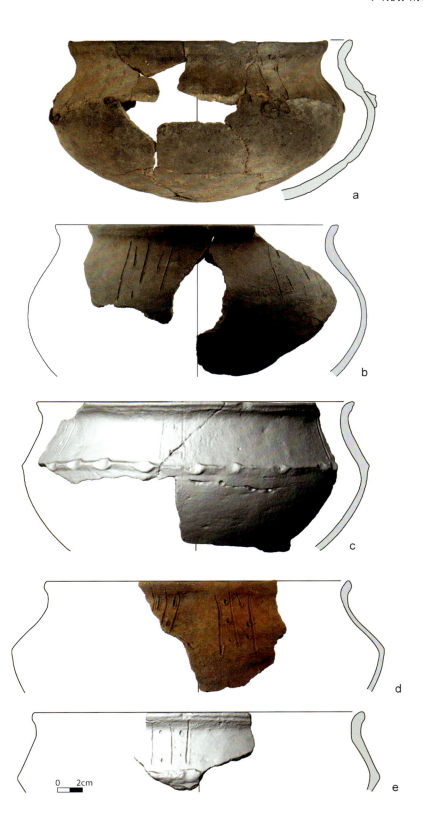

90   B-III-3 with variable rim form and lip. a PAG-13-122; b PAG-8-510; c PAG-12-3; d PAG-12-8; e PAG-10-170.

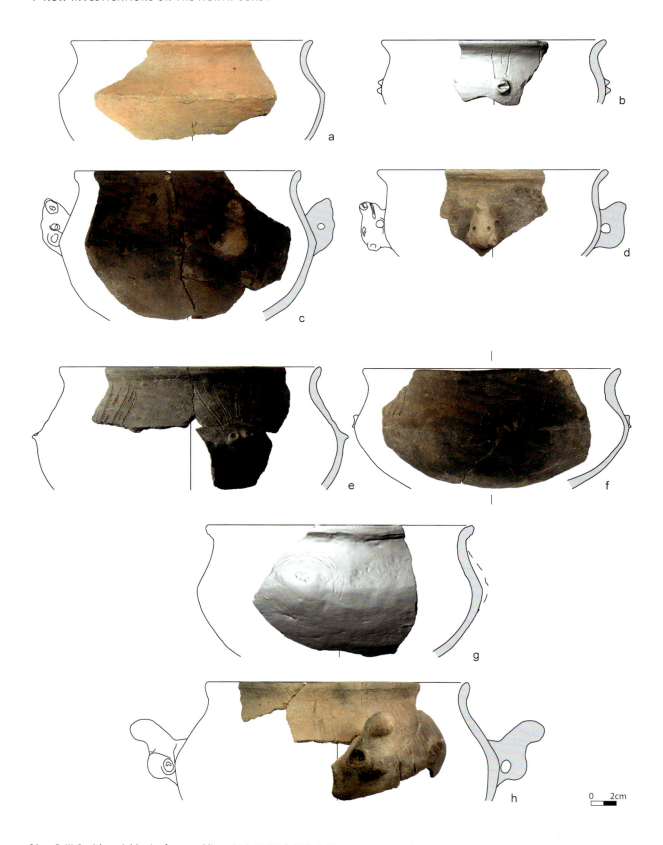

91   B-III-3 with variable rim form and lip. a PAG-15-87; b PAG-6-94; c PAG-53-108; d PAG-8-210; e PAG-15-16; f PAG-12-49; g PAG-17-16; h PAG-15-9.

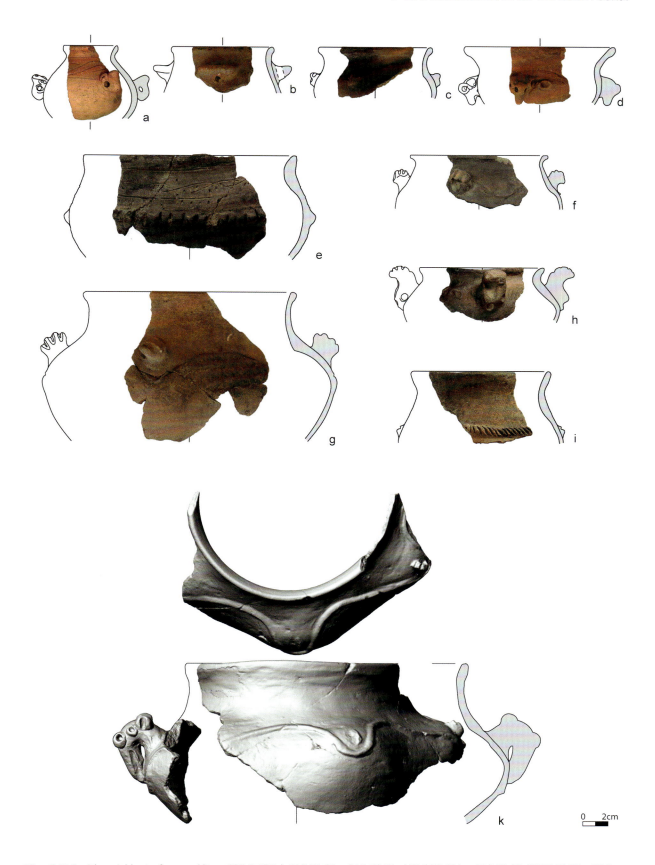

92   B-III-3 with variable rim form and lip. a PAG-8-502; b PAG-71-22; c PAG-53-79; d PAG-53-101; e PAG-53-27; f PAG-17-27; g PAG-44-19; h PAG-44-35; i PAG-53-15; k PAG-17-4.

93   C-II-5 with variable rim form and lip. a PAG-13-10; b PAG-46-64; c PAG-6-225.

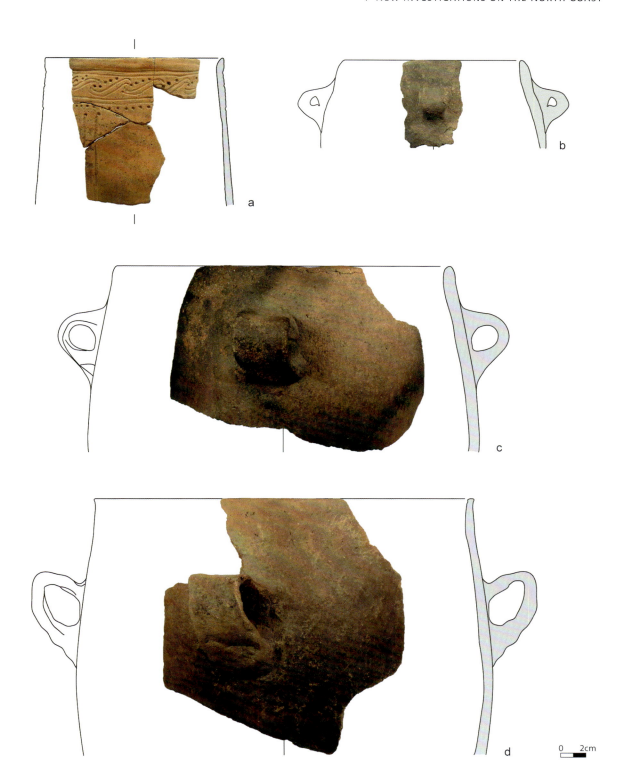

94   C-II-5 with variable rim form and lip. a PAG-53-113; b PAG-6-486; c PAG-10-554; d PAG-15-338.

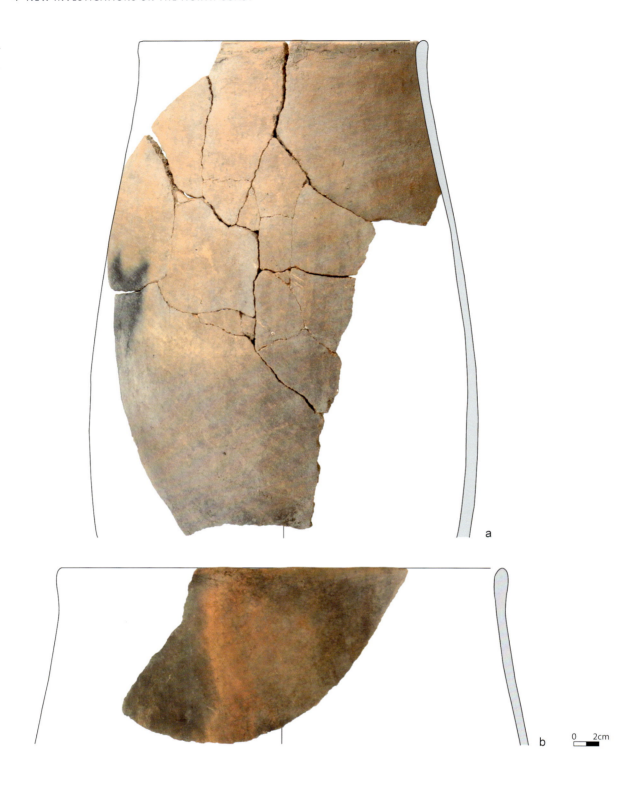

95   C-III-1 with variable rim form and lip. a PAG-12-1126; b PAG-44-12b.

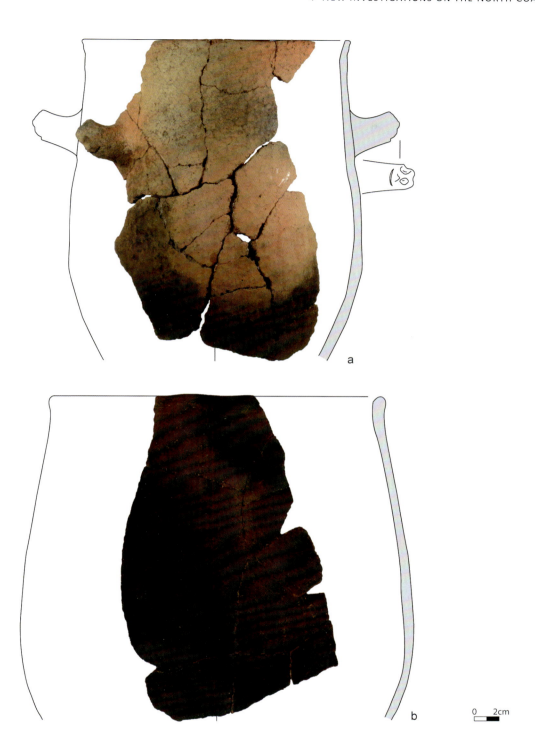

96   C-III-1 with variable rim form and lip. a PAG-17-32; b PAG-46-83.

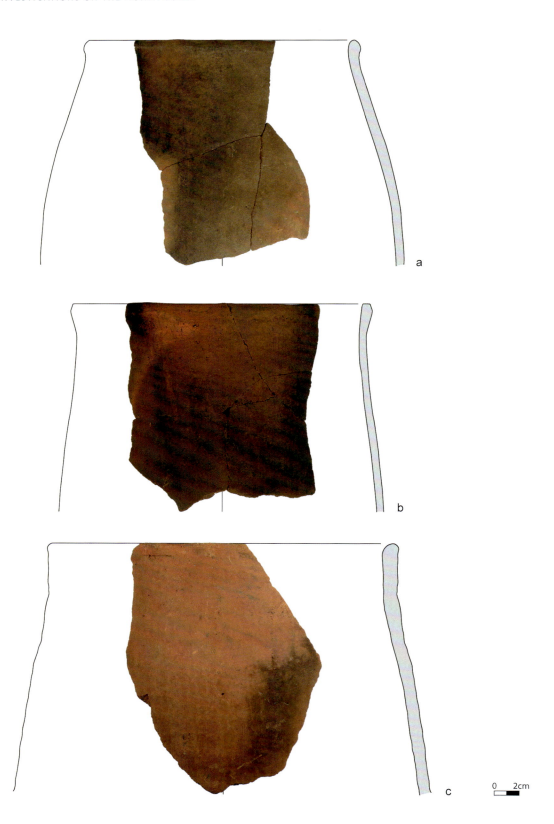

97 C-III-1 with variable rim form and lip. c PAG-59-1; b PAG-53-74; a PAG-15-500.

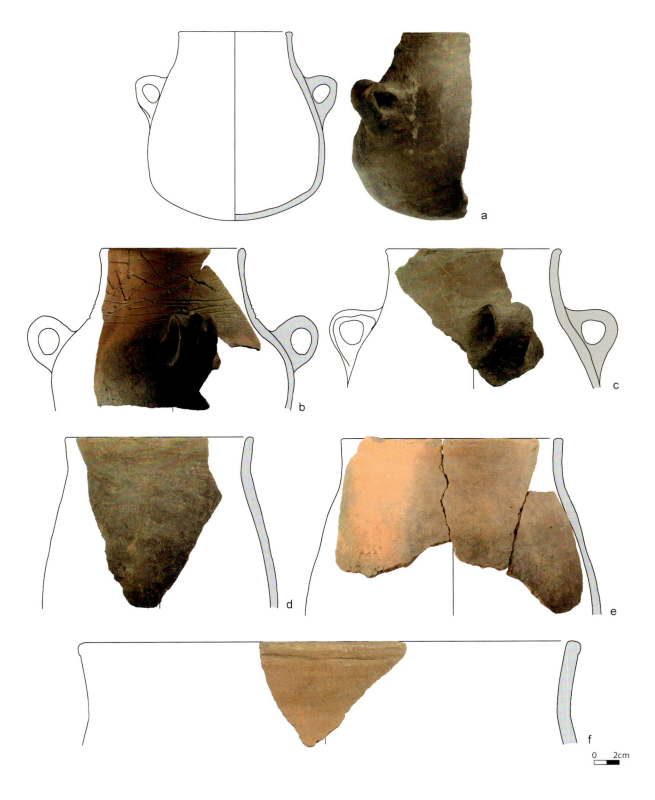

98   C-III-1 with variable rim form and lip. a PAG-12-137; b PAG-44-55; c PAG-12-1123; d PAG-10-259; e PAG-13-3; f PAG-8-38.

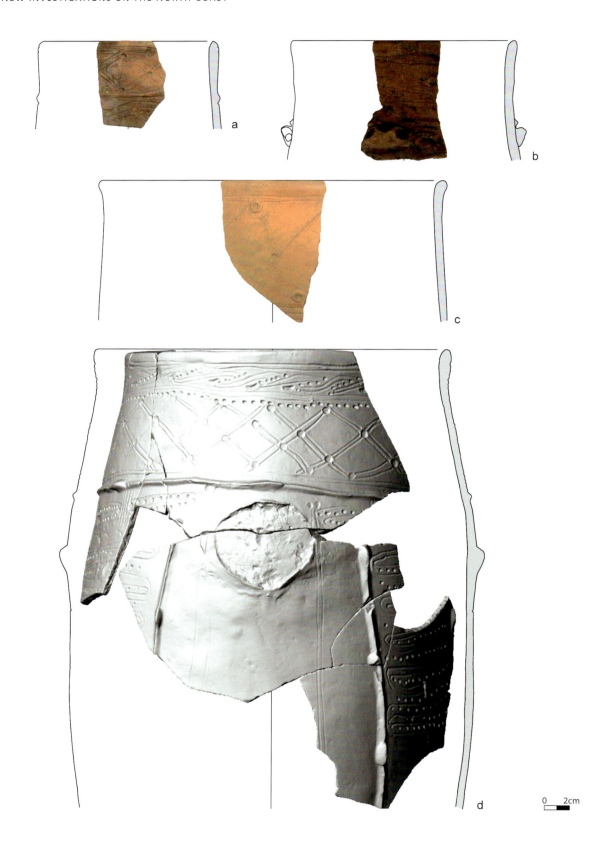

99   C-III-1 with variable rim form and lip. a PAG-44-30; b PAG-71-17; c PAG-17-31; d PAG-46-308.

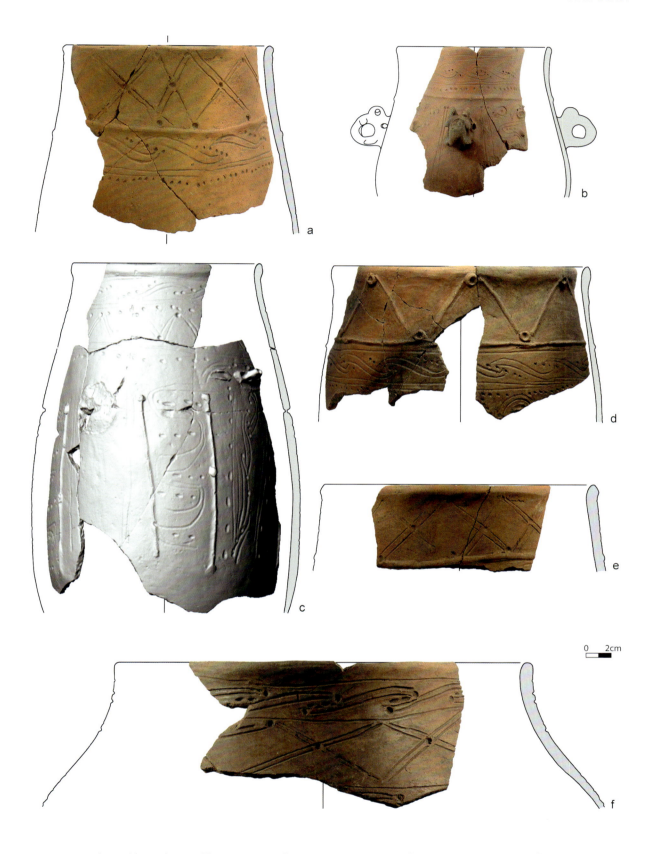

100   C-III-1 with variable rim form and lip. a PAG-53-24; b PAG-40-3; c PAG-53-110; d PAG-46-309; e PAG-46-24; f PAG-53-28.

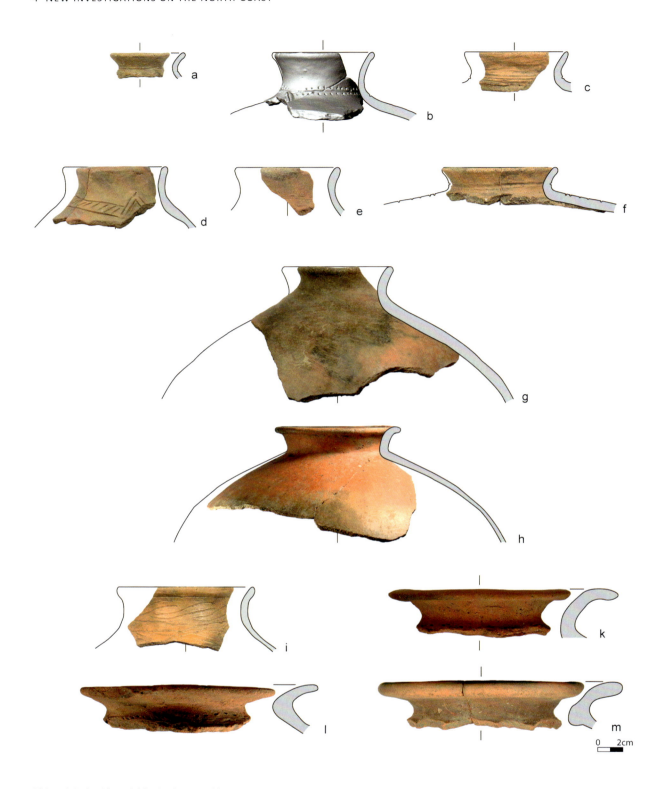

101   C-III-3 with variable rim form and lip. a PAG-8-93; b PAG-17-24; c PAG-8-237; d PAG-44-37; e PAG-114-17; f PAG-6-62; g PAG-15-122; h PAG-44-14; i PAG-8-542; k PAG-71-8; l PAG-44-32; m PAG-17-20.

102 C-III-3 with variable rim form and lip. a PAG-44-51; b PAG-10-164; c PAG-15-2; d PAG-46-67.

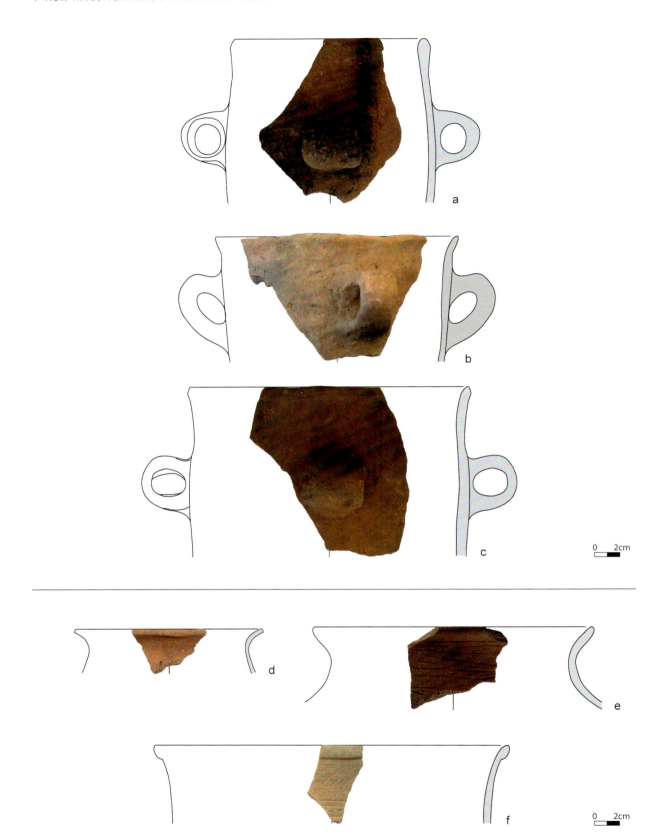

103   C-0 (basic form unkown) Group a and Group b. a PAG-53-83; b PAG-12-396; c PAG-53-99; d PAG-113-18; e PAG-90-80; f PAG-99-52.

Individual Attributes

In this section, individual attributes are examined. First, attributes that do not occur in combination with basic forms will be described. Next, individual attributes are checked for chronological relevance, independent of association with a basic form.

Rim Form/Lip. The stratigraphic analysis suggests that neither rim nor lip form possesses a great chronological significance. The forms show a more or less even distribution within the layers. Rim Form 1 is the most common, followed by Rim Form 2, while Rim Forms 4 and 5 are found only sporadically. The only rim form that shows chronological relevance is Rim Form 6, which is observed on 14 fragments (Figure 104). The rim is exterior folded, relatively rough, and uneven. None of the fragments with this rim form could be assigned to a basic form. This is partly due to the small size of the fragments but also to the irregular shape of the lips, which makes it difficult to determine their position. However, I assume that they are rather shallow, open vessels, possibly A-I. This rim shape can be attributed to the early periods since it is only found in the occupation layers (Inv. 94–149).

Bases. Few bases were documented during the initial identification of diagnostic sherds. This indicates that most bases are rounded and were mistakenly identified as body sherds (see Paap 2002: 37) (Figure 105). When we became aware of this problem and were more familiar with the material, we did a test search of the sherds of Inv. 53, which had been labeled as undiagnostic, and actually found some round bases. I, therefore, assume that other round bases remain unidentified among the undiagnostic sherds.

104   Rim 6. a PAG-139-44; b PAG-114-12; c PAG-114-22; d PAG-139-34.

The other base forms rarely occur (Figure 106). Only three instances of Base b (flat) were found, which seem to occur in connection with the frying pan form. Base c (incurved) occurs eight times. On one of the bases (Figure 106i), two appliqués are preserved, which indicates that this shape was associated with supports. We do not know which basic vessel form is associated with these bases. Two of these base forms come from settlement layers (Inv. 91 and 105), the others from the ceramic layer, where they are concentrated in the lower portion. One example, however, was identified in the upper-most portion of the ceramic layer (Inv. 12). Base d occurs ten times. This seems to be an early phenomenon because seven specimens originate from the settlement layers. The other three specimens were found in the lower portion of the ceramic layer (Inv. 71 and 53).

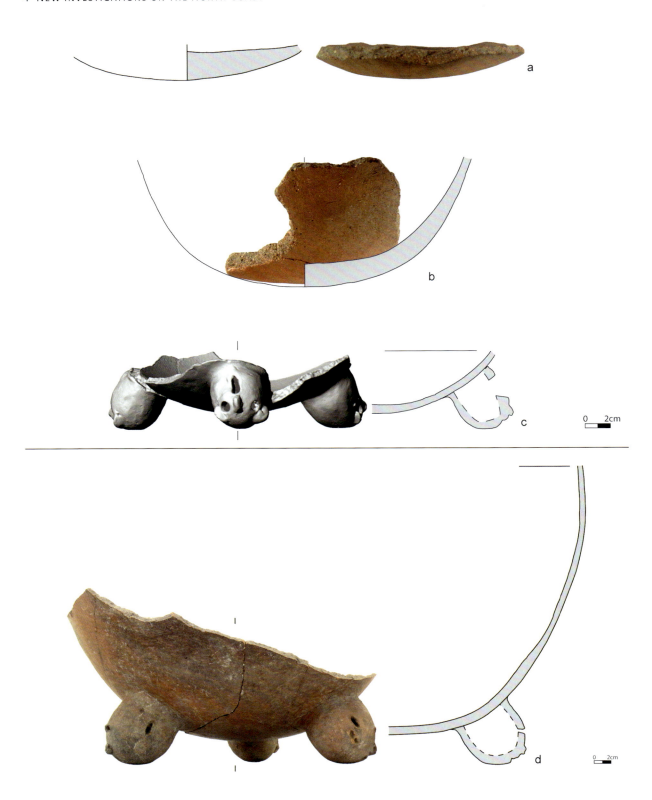

105   Base a. a PAG-53-473; b PAG-53-474; c PAG-17-8; d PAG-13-123.

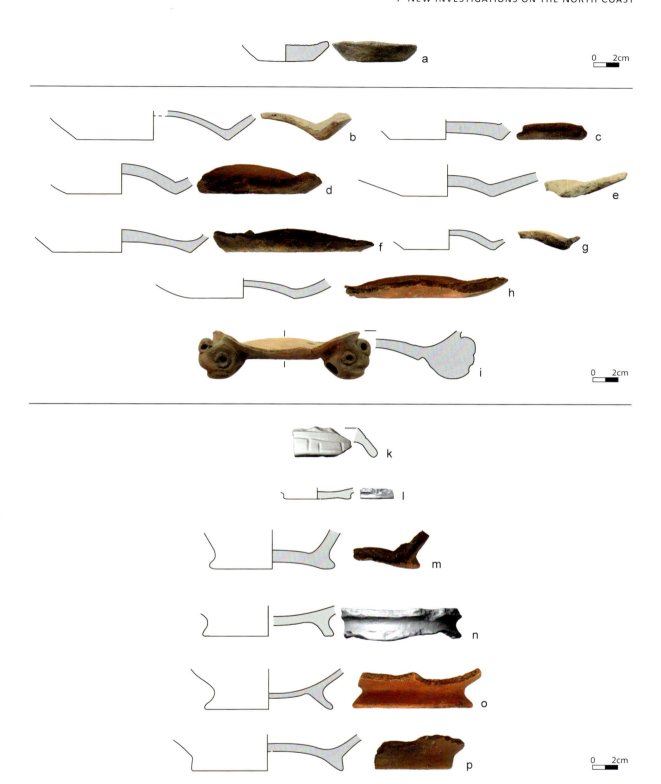

106   Base b, Base c and Base d. a PAG-44-41; b PAG-12-164; c PAG-53-86; d PAG-53-84; e PAG-105-52; f PAG-46-68; g PAG-91-149; h PAG-53-93; i PAG-44-52; k PAG-139-33; l PAG-89-42; m PAG-71-13; n PAG-90-65; o PAG-53-87; p PAG-53-85.

4.4.1.3.2 Incisions

Incisions refer to all modifications created by cutting or displacement techniques. In our case, this includes mainly incisions and impressions, but not joining techniques, where clay is added to the vessel. Of the 868 pieces analyzed, 251 have incisions (28%) (Figure 107). Individual lines and rows of dots are not considered separately here, as they occur in combination with many designs and are used to separate different motifs from one another. On most objects (231), the decoration is applied to the exterior. The lines must have been applied with a pointed object (e.g., a wooden stick, reed, or bone) into the leather-hard, sometimes moist clay (evidenced by thrown-up edges). On some fragments, the lines are smeared over, indicating the surface was subsequently smoothed (Figure 108).

Motif 1 – Cross (Figure 109)

The cross motif is one of the most frequently occurring incisions. It is found on 35 of the 251 fragments (14% of those with incisions). The motif consists of a series of crosses that wrap around the vessel in a horizontal line. Within this motif, there are different varieties. The crosses consist of double lines or single lines, with or without dots. If there are dots, they are located where the lines cross. There is also a version where the cross pattern is appliquéd (see Appliqué Motif 33). The design is located on the exterior of the vessels without exception and always in the upper section. When it occurs alone, it is found directly below the rim. If it occurs in combination with other incised motifs, it can also be located further down. It is especially common to find this motif in combination with a wave design (Incision Motif 3).

Notably, the pattern is not applied very symmetrically. In some vessels, the exact placement of the dots did not apparently play an important role, as they are located to the side of the crossing points (e.g., Figure 109e, h). This observation can contrast with the vessel's quality, especially in the case of PAG-15-683, which exhibits fine temper and regular firing.

The cross motif is present throughout the entire pottery layer. In the settlement layers, only two fragments occur in a single context (Inv. 90). Furthermore, it appears that the variety with dots is more represented in the lower layers of the pottery layer and thus is an earlier phenomenon.

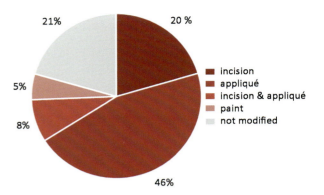

107   Percentages of ceramic sherds with modifications in the sample (F. Fecher).

108   Smeared over incisions: a PAG-15-13; b PAG-8-508; c PAG-46-24 (F. Fecher).

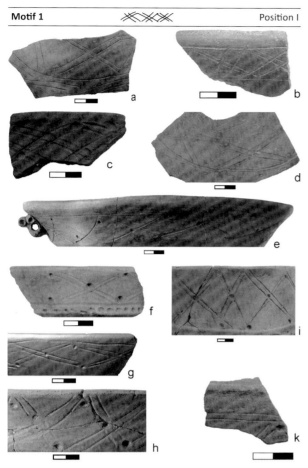

109   Incision Motif 1. a PAG-6-31; b PAG-8-551; c PAG-8-535; d PAG-12-20; e PAG-15-683; f PAG-17-30; g PAG-44-31; h PAG-44-34; i PAG-53-24; k PAG-90-57.

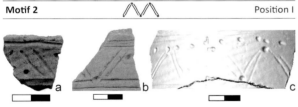

110   Incision Motif 2. a PAG-10-224; b PAG-46-763; c PAG-53-110.

Motif 2 – Zigzag (Figure 110)

There are three examples of the zigzag motif in the sample. The motif consists of two parallel lines that form a zigzag pattern. Dots occur at the corners or between the lines. In two cases, the pattern is located on the upper part of the vessel's exterior. In the third case, the pattern's position is not clear due to the sherd's small size. Since the design is very similar to Incision Motif 1 and occurs in combination with the same motifs, it is probably a variation of Incision Motif 1. The motif only occurs in the ceramic layer.

Motif 3 – Waves (Figure 111)

The wave motif is the most common incision. It occurs on 75 of 251 fragments (30%). The pattern consists of wavy lines that wind horizontally around the vessel in a band. There are different variations. For the most part, the motif consists of two parallel lines running from the lower left to the upper right. In a few cases (e.g., Figure 111e), the wave runs from the upper right to the lower left. The spaces between the waves are often filled with a varying number of dots. Regarding the alignment of the lines, they vary in inclination from steep to flat. In a few cases, the wave consists of a single line (e.g., Figure 111g). Without exception, the pattern is located on the upper part of the vessel's exterior. When it appears alone, it occupies the area below the rim. If it occurs in combination with other incised motifs, it may be located further down on the vessel wall. This motif is commonly found in combination with the cross motif (Incision Motif 1). As with the cross motif, there are differences in the exactness of the design. Some vessels show a very symmetrical design, while other incisions seem to have been executed rather carelessly so that the motif is hardly recognizable. The latter is common in the upper layers (e.g., Figure 111b, c).

The motif is present throughout the unit's entire depth, including the ceramic layer and the settlement layer down to its lowest portions (Inv. 172). No patterns can be observed with regard to motifs changing across layers. The only noticeable variation is that the frag-ments in the lower portions of the pottery layer have sig-nificantly more dots between the wavy lines, while the upper layers of the pottery layer and those from the set-tlement layer show fewer dots.

Motif 4 – Wavy Line (Figure 112)

The wavy line motif occurs six times (2%). The pattern consists of a single wavy line running horizontally. Each undulation is accompanied by one or two punctations. It is located exclusively on the vessel's interior and sits just below the rim. So far, it is not seen in combinations with other motifs. The motif is only present in the ceramic layer (Inv. 8, 17, 44, 46, and 53).

Motif 5 – Scroll (Figure 113)

The scroll motif occurs 11 times (4%). It represents a horizontal S-shaped line. There are punctations in the spaces between the lines. The motif is always on the ves-sel's exterior, and it always occurs in combination with other patterns. The most common combination is with vertical bars (Incision Motif 8). In this case, it alternates with the bars in a horizontal band below the rim. In four cases, it occurs together with Incision Motifs 1, and 3. The motif is present in the lower half of the ceramic lay-er (Inv. 15–53).

Motif 6 – Bars and Dots (Figure 114)

The bars and dots motif occurs 13 times (5%). It con-sists of single, slightly curved bars accompanied by dots. The pattern runs in a horizontal band and is bor-dered by a thin line at the top and bottom. In some cases, there is a line of punctations above and/or below these lines. In 12 cases, the motif is located on the ves-sel's interior; in a single case, it is on the exterior. In all cases, however, it is below the rim. This motif only oc-curs alone. Notably, this motif is executed with very fine lines with relatively shallow incisions. The motif has a certain similarity to Incision Motif 3. It occurs in both the ceramic layer and settlement layers (Inv. 90 and 91).

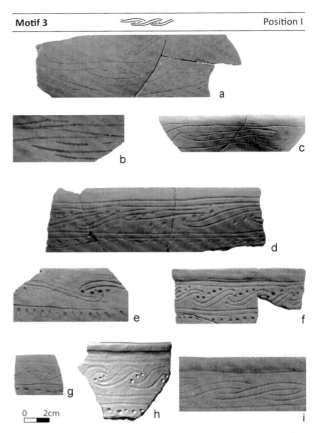

111 Incision Motif 3. a PAG-6-2; b PAG-6-63; c PAG-8-526; d PAG-17-41; e PAG-46-26; f PAG-53-113; g PAG-53-609; h PAG-71-19; i PAG-139-48.

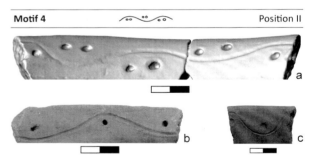

112 Incision Motif 4. a PAG-17-29; b PAG-46-333; c PAG-53-917.

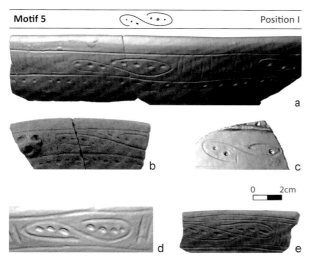

113   Incision Motif 5. a PAG-17-23; b PAG-44-269; c PAG-46-18; d PAG-46-57; e PAG-53-629.

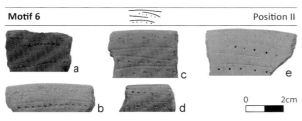

114   Incision Motif 6. a PAG-8-574; b PAG-46-578; c PAG-71-96; d PAG-90-74; e PAG-91-134.

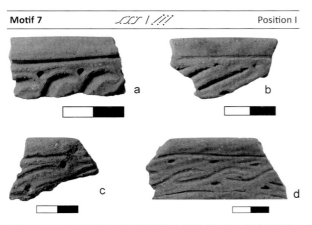

115   Incision Motif 7. a PAG-99-32; b PAG-99-45; c PAG-99-55; d PAG-105-25.

Motif 7 – Diagonal Bars (Figure 115)

The diagonal bars motif occurs 14 times (6%). It consists of diagonal or slightly curved individual lines arranged next to each other. There is a dot at the beginning and end of each line. The pattern runs in a horizontal band and is framed at the top and bottom by parallel lines. It is located exclusively on the vessel exterior, where it sits below the rim. So far, it is not seen in combination with other motifs. In our sample, this motif occurs exclusively in the settlement layers (Inv. 91–142) and thus seems to be an early phenomenon. The number of fragments with this motif is exceptionally high in Inv. 99 (seven fragments).

Motif 8 – Vertical Bars (Figure 116)

The vertical bars motif is found on 14 fragments (6%). It is made up of a series of vertical bars. In one version, there are punctates above and below the lines (e.g., Figure 116b, d). In all cases, it is located on the vessel's exterior, where it appears in different combinations and different positions. It is most frequently (seven times) found in combination with Incision Motif 5, in which case it encircles the vessel rim. In one case, the motif is found in the middle of the vessel's body and in combination with other modifications. In the other cases, the fragments are very small, and its exact position cannot be determined. It is also unclear whether these vessels have other motifs. The motif is represented in the lower portion of the ceramic layer (nine fragments, Inv. 15–53) and the settlement layer (five fragments).

Motif 9 – Vertical Lines with Dashes (Figure 117)

The vertical lines with dashes motif is found on 14 fragments (6%). It consists of vertically running lines with shorter vertical lines in between. The varieties range from two to three lines. In one case (Figure 117d), four lines converge towards the bottom. The motif is always on the vessel's exterior. In 13 cases, the motif is located on the upper half of the vessel. In some cases, it appears in combination with Incision Motif 10, where Incision Motif 9 occurs several times on the vessel, and each time with an unmodified, blank space between the motifs. The motif occurs exclusively in the ceramic layer and is concentrated in the upper portion (Inv. 6–15). Only a single example was identified in Inv. 53.

Motif 10 – Bent Line with Dashes (Figure 118)
The bent line with dashes motif occurs five times (2%). It consists of two curved lines that form a semicircle. The space in between the lines is filled with short lines. The motif seems to be closely related to Incision Motif 9. In three cases, it occurs together with this motif. However, the other two vessels may also be decorated with Incision Motif 9, but this cannot be verified given the small number of examples. The motif is always on the vessel exterior at the widest point. In three cases, a small appliqué is located in the center of the bent lines, while in the other cases, this part is not preserved. Like Incision Motif 9, it is concentrated in the upper layers of the ceramic layer (Inv. 5–17).

Motif 11 – Short Lines (Figure 119)
The short lines motif occurs ten times (4%). It is always on the vessel's exterior. The motif has a dashed line consisting of short strokes. In some cases, these lines are framed by a continuous line at the top and bottom. The motif appears in combination with Incision Motifs 1 and 3. In these cases, it wraps either around the neck of the vessel or around its body. In two cases, the fragments are so small that the exact position or associated motifs cannot be determined. Six of the fragments were found in the upper layers of the ceramic concentration (Inv. 6–15). One fragment is from the ceramic layer (Inv. 44), while the others were found in the settlement layers (Inv. 90 and 105).

Motif 12 – Dots (Figure 120)
The dots motif occurs only three times (1%). It consists of two horizontal, parallel lines with dots in the space between them. The motif does not likely occur in combination with other motifs. However, the fragments are relatively small, so it is difficult to say with any certainty. PAG-17-666 (Figure 120a) has this motif on its exterior, positioned just below the rim. PAG-90-66 and PAG-91-118 (Figure 120b, c) have this design on the interior, also just below the rim. Due to the small number of examples, little can be said about the stratigraphic distribution except that they occur in both the ceramic and settlement layers.

Motif 13 – Diagonal Bars with Dots (Figure 121)
The diagonal bars with dots motif occurs four times (2%). It consists of two horizontal, parallel lines with alternating dots and dashes in the space between them. The motif is always on the exterior, where it forms a band below the rim. The motif does not likely occur in combination with other motifs. However, the preserved fragments are relatively small; thus, it cannot be ruled

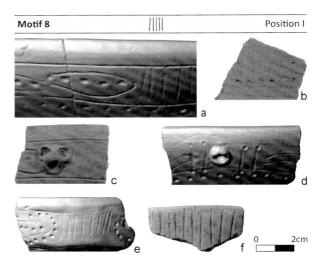

116   Incision Motif 8. a PAG-17-23; b PAG-17-25; c PAG-44-674; d PAG-46-22; e PAG-53-16; f PAG-139-42.

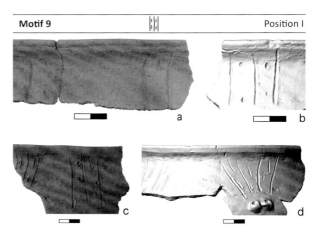

117   Incision Motif 9. a PAG-8-546; b PAG-10-170; c PAG-12-8; d PAG-15-16.

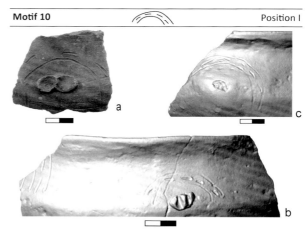

118   Incision Motif 10. a PAG-10-158; b PAG-12-49; c PAG-17-16.

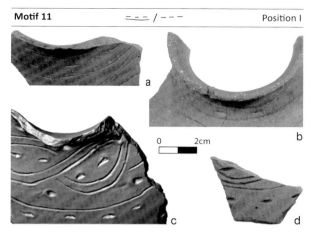

119 Incision Motif 11. a PAG-6-8; b PAG-10-164; c PAG-44-51; d PAG-90-87.

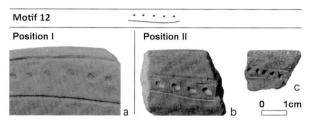

120 Incision Motif 12. a PAG-17-666; b PAG-90-66; c PAG-91-118.

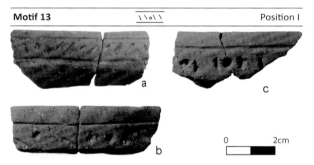

121 Incision Motif 13. a PAG-99-18; b PAG-99-38; c PAG-109-6.

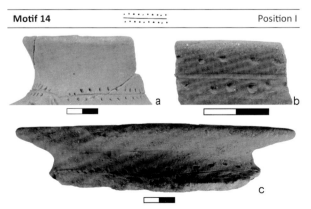

122 Incision Motif 14. a PAG-17-24; b PAG-17-523; c PAG-44-32.

out that other motifs existed on the vessels. The execution of the motif is not uniform. Different pieces differ in the number and sequence of dots and dashes, as well as in their alignment. All pieces were found in the settlement layer.

Motif 14 – Horizontal Line with Dots (Figure 122)
The horizontal line with dots motif occurs seven times (3%). It consists of a horizontal line bordered above and below by parallel dotted lines. The motif is located on the vessel's exterior. In five cases, it winds around the vessel's neck, and, in two cases, it is located below the vessel's rim. Due to the poor preservation, little else can be said about associated motifs. Regarding PAG-17-24 (Figure 122a), it is clear that the line was drawn first, and the dots were added afterward because the displaced clay partially overlaps the line. The motif is concentrated in the lower layers of the ceramic concentration (Inv. 17–71). Two examples come from the settlement layer (Inv. 94 and 114).

Motif 15 – Horizontal Double Line with Dots (Figure 123)
The horizontal double line with dots motif occurs nine times (4%). It consists of two parallel, horizontal lines bordered above and below by parallel dotted lines. The motif is located on the vessel's exterior. In eight cases, it forms a band below the rim. In one case (PAG-91-127, Figure 123d), the fragment is not large enough to associate it with other motifs. PAG-15-59 shows the remains of a dark paint that extends over the rim into the vessel interior (see Figure 170c). Five fragments are associated with small appliqués applied below the rim. Three of them are Appliqué Motif 25. Eight of the fragments are found in the ceramic layer (Inv. 8–71), most of them from Inv. 53. Only one fragment (PAG-91-127) comes from the settlement layer. All three combinations with Appliqué Motif 25 are from Inv. 53.

Motif 16 – Horizontal and Vertical Lines with Dots (Figure 124)
The horizontal and vertical lines with dots motif occurs seven (or possibly four) times. It consists of vertical parallel lines with dots filling the spaces between them. Further parallel lines run perpendicular to the others. Only small wall fragments were preserved, making additional interpretations difficult. Due to the sherds' low degree of curvature, I assume they are relatively deep vessels. The number of dots and lines and their exact position on the vessel are not specified. However, it appears that the motif is always on the exterior, and the absence of rim pieces suggests that it is located on the vessel body. While one example is from the ceramic layer (PAG-15-80, Figure 124a), the others are from the settlement layer. Four fragments are from

Inv. 90. Although the sherds could not be refitted, it is still possible that they come from the same vessel, which would reduce the number of examples of this motif to four.

Motif 17 – Undulating Lines (Figure 125)

The undulating lines motif occurs 11 times (4%). It consists of undulating incised lines with dots or short lines in the spaces between them. The line can be either a single or double line. The motif is always located on the vessel's exterior in the central part of the body. In all cases, it occurs in combination with other motifs and appliqués. The symmetry of the motif does not seem to have played a significant role. In particular, the bends of the line on PAG-53-110 (Figure 125c) are not located directly above one another, and the distances between the lines are irregular. The motif occurs only in the ceramic layer and is concentrated in the lower layers (8 fragments were found in Inv. 44–71).

Motif 18 – Punctates (Figure 126)

The punctates motif occurs four times (2%) and consists of small round circular punctates. They are impressions of hollow objects, perhaps plants. The motif is always on the exterior. The preserved fragments are very small, and only small parts of the pattern are preserved. Therefore, little can be said about vessel shapes, combinations, or positions. However, I assume that the motif is located on the vessel wall. Goodwin (2011: Fig 6.14) illustrates two fragments with this decoration that come from the site PR06 on Roatán. The illustrations reinforce this assumption and show that the motif is found in combination with a raised band. In Guadalupe, the motif only occurs in the settlement layers (Inv. 99, 105, and 142).

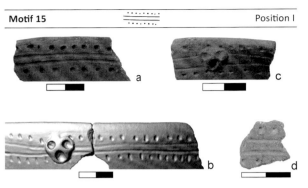

123   Incision Motif 15. a PAG-8-595; b PAG-53-23; c PAG-53-160; d PAG-91-127.

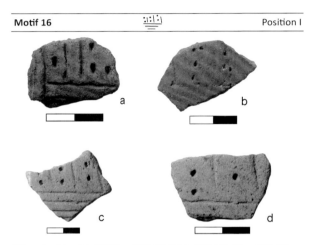

124   Incision Motif 16. a PAG-15-80; b PAG-90-42; c PAG-99-43; d PAG-99-61.

125   Incision Motif 17. a PAG-10-169; b PAG-44-50; c PAG-53-110; d PAG-71-1025.

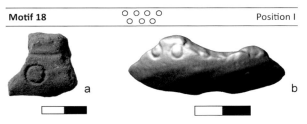

126   Incision Motif 18. a PAG-94-28; b PAG-105-41.

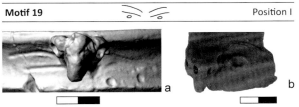

127   Incision Motif 19. a PAG-53-29; b PAG-53-101.

Motif 19 – Wings (Figure 127)

The wings motif only occurs twice. In both cases, it is related to an appliqué showing a bird's head (Appliqué Motif 19). Incision Motif 19 consists of slightly curved lines that run from the bird's head to either side and possibly represent wings. Both fragments are from Inv. 53.

Motif 20 – Striations (Figure 128)

The striations motif occurs three times. They are fine lines that cover the entire vessel exterior, although differ in the design and direction of the lines depending on the vessel. The lines are only lightly incised and do not run strictly parallel but partly overlap. They were possibly applied with a kind of broom or bundle of grass. The three fragments were found in Inv. 6, 53, and 166. Because of the uneven distribution and the differences in execution, I suspect that there is no direct connection between the three examples.

Motif 21 – Curved Line

The curved line motif is a line that winds around the widest part of the vessel body. This motif appears as an incision, appliqué, or as a combination of the two. Since the two techniques are difficult to separate in this case, the motif will be examined more closely in the section for Appliqué Motif 30.

Motif S – Single Motifs (Figure 129)

The single motifs category includes all motifs that occur only once. There are 11 such examples.

Motif 0 – Unidentified Motifs

Thirty-four other incised fragments could not be assigned to a motif. These are small fragments with only a small portion of the design visible, making it difficult to determine the motif, especially since the components, such as lines and dots, are part of several motifs. These fragments were marked "In-0" in the key.

Drilled Holes for Crack Lacing

Some fragments have a drilled hole. This feature has not been included in the classification, as it is a functional element created after initial production. These are holes for crack lacing. They are introduced into the fired clay to repair cracked vessels by making holes on both sides of a crack and lacing them together with a string (Figure 130; see also Figure 70i).

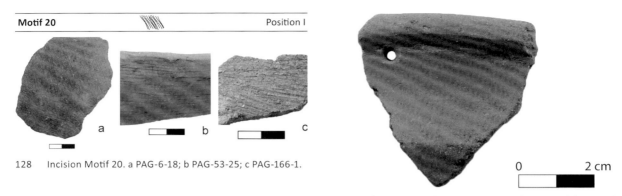

128   Incision Motif 20. a PAG-6-18; b PAG-53-25; c PAG-166-1.

130   Rim fragment with hole for crack lacing (PAG-17-92) (F. Fecher).

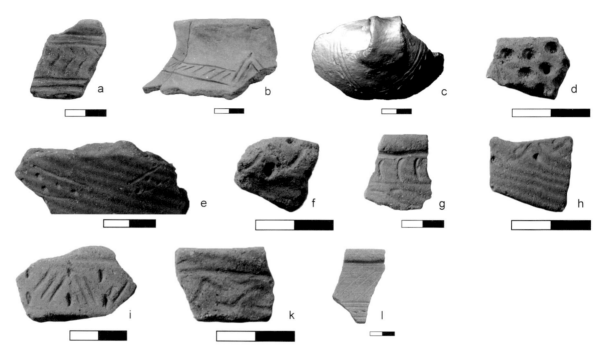

129   Incision Single Motifs (S). a PAG-8-563; b PAG-44-37; c PAG-46-25; d PAG-49-6b; e PAG-90-45; f PAG-94-5b; g PAG-94-30; h PAG-99-14; i PAG-99-23; k PAG-99-25; l PAG-99-52.

4.4.1.3.3 Appliqués

A total of 467 fragments have appliqués or represent appliqués, which corresponds to about 54% of the sample (see Figure 107). Given this high number, it should be noted that vessels always have three supports and probably two handles, which likely leads to an overrepresentation of appliqués. The term "appliqué" covers all modifications that are executed with a joining technique, i.e., those that protrude from the vessel surface. This is the result of applying clay to the vessel surface. In some specific cases, appliqués can also be formed from the clay mass of the vessel itself. When defining an appliqué, the first production step determines the definition. So, if a modification is produced by adding clay as the first step, it is counted as an appliqué, even if incisions are applied to the appliqué later. However, it is not easy to divide appliqués into motifs due to abstraction and the fact that motifs often seem to blend into one another (Strong 1935: 99).

Several observations can be made regarding the appliqué technique. Some appliqués are solid, while most are hollow. This is certainly related to their size. Solid objects would burst during firing above a specific size. Broken supports allow us to observe the different steps in the production process. The hollow supports are made of slabs that are attached to the vessel body. The fact that they are not only smeared on the outside but also the inside shows us that the plates were not yet closed at their end when they were applied to the vessel bottom. Only after they had been attached were they finally closed at their distal end (Figure 131). To prevent the appliqués from bursting during firing, holes are required through which air can escape. The clay displaced in the process is often still preserved, suggesting that the holes are only inserted after the supports have been attached to the vessel body (Figure 132). Presumably, the decoration of these supports was also only applied after they had been attached to the vessel body. In some hollow supports, there are small ceramic balls that make a sound when the vessel is moved.

Motif 1 – D-Shaped Strap Handle (Figure 133)[16]
The sample contains 60 fragments with D-shaped strap handles and thus corresponds to 13% of the applications. They consist of a strap that is attached to the vessel at two points. They are always attached to the upper part of the vessel wall. They exist in different sizes and widths, depending on the size of the vessel, and have different designs. The two attachment points are not al-

16 A selection of representative objects has been chosen to illustrate each motif. Since the original position of the appliqués on the vessel cannot always be reconstructed, they are arranged vertically.

131   Broken supports providing insight into production technique: a PAG-53-1007, b PAG-53-1003 (F. Fecher).

132   Broken support with displaced clay in its interior (PAG-53-1006) (F. Fecher).

137

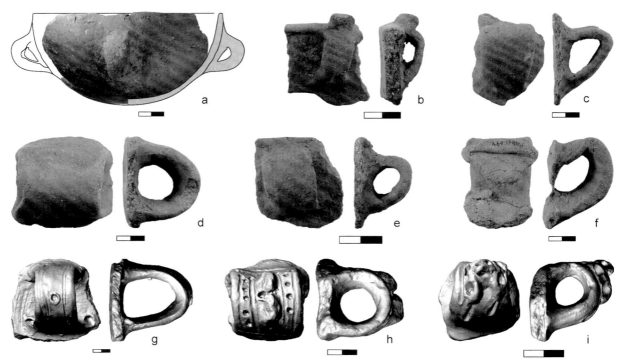

133   Appliqué Motifs 1. a PAG-10-3; b PAG-8-324; c PAG-12-59; d PAG-12-390; e PAG-12-471; f PAG-15-694; g PAG-44-53; h PAG-53-45; i PAG-71-29.

ways located one above the other (e.g., Figure 133b, e), making the handle appear skewed. Some handles are decorated with additional appliqués and incisions. Most of the handles are found on rather coarse vessels without additional appliqués or incisions. The production technique can be observed on broken handles. Apparently, two ceramic strips were placed on top of each other, bent, and then attached to the vessel wall (see Figure 133f). This appliqué is found in the ceramic layer (54 specimens) as well as in the settlement layers (six specimens) (Inv. 6–100).

Motif 2 – Massive Handle (Figure 134)
The massive handle appliqué occurs 12 times (3%). These are solid, elongated handles that only have a small perforation in the center. The handles have different designs. One is undecorated (Figure 134b), while the other fragments show additional incisions and appliqués. Three fragments (Figure 134e, f) have a motif that we will consider in detail later (see Appliqué Motif 18). Three other fragments (Figure 134c, g, and h) have anthropomorphic motifs, each of which has a different design. This appliqué represents frying pan handles, as is clearly seen on PAG-53-37 (see Figure 72g; see also combination analysis in section 4.4.1.3.5).

This appliqué is mainly found in the ceramic layer (Inv. 8–53). Only one example comes from the settlement layer (PAG-149-1, Figure 134h). Since this motif

was initially thought to be a unique form, all specimens in the sample were documented. For this reason, the count of 12 does not correspond to a representative percentage of the overall assemblage.

Motif 3 – Knob (Figure 135)
The knob motif occurs nine times (2%). It consists of a solid appliqué that takes on different shapes ranging from elongated to bulbous. Four objects have additional perforations (e.g., Figure 135c and f). While most appliqués probably represent handles, it is unclear whether PAG-114-23 (Figure 135d) and PAG-139-39 (Figure 135f) are handles or supports. The latter fragment may even be Appliqué Motif 2 (solid frying pan handle). While most of the fragments have no decoration and were probably purely functional, the attentive observer will note a smiling face on the underside of PAG-17-32 (see Figure 96a). Considering the stratigraphy, limited data, and dissimilarity between pieces, no meaningful conclusion can currently be made.

Motif 4 – Conical Plain Support (Figure 136)
The conical plain support motif occurs relatively often. In our sample, there are 15 examples (3%). These appliqués represent supports. They are conically shaped and hollow. At the bottom, they are pressed together, where fingerprints can sometimes be seen on the sides. The distal end forms a small "nose" that would not be func-

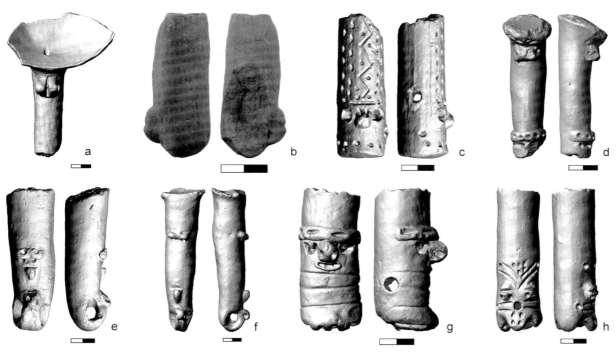

134   Appliqué Motifs 2. a PAG-53-37; b PAG-8-404; c PAG-10-316; d PAG-10-325; e PAG-44-42; f PAG-53-39; g PAG-53-57; h PAG-149-1.

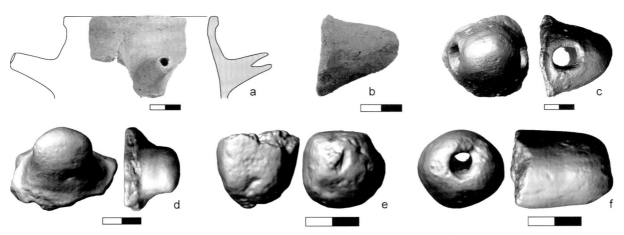

135   Appliqué Motifs 3. a PAG-44-33; b PAG-12-82; c PAG-13-112; d PAG-114-23; e PAG-114-33; f PAG-139-39.

tionally necessary. This feature may represent a strong abstraction of another motif. In addition, perforations are made at the sides for ventilation. Most of these appliqués are undecorated. Only one specimen (Figure 136e) has additional appliqués and incisions. The motif appears throughout the entire ceramic layer but is concentrated in the upper portion. In the occupation layer, fragments that may correspond to this motif were also identified.

Motif 5 – Conical Support with Lateral Slots (Figure 137)
There are seven examples of the conical support with lateral slots motif. They are similar to Appliqué Motif 4

in that they are located at the vessel base and have a conical and hollow form, although they are slightly smaller and shorter. They have elongated slits at the sides. Two examples are also decorated with horizontal lines. So far, they have only been found in the ceramic layer (Inv. 8–46), with no discernible concentration.

Motif 6 – Conical Foot Support (Figure 138)
The conical foot support motif occurs seven times. It is a conical, hollow support. The lower end of the appliqué is shaped like a human foot with small balls representing toes. The motif indicates the function of the appliqué, representing a "vessel foot." Only one specimen (Fig-

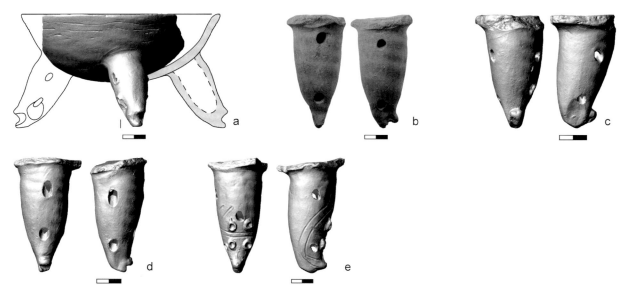

136   Appliqué Motifs 4. a PAG-6-98; b PAG-8-307; c PAG-10-33; d PAG-15-299; e PAG-44-48.

137   Appliqué Motifs 5. a PAG-44-1; b PAG-8-393; c PAG-12-77; d PAG-46-48.

ure 138e) is undecorated. The remaining fragments have incisions. Some of them are decorated with horizontal lines, as in Incision Motif 5. Three other specimens have more elaborate decoration. Regarding the stratigraphy, it should be noted that the motif is only found in the ceramic layer (Inv. 6–44).

Motif 7 – Conical Splayed Foot (Figure 139)
The conical splayed foot motif occurs ten times. The appliqué is similar to Appliqué Motifs 4 and 5. The form is conical and compact. In contrast to the previous conical supports, this appliqué is not hollow but still has several punctures or slits. The distal ends are splayed and resemble a fin. Although it is not clear in all cases, it is assumed that these are supports. Two specimens (Figure 139b, c) have an incised horizontal line; the others are undecorated. The motif is concentrated in the lower layers of the ceramic layer. A single specimen comes from the settlement layer (Figure 139d).

Motif 8 – Vertical Groove Support (Figure 140)
The vertical groove support motif occurs 11 times in the sample. It represents a conical appliqué that serves as a

support in all cases, indicated by the sometimes very worn basal surfaces. This appliqué is also solid. A vertical groove runs through the front side and widens towards the distal end. Above the groove, there is an appliqué with two depressions that Dennett calls the "flaring nostril." We will encounter this appliqué more in the following. There are perforations on the sides. One variety shows additional notches at the distal end (see Figure 140b). Dennett (2007: 69) interprets this appliqué as a highly stylized face, in which the lateral perforations form the eyes and the appliqué the nose. This seems plausible considering the design of the nose in other appliqués (see Appliqué Motifs 10–13) and the similarity to Appliqué Motif 9. Cuddy (2007: 85) interprets these appliqués as manatees.

The motif is concentrated in the upper part of the ceramic layer (Inv. 6–17). However, there are also two fragments from the settlement layer (Inv. 90 and Inv. 105). Dennett notes that "it is perhaps the most common form of support from the site of Río Claro" (Dennett 2007: 69).

Motif 9 – Stylized Face (Conical) (Figure 141)
The stylized face (conical) motif occurs eight times. The appliqué is conical and solid and serves as a sup-

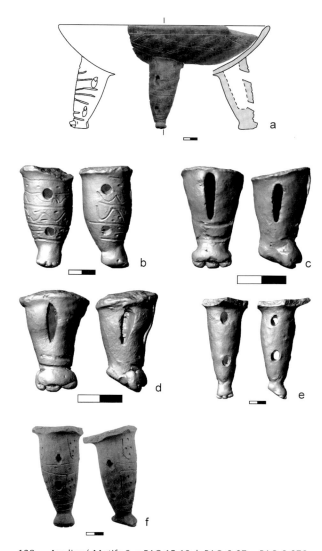

138 Appliqué Motifs 6. a PAG-15-10; b PAG-6-97; c PAG-8-376; d PAG-15-351; e PAG-17-34; f PAG-44-164.

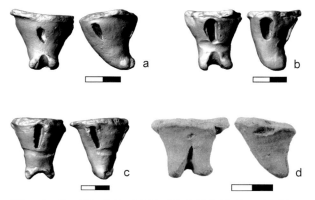

139 Appliqué Motifs 7. a PAG-8-369; b PAG-46-42; c PAG-71-25; d PAG-90-91.

port. It has certain parallels to Appliqué Motif 8. Towards the top, we again find the "flaring nostril" appliqué, and this time, its interpretation as a nose seems more obvious. Underneath, there is a single puncture (mouth) and, at the sides, two punctures (ears). The lower part is only preserved in four cases in which each exhibit two notches. This motif is also concentrated in the upper parts of the ceramic layer (Inv. 8–17). Two specimens come from the settlement layers (Figure 141c, d).

Motif 10 – Detailed Face (Conical) (Figure 142)
The detailed face (conical) motif occurs seven times. The appliqué is conical, solid, and serves as a support. Here, the interpretation as a head is now apparent. The nose is formed by a ball with two cavities. A horizontal slit forms the mouth, and the ears are formed with appliqués. This motif was only found in the ceramic layer, where it is concentrated in the lower portion (Inv. 17–71).

Motif 11 – Stylized Face (Round) (Figure 143)
The stylized face (round) motif is represented eight times in the sample. The appliqué consists of a hollow hemisphere that functioned as a support. It is very similar to Appliqué Motif 9 but differs in the hemispherical shape. As the name suggests, this may also be a stylized face. Like Appliqué Motifs 8 and 9, the appliqué has two depressions, lateral perforations that may symbolize eyes, and a perforation in the middle of the front that may represent a mouth. The appliqués can be found in different shapes and sizes. PAG-6-506 (Figure 143a), for example, is 7 cm high and was undoubtedly part of a large vessel. Inside, there is a ceramic ball that produces sound when the appliqué is moved. Three specimens deviate from the hemispherical shape and are instead slightly oval. Two specimens show additional incisions, which Dennett (2007: 70) describes as a "whiskered man." She believes that the lines suggest a beard or a kind of face painting technique. Appliqué Motif 11 is only present in the ceramic layer (Inv. 6, 8, 10, 53, and 71). All oval varieties were found in the lower portion.

Motif 12 – Stylized Face (Round, Inverted) (Figure 144)
There are nine examples of the stylized face (round, inverted) motif. It is very similar to Appliqué Motif 11; it is essentially an inverted version of it. In addition, the punctures and appliqués are arranged in a slightly different manner. They are also hemispherical, hollow, and serve as supports. The flaring nostril appliqué is found

at the distal end, and above it, there is a puncture that may symbolize a mouth. This motif is also only found in the ceramic layer (Inv. 8–71) but is concentrated in the upper portion.

Motif 13 – Detailed Face (Round) (Figure 145)

The detailed face (round) motif is relatively common (19 pieces; 4%). It shows some similarities to the appliqués described above, especially because it also depicts a human head. However, in this case, the head is far less stylized. In all cases, the appliqué is a hollow hemisphere that serves as a support. The head points either upwards or downwards. Some versions have additional incisions, which Dennett (2007: 70) describes as the "whiskered man" (see Appliqué Motif 11). The motif occurs throughout the entire ceramic layer (Inv. 6–71).

Motif 14 – Old Face (Figure 146)

Four specimens of the old face motif are present in the sample. The appliqué is solid, most likely functions as a support, and represents a head. Compared to the previous motifs, it differs in appearance and production technique. The eyes are not formed by simple punctures but by small bulbs, which are subsequently punctured. The mouth is formed by a line as opposed to a perforation. The motif appears to represent an elderly person with a wrinkled, sunken face, and toothless mouth. It only occurs in the ceramic layer, in Inv. 8, 17, 44, and 53.

Motif 15 – Rounded Tip (Figure 147)

The rounded tip motif occurs only three times, which is a somewhat limited number of examples. Nevertheless, these appliqués stand out due to their unique shape, which is elongated, hollow, and rounded at the bottom. Two of the appliqués, which were probably used as supports, have an appliqué toward the top. All three specimens have additional incisions. In terms of stratigraphy, the specimens are located in the lower parts of the ceramic layer (Inv. 46, 53, and 71).

Motif 16 – Hemispherical Plain (Figure 148)

There are 12 examples of the hemispherical plain motif in the sample. It is very common in Unit 2's assemblage and is represented in each inventory number with several specimens. They are hemispherical, hollow appliqués that function as supports. To allow air to escape during firing, small perforations were made on the sides. A broken specimen (see Figure 131) shows that the appliqué was not formed by hollowing out a solid ball of clay, as one might imagine, but that slabs were

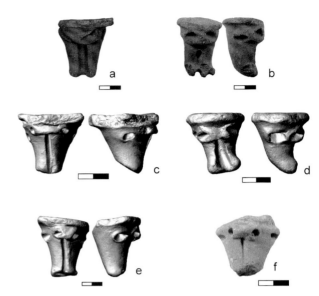

140   Appliqué Motifs 8. a PAG-6-491; b PAG-8-336; c PAG-10-55; d PAG-10-63; e PAG-15-293; f PAG-105-19.

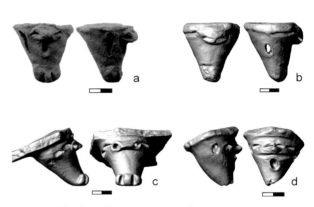

141   Appliqué Motifs 9. a PAG-10-30; b PAG-10-343; c PAG-114-34; d PAG-139-46.

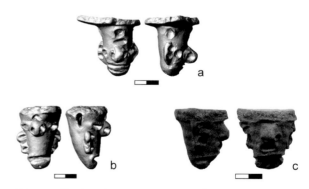

142   Appliqué Motifs 10. a PAG-44-500; b PAG-46-52; c PAG-71-1022.

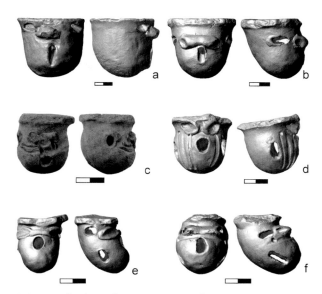

143 Appliqué Motifs 11. a PAG-6-506; b PAG-6-527; c PAG-8-306; d PAG-10-329; e PAG-53-60; f PAG-71-23.

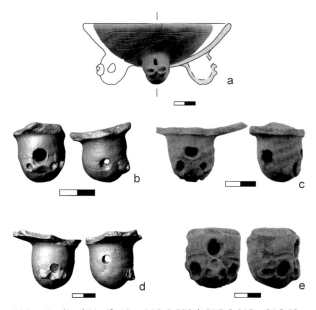

144 Appliqué Motifs 12. a PAG-8-526; b PAG-8-316; c PAG-10-34; d PAG-10-64; e PAG-15-295.

formed and pressed together at the bottom. None of the specimens have additional incisions or appliqués. Only one object (PAG-46-6, see Figure 169f) has polychrome paint and can be assigned to the Bay Island Polychrome style. Regarding the stratigraphy, the motif appears throughout the ceramic layer. Only a single fragmented specimen comes from a settlement layer. It also appears that the specimens of the lower layers are rather egg-shaped.

Motif 17 – Paw/Fin (Figure 149)

The paw/fin motif occurs 13 times in the sample. It is a solid appliqué with several cavities at its distal end, creating the impression of fingers. It is possibly a stylized representation of a hand or paw. Cuddy (2007: 85) interprets this motif as a manatee fin. One variant, which is always associated with Appliqué Motif 31, has an additional cavity on its underside and is attached to the upper part of the vessel body (Figure 149a). There are no clues as to the position of the other variants. Stratigraphically, the motif only occurs in the ceramic layer, where it is concentrated in the lower inventory numbers (Inv. 17–71).

Motif 18 – Serpent Head (Figure 150)

The serpent head motif is represented 81 times in the sample and thus corresponds to 17% of the total appliqués. This high percentage is due to the fact that many motifs that, at first glance, do not appear to be very similar are combined here within a single motif. However, on closer inspection, it becomes clear that there are different variations of the same motif—some detailed and naturalistic, some highly abstracted. The motif represents a reptile head, likely that of a serpent. The head has eyes and an open mouth, from which a curved tongue winds upwards and forms a rounded end. The tongue is accompanied by four teeth protruding from the mouth. PAG-90-90 (Figure 150o) is a clear example that highlights the open mouth and tongue. PAG-15-294 (Figure 150f) and PAG-46-975 (Figure 150l) are two additional examples of such naturalistic representation,

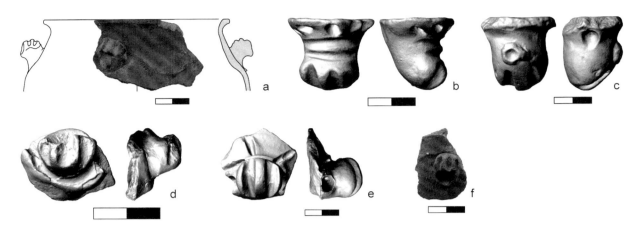

149   Appliqué Motifs 17. a PAG-17-27; b PAG-6-45; c PAG-53-63; d PAG-53-431; e PAG-71-33; f PAG-159-44.

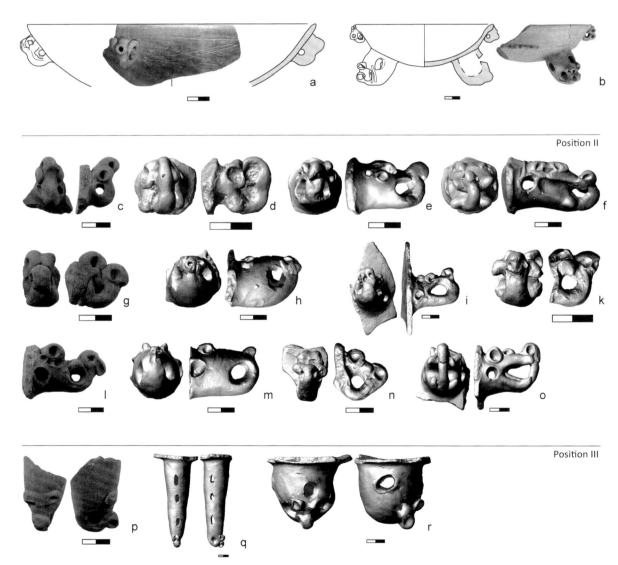

Position II

Position III

150   Appliqué Motifs 18. a PAG-10-151; b PAG-44-15; c PAG-8-349; d PAG-12-418; e PAG-13-124; f PAG-15-294; g PAG-15-323; h PAG-15-347; i PAG-44-47; k PAG-44-162; l PAG-46-975; m PAG-53-35; n PAG-53-995; o PAG-90-90; p PAG-15-476; q PAG-17-35; r PAG-44-45.

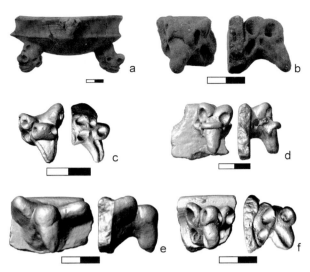

151   Appliqué Motifs 19. a PAG-53-29; b PAG-8-314; c PAG-8-394; d PAG-10-43; e PAG-15-308; f PAG-44-552.

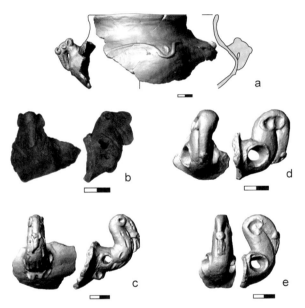

152   Appliqué Motifs 20. a PAG-17-4; b PAG-8-309; c PAG-53-40; d PAG-53-52; e PAG-71-26.

Motif 19, we can observe a small appliqué on the beak, which probably represents nostrils or a biological feature. PAG-53-40 (Figure 152c) is decorated with small lines, perhaps representing plumage. All specimens have a perforation close to the wall, which probably served to hang the vessel. The motif only occurs in the ceramic layer (Inv. 8, 13, 53, and 71).

Motif 21 – Mammal Head (Figure 153)

The mammal head motif occurs 14 times. This also serves as a handle, as it is attached to the body of the vessel. The motif represents an animal head with an elongated snout, and eyes and ears indicated by small clay balls. A line below the snout indicates the mouth. It almost appears as if the animals were grinning. In three fragments, a portion of the vessel wall is preserved, which clearly indicates that the head is attached to the vessel with the snout pointing upwards.

The motif certainly represents the head of a mammal. The snout varies in design, with some specimens showing a long, pointed snout, slightly curved upwards at the end. Because of these characteristics, it appears that they are coatis (*Nasua*). Other possibilities—when comparing them with the species native to Honduras—are the armadillo (*Dasypodidae*), the anteater (*Myrmecophagidae*), or the tapir (*Tapirus*) with a snout that is characteristically curved downwards. Other specimens have a shorter, more rounded snout and may represent the peccary (*Tayassuidae*), opossum (*Marsupialia*), agouti (*Dasyproctidae punctata*), or paca (*Agouti paca*). If it is confirmed that different animals are represented here, the motif may be further subdivided in the future.

The motif only occurs in the ceramic layer, where it is concentrated in the upper portions. Eleven of 14 specimens were found in Inv. 6–15; a single example comes from Inv. 53. Examination of the entire collection of sherds from Unit 2 confirmed this observation. In Inv. 6–15, 11 more specimens were found, while none were found in Inv. 17–71.

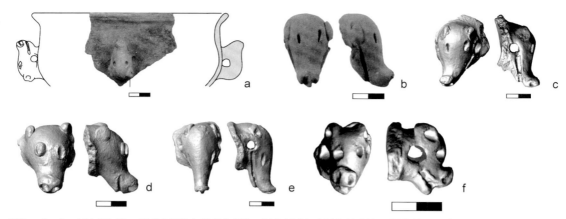

153   Appliqué Motifs 21. a PAG-8-210; b PAG-8-398; c PAG-10-31; d PAG-10-342; e PAG-12-410; f PAG-15-355.

Motif 22 – C-Shaped Lug (Figure 154)

The C-shaped lug motif occurs three times. It is formed by two protrusions, the upper being shorter than the lower. The lower protrusion also has a groove. It is a solid appliqué located on the upper portion of the vessel wall. It was found in Inv. 8–13. It appears to be the abstraction of another motif, possibly a person. Dennett (2007: 127) relates this form to the El Rey Adorno.

Motif 23 – Tubular Lug (Figure 155)

Of the tubular lug motif, only two objects were found. Nevertheless, the motif is briefly mentioned here, as it seems to be common at other settlements in the region and thus is important to reconstruct connections between sites. It is a hollow cylindrical handle with an open distal end and is decorated by several appliqués. This motif bears a certain resemblance to the so-called "rider lug," as noted by Dennett (2007: Fig. 4.29). The two specimens are from Inv. 17 and 44.

Motif 24 – Rim Attachment (Figure 156)

The rim attachment motif appears nine times. This appliqué is located on the vessel lip and consists of one or two small knobs. In one case (PAG-10-24, Figure 156b), the appliqué is relatively large and forms two extended knobs. It is not clear whether this appliqué has a purely decorative purpose or if it is also functional. This motif occurs in the ceramic layer, although it is only observed in Inv. 46 and the layers below it. A single example (PAG-91-143, Figure 156e) comes from the settlement layer.

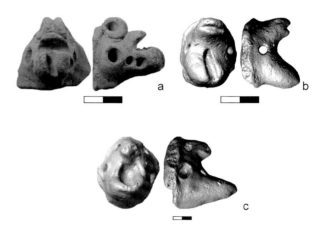

154   Appliqué Motifs 22. a PAG-8-117; b PAG-10-58; c PAG-13-120.

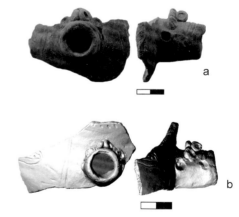

155   Appliqué Motifs 23. a PAG-17-118; b PAG-44-800.

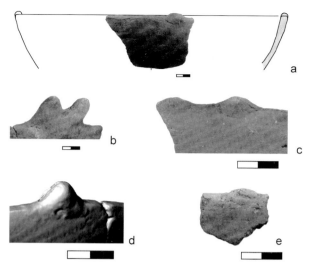

156   Appliqué Motifs 24. a PAG-8-177; b PAG-10-24; c PAG-15-599; d PAG-46-16; e PAG-91-143.

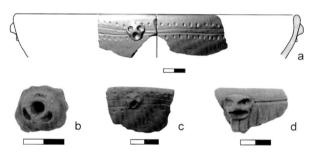

157   Appliqué Motifs 25. a PAG-53-23; b PAG-6-558; c PAG-53-160; d PAG-91-161.

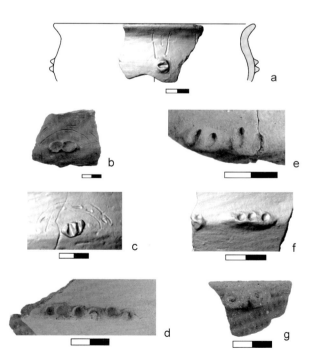

158   Appliqué Motifs 26. a PAG-6-94; b PAG-10-158; c PAG-12-49; d PAG-44-15; e PAG-44-40; f PAG-53-17; g PAG-90-85.

Motif 25 – Plain Nub with Impressions (Figure 157)

The plain nub with impressions motif occurs ten times. It is a small, flat appliqué that forms a hemisphere and has several cavities. Seven examples have three cavities, while the others have four to five. This appliqué is located in the upper portion of the vessel wall, below the rim. In three cases, it is associated with Incision Motifs 5 and 8, and in three other cases with Incision Motif 15. The motifs are concentrated in the lower part of the ceramic layer (Inv. 44–53) and in the settlement layer (Inv. 91 and 105). A unique example with four impressions was found in Inv. 6.

Motif 26 – Nub (Figure 158)

The nub motif summarizes a variety of appliqués that exhibit some differences but are not easily separated. This likely explains their relatively frequent occurrence of 25 examples. The appliqués are small and applied to the vessel's upper portion, often directly below the rim or, in some cases, at the widest part. The unifying principle here is that they are flat forms with small cavities. The number of depressions can vary, and the shape of the object ranges from hemispherical to oblong. Usually, these appliqués are associated with other incisions and appliqués. They mainly occur in the ceramic layer, but five specimens also originate from the settlement layers.

Motif 27 – Band with Impressions (Figure 159)

The band with impressions motif occurs five times. The motif consists of a clay coil that winds around the body of the vessel at its widest point. The coil is a narrow appliquéd band that has been flattened at regular intervals. Two examples are associated with Incision Motif 9. Similar to Incision Motif 9, this motif is concentrated in the upper portion of the ceramic layer (Inv. 10–46).

Motif 28 – Band with Incisions (Figure 160)

The band with incisions motif only occurs twice. Both examples are from the lower portion of the ceramic layer (Inv. 53). Similar to Appliqué Motif 27, the motif is formed by a clay coil that winds around the vessel body. As opposed to impressions, this band has closely-spaced small diagonal incisions.

Motif 29 – Raised Straight Band (Figure 161)

Twenty-three fragments with the raised straight band motif were identified (5%). It consists of a raised band created by applying a thin clay coil. One version of this motif has small nodules at specific intervals. The band can run horizontally or vertically. Based on well-preserved pieces from the ceramic layer, it is clear that the bands are used to separate different motifs from one another. They occur in association with the cross motif

(Incision Motif 1), the wave pattern (Incision Motif 3), and the face (Appliqué Motif 31). In the ceramic layer, this motif is only found in the lower portion (17–71). The fragments from the settlement layers, on the other hand, are very small and do not allow for many associations to be made with other motifs at the moment. Because of this, a more precise statement about the position or association with other patterns is not possible at the moment. The only motif that can be associated is the cross motif, evident in a single case (Figure 161e).

Motif 30 – Curved Line (Figure 162)
The curved line motif has already been encountered in the incision motifs. This is because the motif combines both application and incisions. It consists of a thin appliquéd coil of clay that winds around the vessel body at its widest point. It is occasionally accentuated by incisions. If both techniques are considered to be a single motif, then it appears eight times. The motif is associated with a specific vessel shape, the B-vessel with convexities. Appliqué Motif 17 is often associated with this motif, where it is attached within the loop formed by the coil. The motif appears in the lower portion of the ceramic layer (Inv. 17, 44, and 53).

Motif 31 – Face (Figure 163)
The face motif appears nine times. Like Appliqué Motif 30, it is also a combination of application and incision. The motif represents a face. The nose and mouth are applied, while the eyes and eyebrows are incised on the vessel wall. It is the only motif other than the wings motif (Incision Motif 19) that adds to the appliqué through incisions on the vessel wall. The motif is found on the same vessels as the raised bands (Appliqué Motifs 29 and 30) and is concentrated in the lower layers of the ceramic layer (Inv. 17–71). Two fragments come from the settlement layer (Inv. 91).

Motif 32 – Lattice (Figure 164)
This lattice motif is an appliquéd version of the cross motif and occurs twice. Several coils are placed on top of one

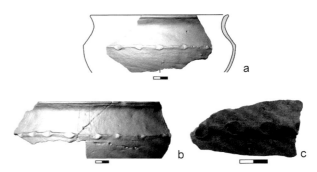

159   Appliqué Motifs 27. a PAG-15-87; b PAG-12-3; c PAG-17-526.

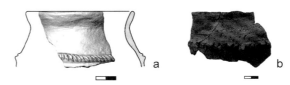

160   Appliqué Motifs 28. a PAG-53-15; b PAG-53-27.

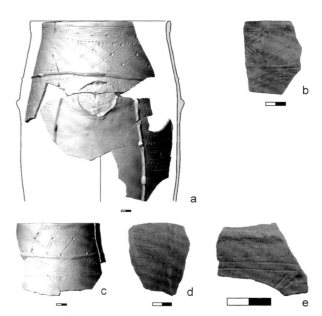

161   Appliqué Motifs 29. a PAG-46-308; b PAG-44-30; c PAG-53-24; d PAG-71-1025; e PAG-90-57.

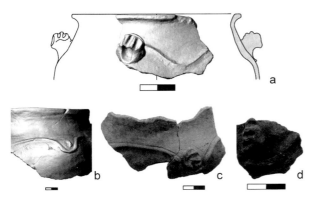

162   Appliqué Motifs 30. a PAG-17-27; b PAG-17-4; c PAG-53-1015; d PAG-71-1013.

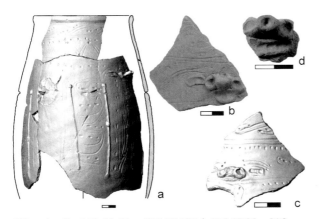

163   Appliqué Motifs 31. a PAG-53-110; b PAG-17-26; c PAG-44-49; d PAG-91-115.

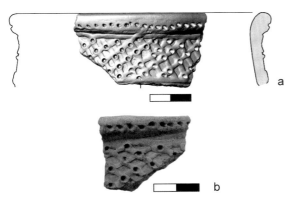

164   Appliqué Motifs 32. a PAG-44-43; b PAG-17-28.

165   Appliqué Motif 33. PAG-17-31.

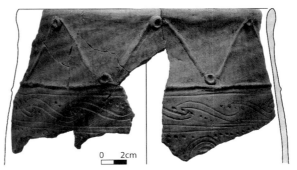

166   Appliqué Motif 34. PAG-46-309.

another so that they cross multiple times. The crossing points are marked by punctures. The pattern is located directly below the rim. Since only small fragments are preserved, little can be said about the vessel shape or associations with other motifs. Dennett (2007: Fig. 4.11) and Strong (1935: Plate 5e), however, each mention a fragment

with this decoration, each of which bears incised wave patterns below the lattice motif. Based on both the sherds from Guadalupe and those in the mentioned publications, I assume this motif exists on either B or C vessels.

Motif 33 – Cross (Figure 165)
The cross motif occurs only once. It is considered here because it is a variety of the already-discussed cross motif (Incision Motif 1). On this vessel, however, the motif is not incised but applied. It runs horizontally below the rim and exhibits small cavities where the crosses overlap.

Motif 34 – Zigzag (Figure 166)
This zigzag motif is similar to Appliqué Motif 33 in that it only occurs once. It is listed here because it is a variety of Incision Motif 2.

Motif S – Single Motifs (Figure 167, 168)
The single motifs category includes appliqués that could not be assigned to any other appliqué motifs and only occur sporadically. There are 49 motifs listed under this category. Twelve additional appliqués could not be assigned to any motif either, as they are too fragmented to identify an actual motif.

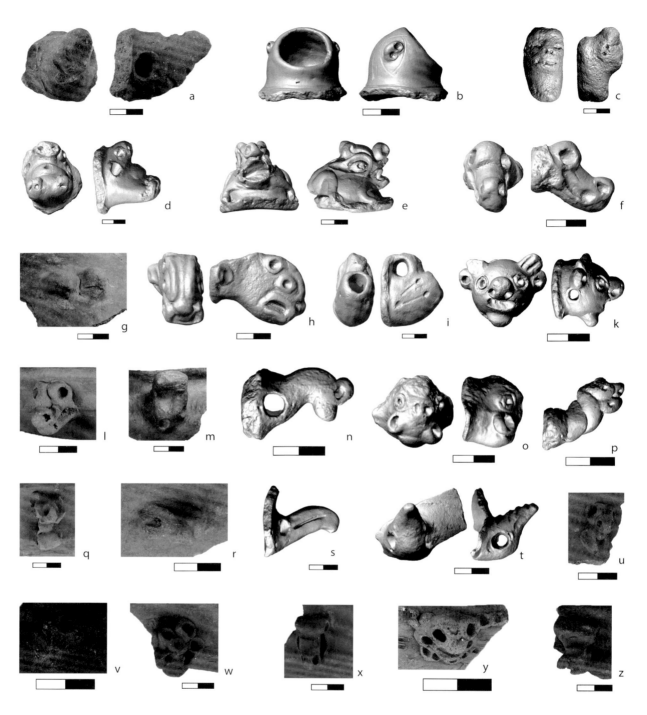

167   Appliqué Single Motifs (S), Position II (Body). a PAG-8-323; b PAG-8-366; c PAG-8-375; d PAG-10-51; e PAG-12-384; f PAG-12-
417; g PAG-13-8; h PAG-13-402; i PAG-15-317; k PAG-17-39; l PAG-44-26; m PAG-44-35; n PAG-44-46; o PAG-46-51; p PAG-46-56; q
PAG-46-59; r PAG-46-66; s PAG-53-58; t PAG-53-62; u PAG-53-78; v PAG-53-79; w PAG-71-6; x PAG-71-7; y PAG-71-10; z PAG-71-12.

Position II (Body)

Position III (Base)

Position 0 (Unknown)

168   Appliqué Single Motifs (S). a PAG-90-23; b PAG-91-106; c PAG-99-53; d PAG-99-56; e PAG-109-21; f PAG-114-29; g PAG-139-49; h PAG-139-50; i PAG-6-513; k PAG-6-550; l PAG-8-401; m PAG-10-35; n PAG-12-308; o PAG-46-45; p PAG-46-47; q PAG-53-49; r PAG-53-1000; s PAG-53-1002; t PAG-71-21; u PAG-71-1026; v PAG-89-40; w PAG-90-84; x PAG-99-15; y PAG-175-1.

4.4.1.3.4 Paint

Compared to fragments with incisions and/or appliqués, painted sherds make up a small percentage of the sample (42 pieces, 5%). Due to their rarity, all fragments with paint from Unit 2 were included in the sample. If a random selection had been made, their percentage would have been much lower. Due to the small number of examples, a detailed classificatory scheme was not developed. Instead, the fragments were divided into just three categories: polychrome paint, monochrome paint, and slip. These are discussed in detail below.

Group I – Polychrome (Figure 169)

Fourteen fragments have polychrome paint or belong to a polychrome painted vessel. In all cases, the paint is black and red on an orange background. The fragments show lines and figurative representations. They also have a very fine temper and are thin; Strong (1935) originally described them as "thin polychrome." This style is now known as Bay Island Polychrome after it was first discovered on the Bay Islands. Strong (1935) assumes that this pottery was associated with ritual activities, as the discovery of a whole vessel at Dixon Site, Roatán, suggests. The vessel was filled with numerous objects such as metal bells, shells, and stone artifacts and is interpreted by Strong as a votive cache. In Guadalupe, this style appears throughout the ceramic layer (Inv. 15–71). Four sherds also come from the settlement layer (Inv. 94). However, in these four examples, the paint is not well-preserved, and thus their assignment to this category is uncertain.

Group II – Monochrome (Figure 170)

Eighteen objects exhibit monochrome paint. Because these fragments are mostly very small, few solid conclusions can be reached regarding this category. As of yet, both black and red monochrome paint have been identified. They include simple lines and abstract representations. Four fragments have red paint at the rim (Inv. 46 and 53). The other fragments cannot yet be meaningfully sorted into subgroups. Most of the objects are located in the lower half of the ceramic layer, while six were found in the settlement layers (Inv. 90, 91, and 94). This is interesting because it agrees with observations that the lower layers are closer to the Selin phase, which is characterized by a larger proportion of painted pottery.

Group III – Slip (Figure 171)

Nine objects have a single-color slip on their exterior. The fragments vary greatly in style. Four of them have the remains of an orange coating. Three of them resemble Bay Island Polychrome and may belong to this style. The fourth fragment (Figure 171a) has a shiny orange coating, which is not typical of Guadalupe's material and which might be an import. The other fragments are also individual examples and do not fit well into the typical local styles. Their slips include shiny metallic (Figure 171d), smooth eggshell-colored (Figure 171c), white (Figure 171g, h), and dark (Figure 171b). Eight of the nine objects come from the settlement layers.

4.4.1.3.5 Combination Analysis

After describing the individual attributes and looking at their stratigraphic distribution, attributes found in combination with one another are considered in this chapter. This study aims to examine patterns in how attributes are combined and, based on this examination, to define groups of attributes that can serve as a basis for the future definition of types (also in combination with the observations of ceramic fabrics). In the next step, attention is given to how the defined groups distribute stratigraphically and if their occurrence can be chronologically defined. The following analysis is guided by form. For each distinct group, one object is selected as a representative example.

Form A

Form A is found in combination with:
– Incisions: 1, 3, 4, 5, 6, 7, 8, 12, 13, 14, 15, 19, and 20
– Appliqués: 2, 4, 5, 6, 10, 12, 13, 15, 18, 19, 24, 25, and 26
– Paint: II (red rim)

In the following, several aspects of these attribute groups will be considered. A particularly diagnostic combination is Form A-I with Appliqué Motif 2: a shallow vessel with no breaks with a solid handle in various designs (Type 1). This type can also have a lip application (Appliqué Motif 24). This type is usually called a "ladle censer" or "frying pan censer" in the literature, although the residue analysis revealed that these vessels were most likely not used to burn incense. In the selected sample, it is only represented twice (see Figure 72g, i) but was observed several times in the remaining diagnostic sherds of the excavation. Since Appliqué Motif 2 stands out from the other appliqués due to its shape and solid body, I assume that each of these appliqués is part of a Type 1 vessel. The oldest example of such a handle was found deep in the settlement layer (Inv. 149). In the ceramic layer, this type of vessel appears throughout (Inv. 8–53). It, therefore, appears to be a persistent form.

As for decoration, Incision Motifs 1 and 3, in particular, often appear with the Form A, namely A-I-4 and A-II-3 (Type 2) (see e.g. Figure 74). These motifs do not appear in association with additional incisions. Both motifs do, however, appear in combination with the reduced version of Appliqué Motif 18 (serpent head) as a handle. Associated supports are Appliqué Motifs 4, 6, 12, and 18 (spherical version). In a single case from the

169   Fragments with polychrome paint. a PAG-15-66; b PAG-17-2; c PAG-17-3; d PAG-44-4; e PAG-44-5; f PAG-46-6; g PAG-53-7; h PAG-53-13; i PAG-71-2; k PAG-71-3; l PAG-94-1b; m PAG-94-4b; n PAG-94-6c; o PAG-94-8b.

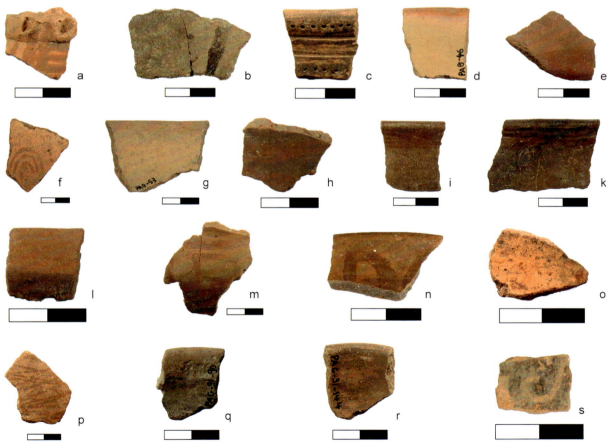

170   Fragments with monochrome paint. a PAG-10-480; b PAG-10-481; c PAG-15-59; d PAG-46-4;e PAG-46-5; f PAG-53-3; g PAG-53-4; h PAG-53-5; i PAG-53-6; k PAG-53-8; l PAG-53-9; m PAG-53-10; n PAG-90-2b; o PAG-91-1b; p PAG-91-2b; q PAG-91-90; r PAG-91-144; s PAG-94-7b.

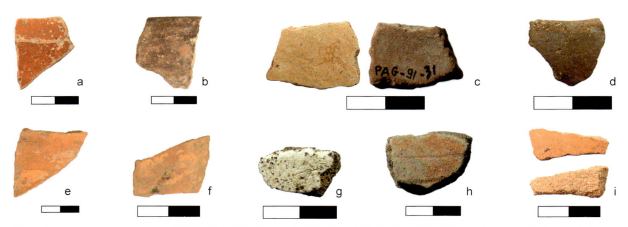

171　Fragments with slip paint. a PAG-53-14; b PAG-90-3b; c PAG-91-31; d PAG-91-56; e PAG-94-5; f PAG-94-9b; g PAG-114-31; h PAG-139-6; i PAG-156-1.

settlement layer (Inv. 114), Incision Motif 3 also appears with the A-I-2 form. These dishes, most of which were likely tripod-dishes, are very typical and diagnostic of the material in Guadalupe. They are found with or without incisions and with zoomorph handles occurring in different combinations. Judging from the size of the appliqués present in our sample, they make up a large part of the ceramic material.

A particularly common combination is a bird's head (Appliqué Motif 19) with Form A-I-2, i.e., dishes with straight flaring walls (Type 3) (see Figure 70d, e, f and Figure 71c, h). This type has no additional incisions. Appliqué Motif 18 (conical version) is a possible support. In two cases, the bird's head is also present on Form A-II-3 and is associated with Incision Motif 19. Appliqué Motif 10 is a possible support for this type.

Another frequent occurrence is Incision Motif 4, which is often associated with Forms A-I-2 and A-II-3 and is always found on the vessel interior (Type 4) (see Figure 71i, k). Because the fragments are relatively small, the exact vessel shape cannot be determined. This type occurs throughout the entire ceramic layer (Inv. 8–53).

Incision Motif 6 also occurs in combination with Form A. In most cases, the decoration is located on the interior below the rim (Type 5) (see Figure 71e). Due to the small size of the fragments, the exact shape cannot be determined for all fragments. However, four fragments are certainly Form A-II-3. Five fragments of this type originate from the settlement layers, and in the pottery layer, they are mainly represented in the lower portions. However, two fragments were also found close to the surface (Inv. 6 and 8).

Another possible combination already mentioned in the analysis of modifications is Form A-I-2 with Incision Motifs 5 and 8, which are often combined with Appliqué Motif 25 (Type 6) (see Figure 75). Appliqué Motif 15 is a possible support and is mainly found in the lower portion of the ceramic layer. One example was also found in

the settlement layer (Inv. 91), suggesting that this type is an early phenomenon.

Another interesting combination is Form A with Incision Motif 7 (Type 7). All of these fragments come from the settlement layers. Although not every example of Incision Motif 7 could be clearly assigned to this form due to the small size of the fragments, I assume that most of them are open vessels and most likely Form A. One relatively large fragment has Form A-II-3 (see Figure 79h), while two finds found during surveys of Guadalupe also show an association with Form A and further indicate that this type may be associated with Appliqué Motif 8. The survey finds include Form A-II-2 (Figure 172). As mentioned above, Form A-II with straight walls was found only in the settlement horizon associated with Incision Motif 13 (Type 8) (see Figure 76a, b). The combination of Incision Motif 7 and Form A is, therefore, certainly an early phenomenon.

Form B

Form B is found in combination with:

– Incisions: 3, 8, 9, 10, 15, 19, 20, and 21
– Appliqués: 1, 3, 17, 18, 19, 21, 24, 25, 26, 27, 28, 30, and 32
– Paint: II

A relatively common combination of attributes is Form B with Appliqué Motif 1 (D-shaped handle). This type of appliqué is particularly common with Form B-I. Vessels with D-shaped handles usually do not have any additional modifications and consist of rather coarse material. Therefore, I assume that these are cookware and storage vessels that did not have a purpose beyond the practical.

Concerning the combination of Form B with incisions, it is noteworthy that, in contrast to Form A, there is no combination with Incision Motif 1 (cross pattern). The most commonly associated motifs are Incision Mo-

172   Survey find with incision motif 7 (M. Reindel).

tifs 9 and 10. Both motifs are closely related and occur exclusively in combination with Form B-III-3. This type can also be associated with Appliqué Motif 21, which served as a handle. Different varieties of Appliqué Motif 26 also frequently occur with this set of attributes. In two cases, the motif is associated with Appliqué Motif 27. In addition, the clay of this type is often very dark, which indicates firing in a reduced atmosphere. Since both decorations, Incision Motifs 9 and 10, and Appliqué Motif 21 are more concentrated in the upper portion of the ceramic layer (except for a single example in Inv. 53), I assume that this type is a temporary and rather late phenomenon. Since the distribution of Incision Motifs 9 and 10 and Appliqué Motif 21 coincide stratigraphically, I further assume that they only occur in combination with each other. In combination with Form B-III-3, it appears they can also be defined as a type (Type 9) (see Figure 91).

The combination of B-III-3 with Appliqué Motif 30/ Incision Motif 21 is also common (see Figure 92f, g, k). In most cases, it is associated with Appliqué Motif 17 as a handle. One specimen (PAG-17-4, see Figure 92k) is associated with Appliqué Motif 20. A striking feature of this combination is the vessel shape, which has convexities. Since this is a specific combination, it can be defined as a type (Type 10). Stratigraphically, it seems to be concentrated in the lower portion of the ceramic layer.

Another diagnostic combination is Form B-II-6 with a wave pattern (Incision Motif 3) below the rim (Type 11) (see Figure 86d, e, f). It appears in the lower portion of the ceramic layer (Inv. 44, 46, and 53).

Another possible type is Form B-I with a red-painted rim (Type 12) (see Figure 83a, b, c). However, the sample of just three fragments is admittedly quite small.

Unfortunately, very few preserved base fragments could be assigned to Form B; thus, it is not clear if this form was associated with supports. The examples that do have preserved parts of the base do not show appliqué scars. Nevertheless, it is still possible that they were also

associated with supports. Both possibilities—with and without supports—have been described for these vessel forms in the Bay Islands (e.g., Strong 1935: Fig. 38).

Form C
Form C is found in combination with:
– Incisions: 1, 2, 3, 5, 8, 11, 14, and 17
– Appliqués: 1, 3, 13, 18, 22, 23, 26, 29, 31, 33, and 34
– Paint: I

Form C is the most challenging group to define. This is because only the upper portion of a vessel is generally preserved, and only a small part of the combined modifications are visible. This hinders a full understanding of the complete spectrum of forms. Concerning possible bases, we do have some with appliqués, which have sizes that suggest they were associated with Form C vessels.

The analysis of attribute combinations has shown that there are at least three typical combinations of shapes and modifications. One combination that occurs several times is Form C-III-3 with Incision Motif 14 winding around the neck. Since only the neck is present in each case, nothing is known about additional associated incisions or appliqués. However, it is possible that this variety is related to the second typical combination: Form C-III-3 with Incision Motif 11 winding around the narrow neck. Incision Motifs 1 and 3 are often found in combination with this second variety (Type 13) (see Figure 102). The order in which the motifs are incised can differ. Incision Motif 11 is sometimes used to delimit the incisions at the bottom of another motif. Vessels with this decoration usually have relatively thin walls. This combination of attributes is mainly found in the upper portions of the ceramic layer.

The second striking combination is Form C-III-1, which has an entire set of associated incisions and appliqués (Type 14) (see Figures 99, 100). Incision Motifs 1 and 3 are located below the rim, which again do not seem to follow any particular order in which they are positioned. Sometimes Incision Motif 1 is at the top, while in other cases, Incision Motif 3 is. These two motifs are usually separated at the bottom by Appliqué Motif 29. In the center of the vessel, Appliqué Motif 31 and Incision Motif 17 alternate and are occasionally separated by Appliqué Motif 29. Sometimes, Incision Motif 5 is also present. Known handle combinations are Appliqué Motifs 18 and 23. This type represents the most intensely decorated vessels. Due to their large size, I assume that they were storage vessels. Judging from their elaborate decoration, they also likely had a symbolic function and were used for special occasions. Ethnohistoric sources mention that the consumption of *chicha* (a fermented drink made from maize or manioc) was an integral part of feasts. These large, highly decorated storage vessels probably served this function. They occur mainly in the lower portion of the ceramic layer. Some decorative elements, such as Appliqué Motif 31, only occur in combination with this vessel form but are also found independently in the settlement horizon; thus, I assume that these vessels are an early phenomenon. It seems that this type was later replaced by thin-walled jars on which similar decorative motives can be found. PAG-10-169 (see Figure 149a) has Form C-III-3 and shows the diagnostic Incision Motive 17 of the supposed *chicha* vessels. While no bases are preserved in Guadalupe, Dennett (2007: 64) mentions that a similar object of this type with basal flange was found in Río Claro.

Most of the remaining vessels of Form C are undecorated and possibly served as storage vessels for domestic use. They are often associated with Appliqué Motif 1, which indicates a utilitarian purpose.

Some vessels of Form C, more precisely Form C-II-1, have polychrome paint and can be assigned to the Bay Island Polychrome style. Since the sample also contains polychrome painted hemispherical supports, it can be assumed that the basic form is associated with them. Several complete vessels of this type have previously been recovered, thus confirming the attribute combination of this type (e.g., Strong 1935: Frontispiece).

4.4.1.3.6 Residue Analysis

Residue analysis was carried out to evaluate if patterns of use could be attributed to the categories defined by the typochronological analysis. The analysis was aimed at checking whether different forms or types were used differently and whether the classification results could be supported by confirming the established categories. Possible confirmation of specific uses for some of the types defined above should also be examined. Working hypotheses were developed for Types 1 and 14 (see below). The analysis was conducted under the direction of Dr. Luis Barba Pingarrón (Laboratorio de Prospección Arqueológica, UNAM). A sample of 23 sherds was tested for chemical residues of phosphates, carbonates, proteins, carbohydrates, fatty acids, and pH, allowing for semi-quantitative observations of their concentration. The techniques applied to identify the respective substances are described in detail in Barba Pingarrón / Rodríguez Suárez / Córdova Frunz (1991).

In general, the analysis showed that all of the analyzed fragments had intensive contact with foodstuffs, which is particularly apparent due to the detection of high concentrations of proteins and carbohydrates. This may be because the vessels were used continuously to prepare or store food or because they were deposited together with food. The values of the detected chemical substances for the different form categories do not vary greatly. Additionally, the analysis does not allow for a more precise differentiation of substances, such as the

differentiation of animal and vegetable proteins. Thus, no specific uses can be proven for the different categories.

However, interesting observations concerning Types 1 and 14 could be made. Type 1 is described in the literature as a censer, and it is assumed that incense or resins were burned in it (Dennett 2007: 44f). A residual analysis should therefore detect fatty acids. Yet, the analyses have shown both carbohydrates and proteins in all three of the analyzed specimens. These observations suggest that resin was not burned in these specimens but that they were used to prepare food, probably as a kind of pan. In addition, the relatively high concentration of phosphates could indicate that they were used to prepare meat. For Type 14, we assumed that the large and richly decorated barrel-shaped vessels might have served as containers for *chicha*, a fermented drink made from maize or manioc. In all five of the tested specimens, carbohydrates could be detected that one would expect to find in such a case. They also have a high concentration of proteins that could be derived from the protein-containing crops. Although these results do not confirm their use as *chicha* containers with certainty, the observations do not contradict such an interpretation. The sample of just 23 sherds is very limited, and further analyses are necessary to make reliable statements.

4.4.1.3.7 Correspondence and Addition to the Existing Classification

Now that the ceramics have been described in detail, a brief comparison with the most recent existing ceramic typology (Dennett 2007) is presented here. This should help the reader to compare the existing classifications. The observations made in Guadalupe are intended to supplement information on the temporal distribution of the types and highlight similarities and differences between the defined ceramic types. Consideration of the regional and interregional distribution of pottery follows in the discussion section (see below).

Type 1 corresponds to Dennett's variety Capiro monochrome: Capiro incensario. Vessels with form B-I-4 und incision 14 or 15 correspond to Dennett's variety Concha Simple Incised punctate: Concha.

PAG-94-5b (see Figure 129f) corresponds to the variety that Dennett describes as Concha Simple Incised Punctate: Zamora. Her definition is based on four objects that date to the period before AD 1255. Concha Simple Incised Punctate: Limpia corresponds to Type 8. We can add to Dennett's definition by indicating that these objects are limited to the Early Cocal period.

Under the variety Dorina Abstract Incised Punctate: Dorina, Dennett combines several forms, decorations, and appliqués. Based on this classification, Types 5 and 11 and all pieces with a wave pattern (Incision Motif 3) would correspond to this variety, which is why I do not consider the classification by Dennett to be very useful at this point. This is especially true since the analysis has shown that these types have a different distribution pattern. Dorina Abstract Incised Punctate: Castilla corresponds to Type 7. Our observations correlate with Dennett's data in that this type can be assigned to the Transitional Selin/Early Cocal period. Dorina Abstract Incised Punctate: Tarros corresponds to vessels with appliqué 32.

Dennett defines any dishes and bowls with a cross pattern (Incision Motif 1) as belonging to Durango Cross-Hatch incised Punctate: Durango. In Guadalupe, they are also associated with the serpent motif and support 6. Judging from the contexts in Guadalupe, this type is not limited to the Late Cocal period, as Dennett suggests, but also occurs in the Early Cocal period.

The Type San Antonio Carved corresponds to Type 14, and Dennett, following Healy, places this type in the Transitional Selin phase. The findings in Guadalupe confirm this but show that these vessels also occur in the Early Cocal phase.

It is noticeable that some types and modes described by Dennett were not found in Guadalupe. These include the Types Capiro Monochrome Incensario and Carpá Combed, the so-called pump heel support, and the rider lug. The latter is described in many sites along the coast and is often found in private collections. On the other hand, there are types common to Guadalupe but absent in Río Claro (or are not mentioned in the publications). These include Types 4, 6, 9, and 10, Appliqué Motif 19 (bird head), and Appliqué Motif 21 (mammal head).

4.4.1.4 Summary

The above analysis shows that the new classification scheme has been successfully applied to the ceramics from Guadalupe. Thus, a new classification system for the systematic analysis of Cocal period pottery is now available for future research. The scheme can also be applied to earlier periods. Compared to the existing classification based on the type-variety approach, the new system has the advantage of being based on clearly and transparently presented definitions and is therefore easily reproducible. It considers form and modification attributes equally and meets the requirements of the material by paying specific attention to the appliqués. Furthermore, it can easily be extended if new attributes are discovered. The numerous illustrations will facilitate the systemic analysis and comparison of ceramics finds in northeast Honduras.

Concerning the interpretation of the context in Guadalupe, the classification analysis has fulfilled its requirements. As already mentioned above, the stratigraphic situation of the excavation in Guadalupe is not entirely clear. One task of the pottery analysis is to clarify the chronological distribution of the pottery and to contribute to the understanding of the stratigraphy. In this respect, the following observations can be made:

1. Within the ceramic layer, there is an observable stylistic development in the ceramics, which supports the assumption that the ceramic deposit accumulated over time.
2. A clear difference can be seen between the pottery accumulation and the pottery of the settlement layers. There are elements limited to the pottery horizon but also to the settlement layers.
3. Some elements can be identified in both contexts.
4. The above observation, combined with the fact that the pottery is generally similar in its execution (focus on appliqués and incisions), suggests that there was no "hard" break between the settlement phases, such as the immigration of a new population.

These points are examined in more detail below. The ceramic layer has no clear internal stratigraphy; no distinct layers could be identified during the excavation. The excavation strategy was also changed after the first year. While the first layers (Inv. 6–15) were excavated by following the inclination of the mound, the excavation of horizontal layers was pursued in the following years, with visible features being excavated separately. Furthermore, one must assume that the upper layers are partially disturbed. Each of these points makes it challenging to make reliable statements regarding the interpretation of the chronological development of the pottery. Nevertheless, I believe that relatively clear differences can be observed in the stratigraphic distribution of some elements. Type 9 is clearly concentrated in the upper layers, where it was very frequently observed during the secondary examination of Unit 2's remaining sherds. The thin-walled vessels of Type C-III-3 with incisions (Type 13) are also concentrated in the upper layers. Such forms are still found in the lower layers, but they do not have the characteristic incisions and thin walls. Type 10 is well represented in the lower layers, whose typical features, appliqué 30 and 17, only occur in this lower part. Type 14 also only occurs in the lower layers. Appliqué 31 is particularly characteristic of these vessels and has not been observed on any other vessel form. However, it is also found in the settlement horizon, so I assume that Type 14 is also represented in this horizon. This brings us to the next point. There is a clear difference between the settlement horizons and the ceramic layer. For the analysis of the occupation layers, we mainly have to rely on incisions and appliqués since reliable statements cannot generally be made about the form. There are elements limited to the ceramic accumulation (e.g., incisions 4, 5, and 9 and appliqués 6, 13, 19, and 21) and those that only occur in the occupation layers, such as form A-II-1, rim form 6, and incisions 7, 13, 16, and 18. At the same time, the number of painted sherds increases in the settlement horizon. However, like appliqué 31, some elements can be found in both areas. These include the serpent motif (appliqué 18), appliqués 8 and 9, and the wave motif (incision 3).

So, what does this mean for the chronological interpretation of the site? The observations confirm what the stratigraphy and ^{14}C dating had already clarified: we are dealing with different phases of occupation. A discernible change of preferred motifs is apparent when we compare the different occupation phases. However, the ceramic style does not suggest a hard break between these phases. This is indicated by the motifs that can be found in all levels and by the style as a whole, which maintains consistent decorative techniques and emphasizes incisions and appliqués throughout the entire context. It is essential to keep in mind that the change of attributes is a slow process that occurs over a long time and is not discernible as a clear break but as a tendency towards change. However, the oldest occupation layers contain a higher percentage of painted fragments, which indicates a transition to the Selin phase. There are distinctive similarities between the layers directly below the pottery concentration (Inv. 74, 89, and 90) and the pottery concentration itself, while the attributes in the layers further below have more apparent differences. This has implications for the interpretation of the stratigraphy. This observation supports the idea that the lower layers of the pottery accumulation are temporally close to the latest occupation layer and are thus also related to the concentrations of *bajareque* and the burials that were introduced from this level.

Considering the ^{14}C dates and the observations above, I conclude the following: In the ceramic layer, two periods can be distinguished that correspond to the Early and Late Cocal phases, respectively. The settlement layers date to the Early Cocal period, with the Transitional Selin period also being represented. The transitions between the respective periods are not marked by disruptions. Instead, they may be due to an orientation towards new exchange partners, etc., but not to the arrival of a new population group.

4.4.1.5 Unique Forms

After a detailed examination of the classification of ceramic vessels, clay objects with less common or unique forms are presented in the following.

4.4.1.5.1 Ocarinas

Seven objects from Guadalupe can be referred to as ocarinas (globular vessel flutes) (Figure 173). "An ocarina is a type of wind instrument, or aerophone, in which sound is produced by the vibration of air. Unlike flutes, ocarinas are not tubes but consist of one or more enclosed, rounded chambers" (Peabody Museum of Archaeology and Ethnology). Of the seven objects, three are complete, and four are fragments. Two of the complete ocarinas were able to be successfully played (see acoustic analysis in Appendix A). For each fragmented ocarina, the mouthpiece is always preserved. With one exception, the ocarinas are figurative, with the majority likely representing turtles.

The following structure is evident based on the complete pieces: The mouthpiece is attached to the hollow instrument body. The upper and lower sides of the body are produced separately and later attached to one other. The slit-shaped air duct leads from the end of the mouthpiece to the underside of the chamber enclosed by the body, where the aperture with the sound-producing edge is located. On the upper half, there are four round fingerholes perforated from the outside to regulate the sound. On both sides of the mouthpiece, there are holes with vertical perforations that probably served to attach the instrument to a cord. In some cases, they also represent the front legs of the turtle. In contrast to the majority of Guadalupe ceramics, the clay used for the ocarinas is very finely tempered. Aerophones are sensitive to irregularities, especially in the air duct and at the aperture. The objects are described individually below.

PAG-8-406 (Figure 173a):
Zoomorphic double ocarina, possibly in the shape of a turtle.
2.5 x 3.6 x 1.6 cm (L x W x H); weight: 8.3 g.
Surface: oxidized; core: reduced.
The head and the front part of the body's left side are preserved. The head contains two adjacent mouthpieces with air ducts leading into separate chambers. The head's left and right sides are made of two separate pieces, each having a mouthpiece. The two chambers of the body each consist of an upper and a lower part with an internal seam where they join. The two eyes each consist of a round puncture with a surrounding punctured circle. A round attachment on the neck probably depicts an additional eye. The edge of the attachment is overlapped by the left eye, indicating that it was applied first. On the left side, part of a vertically perforated suspension hole can be seen. The two separate mouthpieces and the two chambers confirm that it is a double ocarina. In order to make both sides of the instrument playable, there were probably four fingerholes on each side. All published ocarinas from northeast Honduras and, as far as can be

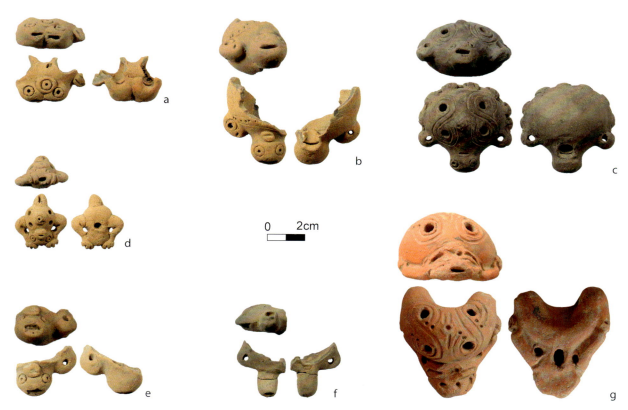

173   Ocarinas (Scale 1:2). a PAG-8-406; b PAG-18-1; c PAG-43-1; d PAG-57-1; e PAG-90-1; f PAG-152-1; g PAG-195-1.

determined, those from Guadalupe, have four finger-holes. The fragment was found in the upper part of the ceramic layer.

PAG-18-1 (Figure 173b):
Zoomorphic ocarina in the shape of a turtle.
4.9 x 3.4 x 3.2 cm (L x W x H); weight: 14.9 g.
Surface: oxidized; core: reduced.

The head and the front right side of the body are preserved. The ellipsoid body is made of two parts. The seam between the upper and lower halves is clearly visible on the inside, whereas it is smeared over on the outside, where it attaches to the head. The eyes each consist of a round punctate surrounded by a circular punctate. The head serves as a mouthpiece with an attached slot-shaped mouth and the air duct. There is an oval attachment with a horizontal slit on the neck. On the right side of the body, a leg serves as a suspension hole. The vertical perforation is pierced from top to bottom and framed by a punctured circle similar to the eyes. Two parallel grooves run from this leg toward the opposite, broken leg. Between the grooves, there is an irregular row of punctures. On the back, part of a perforated fingerhole is preserved; its position suggests a rectangular layout of the fingerholes. On the ventral side, the air duct opens into an aperture. The fragment was found

in the northern profile of Unit 1 in the upper part of the ceramic layer.

PAG-43-1 (Figure 173c):
Zoomorphic ocarina in the shape of a turtle.
4.8 x 4.9 x 3.1 cm (L x W x H); weight: 29.6 g.
Surface: reduced.

The ocarina is likely complete, although it is possible that a small piece detached from the neck. The body is ellipsoid and composed of two parts (top and bottom). The seam where the head is attached has been carefully smeared over. The laterally placed front legs serve as suspension holes. Behind them, the seam between the upper and lower parts of the body is visible and is partially covered by seven small oval attachments with two vertical notches each. The turtle's head serves as the ocarina's mouthpiece, through which air flows to the inside. The eyes consist of round punctates surrounded by a likewise punctured circle. There is a notch on the neck, which, when compared to the other objects, probably served as an attachment point for an appliqué. On the upper side of the carapace, there are four fingerholes in a rectangular arrangement. Opposite pairs of S-shaped incisions border the pairs of holes on the right and left. In the middle of the carapace, there is a small knob with several flat round cavities. The underside has no decoration.

It only has a circular aperture with an edge. The ocarina is easy to play after careful cleaning and produces a warm sound typical of this instrument group. It was found in the lower part of the ceramic layer.

PAG-57-1 (Figure 173d):
    Zoomorphic ocarina.
    3.1 x 2.8 x 2.7 cm (L x W x H); weight: 5.9 g.
    Surface: oxidized.

This piece is very similar to the turtle-shaped ocarinas, but it has arms with hands attached to the head. It is complete. The body is spherical and probably composed of two parts (top and bottom). The head serves as a mouthpiece, while the mouth forms the beginning of the air duct. The eyes consist of round punctates surrounded by punctate circles. There is a round attachment with a horizontal notch on the neck. On the carapace, there are four fingerholes in a rectangular arrangement. In the middle, a round knob with a circular punctate is framed by another circle, similar to how the eyes are formed. On the back, there is a conical attachment with slots on the top. Arms protrude from each side and extend towards the head at an angle. They end in hands or paws with three fingers resting on the side of the air duct. The angled arms that lead to the head form the suspension holes. The ventral side is undecorated but features a circular aperture with an edge.

A very similar ocarina was found by Healy et al. (2010: Fig. 4) during excavations in Río Claro. The object is identified as anthropomorphic because of the arms (Healy et al. 2010: 29). Nevertheless, PAG-57-1 appears very similar to the other turtle-like instruments. It may represent a human-animal mix due to the blending of anthropomorphic and zoomorphic features. The ocarina was found in the same layer as the *bajareque* in Unit 4.

PAG-90-1 (Figure 173e):
    Zoomorphic ocarina in the shape of a turtle.
    2.9 x 3.4 x 2.2 cm (L x W x H); weight: 7.6 g.
    Surface: oxidized; core: oxidized.

The head and front left side of the body are preserved. Presumably, the ellipsoid body consisted of two separately formed parts, with the upper part obviously broken off along the seam. The head is attached to the body, and the joint is smeared over well. The head serves as a mouthpiece where air is blown through into the instrument. The eyes consist of small punctates encircled by additional punctates. On the neck, there is an oval attachment with a horizontal notch. On the bottom, the aperture is not preserved. The fragment was found in the gravel layer directly below the ceramic layer.

PAG-152-1 (Figure 173f):
    Undecorated ocarina.
    2.9 x 2.8 x 1.8 cm (L x W x H); weight: 4.3 g.
    Surface: partially oxidized; core: reduced.

The shape is similar to the zoomorphic turtle-shaped objects but does not otherwise indicate a figurative design. Decoration is not present. The mouthpiece and the front part of the right side with a suspension hole are preserved. The mouthpiece is broken off but fits to the other fragment. The body is ellipsoid and made of two parts that form the upper and lower halves. The corresponding seam is visible on the inside. The mouthpiece is relatively long and bent slightly upward. A slit-shaped air duct begins at its end and is directed towards the aperture on the ventral side, which is still partly preserved. The fragment was found in the settlement layer, approximately at the level of the hardened clay floor (Unit 3 Inv. 148/151).

PAG-195-1 (Figure 173g):
    Crescent-shaped ocarina.
    6.2 x 5.4 x 3.5 cm (L x W x H); weight 27.5 g.
    Surface: oxidized.

The ocarina is complete except for a small part detached from the neck area. The body is crescent-shaped and thus clearly stands out from the other ocarinas. The mouthpiece is formed by a head, and the eyes are indicated by two small punctations. To the left and right of the head, arms rest against the body, the ends of which form hands or paws with three fingers. The arms are perforated and form suspension holes like the other ocarinas. At the top of the body, there are four fingerholes in a rectangular arrangement. Like PAG-43-1, opposite pairs of S-shaped incisions frame two pairs of holes on the right and left, the ends of which are marked by punctations. An additional punctation is located between the fingerholes. The underside has no decoration, only the oval aperture. It is difficult to determine whether the object depicts an animal or a human. The ocarina was found in the settlement layer of Unit 4.

Summary and Comparison. Considering the ocarinas' style and stratigraphic contexts, it is notable that the objects from the lower settlement layers are stylistically different from those in the ceramic layers. In contrast, the ocarina from Inv. 90 (PAG-90-1), the gravel layer just below the ceramic layer, resembles those from the ceramic accumulation. This is another indication of the close connection between the two layers. PAG-152-1 and PAG-195-1, on the other hand, stand out due to their lack of design and differing shapes.

Guadalupe's ocarinas belong to a group of finds already known in northeast Honduras. They are also common in the neighboring culture areas. This is especially true for the Bay Islands, where several ocarinas were found (Healy et al. 2010; Strong 1935: Plate 27 a-c, g). During excavations at Selin Farm and Río Claro, Healy et al. (2010) found two additional ocarinas. The ocarinas from these sites take on anthropomorphic and zoomorphic designs. According to the authors, the latter represent birds, fish, turtles, and manatees. Although the flutes from Guadalupe resemble these finds stylistically, they probably form a distinct local style. A find from Río Claro closely parallels PAG-57-1. Healy et al. (2010) reflect on those that would have played the ocarinas and the circumstances and occasions in which the instruments were used. They consider theories that the ocarinas served a signaling function by imitating animal calls to be less likely. Instead, they see the ocarinas as communication media between humans and "the spiritual world," used during various ritual activities. I think this interpretation is appropriate since it has also been confirmed for other American cultures (see, e.g. Bernier 2009). Additionally, one can imagine that the musical instruments accompanied festivities and dances. The discovery of seven ocarinas in Guadalupe within a relatively small excavation area is striking and is a further indication for our assumption that the location was connected to the performance of ritual activities.

4.4.1.5.2 Figurines

During the excavations in Guadalupe, five figurine fragments were found (Figure 174). All originate from the ceramic layer.

PAG-9-337 (Figure 174a): This figurine is solid clay and measures 4.8 x 1.5 x 5.5 cm (L x W x H). The figure is zoomorphic and largely complete. Only the extremities are broken off. Small applied clay balls indicate the eyes. The figure is crudely crafted; the surface is not polished, and fingerprints are visible. The fragment was found in the upper part of the ceramic layer of Unit 2.

PAG-20-1 (Figure 174b): This figurine is solid clay and measures 8.35 x 3.1 x 2.2 cm (L x W x H). It probably represents the torso of a mammal. The head, arms, legs, and tail are broken off. The fragment was found in the west profile of Unit 1.

PAG-21-662 (Figure 174c): This figurine is also likely a representation of an animal. It is also solid and measures 4.95 x 2.35 x 3.2 cm (L x W x H). Only the front part of the body is preserved. Two fractures mark the locations where the arms were broken off. The head is characterized by a long snout. The eyes and mouth are not highlighted. The surface has several cracks. The clay was probably not carefully burnished, causing it to crack when drying. The figurine was found in the uppermost layer of Unit 3.

PAG-32-325 (Figure 174d): This figurine is solid, measures 7.85 x 2.2 x 4 cm (L x W x H), and consists of a unusual light red clay with beige spots. Given its cylindrical trunk, it resembles figurine PAG-20-1, but in this case, the head is still preserved. It has ears and eyes and a mouth indicated by a slit, while the extremities are broken off. A small puncture marks the anus. Fingerprints are visible on the surface. The figurine was found in the ceramic layer in Unit 4.

PAG-33-1 (Figure 174e): This figurine is solid and measures 6.35 x 4 x 3.45 cm (L x W x H). It may also represent a zoomorphic figure, but only a part of the trunk is preserved. The rear portion and all extremities are broken off. It was found in the lower part of the ceramic layer of Unit 3.

Several authors mention the discovery of clay figurines in our research area. Stone (1934a: 130f) finds a female figurine in Jerico Farm, and Strong (1935: Plate 28) illustrates several crudely fashioned anthropomorphic figurines from different sites on the Bay Islands. Healy (1978b: 60) mentions that "several small ceramic figurines" were found during excavations of Mound 1 at Selin Farm. He illustrates an example that appears to be an anthropomorph (Healy 1978b: Fig. 9). Clark et al. (1982: 29) also report the discovery of ceramic figurines in the Mosquitia. Unfortunately, these ceramic figurines are not usually described in detail, making it difficult to judge whether Guadalupe's figurines are typical or uncommon objects. It is notable, however, that most sources describe anthropomorphic figures, whereas the figurines in Guadalupe mostly represent animals.

Beyond the borders of our research area, clay figurines are widely distributed and known from very different periods and contexts. The variety is so diverse and the sample from Guadalupe so small that it does not seem useful at this point to systematically search for parallels. Nevertheless, it should be noted that figurines are often associated with burials (e.g., Agurcia Fasquelle [1978] for Playa de los Muertos in the Sula Valley, and Snarskis [1984: 209] for Costa Rica). On the Caribbean islands of Los Roques, figurines were associated with ritual activities (Antczak / Antczak 2006). Although this would also be conceivable for Guadalupe, the simple design and crude execution are salient. It is also possible that the objects were used as toys or represent pottery experiments by children.

4.4.1.5.3 Roller Stamps

Three ceramic objects were found that are interpreted as roller stamps (Figure 175). They are cylindrical objects with a hole in the center and exteriors decorated by carvings. They were used to decorate surfaces; the raised areas were covered with paint to create a pattern when rolled over an object. They were probably used to decorate textiles or skin (Alcina Franch 1958). There are no

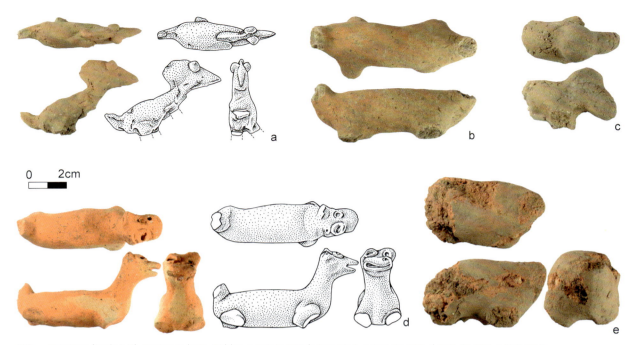

174   Figurines (Scale 1:2). Drawings by B. Gubler. a PAG-9-337; b PAG-20-1; c PAG-21-662; d PAG-32-325; e PAG-33-1.

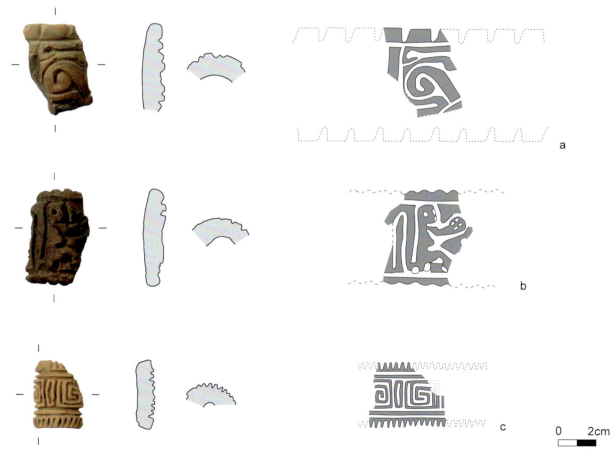

175   Roller stamps (Scale 1:2). Drawings by P. Bayer. a PAG-10-195; b PAG-16-1; c PAG-120-1.

completely preserved examples found at Guadalupe. The fragments are described in the following:

PAG-10-195 (Figure 175a): This fragment measures 4.8 x 3 x 1.2 cm (L x W x H). The object has a geometric pattern in the center that forms a spiral. There are notches at the edges, which, when rolled, result in a crenelated pattern. The object was found in the upper part of the ceramic layer (Unit 2).

PAG-16-1 (Figure 175b): This fragment measures 5.3 x 3.25 x 1 cm (L x W x H). About one-fourth of the object is preserved. The exterior is decorated with incisions. They depict a zoomorphic being (possibly a monkey) sitting and holding an object in its hand. The scene is framed by wavy lines at the top and bottom. The object was found in the upper part of the ceramic layer (Unit 1).

PAG-120-1 (Figure 175c): This object measures 3.8 x 2.6 x 0.9 cm (L x W x H). The exterior is decorated with incisions that create a geometric pattern. The pattern is bordered by a horizontal line at the top and bottom. There are notches at the ends that form a serrated pattern when rolled. The object was found in the eastern part of Unit 4, the periphery of the mound.

Healy (1978a: Fig. 12, 1984a: 234) has also found similar cylindrical roller stamps in Cocal contexts. Clark et al. (1982: 29) mention that they found the fragment of a roller stamp with a geometric design during site inspections near Rio Negro. Numerous roller stamp specimens are known from the Sula Valley. They have geometric patterns, with some of them having zoomorphic figures, possibly representing monkeys. Their motifs are relatively similar to PAG-16-1.

Roller stamps are regionally and diachronically widespread. They have been found in Mesoamerica (Evans 2008: 152; Field 1967), Southern Central America (Abel-Vidor / Bakker 1981; Snarskis 1984), and the Caribbean (Fitzpatrick 2015: 318f) and, as Healy has already noted, "the northeast Honduras specimens could be related to either region" (Healy 1984a: 234). Snarskis (1984: 209) points out that during the El Bosque complex in Costa Rica (100 BC–AD 500), ocarinas, stamps, and figurines are found almost exclusively in higher-rank burials, which is why he suspects that they were connected to ritual or shamanistic activities.

4.4.1.5.4 Spindle Whorls

Fourteen spindle whorls were found in Guadalupe (Figure 176). Eight examples are complete, while six are fragmented, and all have a perforation in the middle. The variety of shapes is surprising. They range from disc-shaped and semi-circular to spherical and pear-shaped. Some are undecorated, while others are decorated with incisions of geometric patterns. All specimens were found in the ceramic layer of Units 1, 2, and 3 at various altitudes. No particular distribution pattern can be identified concerning shapes and decorations.

PAG-6-584 (Figure 176f): 2.3 x 1.95 cm (W x H). 10.4 g. The object is complete. It is spherical and undecorated.

PAG-7-727 (Figure 176k): 1.7 x 1.35 cm (W x H). 2.2 g. The fragment is spherical with a flattened top and bottom. It is decorated with carefully applied incisions consisting of semicircles and geometric lines separated by two parallel lines.

PAG-8-405 (Figure 176h): 2.1 x 2.15 cm (W x H). 7.5 g. The object is a fragment. It is cylindrical and has an incised decoration in the center. Incised punctates are framed by two horizontal lines. The execution of the decoration is not very symmetrical.

PAG-10-553 (Figure 176c): 2.15 x 1.5 cm (W x H). 9.2 g. The object is complete and spherical. It is noticeably flattened at the top and bottom and is undecorated.

PAG-11-312 (Figure 176l): 2.15 x 2.5 cm (W x H). 6.5 g. The object is broken in half. It is a sphere with a slightly flattened top and bottom. It is decorated with a geometric pattern consisting of two parallel horizontal lines and a band of circles.

PAG-15-684 (Figure 176e): 1.45 x 1.6 cm (W x H). 2.5 g. The object is a fragment. The preserved part is cylindrical and widens towards the bottom. It bears no decorations.

PAG-15-685 (Figure 176m): 3.4 x 1.7 cm (W x H). 20.4 g. The object is completely preserved and represents the largest spindle whorl found in Guadalupe. It is hemispherical. Two shallow incised lines run parallel to the upper edge with jab marks between them.

PAG-23-320 (Figure 176n): 2.4 x 3 cm (W x H). 24.2 g. The completely preserved, spherical spindle whorl is flattened at the top and bottom. It is decorated with a symmetrical design consisting of parallel lines, circles, and incised punctates.

PAG-23-695 (Figure 176a): 1.95 x 2.2 cm (W x H). 3.4 g. Only half of the object is preserved. It is almost spherical but not quite symmetrical. It is decorated with shallow, incised, wavy lines.

PAG-31-9 (Figure 176g): 2.1 x 1.9 cm (W x H). 10 g. The completely preserved object is spherical and slightly flattened at the top and bottom. A shallow incised line is visible at its widest point.

PAG-44-2 (Figure 176b): 1.9 x 1.85 cm (W x H). 3.2 g. The object is complete, spherical, and undecorated. Because of the small size and the unspecific shape, use as jewelry or as a bead is possible as well.

PAG-47-1 (Figure 176i): 3.1 x 0.6 cm (W x H). 6.5 g. The object is complete. It differs from all other spindle whorls in that it is flat and wide. The outline is not round but has several edges. It may be a recycled ceramic sherd.

PAG-52-1 (Figure 176o): 2.2 x 2.85 cm (W x H). 8.3 g. The object is broken at its longitudinal axis. It is pea-

176   Spindle whorls (Scale 1:1). a PAG-23-695; b PAG-44-2; c PAG-10-553; d PAG-53-2: e PAG-15-684; f PAG-6-584; g PAG-31-9; h
PAG-8-405; i PAG-47-1; k PAG-7-727; l PAG-11-312; m PAG-15-685; n PAG-23-320; o PAG-52-1.

nut-shaped. The decoration consists of shallow incised lines with small, incised punctates between them.

PAG-53-2 (Figure 176d): 1.5 x 1.6 cm (W x H). 4.3 g. The object is complete and resembles PAG-44-2 in its spherical, undecorated form.

The presence of spindle whorls indicates that textiles were produced in Guadalupe. Together with a wooden stick inserted into the perforation, the spindle whorls form a hand spindle. This was used to produce yarn by spinning together textile fibers. The discovery of a metal needle and bark beaters also attest to the production of textiles in Guadalupe (see chapter 5.1.2.2). Interestingly, for other sites in northeast Honduras, the discovery of spindle whorls is hardly mentioned. For Selin Farm, Healy (1978b: 60) reports the discovery of a single spindle whorl. It is a reworked ceramic sherd similar to PAG-47-1 and was found in Mound 1 with a Basic Selin or Early Selin context. Several bone needles were found in the same context. For the Bay Islands, only a single spindle whorl is mentioned. Strong (1935: 53, 65, Plate 12b) found it in the Dixon site cache. It is a flat stone decorated with incisions. It is unclear if spindle whorls have actually not been found at other sites or if they are simply not mentioned. If the former is true, the discovery of such a large number of spindle whorls in Guadalupe is exceptional and suggests that textile production may have been a specialized activity not practiced at all sites. However, a more complete base of evidence is needed to corroborate such a hypothesis.

4.4.1.5.5 Miniature Vessels

The last category in this section is that of miniature vessels. Because these objects are vessels, they have already been partly discussed in the vessel classification section. In this chapter, however, they will be described again in detail, and their possible significance will be discussed. We found four miniature vessels in Guadalupe (Figure 177). Two of them are complete, while two are fragmented.

PAG-7-345 (Figure 177a): 2.6 x 3.6 cm (W x H). Wall thickness: 2–3 mm. The vessel is fragmented. It is a small bowl with parts of the rim broken off. Three small knobs are attached to the bottom and represent supports. One knob is also preserved below the rim. Thus, the vessel forms a basic shape similar to the large vessels. The vessel is not very carefully worked and has an irregular thickness and surface. Some scratches are visible on the surface.

PAG-13-123b (Figure 177b): 2.00 x 4.6 x 3.5 cm (L x W x H). Wall thickness: 4–6 mm. The vessel is complete. The shape is unrestricted and elliptical and does not reflect the canon of shapes of the large vessels. While its form has some irregularities, the surface is relatively well burnished.

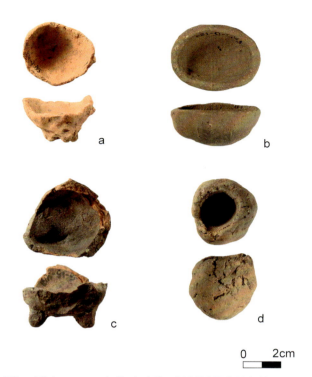

177 Miniature vessels (Scale 1:2). a PAG-7-345; b PAG-13-123b; c PAG-15-417; d PAG-29-458.

PAG-15-417 (Figure 177c): 4.6 x 3.2 cm (W x H). Wall thickness: 4–5 mm. This miniature vessel represents a tripod vessel. The rim is not preserved, and one of the supports is broken off. The shape is rather irregular, and the surface is only lightly burnished.

PAG-29-458 (Figure 177d): 3.5 x 3.25 cm (W x H). Wall thickness: 3–10 mm. The vessel is complete and very irregular, especially concerning the thickness of the walls. It appears that a rough clay ball or cylinder was first formed, and then a hole was pressed into the ball with a finger or a stick.

Several authors report on the discovery of miniature vessels in northeast Honduras. Spinden (1925: 530) writes: "Along small streams sacred places of deposit for votive metates, bowls etc. are encountered. These votive specimens exist in miniature and giant sizes and in all stages of manufacture." Strong found several miniature vessels on the islands and illustrated some of them (1935: Plate 8, Fig. 29). They come from Dixon Hill and Indian Hill. Both sites are characterized as offertory sites and represent a similar situation to Guadalupe (see below). The miniature vessels from these sites were placed together with other finds in deposits. Strong (1935: 55f, 94) describes them as crude and believes that they are models of larger vessels. He also assumes that they were specially made for offertory purposes. They resemble the miniature vessels from Guadalupe in that they are also crude in execution. However, they differ in their form. Strong mainly illustrates cylindrical vessels without tripods. Goodwin (2011: 122) also finds miniature vessels during her investigations in El Antigual on Roatán. They, too, are rather simple and crude. For the mainland, Epstein (1957: 31) mentions the discovery of a miniature vessel at Selin Farm but does not describe it in detail. Begley (1999: 154) mentions two miniature vessels from Jamasquire near Talgua, which probably date to Period V or VI. However, he does not provide further details, either.

Griffin et al. (2009: 83) mention that the Pesh use miniature vessels during certain ceremonies. Due to the archaeological contexts, the ethnographic reports, and the fact that there are also miniature metates found in northeast Honduras, the interpretation of the vessels as votive specimens appears quite logical. Nevertheless, I would like to mention another possible interpretation. Miniature bowls are also known from the Mexican highlands, and ethnohistorical sources show that they were used for spinning (Smith / Hirth 1988). They served as support for the spinning whorls. "These bowls are needed during the thread making process to support the spindle when spinning short-staple fibers like cotton" (Smith / Hirth 1988: 350). The bowls have similar dimensions to the miniature vessels found in Guadalupe and represent hemispherical vessels with supports. The function of Guadalupe's miniature vessels remains unclear. It is also possible that they had multiple functions; perhaps they were initially used for more practical purposes and only later deposited in a ritual context, as is the case with spindle whorls.

4.4.2 OBSIDIAN

After pottery, obsidian is the second-most numerous find group in Guadalupe. Compared to other sites in the region, the large number of obsidian objects makes it an important subject of study. In addition, obsidian is particularly well suited for the reconstruction of material networks because it can be assigned to a specific geological source and thus allows for the reconstruction of links between these sources and pre-Hispanic settlements. In Guadalupe, 767 obsidian objects were recovered, the majority of which are prismatic blades. Other forms were projectile points, casual and bipolar industries, and one blade-core (Figure 178, Figure 179). Apart from obsidian, no other chipped stone artifacts were present in Guadalupe. This large number of obsidian artifacts alone is an interesting result of the research. Such an extraordinary amount of obsidian has not been reported for any other northeast Honduras sites so far. Chemical and technological analyses were carried out for 355 objects at the Mesoamerican Research Laboratory at the University of San Diego, under the direction of

178   Obsidian prismatic blades found in Guadalupe (T. Remsey).

179   Obsidian projectile points found in Guadalupe (T. Remsey).

Geoffrey Braswell and with the participation of Luke Stroth and Raquel Otto. Before the results of the analyses are presented, the panorama of obsidian sources in Middle America is briefly described in the following.

Obsidian Sources in Middle America. Obsidian is a volcanic glass that occurs only in areas with volcanic activity and under certain conditions. The largest deposits are located in the Central Mexican highlands, with Pachuca near Teotihuacán being one of the most intensively exploited sources with its greenish shimmering obsidian (Pastrana / Domínguez 2009) (Figure 180). The most important sources in present-day Guatemala are El Chayal, Ixtepeque, and San Martin Jilotepeque, all of which are located in the southern highlands. Although obsidian sources have been identified in El Salvador, there is no evidence that they were exploited in pre-Hispanic times (Braswell 1999: 1). Three sources are known in

180   Location of raw material sources mentioned in the text (M. Lyons). Map tiles by Stamen Design, under CC BY 3.0. Data by OpenStreetMap, under ODbL.

Honduras: San Luis in the west, La Esperanza in the southwest, and Güinope 35 km southeast of the capital Tegucigalpa. In Nicaragua, there are sources near El Espino and near the Mombacho, but this raw material is not suitable for the production of tools (Braswell 1999: 1). In addition, there are sporadic deposits in the form of pyroclastic bombs, which may have been used in pre-Hispanic times but were only of limited suitability for the manufacture of tools. No obsidian sources further south are known, and obsidian artifacts are very rare (Lange 1984a: 57; Sheets 1994). There are no known obsidian sources in the Caribbean islands either (Fitzpatrick 2013: 122).

The Honduran sources differ in terms of extraction technology and production techniques. In La Esperanza, obsidian was mined in vertical shaft mines. The raw material was further processed mainly into prismatic blades, which is why it is characterized as more Mesoamerican (Sheets et al. 1990). The San Luis source was first described in 1999 (Aoyama / Tashiro / Glascock 1999). It yields only small cobbles and seems to have been used rather locally. It does not appear to have played a significant role in interregional exchange. Güinope was first described in 1990 (Sheets et al. 1990). It is also considered a low-quality source, and the raw material is often only available in the form of small cobbles. In Güinope, there is no single outcrop; the cobbles

are located in colluvial and alluvial deposits. No signs of pre-Hispanic mining were found. In contrast to La Esperanza, the source belongs to a Southern Central America exchange sphere. Due to the small size of the material, it was initially assumed that the raw material would not be suitable for the production of prismatic blades (Sheets et al. 1990: 148). However, the present analyses from Guadalupe determined the on-site production of prismatic blades using Güinope obsidian for the first time. The following observations are based on the investigations of Luke Stroth (2019) and Raquel Otto (2019).

Provenience Analysis. To assign the objects found in Guadalupe to the sources described above, a provenience analysis was carried out, which combined chemical and visual analysis. First, the chemical composition of the samples was determined using a hand-held Bruker Tracer III-V pXRF analyzer. With the help of this device, a sample is bombarded with X-rays for 180 seconds, which causes electrons to be excited and move. However, the electrons immediately return to their original position, emitting energy. Each element emits a characteristic amount of energy. By measuring this energy, the elemental composition of the sample can be determined. The data were collected for the elements manganese (Mn), iron (Fe), zinc (Zn), gallium (Ga), thorium (Th), rubidium (Rb), strontium (Sr), yttrium (Y), zirconium (Zr), and niobium (Nb). After collecting the relative chemical concentrations, multivariate statistical analyses were performed to determine if the artifacts can be assigned to groups based on their chemical composition and thus clarify their provenience. The analysis was carried out in two steps. In a first principal component analysis, only the sample from Guadalupe was considered to determine whether groups can be identified with respect to the elemental composition. This first principal component analysis showed that the Guadalupe sample can be divided into at least two groups concerning its composition. Nb, Zr, Rb, and Sr, are the most significant elements for variation (Figure 181). Once this was determined, the second principal component analysis was performed using a reference sample containing objects from different Central American Sources, including El Chayal (G), Güinope (H), Ixtepeque (G), La Esperanza (H), Otumba (M), Pachuca (M), San Martín Jilotepeque (G), Ucareo (M), Zacualtipan (M), and Zaragoza (M). In this analysis, Y, Sr, Zr, and Nb were significant drivers of variation. This PCA made it clear that Zacualtipan, Zaragoza, and Pachuca were not potential sources. In order to assign the Guadalupe material to the geological sources, Mahalanobis distances Analysis (using the program GSRUN) and Canonical Discriminant Analysis (using the program JMP) were performed. These analyses largely agreed that the artifacts from Guadalupe clustered around La Esperanza, Güinope, and Ixtepeque (Figure 182). For 18 objects, the two methods of analysis did not coincide.

The uncertain cases were additionally examined through visual sourcing with a reference collection. It was based on the evaluation and comparison of optical criteria, including:

"(1) the refracted color; (2) the reflected color; (3) the degree of translucence and opacity; (4) the degree to which refracted light is diffused; (5) the presence, size, color, frequency, and nature of inclusions; (6) the texture and luster of flaked surfaces; and (7) the color, texture, and thickness of cortex" (Braswell et al. 2000: 270 f).

Three people participated in the analysis. The final assignment of the objects to geological sources is based on a combination of the results of chemical and visual analyses. This strategy's exact procedure and its advantages are described in detail in Stroth (2019) and Stroth et al. (2019).

The combination of chemical and visual analysis ultimately yielded the following result for the provenience analysis: 223 pieces originate from Güinope, 122 pieces from La Esperanza, 9 from Ixtepeque (Guatemala), and 1 from Otumba (Mexico). This result is surprising for several reasons. First, as Braswell (2003) has demonstrated, most obsidian used in northern Honduras during the

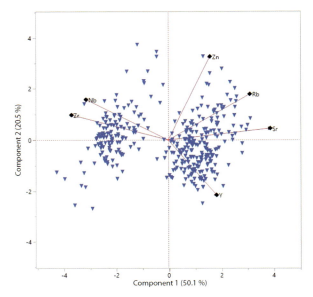

181   Obsidian analysis: First and second principal components (Stroth 2019: Fig. 2).

Selin period comes from La Esperanza. In contrast, most artifacts in the Guadalupe sample come from Güinope. Second, formal tools made of Güinope obsidian are uncommon at other sites. Braswell (2003: 141) states that "there is little evidence for blade production in northeast Honduras, where inhabitants seem to have produced casual flake tools and to have used imported blades." Before these results are discussed in detail, the results of the technological analysis are presented.

Technological Analysis. The technological analysis was carried out by Luke Stroth (2019) and Raquel Otto (2019) and aimed to reconstruct production processes and identify the production steps that took place in Guadalupe, whether they were raw materials or finished goods that found their way to Guadalupe from the respective sources. In order to achieve these goals and to offer a high-resolution approach, the artifacts from Guadalupe were examined for the following attributes (cf. Stroth 2019: 21): source, condition, industry, type, series, platform, retouch, lip grinding, cortex, termination, number of dorsal ridges, bulbar scar, cutting edge, length, width, thickness, bulb thickness, and mass. The technological data were compared for the respective raw material sources to identify different production patterns.

The 355 analyzed artifacts from Guadalupe are composed as follows from a technological point of view: 346 prismatic blades, 3 projectile points, 1 complete blade core, and 5 objects comprising a mix of causal and bipolar industries, whereby some objects belong to more than one technology (casual flakes produced from exhausted prismatic cores and prismatic blades retouched into projectile points) (Table 2). If the technological

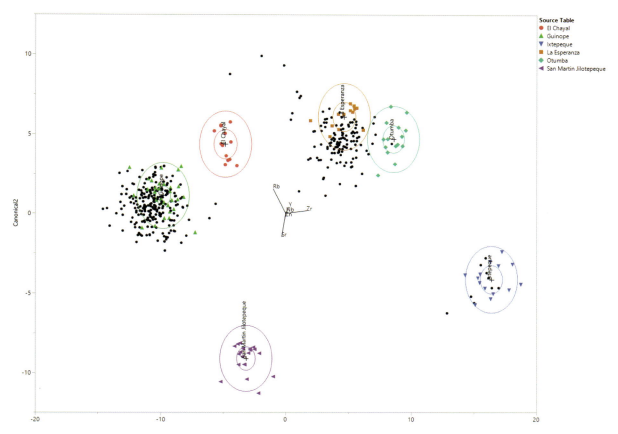

182   Obsidian analysis: Projection of canonical discriminant analysis (Stroth 2019: Fig. 4).

analysis is combined with the provenience analysis, clear technological differences are visible for the respective sources. The data suggest that the inhabitants of Guadalupe were involved in at least two different exchange networks. Blades were produced locally from Güinope material. At the same time, finished blades were imported from La Esperanza and Ixtepeque. Of particular interest is the local production from Güinope obsidian. A prismatic blade core provides evidence of this and, compared to the objects from other sources, a high number of objects with cortex (15.25%; for comparison: 5.74% from La Esperanza and 0% from Ixtepeque). Also, many distal ends (which were actually removed in a finished product) indicate local production.

According to Stroth (2019), the blade core is the first known example from Güinope obsidian. The core is still half-covered with cortex (Figure 183). This could be because the inhabitants of Guadalupe used a hand-held method and left the cortex intact to allow for better handling of the core. Together with the core, 15.25% of the artifacts from Güinope obsidian have cortex. This places this group of materials within the range of 10.3–16.2%, which Clark (1988: 31) indicates as evidence for on-site production. While blades from Güinope obsidian have been reported at other sites (e.g., Braswell 1997; Healy et al. 1996; Lange et al. 1992), Guadalupe is the first site where the production of these blades was proved (Stroth 2019: 2).

Source	Artifacts Total	Blades	Casual	Bipolar	Formal Tools	Blade Cores
La Esperanza	122	119	2	1	2	0
Güinope	223	218	3	3	1	5
Ixtepeque	9	9	0	0	0	0
Otumba	1	0	1	0	0	1
TOTAL	355	346	6	4	3	6

Table 2   Number of obsidian artifact types by raw material source. Artifacts belonging to more than one industry are listed multiple times (after Stroth 2019: Table 5).

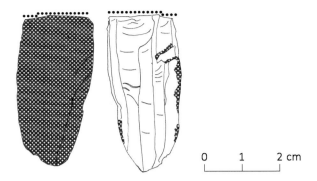

183   Drawing of the Güinope blade core. The spotted area indicates cortex (Stroth 2019: Fig. 8).

The artifacts from La Esperanza and Ixtepeque are imported products. This is indicated by the absence of cores, the relative lack of cortex on the artifacts, and the few distal ends. Most imported products are prismatic blades, but there are also three projectile points (Figure 184). They were apparently "recycled" from prismatic blades. They have retouch, which occurs in only 2.25% of all artifacts. Retouch, therefore, does not appear to have been a local production technique. Another notable piece included in the sample is a casual flake assigned to the Otumba source in Central Mexico, which is about 1400 km away. This find proves contact to Central Mexico, even if it was certainly indirect, and the object reached Guadalupe by down-the-line exchange. This object was also recycled. It was made from an exhausted blade core. Blades from Otumba were not found in the sample.

Another technological observation is that the prismatic blades have pecked and ground platforms, which are diagnostic for the Postclassic. This simplifies the hand-held technique as they are more stable and do not require as much pressure to be applied. It is most likely that the hand-held technique was used in Guadalupe, which is also indicated by the small core size. The metric analysis has shown no significant differences in the quality of artifacts from the different sources. The blades from Güinope are generally somewhat narrower and thinner, which is partly due to the nature of the raw material. The reuse of material and the intensive traces of use on the objects also show that obsidian was still an important commodity that was not available in abundance.

Discussion. The geochemical and technological analysis revealed that the inhabitants of Guadalupe were involved in several obsidian exchange networks. Finished blades were imported from Ixtepeque and La Esperanza. Prismatic blades were manufactured locally from Güinope obsidian. The data from Guadalupe can prove such on-site production for the first time. As de-scribed above, Ixtepeque and La Esperanza are traditionally considered as belonging to a Mesoamerican exchange sphere. Ixtepeque is mainly transported through the Motagua River and along the Caribbean coast into the Maya lowlands (Braswell 2003; Hammond 1972) but was also found in Nicaragua (Braswell 1997; Sheets et al. 1990). La Esperanza was an important source for Central Honduras but was also exchanged into the Maya lowlands (Hirth 1988; McKillop 1996: 55). In Nicaragua, artifacts from this source seem to have been rarely used (Healy et al. 1996 confirm the finding of a single object). Güinope, on the other hand, is clearly oriented towards the south; for the Mesoamerican culture area, this raw material does not seem to have played an important role (Braswell 2003). Of particular interest is the local production of prismatic blades in Guadalupe. The production of prismatic blades is a Mesoamerican technology and is even considered a defining cultural feature (Braswell 1997: 19). About 95% of the obsidian artifacts found in Mesoamerica consist of prismatic blades or products related to blade production (Braswell 1997: 20). The fact that this technology was used in Guadalupe is evidence of contact and technology transfer. The Mesoamerican technology was adapted here to the local needs and further developed by applying the hand-held method. The use and adaptation of a Mesoamerican technology and the use of raw materials from a source described as belonging to the Southern Central American exchange sphere is a vivid example of the fact that the inhabitants of Guadalupe were involved in various cultural and economic networks at different levels.

The considerable amount of obsidian is exceptional and deserves closer examination. For Mesoamerica, an increase in the extraction and production of obsidian tools can be observed during the Postclassic period (Braswell 2003). The fact that the artifacts are no longer concentrated in large settlements, as was often the case during the Classic period, but are widely available, suggests increasing commercialization. Moreover, obsidian is mainly found in coastal settlements, which indicates circuminsular transport (Braswell 2003). Healy (1978a, 1978b) found only two objects in the Selin-period site, Selin Farm, whereas in the Cocal-period site, Río Claro, there were 100. Although the amount had increased significantly during the Cocal period, Guadalupe, with its 757 artifacts, clearly stands out (surface finds were not included and would increase the number to well over 800). We did not find any sites with a comparable amount of obsidian visible on the surface during survey activities. We must therefore assume that the inhabitants of Guadalupe had access to an exceptionally large amount of obsidian. This may have several reasons: 1) It is conceivable that Guadalupe was a kind of trading post where obsidian from different sources was collected,

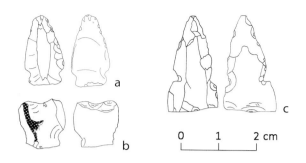

184   Dorsal and ventral surfaces of projectile points produced from prismatic blades (Stroth 2019: Fig. 7).

processed, and exchanged. The coastal location would provide access to maritime trade routes, which gained importance during Period VI. 2) Guadalupe may have represented a site of cultural and ritual importance, where obsidian was brought and deposited together with other objects from different regions. Both theories are discussed in the concluding discussion.

4.4.3 Greenstone

In contrast to obsidian, only a moderate number of greenstone objects were found at Guadalupe, indicating that the material was not as widely accessible as obsidian or ceramics. Nevertheless, the investigation of these objects can provide us with important information about existing exchange networks. Nine greenstone objects were found (Figure 185). Six of them are small tubular beads with a perforation in the middle. They measure between 12 and 26 mm. PAG-7-Pi-1 (Figure 185c) is a ring-shaped bead. PAG-5-Pi-1 (Figure 185a) is a rather elongated bead that was not worked into an exact cylindrical shape like the other beads. PAG-33-Pi-2 (Figure 185f) is a small, flat amorphous object to which no function can be attributed at the moment.

In Middle America, greenstone held a central importance for many societies. The Olmecs had already made intensive use of this material and were masters of lapidary. For the Maya and the Mexica, the color of the stone symbolized fertility (Wagner 2012). Laura Filloy Nadal (2017: 67) noted that "from the Preclassic to the Postclassic period, no raw material in Mesoamerica was more valued and esteemed than greenstone and the objects produced from it." The term greenstone covers various minerals and rocks that have a green to bluish color. In the older literature, the term "jade" is often mistakenly used for all of these stones. In fact, a dis-

tinction must be made between real jade and other rocks with a greenish color, which are not jade in a chemical sense. Jade, in turn, is a generic term for the two minerals, jadeite and nephrite. Other stones with a greenish color can be, e.g., serpentinite, albitite, quartzites, or soapstone (Harlow 1993). It is unclear to what extent pre-Hispanic societies differentiated between these two categories. Bishop and Lange (1988) introduce a distinction between real jade (i.e., jadeite and nephrite) and social jade. They use the term social jade to describe green stones that are not real jade but experienced a similar use and significance to real jade. With this, the authors consider that the pre-Hispanic groups may not have distinguished between real jade and other raw materials with a greenish color, such as serpinite[17] (Figure 186).

Chemical Composition. To examine the chemical composition of the greenstone objects from Guadalupe, eight of the nine objects were analyzed with Raman spectroscopy under the direction of Prof. Dr. Ulrich A. Glasmacher (Institute of Earth Sciences, Research group Thermochronology and Archaeometry, Heidelberg University). For details regarding the methods used, see Appendix B.

The analysis showed that all of the objects are jade, or more precisely, jadeite. Additionally, the minerals muscovite, albite, quartz, and serpentinite were identified. The analyzed objects were composed of combinations of the mentioned minerals in different concentrations (see Appendix B). Furthermore, various organic substances were detected on the samples that were not previously cleaned. The Raman spectra of the respective samples can be found in the appendix.

Provenience. The chemical analysis provides information about the provenience of the objects. The objects likely stem from the Motagua Valley in present-day Guatemala, where the nearest jade source is located (see Figure 180). Jade is only formed under specific geological conditions. Jadeite is formed by the metamorphosis of albite, blueschist or gneiss. High pressure and low temperatures at subduction zones are necessary for the mineral to form (Harlow 1993: 13). Therefore, only a few jade sources are known in the world. On the American continent, only two jade sources were known for a long time. They are located on the USA's west coast and the Motagua Valley in Guatemala (Harlow 1993; Hauff 1993). Recently, jade sources were discovered in the Caribbean, specifically in south-central and eastern Cuba (García Casco et al. 2009) and north-central Hispaniola (Schertl et al. 2012; Schertl / Maresch / Krebs 2007). All of these sources are deposits of jadeite. Nephrite sources are not yet known in Middle America (Wagner 2012).

---

17   For a contrary opinion see for example Filloy Nadal (2017: 67).

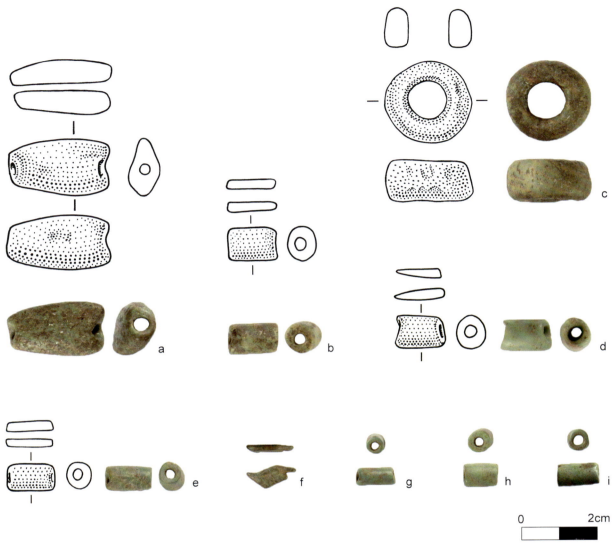

185   Green stone beads (Scale 1:1). Drawings by B. Gubler. a PAG-5-Pi-1; b PAG-5-Pi-2; c PAG-7-Pi-1; d PAG-12-Pi-1; e PAG-15-Pi-1; f PAG-33-Pi-2; g PAG-33-Pi-3; h PAG-42-Pi-1; i PAG-48-Pi-2.

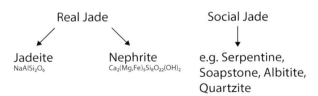

186   Real jade and social jade (F. Fecher).

There is disagreement about the presence of other jade sources in Central America. The discussion was comprehensively presented in the volume on pre-Columbian jade by Lange (1993b). The reason for the ongoing discussion is that there are two major greenstone processing traditions in Central America. In Mesoamerica, presented by the Olmecs and the Maya, and in Costa Rica. The Maya preferred pale green jade, while bluish jade (called "Olmec blue jade") was the preferred material for the Olmecs and in Costa Rica. Visually, the two groups are easily distinguished, and chemical analyses have demonstrated that they actually have different compositions (Curtiss 1993). While the greenish jade could clearly be assigned to the Motagua source in Guatemala, the source of the Olmec blue jade remained unknown for a long time. There are two possible reasons for this: 1) there is another still undiscovered source from which the Olmec blue jade originates, or 2) there are jade-bearing areas within the Motagua Valley that have not yet been discovered and are the origin of the Olmec blue jade. The first hypothesis is called the multiple-source hypothesis. Their proponents (e.g., Bishop / Sayre / Mishara 1993; Reyonard de Ruenes, Margarita

1993) assume that there must be an additional jade source to that of the source in the Motagua Valley. The large amount of greenstone objects in Costa Rica (and their absence in Nicaragua) leads them to assume that it is located in Costa Rica. So far, however, such deposits have not been discovered. Advocates of the single-source hypothesis, on the other hand, argue that there is only one source in the Motagua Valley and that Olmec blue jade can also be attributed to it (e.g., Harlow 1993).

At the beginning of the 21st century, geological reconnaissance has identified previously unknown jade deposits in the Motagua Valley. Among the deposits, there is one that strongly resembles Olmec blue jade in composition and visual characteristics (Seitz et al. 2001). Although the discussion is still not conclusive today, most researchers currently support the single-source hypothesis (e.g., Hoopes 2017; Mora Marín / Reents-Budet / Fields 2017). At the same time, studies from the Caribbean show that sources can still be discovered. Harlow (1993) had described these areas in his contribution as possible sources due to the geological situation. Interestingly, he also mentions the Honduran Bay Islands (Roatán) as an area that meets the geological requirements for the occurrence of jadeite. As Hoopes (2017: 58) notes, areas with jade deposits are geologically dynamic areas where geological processes such as earthquakes or landslides can open up new sources or impede access to old ones. It is therefore not impossible that systematic inspections will lead to the discovery of additional sources. However, as long as no other sources are confirmed, we must assume that the finds from Guadalupe come from the Motagua Valley in Guatemala.

Stylistic Observations. In Lange's (1993a) volume on pre-Columbian jade, he distinguishes four different greenstone lapidary traditions for the Central American mainland: Olmec, Maya, Ulúa (Central Honduras), and Costa Rica. South of Costa Rica, greenstone artifacts are only found sporadically (Stone 1993). Lange does not cover the Caribbean, where greenstone objects represent very important commodities (Rodríguez Ramos 2010). Although the four traditions defined by Lange have some iconographic elements and production techniques in common, they do not develop from or dominate each other. Instead, they differ in their raw material, use, production techniques, and iconography. According to Lange (1993a), greenstone processing begins with the Olmecs around 1200 BC. Jade objects were found mainly in caches under burials and plazas. The Maya processed jade objects from the Late Preclassic to the Postclassic period, with a peak during the Classic period (AD 300–900). They preferred objects made of green opaque jade or albite and used them mainly in architectural contexts, such as caches or construction rituals, as personal adornments, and as grave goods. Jade artifacts

were also found in domestic contexts. Besides the famous jade masks and personal jewelry, another well-known form is the dynastic plaque. These objects are often decorated with a ruler's portrait and inscriptions related to rulership and royal dynasty. The concept of maize as a central plant in Maya cosmology is also associated with these artifacts, represented by the green color and the axe shape (the tool used for clearing a forest to cultivate maize) (Mora Marín / Reents-Budet / Fields 2017: 181).

In central Honduras, 2842 greenstone artifacts were recovered during excavations in El Cajón, which led Hirth and Grant Hirth (1993) to define another greenstone lapidary tradition. The predominant material here is albite, accompanied by a small amount of real jade. The current state of research suggests that processing was most intense from AD 400–600. The contexts mentioned are public rituals, caches in architectural contexts, and personal adornment. Common object classes are beads, pendants, pectorals, and earflares. Besides zoomorphic and anthropomorphic imagery, the human dwarf or hunchback is a frequent motif.

The fourth and last processing tradition Lange mentions is that of Costa Rica. It is also the one that raises the most questions. It takes place between 300 BC and AD 700, and unlike the other traditions, many other green stones were elaborately processed here in addition to jadeite and albite. The objects mainly come from burial contexts where they served as personal adornment. The distribution of the objects is limited to northern Costa Rica and its Pacific coast. One form that appears frequently is that of the axe god. These are celt-shaped pendants with stylized zoomorphic heads. Other common motifs are bird heads, dogs, jaguars, crocodiles, serpents, and frogs. The iconography is more an expression of animistic beliefs than dynastic histories and rulership as seen by the Maya (Stone 1993). Interestingly, many dynastic plaques were found in Costa Rica that could be assigned to the Maya area because of their hieroglyphic inscriptions. In Costa Rica, these objects were reworked and fit to local needs. The researchers assume that the Maya artifacts were popular mainly because of the raw material, their shape, and the exoticism that was attached to them. However, further processing of the material into local forms shows that the objects were not appreciated as such (Mora Marín / Reents-Budet / Fields 2017).

As an addition to Lange's conclusions, a few aspects regarding greenstone artifacts from the Caribbean are mentioned here. Preferred materials were jadeitite, serpentinite, turquoise, and radiolarian limestone. While jadeite found in the Caribbean has long been believed to originate in Guatemala, the discovery of several jade sources in the Caribbean itself allows for a new perspective. The material was mainly processed into celts and zoomorphic pendants; the axe god motif is also known (Rodríguez Ramos 2010).

There are also numerous greenstone objects found in our area of study. Most of them come from looting, are privately owned, and have not yet been systematically investigated. However, finds are often mentioned in archaeological reports, and some are stored in museum collections. Data from these different types of sources will be briefly presented here, along with an overview of greenstone finds in northeast Honduras.

Spinden's report (1925: 530, 534) is one of the first archaeological texts to report on greenstone finds in our study area. He mainly mentions long beads and celts, which he finds in burial contexts. Stone (1941: 47ff) also reports several finds in Trujillo's surroundings and in the Aguán Valley (for example, see Stone 1941: Fig. 39, 40, and 43). Many of these pieces are now stored at the NMNH and can be found in the digitized database[18]. Although there are no precise provenience data available, these artifacts give a good impression of the type and quantity of greenstone objects from northeast Honduras. They are mainly long, tubular beads, but there are also some axe gods, which are typical for Costa Rica. During excavations at Jerico Farm (1934a), Stone found a tubular jade bead and an axe god associated with a burial, as well as the head of another axe god. Strong (1935: 148) writes, "A little carved jadeite and great numbers of green talc artifacts occur in this coastal region. Near Puerto Castilla local diggers have obtained great numbers of large and small anthropomorphic celts and beads, especially very massive and long cylindrical types made of green talc." On Roatán, he found numerous greenstone objects in the Dixon Site offertory vessel. Among them are beads, pendants, anthropomorphic and zoomorphic carvings, spindle whorls, and a ring. According to Strong, none of the objects are made of jade but of talc, diopside, marble, calcite, and serpentine[19]. A serpentine source was discovered on the island, which may have served as raw material for some artifacts (Harlow 1993). Feachem (1940) mentions that Guanaja once had "idols" made of greenstone. During excavations, he also found a greenstone amulet showing a bearded man. A greenstone bowl found at Wankybila (Strong 1934) is now in the NMNH collection (catalog number A373427-0). In the Culmí Valley, Begley (1999: 174) found 20 greenstone artifacts. They are not jadeite but soft stones with a Mohs scale of 3. The shapes include tubular beads, small figurine pendants, and unworked chunks. He noticed a decrease in size from Peri-

od V to Period VI beads, as Healy (1978a) had also noticed. Begley (1999: 175ff) further reports on a greenstone source at the Tulito River (a tributary of the Paulaya River), which might have served as a possible source for the artifacts. X-ray diffraction analysis of samples from this source has shown that it is detrital muscovite.

Some greenstone objects can currently be found in the Museum of the Fortaleza de Santa Barbara in Trujillo, which houses a small pre-Hispanic section. However, they are not associated with contextual data. Nevertheless, they also comprise long tubular beads and celt-shaped objects. A second, more extensive collection is housed at the "museum" Rufino Galán, a private collection in Trujillo. Although there are doubts as to the authenticity of some of the pieces, the quantity is impressive, and the forms correspond to those in archaeological publications. Begley, who worked in the Mosquitia for a long time, also visited this collection and estimated that the pieces came from the area around Sico (Begley 1999: 176). Christine Woda, who conducted studies in the Río Plátano biosphere reserve on behalf of the GIZ (German Society for International Cooperation) and in cooperation with the IHAH, reported similar finds. Greenstone objects were also found during site inspections as part of the Guadalupe Project. In Coraza Alta, located between Guadalupe and Trujillo and directly next to a river, many worked stones were found, which leads us to believe that stones were processed in situ. Some greenstone artifacts were also among them, which were possibly produced locally (see Figure 46). Along the course of the river, several rocks were found with elongated grooves. These are most likely the result of grinding processes associated with stone tool production.

All of these observations make it clear that we can define another greenstone lapidary tradition for northeast Honduras, at least for the Selin and Cocal periods (AD 300–1525). Predominant forms include beads with different shapes and sizes depending on the period, and celt-like pendants, which are strongly reminiscent of the axe gods in Costa Rica and suggest a great proximity to this tradition. Another similarity to Costa Rica is the intensive use of social jade. How do the finds from Guadalupe fit into this scenario? It is a small sample consisting of simple, undecorated beads. Iconography is absent, which makes it difficult to classify them. It can be stated, though, that the beads from Guadalupe correspond to the shape canon of the Cocal period due to their small size, which is in stark contrast to the long beads of the Selin period. Similar beads were found in Río Claro and

---

18 Under catalog number A448218-0, for example, two boxes with numerous greenstone artifacts can be found. These were dis-

covered in Colón by Doris Stone and Richard Davis. More objects can be viewed under the numbers A448230-0 and A448214-0.
19 No information is provided about the analytical methods used.

on the Bay Islands. However, what is astonishing is that our finds are real jade, while the other (analyzed) artifacts from the northeast are all made of softer stones, probably from local sources. The presence of jadeite indicates that the inhabitants had links to the Motagua Valley or some other distant source. The fact that this raw material is present in Guadalupe makes this site stand out from the others. Whether the objects were imported as finished products or were manufactured locally remains open. It is known that the raw material from Motagua was exchanged over long distances (Wagner 2012). The finds in the remainder of northeast Honduras prove that the region's inhabitants were quite familiar with greenstone processing techniques, while the finds from Coraza Alta provide an idea about the local greenstone processing tradition. Thus, the possibility that the raw material was imported from the Motagua Valley and that the objects were manufactured somewhere in our study area cannot be excluded. In the following, technological observations are covered.

Technological Observations. Jade is a very hard stone (6 to 7 on the Mohs scale). The hardness of the material makes it difficult to process. Tools made of equally hard or harder rock or other material, such as abrasive powders, must be used to work it. There are no technological studies available so far for finds in northeast Honduras, so we have to rely on studies from other areas. Digby (1972) and Easby (1968) mention some jade working techniques used by the Maya and in Costa Rica. Pecking could be used to produce a rough form, in which a directed blow from a rock hammer would chip material away, or a pointed stone would be used as a chisel. Another method is sawing using string saws (mainly in Costa Rica), a thin piece of wood, or slate. Together with a cutting agent like sand, the object was worked on until it was cut through. Usually, the object was cut from two sides. Incisions could be made with a pointed piece of obsidian (Wagner 2012). In order to drill holes, wooden drill bits were used. Together with sand or powdered obsidian, a hole could be created. "As the cutting powder worked free from the end of the drill and spread round the side of the bit, it tended to widen the diameter of the hole, producing a conical depression" (Digby 1972: 15). If this technique is applied from both sides, an hourglass-shaped depression is created. This technique was mainly used for small drill holes, for example, for beads. Healy (1978a) observed this technique on beads from Río Claro. That this technique was also used in Guadalupe can be seen especially well on bead PAG-12-Pi-1, which has the characteristic hour-glass-shaped depressions (Figure 187). A second method for creating holes was the use of a tubular drill, which consisted of a hollow reed, cane, or even a bird bone. "This was armed in the same way with an abrasive powder, and its action was to

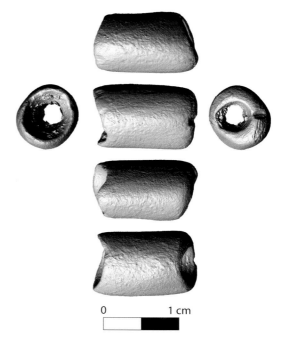

0   1 cm

187   3D Model of jade bead (PAG-12-Pi-1). The hour-glass-shaped perforations are especially visible here (P. Bayer).

cut a circular trench leaving a cylindrical core" (Digby 1972: 15). This method can only be used for objects larger than 1.5 cm in diameter. Finally, the objects were usually polished with a soft material such as wood or leather together with a fine abrasive powder. Interestingly, Easby (1968: 26) states that jade processing with these methods is not as time-consuming as one might imagine. In experiments, jade was sawed a quarter of an inch (0.6 cm) deep in one hour.

4.4.4 GROUND STONE

The excavations in Guadalupe have brought to light 116 ground stone tools of various sizes and raw materials. Stone tools can give us important information about activities that took place in Guadalupe. In contrast, their stylistic comparisons can provide us with information about connections to other sites or regions. In a first step, worked stones and those that show traces of use visible to the naked eye were separated from unworked stones. All worked stones were measured, described, and photographically documented. Some diagnostic artifact groups stand out and are described in detail below. The stones not described here only have light traces of processing, or their purpose cannot be defined (e.g., stones for burnishing, pounding, etc.). These are only briefly addressed.

Celts. Thirteen celts were found in Guadalupe (Figure 188). One object (PAG-46-Pi-1, Figure 188f) is relatively large, 11.9 cm long and 9 cm wide, and made of

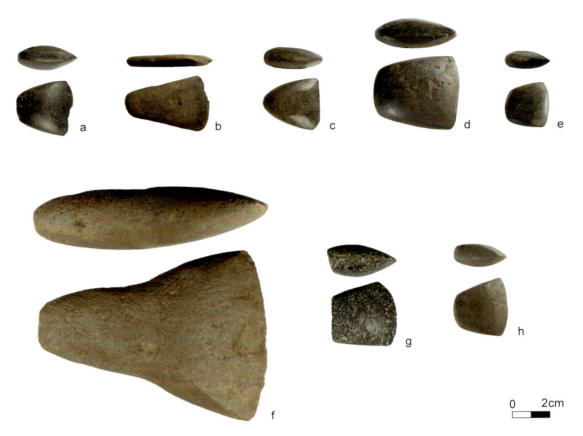

188   Celts (Scale 1:2). a PAG-8-Pi-1; b PAG-11-Pi-1; c PAG-15-Pi-2; d PAG-42-Pi-2; e PAG-44-Pi-1; f PAG-46-Pi-1; g PAG-81-Pi-1; h PAG-221-Pi-1.

rough stone. One can probably assume that it was used for chopping wood. The other celts are remarkably small. The smallest object measures only 2.3 x 2.2 cm (PAG-44-Pi-1, Figure 188e). The others do not exceed a length of 4.5 cm. Most of these "miniature celts" are made from a fine, hard stone and have been carefully polished to a shiny finish.

Stone celts are widespread throughout Central America and the Caribbean and have existed since the earliest periods. Celts are traditionally associated with sedentarism and agriculture. They are used to clear forests and to create space for planting (Snarskis 1981: 29). In the Olmec period, they already presented a symbolically significant form closely linked to the iconography of fertility. The Maya adopted this association, and there is even evidence that their stone stelae were also perceived as celts (Taube 2005). The celt seems to have been an important form in Costa Rica as well because many greenstone objects are found in the form of so-called axe gods, celt-shaped objects with zoomorphic heads. Similar objects were also found in our study area (see below). While such axe gods were not found in Guadalupe, the presence of many small celts is particularly striking. Objects with similar dimensions are known from Río Claro

(Healy 1978a: Fig. 14) and Roatán (Strong 1935: Plate 13, 16). Such miniature celts have been found in many different contexts throughout Central America in Mexico (Diehl 2004; Pollock et al. 1962), Guatemala (Aoyama et al. 2017; Inomata / Triadan 2015; Willey / Olsen 1972), Nicaragua (Bovallius 1886; Healy / Pohl 1980), Costa Rica (Lothrop 1963), and Panama (MacCurdy 1911; Lothrop 1950). The analysis of use-wear of objects from Ceibal, Guatemala, has shown that such small celts were used for wood carving (Aoyama et al. 2017). This analysis confirms the assumptions of previous authors (e.g., Healy / Pohl 1980: 283). Willey and Olsen (1972: 132), on the other hand, assume they are cutting tools. Besides a practical use as a tool, miniature celts were found in ritual contexts (Aoyama et al. 2017), as were the objects from Roatán, which were found together with other objects in the votive cache in Dixon Site. Strong (1935: 65) states that he was not able to identify any traces of use on the objects.

Bark Beaters. Two bark beater fragments were found (Figure 189). They are oval stones with flattened upper and lower surfaces. They have an encircling groove that wraps around the side, allowing for the attachment of a handle. The underside is carved with parallel striations.

Such artifacts are referred to as bark beakers, which were used to pound tree bark to produce barkcloth. This type of bark beater is widespread throughout Central America and can be found from Mexico to Colombia (Strong 1948b: 129f). In northeast Honduras, such artifacts have been found at several sites, including the Guaimoreto Lagoon (Stone 1941: Fig. 41), Selin Farm (Healy 1978b: Fig. 11), Marble Hill on Guanaja, and Indian Hill on Barbareta (Strong 1935: Plate 16). Griffin et al. (2009: 64f) mention that until the 1960s, the Pesh used the bark of the *tunu* tree to make cloths. These cloths were also used in some ceremonies. Today, this tree is no longer found in the territory inhabited by the Pesh, and barkcloth is no longer produced.

Metates. Seven metate fragments were found (Figure 190, 191). Six fragments belong to large, flat, and heavy stones with a clearly concave surface. Two of the fragments have a rather high rim. Such stones were used as grinding stones on which food was ground with hand-stones (manos). The seventh fragment (PAG-5-Pi-6, Figure 190a) is curved and slightly grooved on both sides. It once represented the tongue of a reptile's head that would have adorned a three-legged metate (Figure 192; see also Stone 1941: Fig. 34). Such elaborately carved metates are typical for Southern Central America, and Ursula Jones (1992) has convincingly demonstrated that their existence is limited to this culture area. Thus, it can be considered a typical cultural feature. Therefore, the presence of this artifact in Guadalupe can be interpreted as an important indication of connections to the south. Several animal-headed metates are known from northeast Honduras, but they are primarily found in museum collections without a clear context. They are especially known in the Mosquitia, where they reach a height of 1.50 m and are sometimes interpreted as seats. During excavations in the so-called Ciudad del Jaguar, a deposit with several dozen metates was unearthed (Fisher et al. 2016: 22f).

Manos. In Guadalupe, 29 manos (handstones) were found (Figure 193). Nine of them are complete, while the others are fragments. Most of the objects are oval-shaped and have smooth, worn surfaces. The length of the complete objects ranges from 8.3 to 18.5 cm. Manos were used for grinding food (e.g., maize, grains, etc.) on an underlying metate. The presence of a rather large number of manos and metates in Guadalupe is an indication that agricultural products played an important role in subsistence.

Pestles. Two pestles were among the stones (Figure 194). They have a length of 5.5 cm and 4.2 cm and have a diagnostic cylindrical shape thickened at the lower end. Stone (1941: Fig. 41, p. 51f) reports the discovery of such a pestle near Guaimoreto Lagoon and assumes they were used for polishing. However, I instead assume that they were used for crushing or grinding food or oth-

189   Bark beater (Scale 1:2). a PAG-31-Pi-4; b PAG-53-Pi-1.

190   Metates. a PAG-5-Pi-6; b PAG-9-Pi-4.

er substances. Dennett (2007: Fig. 5.6) shows another specimen from the Mosquitia and refers to the similarity with elaborate finds from the Atlantic watershed in Costa Rica. In the Caribbean, there are also elaborate pestles similar to those in Costa Rica (e.g., NMNH catalog numbers A231421-0 and A231419-0).

Others. The remaining stones include gravels that may have been used for smoothing, stones used for pounding, and those that cannot be clearly assigned a specific use. Several pumice stones were also found. Some of them have semicircular grooves that are a few millimeters wide (Figure 195). These grooves are likely the results of the stone being used to manufacture a tool, e.g., for burnishing or grinding. Judging by the size of the grooves, they could have been grinding stones for arrow shafts or other thin wooden sticks. A second possibility is that the grooves did not result from tool man-

191   Metates (Scale 1:3). a PAG-17-Pi-2; b PAG-29-Pi-2; c PAG-29-Pi-3; d PAG-120-Pi-1.

192   Three-legged metate with reptile head in the Museo de Antropología e Historia de San Pedro Sula (F. Fecher).

ufacture but were intentionally introduced to fulfill a specific function. It is conceivable, for example, that the grooves served to fix a cord and the stone was used as a float for fishing nets. Several white quartz stones were also among the finds. Today this stone is still used in the region to grate manioc. For this purpose, several small stones were embedded in a wooden board and used as a grater. Whether the quartz in Guadalupe also served this purpose remains uncertain. Finally, two small crystals were found. They measure 10 x 1 mm and 13 x 3 mm. From other contexts, it is known that such crystals were used to create small perforations.

193   Manos (Scale 1:3). a PAG-9-Pi-3; b PAG-16-Pi-1; c PAG-16-Pi-3; d PAG-46-Pi-10; e PAG-53-Pi-2; f PAG-53-Pi-6.

194   Pestles (Scale 1:2). a PAG-5-Pi-5; b PAG-23-Pi-6.

195   Ground stone artifacts (Scale 1:2). a PAG-33-Pi-4; b PAG-40-Pi-2; c PAG-45-Pi-1; d PAG-46-Pi-8.

4.4.5 METAL

Only a few metal objects from archaeological contexts in northeast Honduras are known, so the discovery of metal objects in Guadalupe is of great importance. Metal objects are of particular interest since they became increasingly popular during Period VI and were exchanged over long distances. The chemical composition and stylistic comparisons provide hints about their origin. Three metal objects were found in Guadalupe: a needle and two bells (Figure 196). One of the bells and the needle were analyzed under Prof. Dr. Andreas Hauptmann (German Mining Museum Bochum). Both objects were examined with a scanning electron microscope for their chemical composition. This is done by directing an electron beam onto the object to be examined. This electron beam causes electrons to be emitted by atoms, so-called secondary electrons. These are detected and used to create an image of the object. The emission of secondary electrons also produces X-rays when the atoms compensate for the lost electrons and repair themselves. These X-rays are characteristic of the respective types of atoms present in the sample. By measuring the characteristic X-rays, the chemical composition of the sample can therefore be determined. The whole process is non-destructive.

The needle (PAG-11-Me-1001, Figure 196a) measures 123 x 3 x 3 mm. It has a drop-shaped eyelet at one end, while the other end is pointed. The surface is uneven and rough due to corrosion. The examination with the scanning electron microscope showed that the needle is made of tin bronze, an alloy of copper and tin. The needle was found in the upper level of the ceramic layer of Unit 1 and was associated with ceramic fragments.

The first bell (PAG-8-Me-1000, Figure 196b) measures 8 x 15 x 9 mm. The bell is egg-shaped and hollow. The body narrows towards the bottom and is divided into two wings by a slit. One wing is broken off from the broadest point downwards. The clapper was not preserved, and the upper end is marked by a small platform on which a loop is attached. The loop seems to be fixed to the platform with a thin wire. The object is heavily corroded, which is evident from the greyish-green color and the rough surface. The object is very fragile. The analysis with the scanning electron microscope showed that the bell is made of copper. No traces of gold were found. The object is from the upper part of the ceramic layer from Unit 2. A particular context was not noted.

The second bell (PAG-42-Me-1, Figure 196c) measures 10 x 17 x 9 mm. It is very similar in shape to the other bell. It also has a ring platform, and the loop is fixed with an additional wire. However, the body is somewhat rounder. Both wings are preserved, although the widest part of the wings is quite porous. The bell is a surface find, so there is no more detailed information

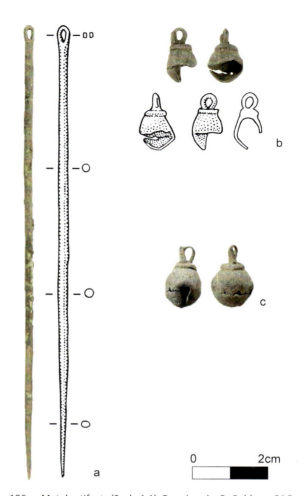

196   Metal artifacts (Scale 1:1). Drawings by B. Gubler. a PAG-11-Me-1001; b PAG-8-Me-1000; c PAG-42-Me-1.

about its context. Thus, no analyses were carried out. However, due to the surfaces' remarkable similarity, the bell is also likely made of copper.

Geographical assignment of the objects is difficult. For this purpose, we look to the various metal production centers in Central America. According to the current understanding, the origins of metal processing can be traced to the central Andes. Hammered gold beads were produced there around 2000 BC at the latest. The melting process was developed around 1000 BC. Apparently, knowledge of metal processing was brought from Peru to Colombia, where the first metal artifacts date to around 400 BC (Jones / Kerr 1985: 11). This is also where the lost-wax technique was developed around 400 BC. From Colombia, this technique reached Panama and Costa Rica around AD 500, probably by sea. The earliest objects were found along the Caribbean coast. A long tradition of metalworking developed here, and masterful objects were produced. Sitio Conte in Panama is particularly emblematic of gold processing in Southern Central America. Beginning in the 5th century AD, burials were furnished with abundant grave goods (Lothrop 1937). A special feature of the metal objects from Southern Central America is the use of a copper-gold alloy, also called *tumbaga*. The alloy has a lower melting point than gold but is harder (Bray 1985: 77). Most of the objects are looted and lack an archaeological context. According to Quilter (2003: 1), "the number of gold objects scientifically excavated from the region (excluding Sitio Conte) could easily fit on a standard dining room table." The metal objects in Southern Central America have mainly been analyzed with regard to their function and meaning, whereas only a few studies deal with their production (Durando 1959; Lothrop 1963; Stone / Balser 1958). One exception is Patricia Fernandez Esquivel's (2010) work, which examines 200 objects from Costa Rica and Panama and 80 possible raw materials sources in Nicaragua, Costa Rica, and Panama. She uses X-ray fluorescence spectroscopy (XRF) and a scanning electron microscope with energy dispersive spectroscopy (SEM-EDX). With these methods, she obtains information about alloys, technology, and geochemistry.

A second production zone is known in West Mexico. However, the metalworking tradition here did not begin until around AD 800. Dorothy Hosler (1997) supports the theory that metal objects from Southern Central America or Colombia were initially traded to West Mexico by sea until the knowledge of processing finally arrived, and objects began to be produced locally. The Mixtecs, for example, are particularly well-known for their high-quality gold processing (Jones / Kerr 1985: 11). As in the whole of Central America, metal was used here mainly to make jewelry and ritual objects, while only a few tools were crafted. Particularly common objects include bells and axes, both of which were used as currency during the Postclassic period (Hosler 1997). Another typical feature of objects from West Mexico is the use of copper or tin bronzes (copper-tin or copper-arsenic bronzes) (Hosler 2013: 237). The composition of finds was investigated early on, mainly by microscopic studies (e.g., Lothrop 1952; McLeod 1945; Root 1953). The work carried out by Dorothy Hosler and Andrew Macfarlane (Hosler 1999; Hosler / Macfarlane 1996) represents an outstanding contribution. This is a lead isotope analysis in which 15 sources in West Mexico, Oaxaca, and Veracruz and 171 artifacts from nine sites in Mexico and Belize were sampled. The study was able to show that for many of the artifacts examined, even those from Belize, the raw material came from West Mexico.

For a long time, it was believed that no metal objects were processed in the Maya Lowlands. However, recent research has shown that metal objects were also cast in some Postclassic Maya centers, such as Mayapán or Lamanai, although it is possible that the material was recycled (Hosler 2013; Simmons / Shugar 2013a).

In the Caribbean islands, both ethnohistorical and archaeological sources suggest that metal smelting knowledge was not present. Gold was processed locally but only by hammering. Nevertheless, numerous *guanín* objects were found, which played an important role as status symbols for chiefs. *Guanín* is a copper-gold alloy known in Southern Central America as *tumbaga*. These objects most likely found their way to the islands from the mainland but were not produced there (Valcárcel Rojas / Martinón-Torres 2013). Again, there are only a few objects with a secure archaeological context. A list of these objects, including the respective studies carried out, can be found in Valcárcel Rojas and Martinón Torres (2013).

Some researchers assume that there was a metal production zone somewhere in southeastern Mesoamerica. Lothrop (1952: 22) already suspected that there must have been a metal production zone on the Atlantic coast of Guatemala or Honduras[20]. "Not long before the arrival of the Spaniards, however, a local copper-casting industry had been established on both sides of the Atlantic frontier between Guatemala and Honduras, extending to the Bay Islands." Abbas Shatto (1998: 27) and Hosler (2003) also consider it likely that metal was processed in Honduras. Simmons and Shugar (2013b: Fig. 1.1) define a southeastern Mesoamerican metalworking zone as encompassing eastern Guatemala and western Honduras. According to Hosler (1999: 14), metal finds from southern Mesoamerica are stylistically more similar to those from Southern Central America. This causes her to believe that the knowledge of metal production in southern Mesoamerica may have been brought there by a land route from Southern Central America.

A short summary of the evidence for such a production zone is given here. Ethnohistorical reports contain several references to the production of metal in Honduras. There are reports that metal objects were traded from Honduras to Yucatán. Furthermore, Honduras was known as "the land of gold, feathers and cacao" (Roys 1943: 55). There are also indications of metal production in northeast Honduras. There are reports of the presence of gold mines in the vicinity of Trujillo (Lara Pinto 1980: 100). Metal bells and hatchets, possibly made of *tumbaga*, were delivered by the indigenous people as tribute to the Spanish, again indicating that there was pre-Hispanic local production (Lara Pinto 1991: 228). Columbus

---

20 Lothrop does not clearly state on which observations he bases this assumption. One criterion, however, is the presence of numerous metal artifacts in this region.

reports copper ore on Guanaja (Lothrop 1952: 25) and mentions the remains of metal processing on the island. In the trading canoe mentioned by Ferdinand (see chapter 2.5.4), metal axes and utensils for metal processing were also observed (Lara Pinto 1980: Table 1). Although ethnohistorical sources must generally be treated with caution (especially when it comes to precious metals), there are also a few references to metals in the archaeological context. However, these references are limited to western Honduras in the region around Naco. In the Quimistán Cave, a deposit of more than 800 bells was found during excavations under Blackiston (1910). They have various shapes and designs. It is not clear from the text if the bells were analyzed for their chemical composition, but Blackiston states: "The copper of which these bells are constructed contains gold in small quantities" (Blackiston 1910: 539). Besides the bells, native copper was also found, as well as strips of beaten copper. Together with the enormous number of objects, these are strong indications of local production. Copper mines are known in the cave's vicinity (Blackiston 1910: 539; Urban et al. 2013). This assumption is again supported by Cristobal de Olíd's ethnohistorical report, in which he states that the indigenous people of Naco offered him copper when he arrived (Lara Pinto 1980: 56). During excavations at El Coyote, also located near Naco, signs of local copper production were found in 2002. These include copper ores, slag, and remains of possible furnaces in the form of vitrified adobe (Urban et al. 2013). In addition, different production steps were identified, such as the crushing of ores and the processing of slag. The actual melting of copper and the production of copper artifacts could not be proven. No copper artifacts were found either. Furthermore, the dating of the features is problematic. While parts of the settlement date to the Classic period, many radiocarbon dates also yielded a historical date, and it is not clear with which period the copper production is associated.

Can our finds be assigned to one of these production zones? If the needle were to be assigned, both the chemical composition and the style would most likely point to an origin in West Mexico. Needles belong to a class of objects that is frequently found in this region. Their design strongly resembles the so-called loop-eye needles, where a tab of metal is formed into a loop and fixed to the needle shaft (Hosler 1988: 200f). These needles were often made of copper-arsenic or copper-tin bronzes, which are more flexible than pure copper. Whether the needle was actually produced in West Mexico and how it found its way to Guadalupe must be examined by further studies. While the needle points toward connections to West Mexico, it is difficult to classify the bells. Throughout Central America, metal bells were very popular during Period VI. They were regarded as a status symbol and were attached to clothing for dances, festivals, and rituals to produce a sound. As Hosler (2010: 455) states,

> "we know from ethnographic and sixteenth-century ethnohistoric data that bell sounds were considered sacred and creative. They protected their wearer from malevolent influences; they replicated the sounds of thunder and rain, and the rattle of the rattlesnake; and they promoted human and agricultural fertility."

Bells were also used as means of payment (Simmons / Shugar 2013b: 7). From a stylistic point of view, the bells from Guadalupe are very similar to some bells that Strong (1935: Plate 9) found on the Bay Islands in the Dixon Site votive cache. However, the origin of these bells is also uncertain. Considering a larger geographic area, they resemble Lothrop's (1952: 90) D3 type (pear-shaped bell with platform). Lothrop mentions Arizona, West Mexico, Guatemala, and the Bay Islands as regions where this type occurs. Copper as a raw material does not reliably narrow down possible regions of origin either. Although copper was a frequently used raw material for the production of bells in West Mexico, it was also used in Southern Central America even though *tumbaga* was predominant here. A larger base of data would be necessary to make a reliable statement. It must also be considered that, concerning the bells, there is the possibility of a local or at least nearby production site.

4.4.6 VERTEBRATE FAUNA

Faunal remains were present in Guadalupe in very large numbers. They can provide us with important information about the subsistence strategies of the inhabitants and possible indications of food exchange networks. The analysis of the vertebrate fauna was carried out by Dr. Nayeli Jiménez Cano (Universidad Autónoma de Yucatán). However, only preliminary studies could be realized. A detailed analysis was planned for the 2020 field campaign but had to be canceled prematurely due to the COVID-19 pandemic. The preliminary study aimed to determine the taxonomic composition of a sample to draw conclusions about the economy and culture of the inhabitants of Guadalupe.

Investigations were carried out on Inv. 7 and 52 from excavation Unit 1. The sample consisted of 755 objects. Before identification, the material was carefully cleaned with soft brushes. The identification of the material was performed with the help of manuals and specific literature (Gilbert 2003; Gilbert / Martin / Savage 1996; Hillson 1999; Olsen 1964, 1968, 1982) and online resources (BoneID). At this point, it must be mentioned that, during the field campaign, no reference collection was available, which would have certainly helped to determine the bones more precisely. The identification of the objects was performed according to the Number of Identified Specimens (NISP). In addition, observations were made on the taphonomy and traces of processing.

Taxonomy. The analyzed bones were generally in a relatively good state of preservation, which facilitated their identification. Among the bones, the most abundant group of animals is fish with 63.31% (NISP = 478), followed by mammals with 22.91% (NISP = 173). Reptiles with 13.25% of the total sample (NISP = 100) were a minority group, and birds with only 0.53% (NISP = 4) were the least represented group in the zooarchaeological complex (Table 3).

Taxon	Common Name	NISP	%NISP
Squaliformes	Shark	3	0.40
Rajiformes	Ray/Skate	2	0.26
cf. *Megalops atlanticus*	Tarpon	8	1.06
Centropomus sp.	Snook	11	1.46
Carangidae	Ray-finned fish	18	2.38
cf. Sparidae	Sea breams	2	0.26
Teleostomi	Bony fish	434	57.48
Total Fish		**478**	**63.31**
cf. Cheloniidae	Sea turtle	84	11.13
Chelonidae	Sea turtle	1	0.13
Testudines	Turtle	4	0.53
Sauria cf. Iguanidae	Iguana	5	0.66
Reptilia	Reptiles	6	0.79
Total Reptiles		**100**	**13.25**
Aves	Birds	4	0.53
Total Birds		**4**	**0.53**
Dasypus novemcinctus	Armadillo	29	3.84
Rodentia cf. Agutidae	Agouti	6	0.79
Mammalia cf. Rumiante	Ruminant	1	0.13
cf. Phocidae?	Seal	1	0.13
cf. Marine mammal	Marine mammal	1	0.13
Mammalia	Mammal	135	17.88
Total Mammals		**173**	**22.91**
TOTAL		**755**	**100**

Table 3   Taxonomic list of vertebrate fauna from Unit 1 (Inv. 7 and Inv. 52) (N. Jiménez).

The ichthyofauna is notable for the presence of indeterminate Osteichthyes (bony fish). Within this group, vertebrae are notably abundant comprising 51.72% of the bony fish sample. The sample is also rich in cranium elements (27.46%) and fin elements, especially spines (20.82%). This skeletal frequency pattern corresponds to the local consumption of the fish in the settlement, as the representativeness indicates the presence of complete specimens. On the other hand, the presence of skeletal elements with hyperostosis, such as the radii of the fin and the cleithrum bones, should be noted (Figure 197). This characteristic also indicates the presence of large animals in the sample since hyperostosis is usually associated with larger specimens. The taphonomic marks in this group are restricted to thermal affectation marks, including burning and calcination.

Mammals were the second most abundant group in the site's sample. Armadillos stand out within the sample, represented mainly by dermal plates (Figure 198). Other taxa that make up the Guadalupe mammal sample include large rodents such as agoutis, ruminants, marine mammals, and possibly the presence of a tropical seal represented by a premolar. The reptiles from the Unit 1 context are mostly sea turtles (11.13%) (Figure 199). This group is composed of carapace fragments and long bones. Other reptiles present in the sample are iguanas and indeterminate turtles. Within the studied sample, birds represent a marginal taxonomic group since only four remains were recorded (0.53 % NISP). The site's sedimentological characteristics may have affected their representativeness in terms of taphonomy since the birds have fragile skeletons. However, in Selin Farm, the only place from which subsistence studies are available for comparison, few birds were found, even though the conservation conditions were very good (Healy 1983). This suggests that birds did not play an important role in subsistence.

Artifacts. Bone artifacts were found in different inventory numbers. All originate from the ceramic layer. They include bones with incisions, teeth with perforations, and a bone figurine (Figure 200). These objects are briefly presented here. An elongated, pointed bone fragment from Inv. 10 has ornamental incisions (Figure 200e). Another fragment from Inv. 10 also has parallel incisions with differing intervals. A part of the object is broken off, which is why not all incisions are preserved. A particularly interesting find is an anthropomorphic figurine made of bone. It measures 3 x 6.2 x 1.9 cm and was worked from a single piece but is broken into several fragments. The material is very fragile, which is why we were not able to draw it. Instead, a high-resolution 3D scan of the fragments was made. The figurine could thus be virtually reassembled (Figure 200g). It depicts a person with a rather triangular head. The nose is very prominent, whereas shallow carvings indicate the eyes and mouth. The upper part of the body has elaborate arms resting on the body. The fingers are also indicated. The

197   Hyperostosis of cleithrum bones of bony fish (N. Jiménez).

198   Armadillo dermal plates (D. novemcinctus) (N. Jiménez).

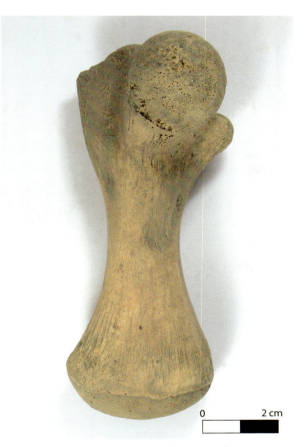

199   Sea turtle (Cheloniidae) femur (N. Jiménez).

right arm is broken off. The legs have several convexities. This figurine is a unique find as it presents the first bone figurine found in our research area. Apart from these artifacts, four teeth with perforations were found (Figure 200a-d). Two of the teeth are probably from marine mammals. The perforations are located in the root and suggest that the objects were used as pendants.

Although the studied sample is small, some observations can be made about the exploitation and consumption of fauna in Guadalupe. It is a very taxonomically diverse sample. It is important to highlight the use of nearby sites for the capture of fauna resources since the vast majority of the animals identified are coastal animals. Among them, it seems that fish played an important role in the diet of the site's ancient inhabitants. It is also interesting to mention the large size of some

fish and turtles present in the zooarchaeological material. It is also interesting to observe the use of animal remains as raw material to make artifacts. This is evident in the teeth, as premolars and canines were perfo-

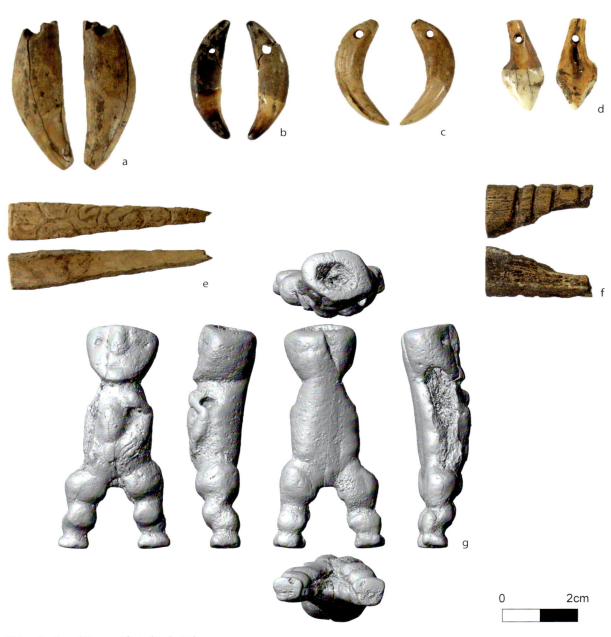

200   Teeth and Bone artifacts (Scale 1:1).

rated and polished with a clear intention of anthropic use. In general terms, the archaeological fauna of Inv. 7 and 52 of Unit 1 of Guadalupe offers an outline of the rich fauna that its ancient inhabitants used during the Cocal phase. Without a doubt, future zooarchaeological studies at the site will be beneficial to deepen our understanding of exploitation, consumption, and use of these resources.

4.4.7 Invertebrate Fauna

Like animal bones, an analysis of mollusks can provide information on subsistence and production strategies. Since certain mollusks only occur in specific habitats, they also give us an idea about the parts of the environment exploited by the inhabitants of Guadalupe. The analysis of the mollusks was carried out by Dr. Nayeli Jiménez Cano (Universidad Autónoma de Yucatán) and Annkatrin Benz (University of Bonn). Taxonomic and taphonomic studies were carried out, and anthropic marks were analyzed. As a material basis, the mollusks from Units 1 and 2 were analyzed, whereby individual objects from Unit 3 were included for comparison purposes. In Units 1 and 2, a total of 4309 mollusk fragments were identified.

Prior to the analysis, the material was carefully cleaned in a dry state. This was followed by taxonomic identification, carried out according to the Number of Identified Specimens (NISP). Manuals and catalogs were consulted in order to identify the mollusks. These included Abbott (1974), Abbott / Morris (1995), Andrews (1969), Elvir / Goodwin (2018), García Cubas / Reguero (2004), García Cubas / Reguero (2007), Gutiérrrez Castillo (2015), Humfrey (1975), Keen (1971), López / Urcuyo (2008), López / Urcuyo (2009), Martens (1890-1901), Hicks / Tunnell / Withers (2010) and Vokes / Vokes (1983), as well as the World Register of Marine Species website (World Register of Marine Species). In order to detect possible changes in use, the number of species identified was recorded for each inventory number. Traces of use were studied with a digital microscope (DinoLite AM7815MZT).

Taphonomy. The material is not well preserved in general. On the one hand, this is due to natural, taphonomic processes that have transformed the material into a floury, porous state. This is particularly true for the genus *Crassostrea*, which, due to the taphonomic processes characteristic of these taxa, showed a more pronounced state of erosion, during which calcium carbonate was often exposed. On the other hand, the condition is due to thermic processes—in some cases, direct contact with fire—that affect the mollusks' internal structure. This condition can be observed, in particular in bivalve mollusks coming from the ceramic layer, where a certain percentage of each inventory number has these characteristics. Further studies are needed to identify the cause of these thermic alterations. Jiménez Cano assumes that the shells were exposed to fire for an extended period: possibly for food production, after consumption, such as in connection with waste incineration, the extraction of lime, or termination rituals.

Taxonomy and Habitat. The shell remains of Units 1 and 2 are assigned to 37 different families belonging to both bivalves and gastropods. By far, the most common are bivalves of the family Ostreidae (especially *Crassostrea* sp.), also known as oysters. Objects of the families Glycimeridae (*Glycymeris* sp.), Strombidae (*Strombus pugilis*), Turbinellidae (*Turbinella angulata*), Neritidae (*Nereina* cf. *Punctulata*), and Veneridae are also common. The exact identification can be found in Table 4 and Table 5. The mollusks come from different habitats, which can be distinguished by their salinity. Freshwater (rivers), brackish water (lagoons), and saltwater (sea) are represented. Freshwater mollusks only comprise a small portion (2.7%) of those from Unit 2, whereas 14.8% come from the sea and 82.5% from brackish water.

Class	Family	Taxon	5	7	9	11	14	16	43	47	52	58	62	70	77	82	116	129	130	NISP
IDENTIFICATION			**INVENTORY NO.**																	
Bivalvia	ARCIDAE	Anadara brasiliana			3	7	2													12
		Anadara ovalis				5	2													7
		Anadara secticostata			1	1	1	1												4
		Anadara sp.			2							1								3
		Arca zebra				3														3
	CARDIIDAE	Cardiidae indet.			2	1														3
		Acrosterigma magnum						4	2	1	2									9
		Trachycardium sp.						1												1
	CHAMIDAE	Chamidae indet.				1		1						1						3
		Arcinella sp.											1							1
	GLYCYMERIDIDAE	Glycymeris sp.			3							11								14
		Glycymeris undata	1	2	10	28	9	9	2	14	16	7	13	2						113
	LUCINIDAE	Lucinidae indet.											4							4
		Codakia orbicularis			3	5	9	5		2	3	2								29
		Phacoides pectinatus					1													1
	MACTRIDAE	Mactrellona alata					1													1
	OSTREIDAE	Crassostrea sp.	5	25	34	53	17	2												136
	PTERIIDAE	Isognomon sp.								2										2
	VENERIDAE	Chionopsis sp.			2	4	3	1	3	1	5		1	1						21
		Hysteroconcha lupanaria			1															1
		Megapitaria maculata			7	3		8												18
		Tivela mactroides			5	10	2	2												19
	indet.	indet.			1	1	4	1	3		1		1	3	1	1				17
Gastropoda	AMPULLARIIDAE	Pomacea flagalatta						1												1
	CASSIDAE	Cassidea indet.																1		1
		Cypraecassis testiculus		1	1	3	1	1												7
		Semicassis granulata	1		1		1	5			1	2								11
	CONIDAE	Conus sp.			2	1		1												4
	MELONGENIDAE	Melongena cf. melongena		2	7	3	1	8	11											32
	MURICIDAE	Siratus sp.					1	1												2
	NATICIDAE	Polinices cf. hepaticus			1															1
		Polinices sp.	1			1								1						3
	NERITIDAE	Neritina usnea			1	1														2
		Nereina punctulata			8	6	6	4	3	3	3	2	1	2						38
	OLIVIDAE	Oliva sp.				2														2
	PACHYCHILIDAE	Pachychilidae indet.				2														2
	STROMBIDAE	Strombidae indet.						1												1
		Lobatus costatus	1																	1
		Lobatus gigas						5												5
		Lobatus raninus	1		1			2	2		2									8
		Lobatus sp.																		0
		Strombus pugilis	16	4	3		7	18	6		1		1							56
	TEGULIDAE	Cittarium pica			4		2	1	5								1			13
	TURBINELLIDAE	Turbinella angulata		2	4	6	5	4	3	15	9		1							49
		Vasum muricatum		2						1										3
	indet.	indet.	5	19	7	2	2	7	3	1			1							47
Polyplacophora	indet.	indet.						2												2
Anthozoa	indet.	indet.			3		7	8	2	7	4	4	3	4	2		1		1	46
TOTAL			31	61	114	159	83	99	47	45	57	18	30	10	1	1	1	1	1	759

Table 4 Taxonomic list of molluscs from Unit 1 (A. Benz).

IDENTIFICATION			INVENTORY NO.														NISP
Class	Family	Taxon	6	8	10	12	13	15	17	44	46	53	71	89	90	139	
B i v a l v a	ARCIDAE	*Anadara* cf. *brasiliana*					3		2								5
		Anadara notabilis					2										2
		Anadara ovalis			1		2										3
		Anadara secticostata						1	1								2
		Anadara sp.				1			1								2
		Andara brasiliana				2											2
		Arca zebra						3									3
		Arcidae indet.			2												2
		cf. *Anadara*			1				6								7
		cf. *Anadara brasiliana*						5									5
		cf. *Anadara ovalis*													1		1
	CARDIIDAE	Cardiidae indet.	1	3	1	10			5								20
		cf. *Dinocardum*		2													2
		Laevicardium serratum						1									1
		Trachycardium cf. *isocardia*			1			1									2
	CHAMIDAE	Chamidae indet.						1	2								3
	GLYCIMERIDIDAE	*Glycymeris* sp.		6	24	16	4	28	17	7	5	2			4		113
	ISOGNOMONIDAE	*Isognomon* sp.		3	15	5	2										25
	LUCINIDAE	cf. *Codakia orbicularis*				1											1
		Codakia cf. *orbicularis*			2												2
		Codakia orbicularis						1	8	2							11
		Codakia sp.		12													12
		Lucinidae indet.						1									1
		Phacoides sp.					2										2
	OSTREIDAE	*Crassostrea* sp.	2	28	421	711	76	585	38	77	33	1					1972
		Ostreidae indet.	67	1	510												578
	PSAMMOBIIDAE	Psammobiidae indet.			1												1
	SOLENIDAE	Solenidae indet.				1											1
	SPONDYLIDAE	*Spondylus* sp.			1	2			1								4
	TELLINIDAE	*Tellina* sp.			2												2
	VENERIDAE	cf. *Anomalocardia*				1											1
		cf. *Chionopsis*			1	15		4	7						1		28
		cf. *Megapitaria*			11												11
		cf. *Megapitaria maculata*		3		21		8									32
		Donax sp.				1	1		7								9
		Megapitaria maculata					2										2
		Prototheca indet.					1										1
		Tivela sp.				5		12	3								20
		Veneridae indet.	2	7	16							2					27
	indet.	indet.				6		11	32	10					5		64
G a s t r o p o d a	BULIMULIDAE	Bulimulidae indet.			2												2
	CASSIDAE	Cassidae indet.						2		1							3
		cf. *Semicassis granulata*			1	3			1								5
		Semicassis granulata				1											1
	CONIDAE	Conidae indet.		5		1			2								8
	CYPRAEIDAE	cf. *Macrocypraea zebra*				1											1
		Cypraeidae indet.		1					3								4
	DECAPODA	*Decapoda*			1												1
	FASCIOLARIIDAE	*Fasciolaria* sp.							2								2
		Fasciolariidae indet.								8							8
		Triplofusus giganteus										3					3
	FISSURELLIDAE	Fissurellidae indet.			2			1									3
	GASTROPODA	*Gastropoda marino*						1			14			2		2	19
	MARGARITIDAE	Margaritidae indet.			1												1
	MELONGENIDAE	cf. *Melongena melongena*		18													18
		Melongena melongena			14	13		8	12	3	2						52
		Melongena sp.						1			4						5
	MOLLUCA	Mollusca indet	46	25		3											74
	MURICIDAE	Muricidae indet.						1									1
	NATICIDAE	Naticidae indet.		1				1									2
		cf. *Naticarius canrena*						1									1
	NERITIDAE	*Nereina* cf. *punctulata*			14	9		11	5			1					40
		Nereina punctulata						1									1
		Nerita cf. *usnea*			1												1
		Neritidae indet.			3			3									6
	NOETIIDAE	Noetiidae indet.	1														1
	OLIVIDAE	*Oliva* sp.					2										2
		Olividae indet.						3									3
	PACHYCHILIDAE	*Pachychilus* sp.		1				1	1								3
	STROMBIDAE	cf. *Lobatus gigas*		12	1							1					14
		cf. *Strombus pugilis*		13													13
		Lobatus costatus						1				3					4
		Lobatus gigas						4									4
		Lobatus raninus				1				1	2						4
		Lobatus sp.							1								1
		Strombidae (grande)						1									1
		Strombidae indet.	24	22	4	1		16	7	1	3						78
		Strombus cf. *pugilis*			2							1			1		4
		Strombus cf. *pugilis?*	20														20
		Strombus pugilis			30	5	6	9	4	8	2						64
		Strombus sp.				3											3
	TEGULIDAE	cf. *Cittarium*		1													1
		Cittarium pica			1	5	2	1									9
	TURBINELLIDAE	*Turbinella angulata*			18		4	2	7		9	26	3		1		70
		Turbinellidae indet.		1													1
		Vasum muricatum			3			1									4
	TURRITELLIDAE	Turritellidae indet.						2									2
	indet.	indet.	14	45	24	1	2	5		32		38	9				170
TOTAL			163	166	1106	845	115	747	158	116	78	36	3	2	13	2	3550

Table 5   Taxonomic list of molluscs from Unit 2 (N. Jiménez).

The abundance of bivalve mollusks living in brackish water, such as Ostreidae (*Crassostrea* sp.) and Isognomidae (*Isognomon* sp.), or Gastropoda, such as *Melongena* sp., exemplifies the intensive use of this habitat. In general, lagoons and mangrove forests are a habitat for many animals and have a great diversity of species. The closest large lagoon in our study area is the Guaimoreto Lagoon east of Trujillo, in which several nearby archaeological sites have been identified (Healy 1978b). The mollusks may have been brought to Guadalupe from the lagoon. It is also conceivable that, in pre-Hispanic times, the mangrove forests along the coast and especially in the estuary of the rivers that drain into the Atlantic Ocean were more extensive. This hypothesis would have to be investigated by further research.

While the mollusks from the sea represent a smaller proportion, they have a greater diversity of species. Most of them come from shallow marine zones. For example, conches like *Semicassis granulata* or *Cittarium sp.* and bivalves like *Donax sp.* can be found on the beach. Conches such as *Fasciolaria, Triplofusus giganteus, Turbinella angulata,* and *Vasum muricatum* and bivalves such as *Anadara, Codakia, Dinocardum, Megapitaria,* and *Glycymeris* live in shallow water. Among the species that inhabit moderate depths, conches such as *Strombus pugilis* and *Lobatus gigas* are identified. Species that inhabit greater depths are shells (*Laevicardium*) and small snails (*Neritina* cf. *usnea* and *Oliva* sp.). Four shells of the genus *Spondylus* are also observed that cannot be identified at the species level due to their poor preservation and the lack of reference material. Spondylus mollusks usually live at depths of up to 60 meters and are firmly attached to a substrate, which is why they can only be extracted using specific diving techniques. Nevertheless, Jiménez Cano mentions that these species can also be found on the beach during special climatic events, at least on the Pacific coast.

Consumption and Use. The mollusks found in Guadalupe played an important role in the diet of its inhabitants. The big conches like *Lobatus gigas* or *Turbinella angulata* have an especially high nutritional value and protein content. Up to 1 kg of meat can be obtained from four conches. They are present in almost all layers of the excavation and seem to have been an important foodstuff during the entire occupation. The freshwater snail *Nereina punctulata* and the marine specimens *Glycymeris cf undata* were also consumed the entire time. It is notable that from Inv. 16 (Unit 1) and 17 (Unit 2) onwards, a greater diversity of species prevails than in the older layers. It is possible that, at this point, the subsistence strategy changed to collecting different species. Many mollusks show traces of processing, which is due to the removal of the meat as food. These are blows usually carried out at the ventral margin of the bivalves or at the vertex of the gastropods to extract the flesh (Figure 201a).

Processing traces were found on 84 objects that were not related to food extraction. Some bivalves were found with a coarse perforation in the center of their shells (Figure 201c). In Key Marco, Florida, such bivalves were found attached to a net (Gilliland 1965: 80-82). In the Caribbean region, this artifact group is therefore also referred to as net weights (Keegan et al. 2009). If several shells are attached to the net, the weight is sufficient to pull the net down. Other bivalves have scratch marks along their edges, suggesting that these objects were used as tools for scraping or scratching. Hasemann, Lara Pinto and Sandoval (2017: 131), for example, report that bivalves were used to scrape off the peel of yuca in the Caribbean. A study by Ciofalo et al. (2020) analyzes starch residues on the shells and shows that they were used for processing a wide range of food products in the Greater Antilles. Rye (1981: 86) shows that shells can be used in ceramic production to remove excess material and smooth the surface when leather-hard. Residue analyses would be necessary to clarify which materials were processed with the shells at Guadalupe. The shells of the large marine gastropods, especially *Turbinella angulata*, were also used for artifact production. They were formed into elongated oval, trapezoidal, and L-shaped artifacts, the use of which remains unclear (Figure 201g). One could imagine the elongated oval artifacts to be used as spoons or the like. The negative of such an artifact is visible on a large conch (Figure 201i). An almost complete specimen of a *Turbinella angulata* has a small oval hole that allowed the conch to be attached to a rod (Figure 201h). Similar devices are well-known from the Caribbean region and are often referred to as hammers or picks (Gilliland 1965: 83-92). Another object is long and pointed and possibly represents a perforator (Figure 201e).

Only a few objects with an ornamental character were found. Among others, an almost complete pendant made of an olive shell and two other fragmented pendants with a central perforation were documented (Figure 201d). Similar objects were found by Strong (1935: Pl. 15) in the votive cache on Roatán. One of the more unique finds from Guadalupe is a worked piece of a large marine snail wing made to resemble the fang of a mammal (Figure 201f). It is also conceivable that the bivalves with a central perforation were used as ornamental pendants. Some specimens have a very symmetrically shaped perforation (Figure 201b).

The analysis shows that mollusks were used intensively as raw materials in Guadalupe. They were a source of nutrition but also a means of tool and jewelry production. For this purpose, different species were collected and different habitats exploited. It seems that the inhabitants made use of a large component of the resources available to them and employed them in many different ways.

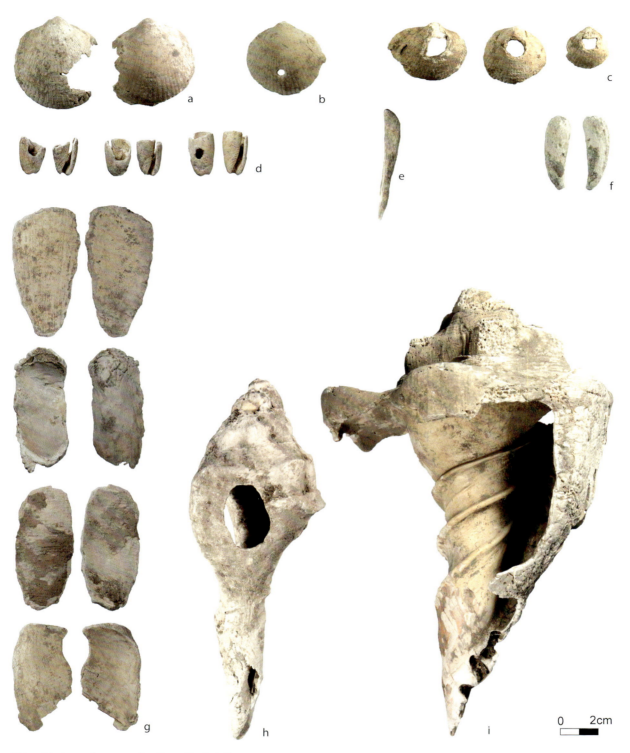

201   Bivalve and gastropod artifacts (Scale 1:2).

5 Discussion

In the previous chapters, the results obtained from the excavations and surveys in Guadalupe and the surrounding area were presented in detail. These finds and features form the basis for our understanding of the local society and the reconstruction and examination of possible networks that Guadalupe's inhabitants were involved in, which connected northeast Honduras with neighboring areas. The theoretical framework for the interpretation of the data is provided by network theory. Network theory views archaeological settlements as nodes in a network connected through links representing a certain kind of interaction. The present study aims to reconstruct such links between sites based on material culture and cultural practices using the concept of similarity and the application of compositional studies. Thoughts on the kind of interaction displayed through the identified links are presented. In this case study, the Cocal-period settlement of Guadalupe is considered the central node within an ego network, and all possible links that it had with other settlements, geological sources, and regions are examined. To do so, it is first necessary to characterize the settlement of Guadalupe and its inhabitants more precisely. Based on this, regional and interregional networks are examined, i.e., the links that existed between Guadalupe and other nodes and networks on different spatial levels and in different directions.

5.1 The Central Node: Guadalupe and its Inhabitants

As a first step, we will take a closer look at Guadalupe and its inhabitants during the Transitional Selin and Cocal periods (AD 900–1525). As previously described, an ego network, in which the settlement of Guadalupe represents the central node, is the primary focus of investigation. Based on our research results presented above, the goal of the analysis is to reconstruct all existing links between Guadalupe and other nodes, which consist of archaeological settlements and geological sources of raw material. Therefore, it is essential to characterize Guadalupe more precisely and consider the information that we have about the site and its inhabitants. Only if we understand autochthonous developments can we understand the links that existed to other sites. In

order to do so, the function and occupation history of Guadalupe is discussed. Economic elements are considered, such as subsistence and production of goods, but also cultural and sociopolitical aspects, including architecture and burial customs. It should be noted that these aspects are not assumed to be strictly separate. Every interaction also has a social component since they occur between humans as social beings. The boundaries between these categories are fluid. In the following, they are considered more in terms of orientation than strict definition.

5.1.1 Chronology, Structure, and Function of the Site

The radiocarbon samples found in Guadalupe during the excavation help us define the time frame of interest more precisely. They cover a period from AD 430–536 (cal 1 sigma) to AD 1471–1622 (cal 1 sigma) (see chapter 4.2.2). While the three early dates (Samples 71, 96, and 104; see Table 1) are difficult to explain and do not currently allow for any meaningful interpretation, continuous use of the site from AD 900 onwards is apparent. This agrees with the finds' stylistic analyses, especially the ceramics. This occupation may have also started somewhat earlier, as the lower layers are poorly documented by radiocarbon dates. At that time, the location was used as a settlement. The presence of postholes, traces of houses, and isolated finds testify to regular settlement activities. An occupation layer is marked by a hardened clay floor and a hearth and dates to around AD 1100. Several pits were probably excavated in the western part of the excavation trench at this point, possibly already in connection with ritual activities. In the middle of the 13th century, burials were interred. Some of them were covered with fragments of *bajareque*. A layer of gravel may indicate that the site was abandoned as a settlement. Subsequently, pottery and other finds were repeatedly deposited where the deep pits were once placed. The large number of shells and animal bones between the ceramic artifacts suggests that the deposition was related to the consumption of food and drinks. It is reasonable to assume that ritual activities related to the burials took place here. In the following, I demonstrate that we are most likely dealing with the remains of feasting. The horizontal extent of the deposited artifacts ends where the burials are interred and does not entirely cover them. Furthermore, we must assume that the deposits do not represent a single event but an accumulation over several years. This, in turn, means that ritual activities were performed here periodically, and the site became an important, central and visible place where people gathered repeatedly and deposited various goods, possibly as offerings or gifts for the dead. The location was apparently visited over centuries until the end of the Cocal period, with the activities ending around AD 1500. Although it cannot be excluded, abandonment of the settlement and the cease of activities related to Spanish arrival is not yet proven.

We can, therefore, clearly distinguish two different functions of Guadalupe: an initial use as a settlement site between about AD 900 and 1250 and a subsequent use as a burial site and place for ritual activities and festivities that were probably related to these burials. We can assume that this central place was surrounded by an extensive settlement on the elevated terrace during both phases. This is indicated by the surface pottery, which contains specimens from the Transitional Selin to the Late Cocal phase. Throughout these years, the terrain where the school is currently located must have occupied a central location within the settlement in both a geographical and symbolic sense, which is determined by the important activities that took place here.

5.1.2 LOCAL ECONOMY

5.1.2.1 Subsistence

Data on subsistence are essential to understand how the inhabitants used and interacted with their environment. The findings in Guadalupe testify to a rich and diverse diet of the pre-Hispanic inhabitants. Obviously, the people used all of the surrounding ecozones, such as the open sea, brackish water, and freshwater, and the land with its fertile coastal plain and the cordillera forests. Given the location by the sea, aquatic resources played a significant role in the diet of the pre-Hispanic population. This is demonstrated by the large number of mollusks and fish bones. Freshwater bivalves and snails, as well as fish and mollusks from different parts of the sea, including brackish water, shallow waters near the coast, and deeper waters, were collected. The collection techniques used are still uncertain. If the perforated bivalves represent net sinkers, this would prove the presence of fishing nets. Although it is reasonable to assume that such nets were used, the tropical-humid climate does not allow for their preservation. There is evidence for the use of fishing nets in the Maya region (Foster 2002: 312), and they were also widespread in the Caribbean (Antczak 1991: 507). Spindle whorls provide evidence for the pro-duction of textile threads that could have been used to manufacture nets. Other possibilities would be line fishing or the use of spears or arrows. Metal fishing hooks were found, for example, in Los Naranjos and the Sula Valley (Stone 1957: Fig. 64c; Strong / Kidder / Paul 1938: 41). Today, the Pesh use the poison of a native plant to kill fish in rivers (Griffin / Escobar Martínez / Hernández Torres 2009: 34). Whatever method was used to extract the animals from the water, the skeletal frequency pattern of fish and mollusks with percussion marks show that they were processed and consumed locally. The only subsistence data available for comparison from an archaeological site in the region are those from Selin Farm (Healy 1983). By comparing the data, it becomes clear that Guadalupe has a greater species diversity regarding mollusks. However, when it comes to quantity, a comparison is problematic because, in Selin Farm, the species were identified, but the individuals were not counted.

The presence of numerous animal bones indicates that hunting also played an important role in Guadalupe. The sample analysis reveals that, in addition to fish, mammals and reptiles were preferred, while birds played a minor role in the diet. Thus, the subsistence pattern in Guadalupe corresponds to that of Selin Farm, where mollusks and fish were also the primary food sources, while birds were rarely consumed. We have to keep in mind that the sample from Guadalupe is relatively small and could not be determined based on a reference collection. Nevertheless, there are striking similarities between the fauna in Guadalupe and Selin Farm. For example, jack (*caranx hippos*) seems to have played an important role in the diets of Selin Farm and Guadalupe. Jack is a large fish that can grow up to 113 cm long and weigh 15.8 kg. Healy (1983: 44) notes that "modern marine fishermen consider the jack to be a hard-fighting fish when caught, suggesting that H-CN-5 inhabitants were skilled fishermen." Tarpons (*Megalops atlanticus*) and snooks (*Centropomus* sp.) are common in both samples. Sharks (*Squaliformes*) and rays (*Rajiformes*) are present in both samples but rare. Among the mammals, armadillos (*Dasypus novencinctus*) and agoutis (*Rodentia* cf. *Agutidae*) played an important role in Selin Farm and Guadalupe. Regarding reptiles, mainly turtles (*Chelonidae*) and iguanas (*Iguanidae*) were hunted in both locations. The latter are considered a delicacy by the current local inhabitants. An open question remains as to how the animals were hunted. In Guadalupe, obsidian arrowheads have been found, which may indicate hunting with bow and arrow. The use of traps or slingshots would also be conceivable. Blowguns and arrows soaked in poison, as the Pesh used before the introduction of firearms, is another possibility (Griffin / Escobar Martínez / Hernández Torres 2009: 31).

If we compare the subsistence pattern of the Cocal period in Guadalupe with Selin Farm, we see clear similarities. Various resources from different ecozones were used. Similar species played an important role in nutrition. The data suggest that the subsistence pattern in the coastal settlements hardly differed between the Selin period and the Cocal period. Detailed studies of animal bones in Guadalupe are necessary to corroborate this assumption. However, a drastic change in the subsistence pattern, as Healy (1983:53) assumes took place at the beginning of the Cocal period in connection with the abandonment of the Selin-period settlements, is not currently supported by the data.

Furthermore, the presence of numerous manos, metates, and pestles indicates that plants were also important for nutrition. Two plants played a predominant role in subsistence in Middle America: maize and manioc. While maize was considered a staple food, especially in Mesoamerica, and was firmly anchored in the society's worldview and religion, it is assumed that, in Southern Central America and the Caribbean, manioc was the most important staple food (Keegan 2013: 72). In Costa Rica, it was cultivated around 1500 BC at the latest (Linares 1979). The presence of small quartz stones in Guadalupe, which today are embedded in a wooden board to grate manioc (manioc grater teeth), could indicate that manioc was also processed here. At the moment, however, the data is not sufficient to make reliable statements. Identifying the plants cultivated in Guadalupe and those that were fundamental for subsistence can only be clarified by future botanical studies.

The analysis results show that the inhabitants of Guadalupe used all resources available to them from diverse ecological regions. Healy (1983) divides these zones for Selin Farm into lowland forest, mangrove-coastal zone, and freshwater marsh-lagoon estuary. For the inhabitants of Guadalupe, the first two zones were especially important environments. The elevated areas of the cordillera in the south also played a major role in subsistence. The tropical lowland forest was home to rodents like agoutis. There were also deer in the area in pre-Hispanic times, which were found in Selin Farm but not in Guadalupe. Numerous other animals were present and certainly abundant. The forest also provided wild plants and herbs that could be used as food supplements. The presence of celts suggests that parts of the forest were cleared for agriculture.

The coastal mangrove zone includes the coast, which may have been populated by mangroves in the past, the shallow waters near the coast, and deeper parts of the ocean. This area provides a habitat for many different species. Species native to this area include oysters, which are present in Guadalupe in large numbers, and numerous other mollusks and fish. The sea turtle is also native

and would have been a significant source of meat. The green turtle (*Chelonio mydas*), documented at Selin Farm, can weigh more than 200 kg (Spotila 2004). Ethnographic studies from the Mosquitia show that it played a central role in the diet of the Miskito ethnic group (Nietschmann 1973). Cuddy (2007) mentions that manatees played a vital role in the subsistence of the north coast; in Guadalupe, evidence for their use could not yet be determined with certainty, whereas it has been proven in Selin Farm (Healy 1983). Although this habitat could be exploited with simple diving, the settlement of the Bay Islands at about 60 km away and Columbus' report (1959) prove there were also canoes.

In sum, Healy (1983: 50) states that "in pre-Columbian times the region of northeast Honduras provided an exceedingly rich, complex natural environment ideal for a broad-based, generalized subsistence strategy exploiting both land- and sea-based resources." The use of diverse ecozones enabled a varied and balanced diet. In addition, by using a wide variety of resources, the risk of overexploiting certain ecozones is low. The activities related to fishing, hunting, and farming were undoubtedly an integral part of village life and would have structured activities and social interaction. As Healy (1983) already noted, the food supply was somewhat different depending on the season. In the rainy season from June to October, fish withdraw into the sea, causing hunting and the procurement of seasonal wild plants to become more important for the assurance of food. In the dry season, in turn, fishing was more important. For the Mosquitia of the Atlantic coast of Nicaragua, where similar climatic and environmental conditions prevail, Magnus (1978) suggests that the coastal sites were temporary fishing camps and that inland sites were agriculture-based. We can assume that this was not the case for Guadalupe, as the presence of fish and animal bones are evidence for foraging during both the rainy and dry seasons. The extent to which agriculture was practiced is challenging to determine at the moment. However, the coastal strip near Guadalupe is very narrow and does not provide the possibility of cultivating enough food to feed large population groups. Larger agriculturally oriented centers certainly existed in the Aguán Valley and were in close contact with the coastal area based on the similarity of material culture (see section 5.2.1).

5.1.2.2 Production

Because material networks are primarily investigated, the examination of production activities at Guadalupe is central to the study. It is useful to identify which products were produced in Guadalupe itself and which were imported. These considerations help to reconstruct the trajectory and direction of links. The finds indicate that the pre-Hispanic inhabitants of Guadalupe used a wide range of raw materials to craft products. In the best cases, both tools used for production as well as the final product of their implementation are preserved, providing evidence that local production took place. In some cases, only the production tools are preserved in the archaeological context, while the final product is not because it was either brought elsewhere or made of perishable material. If only a product can be identified, but no tools, production waste, or activity areas, the product may have been imported instead of locally produced.

The sheer quantity of pottery found in Guadalupe in the excavation and on the surface suggests that pottery was produced locally. Clay deposits are found near Guadalupe, and as a material for temper, shells, sand, or plant remains could be used. During the excavation, we also found wasters, objects that were only partially fired and almost disintegrated during washing. These are a clear indication of local production, as it can be assumed that such defective objects were not transported over long distances. However, no evidence of activity areas or tools related to pottery production could be found in Guadalupe apart from the presence of small, smooth stones that could have been used for burnishing. However, the identification of ceramic production sites is very difficult throughout Central America. The easiest way to identify such sites is usually through the presence of kilns. In Central America, this has only been successful in a few locations so far (Minc 2010). The rarity of kilns suggests that ceramics were fired in open fires or firing pits. However, such a production method would be difficult to prove in an archaeological context. The pottery's surface characteristics from Guadalupe indicate that ceramics were—at least to a large extent—fired in an open fire. This is indicated by discolorations on the surface caused by a lack of control of the firing atmosphere associated with open firing.

Who produced the ceramics, and how was the production organized? Guadalupe's ceramics do not appear to be very standardized. There is a particular canon of forms, but there are significant differences in their execution. Motifs are recurrent, but there is great variation in their design. I, therefore, assume that the ceramics were not produced centrally but possibly at the household or community level, which, at least as far as ceramic production is concerned, indicates a non-centralized network. I further assume that ceramic vessels were a widespread commodity during the Cocal period and that they were available to a large part of the population. They were used in everyday life as storage, cooking, or serving vessels. In Guadalupe, we also see the intentional deposition of ceramics, an action that gave them a new function. Everyday objects were transferred into a ritual

context. However, because numerous supports show clear signs of wear, which can only have resulted from prolonged use, it is clear that the ceramics were not explicitly produced for ritual deposit but that they are everyday vessels. This assumption is also supported by the residual analysis, which detected a high concentration of residues in the vessels.

The obsidian has already been discussed in detail above. The studies have shown that obsidian from Güinope was locally processed from cores into prismatic blades. In this case, the characteristics of the products themselves (the presence of dorsal ends, a core, and objects with cortex) give us information about their local processing. The production of these prismatic blades requires a specific technology that came to Guadalupe from Mesoamerica, possibly with the products themselves. It is not clear who processed the obsidian in Guadalupe. Evans (2008: 105) mentions that blade production is a complex technique mastered only by specialists. Concurrently, the foreign technique is adapted to the local conditions by responding to the peculiarities of the material from Güinope (Stroth 2019). Besides obsidian, we can also prove that there was the production of tools made of perishable material like mollusks. Although the function of these tools can only be partially reconstructed, it can be assumed that the abundant raw material was used for various purposes. It cannot yet be proven that the stone tools were produced in Guadalupe, but the nature of the objects, their weight, and the abundant availability of the raw material suggest that at least some were produced locally or near Guadalupe. As already presented in chapter 4.4.3, we can assume that a distinctive lapidary tradition existed in northeast Honduras, which is confirmed by the numerous greenstone objects and the elaborately worked metates with zoomorphic heads. The numerous stone tools, greenstone objects, and the stones with elongated grooves found in Coraza Alta along the river identify this site as a lapidary production center, and the tools found in Guadalupe were probably produced there.

The production of various products can be deduced from the presence of some tools, such as those used to prepare food, like manos, metates, pestles, etc. This is especially true for the production of textiles. The spindle whorls, needle, and bark beaters are evidence of different steps in the processing of textile fibers. Bark beaters were used for the mechanical compaction of plant fibers, while spindle whorls were used for spinning individual textile fibers into a thread. The needle testifies to the sewing or embroidering of finished fabrics. Which raw materials were processed here? Bast fiber is the raw material for barkcloth, which is located just below the bark of a tree. Ethnographic studies show that the Pesh used the Tunu tree's bark, native to northeast Honduras, to produce barkcloth (Griffin / Escobar Martínez / Hernández Torres 2009: 64f). The bark is removed from the tree in large strips. The fibers are then removed from the bark and soaked in water. They are beaten and compacted with the bark beaters to produce a solid fabric. Several strips of bark bast can be joined together by beating them to produce a larger sheet. The sheets can be used as clothing, blankets, curtains, etc.

For spinning a thread, other raw material is necessary. Since there were no camelids in pre-Hispanic Middle America, plant-based fibers were the next best option. Cotton would be the obvious raw material, and it would be suitable for the climatic conditions. The size and shape of the spindle whorls would also correspond to this raw material. McCafferty and McCafferty (2010) describe that different spindle whorls are required for processing certain materials and that the shape of the spindle whorls affects the quality of the yarn. In general, the smaller the whorls, the finer the yarn. The speed and duration of spindle rotation are influenced by the diameter and height of the whorls. A wider, flatter spindle whorl produces a slower spin than a narrower, higher spindle whorl. The size of the perforation also correlates with the thickness of the yarn produced. Parsons (1972) establishes a typology for spindle whorls from the Central Mexican highlands, distinguishing between two types. Small spindle whorls were used for processing cotton, while larger spindle whorls were used for processing coarser maguey fibers. The Guadalupe spindle whorls, with a maximum diameter of 34 mm, all fall into the first group, and it can probably be assumed that fine fibers, most likely cotton, were processed in Guadalupe. Additional possibilities would be feathers, animal hair (e.g., rabbit hair), or even human hair (McCafferty / McCafferty 2010).

After spinning the threads, they were processed into fabrics in various ways. One of the most common joining techniques is weaving on a loom. For the Andean region and Mesoamerica, a portable loom (also called backstrap loom) was tied around the hips. It consisted entirely of organic material, leaving no traces in the archaeological context (Foster 2002: 317; Stone-Miller 1992). Beyond this, the chaîne opératoire of textile production includes numerous steps and tools that are no longer visible in the archaeological context today, such as combs for preparing wool or the wooden parts of the spindles, which have to be built from a straight, durable and splinter-free wood (Beaudry-Corbett / McCafferty 2002: 60). Dyes may have been used to color the textiles, which can be obtained from vegetable, animal, or mineral raw materials. How textile production was organized is uncertain. However, we know both from the Andean region (Murra 1962) and from excavations in Joya de Cerén in El Salvador (Beaudry-Corbett / McCafferty 2002: 60; Foster

2002: 316) that textiles for daily use were produced at the household level. The relatively large number of spindle whorls found in Guadalupe in a small area supports this assumption. Nevertheless, we must again consider that the context is not a domestic one but a ritual one. It is also true that the spindle whorls were given a new meaning by being deposited in a ritual context.

As shown in the example of textile production, numerous plants and perishable raw materials were used in pre-Hispanic times for the production and processing of objects. These objects may have been of enormous importance, but evidence of their existence can no longer be identified in the archaeological record. Studies show that about 90% of the exchange in pre-Hispanic times took place with perishable materials that are not preserved in tropical climates (Lathrap 1973). Because we are not typically confronted with them in archaeology, we sometimes forget the importance of such resources. I would like to illustrate this with an example. Abrasive powder is needed for processing greenstone. Fine obsidian powder or sand can be used, among other materials. The Aztecs preferred a specific sand for processing greenstone. To secure access to the fine abrasive powder, they took over or subdued the area from which it came (Easby 1968: 24). In the archaeological context, the importance of this raw material and the consequences of its use in sociopolitical actions could not be proven.

Although definitive statements regarding perishable materials cannot currently be made, I would like to address several aspects of the subject. Woods were among the more abundant perishable materials that played a role in Guadalupe. Honduras is home to several tropical hardwoods that are valued today for their resilience. They were a popular raw material in the past and found use in the manufacture of tools, boats, and architecture. Palm leaves and grasses may have been worked into ropes, mats, baskets, bags, and other containers that played an important role for storage and, unlike heavy pottery, for transport. Several ritual baskets from the Sacred Cenote in Chichen Itza are still preserved (Foster 2002: 317). Today, palm leaves are used to cover roofs, and they were undoubtedly used for architecture in the past. Fishing nets and their use are already discussed above. Other conceivable perishable materials include dyes, resins, medicinal herbs, furs, and feathers. Today, the coastal inhabitants use the sticky fruit of a specific tree as an insect trap. Some ethnohistorical sources mention that cacao was cultivated in Honduras, which was highly valued in Mesoamerica and even used as a means of payment during the Postclassic period. Ethnohistorical sources also report that Honduras was known as "the land of gold, feathers and cacao" (Roys 1943: 55).

Even though we can only reconstruct a fraction of the products and production activities that once took place in Guadalupe and its surroundings, the existing data demonstrate that the inhabitants had many different resources at their disposal and used them in many different ways. It seems that they lived in an environment with abundant resources that ensured the population's supply of commodities and did not require the import of basic foods. At the same time, the goods produced certainly played an important role in creating networks in which they were exchanged.

5.1.3 CULTURAL ASPECTS

5.1.3.1 Architecture

During the excavations in Guadalupe, we found evidence of pre-Hispanic architecture, including postholes, stone rows, clay floors, and *bajareque* fragments. Observations on the architecture and its contextualization in northeast Honduras are presented in detail by Jill Mattes (2019). These features, combined with information from ethnohistorical and ethnographic reports, provide an idea of what the pre-Hispanic buildings may have looked like: The foundations consisted of lines of river cobbles. Similar stone rows were found in Guadalupe and other sites in the area and are mentioned in ethnohistorical reports. Several vertical wooden posts served as a basic framework for the structure. Horizontal rods were placed between the posts. The imprints in the *bajareque* pieces in Guadalupe indicate that they must have been very straight materials, such as reed (see Figure 32). These reed canes were attached to the vertical posts with lianas and possibly with cords made of plant fibers. The framework, consisting of wooden posts and reed, was then covered with clayey earth. Even today, earth is used for traditional house building; it is extracted from the building surroundings and does not undergo any special preparation. After application, the earth was smoothed from the outside, indicated by smoothing marks on some fragments (Figure 202). The house floor consisted of compacted earth, just as the hardened clay floors in Guadalupe indicate. This feature is still prominent in the region today (Mattes 2019: 78). No information about roof construction is available from the excavation. However, in ethnohistorical sources, and as is evidenced in recent buildings, roofs are often built with wood and palm leaves (Figure 203).

The combination of vertical and horizontal elements suggests that buildings must have had a rectangular shape. The size of the building, however, is unclear. The excavation area in Guadalupe is too small to reconstruct a ground plan based on the postholes. In the few available ethnohistorical sources about the Mosquitia from the 18th and 19th century, the longhouse is mentioned as a typical building form (Bard 1855: 295; Bell 1899:

202   Bajareque fragment with smoothing marks on the exterior (Mattes 2019: Plate 1).

123, 161; M. W. 1752: 291 f.; Young 1842: 98) (Figure 204). These are houses of up to 26 m in length and 10 m in width, which accommodate several families or extended families. Their sides are usually open. Bell (1899: 84, 292) describes that in a Misquito village and a settlement near Cabo Gracias a Dios, only the chief's house had *bajareque* walls, while the other buildings were open. In this case, the presence of *bajareque* walls seems to be linked to a particular social status.

From the archaeological record of northeast Honduras, little architectural data is available that lend themselves to comparison. It is assumed that buildings were constructed from perishable material throughout the entire area, as is common in Southern Central America. Some reports mention buildings made of stone (Moreno 1525, quoted in Lara Pinto 1980: 122; Strong 1935: 213). However, such buildings have not yet been identified in the archaeological record. Components that are usually

203   Modern bajareque building in Guadalupe (P. Bayer).

preserved include platforms that served as substructures for buildings (Figure 205), stone rows as foundations, and, in a few cases, fragments of *bajareque* or clay floors (e.g., Begley 1999: 212f; Healy 1978a: 19, 1978b: 59; Strong 1934: 34). If we assume that the platforms served as substructures and that the superstructures had similar dimensions, it is quite possible that longhouses did exist. This is especially valid given that some mounds in sites like Rio Arriba 2 measure up to 80 m in length. Healy (1978a: 19) discovered stone alignments in Río Claro, which he identifies as belonging to a longhouse. At the same time, the many smaller platforms indicate smaller buildings. The contemporary houses in our study area are mainly small (see Figure 203). The kitchen is often the only part still built in the traditional *bajareque* style as an annex to the main house.

   The comparison of archaeological, ethnohistorical, and ethnographic sources provides us with information on pre-Hispanic architectural techniques. However, the sizes of the pre-Hispanic buildings in Guadalupe remain unclear and can only be clarified with extensive excavations. This is particularly interesting because it can provide us with information about the social organization within a society. In Guadalupe, we have to keep in mind that the *bajareque* concentrations are very likely related to the burials, i.e., they may represent a particular type

of architecture, which opens up new possibilities of interpretation. In the following chapter, the site's ritual function and the elements associated with it are covered in greater detail.

5.1.3.2 Feasting and Burial Rites

In the previous chapters, it was repeatedly mentioned that the ceramic accumulation in Guadalupe was related to ritual activities and feasting. This aspect is discussed in more detail here. In summary, we assume that the finds and features depict the following: The excavations in Guadalupe uncovered a central place where gatherings and ritual activities took place. The ceramic accumulation, intermixed with food remains and broken and intact artifacts, testifies to festivities that took place there. The stratigraphy suggests that these festivities were related to the burials found interred at the edge of the pottery accumulation. Since these skeletons are not complete but missing individual bones, one hypothesis that explains this pattern is the assumption that the interments were repeatedly opened to extract bones for ritual use. In this section, I discuss the available sources on burial rites in northeast Honduras, define what we understand by feasting, and explain why the finds and features in Guadalupe indicate such activities. Ethno-

204   Paya longhouse on the Guayambre River (Bard 1855: 295).

graphic sources confirm that feasting played an important role for societies in Southern Central America.

Burials in Northeast Honduras. In northeast Honduras, only a few burials have been found so far, and most of them were uncovered in the early years of research. Often, the skeletons were not described in detail nor sufficiently documented, or research results were not published. In addition, the finds could not usually be assigned to any specific period. These circumstances have limited our understanding of burials in northeast Honduras today. The burials from Guadalupe are the first that can be assigned to a secure context due to their careful excavation and subsequent examination by physical anthropological studies.

Descriptions of burials on the Bay Islands only concentrate on a few sites but cover very diverse burial customs. In Black Rock Basin on the north coast of Utila, Junius Bird found eight urn burials containing bones. Bird's observations are summarized by Strong (1935: 20-28). Several skulls, apparently from children and adults, were located near the large urn burial vessels. Individual long bones were associated with the skulls. One of the urns was also encircled by skulls. It is interesting to note that the urns were associated with a black occupational layer consisting of dark earth, numerous ceramic sherds, and other cultural debris. Based on Strong's ceramic descriptions, one can conclude that at least the upper layers date to the Cocal phase. He visited the same site a short time later. However, apart from a few individual human bones, no other burials were found (Strong 1935: 28). Feachem (1940: 181f), who visited the site in 1939 with the same guide as Bird, also mentions the discovery of an urn.

In the 80 Acres site on Utila, seven skeletons were found by Kidder, Eckholm, and Stromsvik when the construction of an airfield affected the site. The details are summarized by Epstein (1957: 22-33). The skeletons were located within a mound that the archaeologists more closely examined. Apparently, there were different burial rites present within the same mound. Three of the skeletons, all of them children, were placed in urns, while others were extended and flexed but only partially preserved. The description of the stratigraphy is remarkably similar to Guadalupe's. The first 60 cm of the mound consisted of dark earth with numerous ceramic sherds mixed with animal bones and obsidian fragments. Below this, the earth became lighter, and there were signs of settlement horizons, including a possible house floor. Below these layers, the skeletons were found. Unfortunately, the excavation was not carried out carefully enough to identify possible grave pits. Thus, it remains uncertain whether the skeletons were inserted from the upper layers. The dating of the burials is also difficult, but according to Epstein, most of them probably date to the Selin period (see Epstein 1957: 31). The 80 Acres site can generally be dated to both the Cocal and Selin phases (Epstein 1957: 23). Epstein (1957: 30f) notes that deposits of beach sand were found in both 80 Acres and Black Rock Basin in connection with the burials.

In Difficulty Hill on Roatán, Begley (1999: 178) came across several burials, which he describes as a possible burial ground. According to Begley, the skeletons were located close to the surface, making it challenging to identify burial pits. The burials were extended, and their poor preservation prevented further analysis. Only one

205   Modern house built on a pre-Hispanic platform. This picture gives an idea of how the platforms might have been used in pre-Hispanic times (F. Fecher).

of them had grave goods in the form of a ceramic "drum" and a copper bell. The skeletons date to the Cocal period.

The Charlie Brown site at the western end of Roatán is a settlement that extends over several terraces. Two burials were found in one of the terraces during test excavations (Cruz Castillo / Orellana 2000). Both skeletons were extended. One was an adult male and was positioned in a north-south orientation. The second skeleton was an adult female located immediately next to the male in an east-west orientation. Other burials, which were not excavated, were located below the skeletons. No further details are provided about other find circumstances or associated materials.

On the mainland, burial reports mainly concentrate on the region around Trujillo. Spinden mentions the discovery of eight inhumations in a low hill near Trujillo (km 20 of the then Trujillo Railroad), "8 bodies were uncovered in both flexed and stretched-out positions. One had been dismembered, and the arms and legs were laid across the body. With these burials, some long beads of jade were obtained" (Spinden 1925: 534). In 1931, during excavations of mound 10c (referred to as mound C by Healy) in Selin Farm, Bird came across an extended child burial, whose age he estimated to be three to five years. The skeleton was in very poor condition (Epstein 1957: 45f; Healy 1978b: Fig. 13). It was located 213 cm below the mound's surface and was introduced from the layers above, which could be seen due to the grave pit cutting through the house floor above. No grave goods were found. During excavations under Healy in the 1970s, more single human bones were found in the same mound (Healy 1978b: 64). In William's Ranch, also dating to the Selin period, a skeleton of an adult male was found in the depression surrounding the settlement. "The body had been weighted to the bottom of its watery grave by a pair of rocks attached to the upper and lower extremities" (Healy 1975: 65). No further information is provided.

Stone (1934a) found two skeletons in Jerico near Trujillo. They were inside a mound and seem to have been associated with architecture. She gives no further information about the burials except that they were in a very poor state of preservation. Close to the burials, she found a ceramic vessel containing an axe god and a greenstone bead, as well as a slate disc which had apparently once served as a cover for the vessel. Due to the limited information on the location provided by Stone, it remains unclear which site she is referring to. It may be Jerico Farm, where additional burials were found during excavations directed by Cruz Castillo (2007). However, these were not investigated further due to their poor state of preservation. According to Cruz Castillo, all burials were in an extended dorsal position and were associated with ceramic fragments and lithic material, as well as obsidian. The site dates to the Cocal period.

These reports demonstrate that very different burial customs exist within a small area, namely the Bay Islands and the adjacent mainland. Skeletons were found in mounds, on terraces, and, in one case, in a depression. Burials are interred in flexed or extended positions with different orientations. There are urn burials, individual skulls, and long bones. Together with signs of dismemberment described by some authors, these point to secondary burial practices. In most cases, grave goods are not found, or they turn out to be single pieces, as in the case of Jerico. At present, due to the patchy information base, it is difficult to judge whether the high diversity of burial practices are due to chronological differences or the result of other factors, such as spatial or social differences. For example, urns have only been found on the islands so far, and it seems that mainly children were buried in this way.

Of particular interest is that some authors mention the association of burials with a dark cultural debris composed of ceramics, bones, and other artifacts. Another such context is described by Strong (1935: 86-111) at Indian Hill Site 1 on Barbereta Island east of Roatán. The site consists of an approximately 1 m thick accumulation of closely packed ceramics measuring 20 m in diameter. Strong emphasizes that the ceramic fragments are broken into large pieces, which is why some vessels could be reconstructed. Based on Strong's extensive illustrations, most of the pottery can be attributed to the Cocal period. He also found several Bay Island Polychrome sherds and depicts handles of Type 1 vessels ("frying pans"), miniature vessels, and ocarinas in the shape of turtles very similar to those from Guadalupe. Individual Selin-period sherds are also illustrated (Strong 1935: Fig. 24a, 28b). The pottery was mixed with shells, animal bones, which include two perforated feline teeth and stone tools. Although no burials were found, Strong discovered individual human teeth and bones, which leads him to believe that there must have been some kind of associated burial. It must be mentioned that Strong's observations are based on a test excavation, which, according to the author himself, was not very systematic. In addition, the site had already been severely disturbed by looting and earlier excavations under Mitchell-Hedges. Compared to Guadalupe, it is striking that a very similar context is described and that the inventory of finds is quite similar. The human teeth and bones indicate burials that have not yet been discovered due to the unsystematic excavation work.

A similar situation is reported for Dixon Site on the adjacent island of Roatán. Here, Strong (1935: 51-72) describes a concentration of ceramic sherds distributed over an area of about 10 m. In the center, the concentration reaches a thickness of 70 cm, thinning out towards the limits. In the center of the accumulation, he found the offertory cache mentioned earlier in the form of a complete Bay Island Polychrome vessel filled with 487 objects, including greenstone beads, metal bells and other copper objects, shell artifacts, and stone celts (for a complete list, see Strong 1935: 53). Strong interprets Indian Hill 1 and Dixon Site as offertory sites. Furthermore, he assumes that the pottery accumulations in such offertory sites were caused by the long-term and periodic use by the islands' inhabitants and that they accumulated over a long period (Strong 1935: 146). Another similar situation exists at Finca Galindo on Roatán. Véliz et al. (1977) found a markedly high concentration of ceramic sherds together with dark humic earth and obsidian fragments during test excavations. Like Guadalupe, the site is located near the coast on a slightly elevated terrace next to a river. Based on the pottery, the site dates to the Cocal phase.

A connection between the accumulation of ceramic sherds and ritual contexts is apparent. Some of these pottery accumulations are associated with burials, while, in others, human bones indicate that burials may be located below the pottery concentrations. While this phenomenon has not received much attention so far, Strong believes that these are offertory sites and that the accumulations are related to ritual activities. I would like to pursue this idea in the following by showing that these are remnants of festivities, which, in some cases, were associated with burials.

Definition of Feasting. How do we define the term "feasting"? Michael Dietler and Brian Hayden (2001: 3) define feasting as "events essentially constituted by the communal consumption of food and/or drink." In a broader definition, they mention that it is often particular food distinct from the everyday domestic staples. Moreover, the food is eaten together during a special occasion (Hayden 2001: 24). This communal, occasion-based consumption of food is, therefore, the main focus. Furthermore, feasting is regarded as a form of ritual activity, which distinguishes it from everyday activities. They may also be accompanied by dramaturgical effects, such as music, dances, and intoxication, to underline this ritual significance. Special occasions in which feasts have been performed include major life events, such as birth, initiation, marriage, or death, ancestor veneration, political events, such as war and chiefly succession, or those related to subsistence, such as the sowing of seeds or the beginning of the rainy season (Dietler / Hayden 2001; Junker 2001: 271). The exchange of food and the distribution of food surplus can also be an important cause for feasting (Piddocke 1965). Apart from giving importance to these events and anchoring them in the society's memory through celebration, feasting is linked to important sociopolitical aspects. The coming together of many people is used for status display or display of wealth, obtaining prestige, status enhancement of the host, or to negotiate or strengthen social relations. "Feasting constitutes part of a central domain of social action; people actually negotiate relationships, pursue economic and political goals, compete for power, and reproduce and contest ideological representations of social order and authority" (Dietler 2001: 65). Feasts can play an important role for prehistoric societies without writing systems in particular, as they can also have a juridical character. The transfer of rights and property, marriages, and other types of contracts cannot be recorded in writing. However, the presence of many guests serves to attest these actions in so far as several people attend the events and act as witnesses to decisions and agreements (Piddocke 1965: 257). Witnesses who pass on the news to those not present also serve as disseminators of the information, distributing it among the population.

Hayden considers feasting an important social practice that is widespread and has its origins in the early periods of cultural development (2001: 24f). It constitutes a special form of social interaction and can be a vital factor for the emergence of social hierarchy (Chacon / Mendoza 2017). Even today, feasting is still a significant aspect of many societies. Consider the feasts held in relation to the Christian sacraments. For some societies, feasting and the prestige associated with it is so essential that the hosting of festivities can plunge families into poverty, as is the case for the Luo in Kenya (Dietler 2001). In recent years, feasting has also been increasingly recognized as a relevant analytical concept in the archaeology of pre-Hispanic societies. Furthermore, the importance of the sociopolitical mechanisms of feasting has been demonstrated (e.g., Brown 2001; Hendon 2003; Lau 2002; LeCount 2001; Vaughn 2004).

Feasting in Archaeological Contexts. Festive activities leave traces and are often preserved in an archaeological context, even if they are often not identified as such (McOmish 1996). Hayden (2001: 40f) lists several features encountered in archaeological contexts that indicate feasting. In particular, he emphasizes the presence of an extraordinarily high number of vessels and food remains and their accumulation or deposition. He also mentions the presence of prestige items and ritual paraphernalia, which were related to dramaturgical effects, such as incense burners or musical instruments. Hayden also mentions the intentional destruction of objects. Most of these elements are observable in Guadalupe. The ceramic layer consists of a considerable number of vessels and food remains. The tremendous amount of pottery and the presence of large fragments indicate that it is not common domestic refuse as is present in the older layers below the pottery accumulation. Particularly in the lower part of the accumulation, the vessel fragments lie in conjunction with one another, indicating

intentional deposition or in situ destruction. The numerous bones and shells further demonstrate that the ceramic deposition was connected to the consumption of food. This is also suggested by the ceramics' residue analysis and the lipid residues discovered on the greenstone beads. Furthermore, we encountered several very large vessels in Guadalupe that may have been used for storing and serving food, possibly alcoholic beverages. In addition to the vessels and food leftovers, the ocarinas are musical instruments that indicate ritual performances that may have accompanied the festivities. The presence of polychrome pottery in the Bay Island Polychrome style is also known only from special contexts so far, not from simple households. Some of the ground stone tools may have been used for food preparation. All in all, the nature of the finds in Guadalupe suggests that they are the remains of feasts.

One question that arises is how the accumulation formed. Is it the result of a single event or periodic activities? Were the objects deposited in situ or just accumulated here? The first question was already addressed above. The accumulation did not develop due to a single event but through recurring depositions. This is chiefly indicated by the volume of the accumulation itself and the radiocarbon data, suggesting formation between AD 1300 and 1450. With regard to the second question, a conclusive interpretation is difficult. It appears that the vessels were both deposited in situ and collected here after being broken elsewhere. Especially in the lower layers, vessel fragments are found in conjunction, which indicates that they were deposited or broken in situ. It is notable, however, that we have not been able to reconstruct complete vessels so far. This might be due to the narrow excavation trench, which could result in fragments of the same vessel lying outside of the excavation limits. It is especially apparent that fragments of the same vessel in the upper layers were found in different levels with some distance between them. It remains unclear if this indicates that the vessels were broken somewhere else and then deposited in the mound or if this is due to disturbance of the upper layers, or if the fragments simply fell away from each other due to the slope. In any case, both scenarios are possible, and it may be a combination of the two. Junker (2001: 285) describes, for example, that the remains of festivities (e.g., bones and broken vessels) in the Philippines were repeatedly swept up into a pile. As a result, an archaeologically recognizable midden formed over time.

Another interesting phenomenon is that, apart from the objects that we can easily associate with festivities (ceramics, leftovers, instruments, etc.), some cannot be directly associated with a festive context at first glance, such as obsidian blades, bark beaters, spindle whorls, needles, bells, and greenstone beads. On the one hand, they are household items associated with production activities; on the other hand, they are personal adornments. It is reasonable to assume that these are either offerings deposited during festivities or, more specifically, grave goods for the deceased. Recall that no objects were found directly associated with the burials. The accumulation of objects may be a kind of collective grave good. By depositing them in the ritual context of the festivities, the objects are transformed; they are given a new meaning and they become part of a symbolic sphere that exceeds that of mere practical use.

One last aspect that needs clarification is the observation that at least some of the burials in Guadalupe were obviously related to architecture. As described above, one of the burials is located directly below a concentration of *bajareque*. Its location clearly coincides with the extension of *bajareque* fragments, so it must be assumed that the *bajareque* was spread over the burial. At the moment, it is not clear whether the *bajareque* came from a building standing in situ or whether the fragments were gathered at this location. Nevertheless, the topic is interesting. References to the connection between burials and architecture can also be found in ethnographic sources and are discussed in the following.

Ethnographic Sources. Ethnographic sources confirm the fact that feasts played an important role in the societies of northeast Honduras. They also attest that funerals were an important occasion for such celebrations and shed light on several questions raised in connection with the interpretation of the findings in Guadalupe.

Eduard Conzemius's (1927: 300f) notes provide information about the Pesh by combining his own observations with information from historical reports. He relates that when a person dies, the corpse is wrapped in a cloth made of tree bark and placed in the house where the deceased had lived. The house is then abandoned. If several people die within a short time, the entire settlement is abandoned. A canoe serves as a coffin in which the person is buried. Grave goods are given to the deceased. These are objects that they used during their lifetime, such as tools, weapons, or tobacco, and are to accompany them on their journey to paradise. However, only "items that are broken or of little use"[21] are buried (Conzemius 1927: 300). In the past, the deceased's animals were also killed, and his fruit trees and cultivations were destroyed. Feasts are held three, nine, and 30 days after the date of death. After one year, the main celebration follows. Conzemius (1927: 301) describes these gatherings as "orgies that are accompanied by strange dances, food and chicha"[22]. He also mentions offerings of food and *chicha* to the evil spirits so that the deceased

is not disturbed by them during his journey. Chapman (1958: 132-139) makes similar interesting observations by evaluating various historical accounts. She mentions that the dead were often buried in buildings that are subsequently abandoned. In some cases, buildings are even built over the graves. She also mentions the use of boats as coffins. When a person dies, all possessions are destroyed. She also summarizes reports of Pesh festivities that testify to the fact that such events were accompanied by the constant drinking of alcoholic beverages and numerous rituals. Recent ethnographic studies on the Pesh prove the importance of funeral celebrations (Griffin / Escobar Martínez / Hernández Torres 2009: 78-81). During funerals, ceremonies are performed by a shaman. They include the preparation and consumption of specific foods and drinks such as *chicha* made from corn or manioc and the provision of food for the spirits of the deceased. To this end, various instruments were played to call upon the spirits. On the 9th day after the day of death, a festival is held where the village community gathers to consume food and drink and dance together. The remains of the festivities are then collected and deposited at a specific location.

Regarding the Sumu and the Miskito, who also live in northeast Honduras today, Conzemius (1932: 156) describes a secondary use of human remains: If a man dies, he is buried. After a year, his widow opens the grave to remove a portion of the bones. The bones are cleaned and dried. Afterward, the woman carries the bones with her in a bag for one year. Although caution is required when linking these observations to the findings in Guadalupe, as we currently assume that the Sumu did not inhabit the area around Trujillo in pre-Hispanic times and that the Miskito are an ethnic group that only formed after the Conquista, this report still offers an interesting perspective on the findings in Guadalupe. Whether such a secondary use took place in Guadalupe remains unclear at the moment.

Some elements described above certainly go back to Christian-influenced ideas, such as that of the preparation of the deceased for their journey to paradise. At the same time, we find important elements in the ethnographic sources, that we also find in the archaeological context in Guadalupe and which apparently date back to pre-Hispanic times. The reports show that funeral celebrations played a central role and were held periodically. Recent studies mention that food leftovers from the feasts were collected and deposited at a specific location. Interestingly, the deceased was given broken objects or things of little value, and all of his possessions were destroyed. Guadalupe's deposit may reflect this partial de-

---

21 Translation from Spanish by the author.

22 Translation from Spanish by the author.

struction of objects and the deposition of both the deceased's possessions and leftover food from festivities. Furthermore, the mention of architecture in connection with burials is notable.

Summary. The current state of research shows that many different burial customs existed within a small area in pre-Hispanic times. This is also true of many regions in Southern Central America. In order to interpret the differences and recognize patterns, detailed studies are needed that carefully interpret the archaeological situation and include physical anthropological studies. Previous research has shown that several sites throughout northeast Honduras have inhumations associated with an accumulation of pottery fragments and other objects. This phenomenon has not yet received much attention. Based on the excavations in Guadalupe and the careful documentation and interpretation of the contexts, I assume that these findings are the remains of feasts that took place in association with the burials. Ethnohistorical sources confirm the importance of festivities in the event of death and mention details recognizable in Guadalupe. Remarkably similar contexts have been recorded in Costa Rica, where ethnohistorical sources also confirm the importance of funeral celebrations (see section 5.3.2).

The festivities in the center of the pre-Hispanic settlement of Guadalupe must have presented a visible and audible event, a central happening, the preparation and execution of which structured communal life in a certain way. Dancing and playing music together is an intense experience that engages all of the senses and leaves a lasting impression. Celebrations, then, form a special kind of social interaction that creates a sense of community and serves as a "social glue" (Gamble / Gowlett / Dunbar 2015: 105). In Guadalupe, it was not only the interaction between the living that was celebrated but also the connection to the dead, who seem to have been an integral part of society. Moreover, the accumulation of the feast's remains was always present and visible to the inhabitants of Guadalupe. The visible remains were part of daily life and, like a monument, occupied a central place in the society and kept the memory of the deceased alive. It is difficult to reconstruct if only the inhabitants of Guadalupe attended these activities or if they were a regional event in which guests from other settlements participated as well. However, the various goods present in Guadalupe show that not only locally produced objects were deposited. Whether the other items came to Guadalupe through exchange relationships or were brought directly by visitors as gifts remains unclear. Other questions that arise in this context pertain to the modes of event organization (central organization or organization by relatives of the deceased/households), the sociopolitical effects, and the signifi-

cance for the identity of the inhabitants. The findings in Selin Farm, which Goodwin (2019) also interprets as remains of ritual feasting, indicate that feasts have a long tradition in northeast Honduras and are not just a phenomenon of the Cocal period.

5.1.3.3 Belief System

The belief system of a society is closely related to festivities and rituals. Reconstructing the belief system of pre-Hispanic groups without having written sources available is difficult. There is no known "pantheon" of gods for our field of research, as is recorded for the Aztecs or the Maya, for example. However, in order to approach the subject, we can look for evidence in the iconography. In our case, ceramics generally have the most iconography. We can also consult ethnohistorical and ethnographic reports that may help to develop ideas about what the belief system may have been like in pre-Hispanic times.

The ceramics from Guadalupe primarily depict animals and anthropomorphic figures and incised wave-shapes, cruciforms, and other abstract forms. The chapter on ceramics has already addressed possible identifications of the animals. In the following, I will go into more detail about these interpretative approaches. There are some uncertainties connected to the identification of the animals. Although some authors provide supposedly unambiguous identifications (e.g., Cuddy 2007; Strong 1935), there is still room for interpretation, which is evident from the fact that several authors provide different interpretations for the same motif. Motif 8, for example, is interpreted by Dennett (2007) as a highly stylized face, whereas Cuddy (2007) recognizes a manatee fin. Reliable identification is complicated because often only animal heads are depicted, while whole animals are rare. Moreover, these are not naturalistic representations; the animals are depicted with a certain artistic freedom or reduced to a few characteristics. In the sample analyzed in this work, I believe that the following animals are frequently depicted: Birds (Motif 19, possibly curassows or a vulture species due to the accentuated protrusion on the nose), pelicans (Motif 20), serpents (Motif 18), coatis (Motif 21 with long snout), and possibly opossums or skunks (Motif 21 with short snout; alternative interpretations: peccaries or agoutis). The individual motifs include a feline (Figure 167h), a tadpole metamorphizing into a frog (Figure 167e), and possibly a sloth (Figure 168y). Furthermore, the ocarinas represent turtles, and a monkey is depicted on one of the roller stamps. In the ceramic fragments that are not part of the studied sample and, therefore, have not been described in detail so far, there is another common motif that consists of a round head with small ears and an open mouth with large protruding teeth (Figure 206; see also Figure 59). This may depict a feline, such as an ocelot, jaguar, or margay. This interpretation is supported by the emphasis placed on the lip, which retracts when predators bare their teeth. Some appliqués have finely engraved dots that indicate the spotted coats of these species (Figure 206b and d). All of the mentioned animals were native to pre-Hispanic northeast Honduras (see Dennett 2007: Table 1.1 and 1.2). It is also notable that some animals have a cranial protuberance on their forehead (Figure 207; see also Figure 59). The turtle ocarinas have a similar attachment on their necks. This is also true of the manatee-lugs typical of the Selin period (see Figure 53; Healy 1978b: Fig. 7D). This may be the exaggerated depiction of a biological feature. It is also possible that these protuberances have a symbolic meaning. Similar cranial protuberances can be found in animal head appliqués (*adornos*) from the Caribbean islands (e.g., Waldron 2016: Fig. 7.58). If we compare the animals represented in the appliqués to the subsistence data from Guadalupe and Selin Farm, it is striking that fish and mollusks, which played a central role in subsistence, are not represented. Apart from some supports that may represent fins of fish or marine mammals (see Appliqué Motifs 7 and 8), they are absent.

Birds, in contrast, were apparently rarely consumed at both sites but make up a large proportion of the appliqués. Coatis were not found in Selin Farm either and have not been identified in Guadalupe's bone assemblage. It can be assumed that felines and serpents did not play an important role for subsistence either. Thus, it seems that ceramics do not primarily represent the animals that were consumed. Obviously, these representations do not have an economic meaning but a symbolic one. Felines and serpents are impressive, threatening animals. Birds are masters of the sky, a space that remains inaccessible to humans. The pelican connects land, air, and sea, and the transitioning tadpole represents the connection between land and water.

A similar pattern was identified in societies in Argentina's Entre Ríos area (Bonomo / Politis 2016). Here, too, monochrome ceramics are decorated with zoomorph appliqués. However, unlike the appliqués in Guadalupe, they are designed in detail and can be assigned to specific species based on the illustration of biological characteristics. Very similar to Guadalupe, many birds were depicted but were rarely consumed. Fish, which played an essential dietary role, were not depicted on the ceramics. Thus, animals with a symbolic value, as opposed to an economic one, were represented here as well. Portrayals of dangerous and poisonous animals were predominant, while parrots were also occasionally depicted, which are similar to humans due to their linguistic abilities and the fact that they could be domesticated

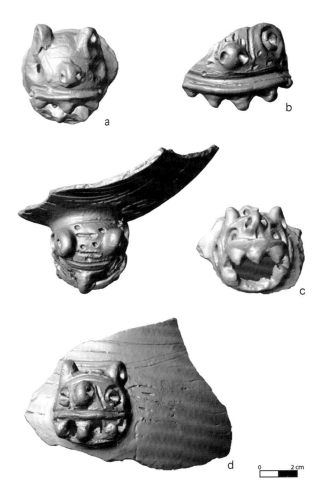

206   Appliqués representing feline heads. a PAG-29-556; b PAG-30-302; c PAG-21-633; d PAG-31-3 (P. Bayer, L. Edvesi).

(Bonomo 2012: 33). The authors explain the phenomenon that in the worldview of many societies from the South American lowlands, animals had the same status as humans. They also refer to studies by Reichel-Dolmatoff (1971) and Descola (1997). Politis (2016: 155) provides an insightful summary of these studies:

"[...] there is a general perception among Amazonian people that animals have status similar to humans, and, therefore, their hunting, processing and consumption is restricted and mediated by ritual complexes and is therefore performed within a multifaceted ideational framework. The basic western dualism between humans, on the one side, and animals, plants and the environment, on the other, simply does not exist within the Amazonian cosmology. Animals are considered to be related to each other and to humans in much the same way in which humans are related to one another."

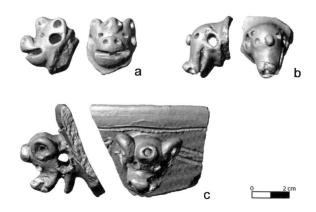

207   Zoomorph appliqués with cranial protuberance (P. Bayer).

I believe that a similar worldview is also manifested in the ceramics of Guadalupe. This is indicated by the fact that human and animal heads are represented together on a single vessel, or elements of different animals occur on the same vessel. There do not seem to be any fixed rules of combination; both motifs have the same significance, and they are not hierarchically separated. Fins of marine mammals are depicted on the ends of supports and are analogous to human feet. Healy et al. (2010) believe that the animal representations in Guadalupe's ceramics are based on an animistic worldview in which nature, humans, and animals alike have a soul or spirit. Today, the Pesh also believe that various elements of nature have spirits within them, that "every ceiba, every mahogany tree, had a spirit"[23] (Griffin / Escobar Martínez / Hernández Torres 2009: 72). Cuddy (2007) considers that the animals depicted on the ceramics may be protagonists of myths. In the Caribbean region, it has been proven that certain animals were associated with a particular symbolism and played specific roles in rituals. Frogs, for example, are associated with the Pleiades and are interpreted as announcers of the rainy season (Waldron 2016: 189f). Likewise, in many indigenous societies in the Americas, there is a belief in an alter ego that manifests itself in animal form.

Detailed zoological studies of the material from Guadalupe will undoubtedly be helpful in the future to identify and compare the animals depicted on pottery and those that were consumed. Whatever the ideas and worldviews were behind the representation, it is clear that the natural environment played a central role for their producers. This can also be seen in the wave patterns that represent water. It is the close interaction with the surrounding environment that we see portrayed on the ceramics. People were closely connected to their en-

vironment and considered it worthy of portrayal on their ceramics. This phenomenon can be observed in many Southern Central American areas and the Caribbean (e.g., Linares 1968; Lothrop 1926; Stone 1977; Strong 1948a; Waldron 2016). Similar worldviews may have been expressed in Guadalupe.

5.1.4 SOCIOPOLITICAL ORGANIZATION

The sociopolitical organization is a core issue in Southern Central America's archaeology and mainly revolves around why so-called complex societies did not develop in this area. In a sense, this perspective was even the reason for defining the culture area. As explained above, the traditional perspective on social complexity primarily concerns social hierarchy. In order to describe the presence of a hierarchy that does not compare to the strongly hierarchically organized neighboring societies in the west, but also does not indicate an egalitarian society, many authors prefer to use the term "chiefdom," which has become established in the archaeology of Southern Central America and the Caribbean. In the Caribbean, the term "cacicazgo," is mainly used to express the same meaning. For northeast Honduras, it is also assumed that the population was organized in chiefdoms during the Cocal period (Begley 1999; Cuddy 2007; Healy 1978a, 1984a). However, there are two fundamental problems inherent in this term that are similar to the issues surrounding the concept of complex societies. On the one hand, the concept of a chiefdom is originally based on an evolutionary model of linear development, where it describes the level of a sociopolitical form of organization between egalitarian societies and the state (Oberg 1955; Service 1962), an outdated perspective that we now know to be invalid. In this model, chiefdoms are regarded as a precursor to state-organized societies. While many authors are aware of this problem and distance themselves from this evolutionist concept (e.g., Begley 1999), a second problem remains. There are numerous other possible forms of sociopolitical organization between egalitarian and state-organized societies. To apply the term "chiefdom" is highly simplistic in that there is no scope for conceptualizing the differences between these forms of organization, which are to be identified and analyzed. This raises the question as to which extent the term's application has any additional analytical value or if it even counteracts a detailed study (Cooke 2005: 151; Curet 2003; Wilson 2007: 111).

When dealing with the emergence of complex societies, we must, therefore, first ask ourselves what we ac-

23   Translation from Spanish by the author.

tually understand by complexity. In the present discourse, complexity is usually equated with hierarchy, i.e., a hierarchical social structure that divides society into groups according to power, property, or skills (see chapter 3.2.2.4). However, complexity can also take on forms other than a vertical hierarchy, which, in an archaeological context, would be traditionally identified by differences in architectural forms, settlement size, or grave goods. Thus, we must pursue new ways of describing societies and understanding how they function. An interesting approach can be found, for example, in the writings of Severin Fowles (2018). He argues that a society without social hierarchies can also be a "complex" society. Maintaining social simplicity can be a conscious, active choice, and particular strategies are needed in order to achieve it, such as imposing sanctions on people who want to usurp too much power. Thus, simplicity can be very complex. It can even cost more energy to consider and weigh each voice in contrast to enforcing the judgment of a ruler. In recent years, approaches have been developed that ask questions about the reasons for the emergence of alternative social formations (e.g., Hoopes 2005; Sheets 1992). Questions have also focused on the consequences that these forms of organization have in contrast to neighboring state-organized societies and whether they afford advantages, such as greater stability (Sheets 1992: 16).

What signs exist in Guadalupe to reconstruct the sociopolitical organization? The poorly preserved and hardly recognizable surface architecture gives us little evidence of social hierarchies in the classical sense. The burials do not initially allow conclusions to be drawn about hierarchies due to the lack of individual grave goods. Instead, the ceramic accumulation can be interpreted as a common grave good. The ancestors are buried together in one place, and through the clearly visible marking of the gravesite, they remain part of the social memory. It is not individuals who are honored here but the deceased who are remembered collectively. The ceramic's iconography also does not emphasize the existence of a ruling class. Instead, the iconography emphasizes the importance of the natural environment, which is apparently related to an animistic world view. No individual rulers are depicted here, as is the case for the neighboring Maya, for example. The pottery also has similar motifs but lacks a high degree of standardization, indicating more decentralized production. Presumably, this is not a strongly centralized network in which one or a few nodes are characterized by a high degree of connectivity. It instead seems that the settlements are well-connected to each other, with a more or less even distribution of connectivity.

However, we can identify elements that certainly had an important meaning for the inhabitants of Guadalupe

and the organization of society. It can be assumed that Guadalupe's festivities played a vital role in the sociopolitical organization and structured communal life in a significant way. The holding of festivities requires a certain amount of organization, food must be provided, rituals must be performed, and the course of events must be determined. Festivities can serve as an important framework for negotiating status or social position and can act as a motor for social change, i.e., they can serve as an explanatory approach to the emergence of certain forms of social complexity (Dietler / Hayden 2001). A second aspect that characterizes the pre-Hispanic inhabitants of Guadalupe and certainly had an important role in the organization within the society is a high degree of interconnectedness and connectivity. The presence of objects originating from distant regions, such as obsidian from La Esperanza, Ixtepeque, and Otumba, and the presence of jade beads from the Motagua Valley, points to a certain degree of complexity as defined in the context of this writing. The inhabitants of Guadalupe had access to objects from distant sources, were well connected, and were involved in various networks.

In summary, there is little evidence available that would suggest a hierarchical society in Guadalupe in a classical sense. At the moment, we have to assume that we are not dealing with a strongly hierarchical society in the form of vertical social classes. Other elements played an important role in society and were necessary for its organization, such as the holding of feasts that celebrated and enforced the connections between individuals and to the ancestors, who were worshipped and commemorated collectively. In the next chapter, we examine this aspect of connectedness on a broader scale and look at the question of sociopolitical organization on a regional level.

5.2 Regional Networks

After characterizing Guadalupe, the central node, and considering its function and economic and cultural aspects, the networks in which this node was integrated and the relationships and links it maintained with other nodes and networks are examined. I suggest that at least two networks can be identified on a regional level that were closely related to each other, where one represents a subnetwork of the other. On the one hand, we can retrace a coastal interaction system that encompasses the immediate surroundings of Guadalupe. It could presumably be reached within a day's journey and thus belonged to a closer field of interaction (Figure 208). This network is characterized by particularly compelling similarities in find material, especially ceramics, and

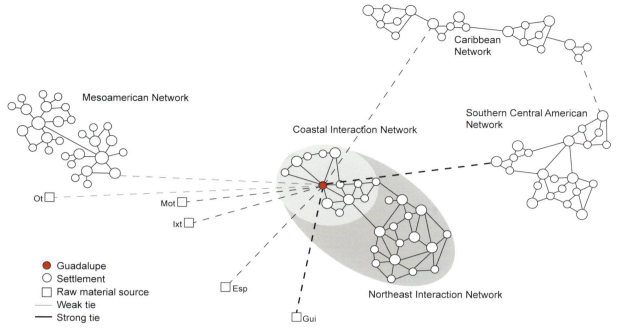

208   Schematic depiction of the different networks Guadalupe was connected to. Note that the graphs do not illustrate the actual network structure but are to be understood as a schematic representation of the networks and their subnetworks. Dotted lines indicate indirect links (F. Fecher).

thus suggests the existence of strong ties (see chapter 3.2.2). On the other hand, the current state of knowledge suggests that this network was part of a larger tradition that united the inhabitants of northeast Honduras and is reflected in similarities in architecture, material culture, and iconography. The degree to which these two systems of interaction can be reconstructed, the extent to which the inhabitants of Guadalupe were involved in them, and the location the inhabitants occupied within these networks are the subject of this chapter.

5.2.1 Coastal Interaction Network

Spatially, the first network covers the area ranging from Betulia in the west to the Guaimoreto Lagoon in the east. Towards the south, it includes the coastal Cordillera Nombre de Dios and the northern part of the Aguán Valley (see Figure 50). This extent corresponds to the area that the pre-Hispanic population, who did not have vehicles or pack animals, could reach within a day's walk. Depending on the terrain and the load carried, this could be a distance between 21 and 30 km (Hirth 2012: 648). Apart from traveling by foot, we know that the inhabitants of the region used canoes. Among the places that could be reached by canoe within a day certainly include the Bay Islands and other locations along the coast to the west and east. Future studies may identify more settlements along the coast as belonging to this

network. Due to strong similarities in the material culture, this area likely belonged to the "near environment" of Guadalupe's inhabitants.

The available information on existing sites and the reconstruction of this network is based on various sources. Publications from the first half of the 20th century do indeed examine and discuss the area but do not usually provide a precise location; thus, it is difficult to reconstruct the exact position of the described sites (Spinden 1925; Stone 1941; Strong 1935). Healy produced the first reliable data in the 1970s (1974b, 1975, 1978a, 1978b, 1984a). The Cuyamel Caves, Williams Ranch, Selin Farm, and Río Claro are described especially well in his publications. During surveys, he comes across additional settlements but does not describe them extensively. Selin Farm was later examined again by Whitney Goodwin (2019) via excavation, and Río Claro has been further studied by Dennett (2007). In the survey project, Costa Norte, directed by Robert Sharer (Sharer / Sedat / Pezzati 2009), some sites are briefly described, and a chronological classification based on surface material is presented. The IHAH conducted additional surveys. The results are available as reports in the IHAH archive. Lastly, surveys were conducted within our own project framework, which mainly focused on the coastal strip (see chapter 4.3). Here, too, the dating of the respective settlements is determined based on surface finds.

The information available from these sources paints the following picture: On the coastal section between

209   Location of Betulia and Río Coco. Note that there is no flat coastal plain between the two settlements but that the cordillera descends steeply towards the coast (Google Earth, F. Fecher).

Betulia in the west and Guaimoreto Lagoon in the east, there are few but significant settlements located at specific intervals. The pre-Hispanic settlements are usually found where the modern settlements are located today. They are preferably situated where rivers drain into the Atlantic Ocean and where depressions in the coastal cordillera allow easy passages into the Aguán Valley to the south.

To the west of Betulia, coastal settlements have not yet been registered. The cordillera slopes steeply towards the coast here and does not form a plain, as is the case further east (Figure 209). There are also no larger rivers. Today, there is no road leading west from Betulia; one can only travel along the coast by boat. The next modern settlement to the west is Rio Coco, located where the coast widens to a narrow plain. This area has not yet been systematically investigated due to poor accessibility. Signs of pre-Hispanic settlement are likely to be found here.

Most of the settlements registered along the coast date to the Cocal period, and most of them are located where modern settlements exist today. Whether this is due to continuity during the colonial period or to the favorable conditions of these locations is still not clear. Coraza Alta is an exception. It can be dated to the Selin period based on the surface pottery. Cruz, the site that Healy (1993) also identified as Selin phase, may be related to this site. Coraza Alta is a relatively large settlement that extends over about 0.2 km² west of Quebrada Corozo Alto and consists of several clearly recognizable settlement mounds. The discovery of numerous ground stone artifacts, several greenstone objects, and stones with evidence of grinding suggest that stone objects were produced in Coraza Alta (see Figure 46, Figure 47 and Figure 48). Interestingly, ground stone objects such as manos and metates, which were used in a domestic context, and fine greenstone beads, which were used as jewelry, were both apparently produced here. There seems to have been no separation in production between everyday objects and wealth objects. Additional Cocal-period lithic production sites were identified in Jerico and Agua Amarilla (Sharer / Sedat / Pezzati 2009).

Several settlements have been discovered in the area surrounding Guaimoreto Lagoon, where the coastal strip widens. Most cannot yet be dated. Only two settlements have been identified with occupation dating to the Cocal period. Selin Farm, the type site for the Selin phase, is the best-researched site in this area. With its mangrove forests serving as a home to a diverse array of species, the lagoon was undoubtedly considered a welcome source of food and made its surroundings a preferred settlement area during all periods.

In the south, the expansive, fertile Aguán Valley extends parallel to the coast. It is drained by the Aguán River, which flows into the Atlantic Ocean at Santa Rosa de Aguán. Today, the valley is used intensively for agriculture, and, presumably, it was also used as such in pre-Hispanic times. Currently, we can only speculate about the kind of plants cultivated. Edible plants were certainly included, but crops such as cotton and cocoa would also be conceivable. Bergmann (1969: 94f) shows that the Aguán Valley served as a cacao-growing area during the colonial period. Systematic surveys have still not been carried out in the Aguán Valley, and it is assumed that modern agricultural and settlement activities have destroyed many settlements. Nevertheless, we are aware of some significant settlements, all of which are located on the valley's northern edge. Again, most known sites date back to the Cocal period, including Panamá, Los Cocos, and Puerto Rico. Río Claro is considered the largest known settlement in the Aguán Valley. Here, more than 50 mounds with lengths of up to 50 m extend over an area of 450 x 190 m. A ditch surrounds a part of the settlement. Due to the settlement's size, Healy (1978a) believes that it could be the center of the *Papayeca* chiefdom, as reported by ethnohistorical sources (see below).

However, the site Rio Arriba 2 exceeds all known sites in the Aguán Valley in size. Several platforms measuring up to 80 m long are arranged around central plazas. On one side of the site, there are terraces fortified with stones. Considerable effort was invested in shaping the landscape here. A paved walkway runs through the settlement and, according to local informants, leads to the coast. This presents an important indication that the coastal settlements were connected to the settlements in the Aguán Valley. Rio Arriba 1, located directly adjacent to Rio Arriba 2, is also a large site that dates to the Selin period. Here, too, several mounds with sides reinforced with stone cobbles testify to a considerable population. Apart from Rio Arriba 1, only small villages, such as La Brea or San Esteban, are known to have existed during the Selin period in the Aguán Valley. They do not have visible architecture (Sharer / Sedat / Pezzati 2009).

Such large settlements transform our idea of the pre-Hispanic groups living in the Aguán Valley that prevailed in the past. Until now, the area did not appear to be densely populated. Apart from Río Claro, only small settlements were known, and it was assumed that most of the population was located on the coast (Goodwin 2019: 28). However, recent surveys have shown that the Aguán Valley was a center of large and densely populated settlements and that Río Claro was not the only sizeable example. The valley must have had a considerable population during the Cocal period, which is confirmed by ethnohistorical sources (Lara Pinto 1980: 63).

The attractiveness of the valley as a settlement area is related to its climatic conditions and geographical location. It offers ample area for agricultural activities, and the Aguán River provides sufficient water. At the same time, it forms an important transport route to the Atlantic. Crossing the Cordillera Nombre de Dios, the coast can be reached in a few hours where marine resources are available. There are several indications for the existence of these connecting routes. Firstly, the location of the settlements in both areas indicates that the

mountain passes in the cordillera were used as navigable routes. In fact, the settlements on the coast are located directly on the northern side of these passes, and, in the Aguán Valley, they are located in the northern part of the valley. During our surveys, we were able to register the settlements Colonia Suyapa and La Polaca. Both sites lie along these routes that connect the coast to the Aguán Valley and may have served as waystations. Finally, the existence of physical paths clearly indicates lively exchange that must have existed between the inhabitants of the coast and those of the valley.

The Bay Islands were undoubtedly part of this network. This is especially true of the nearby islands of Guanaja and Roatán, which are plainly visible from the mainland on a clear day. These islands can be reached by canoe within a day. Ethnohistorical sources confirm a close relationship between the inhabitants of the islands and the coast around Trujillo when the Spanish arrived (Lara Pinto 1980: 78, 1991: 234).

The interaction's intensity is reflected by the close similarities in the material culture, especially in the ceramics. Almost identical forms and motifs to those in Guadalupe were found in the Aguán Valley and the Bay Islands (Figure 210). The close connection to the islands is also evident in the distinctive categories of material culture found in both areas. These include zoomorph ocarinas, miniature vessels, metal bells, and the presence of Bay Island Polychrome Vessels. It also becomes evident in the existence of ceremonial sites where objects were repeatedly deposited over an extended period (Strong 1935: 146). Although the same motifs frequently appear when comparing the material culture in this region, they can differ slightly in their execution. At the same time, there are particular forms that only occur in certain settlements and are not found in others. Taken together, these criteria indicate that people were in contact with each other and connected by a similar worldview, which is expressed in ceramics. It does not suggest that there was strong centralization.

Can we define the nature of the interaction that took place between the inhabitants of this region? To design a reliable model, more data, especially from the Aguán Valley, is necessary. What is clear, however, is that marine resources were extracted along the coast. The discovery of marine gastropods in sites in the cordillera suggests that these resources were not only exploited locally but that they were also brought to the hinterland. A similar exchange network in which *strombus gigas* were transported from the coast to the hinterland has been identified in northern Venezuela (Antczak 1998: 215-218). In return, agricultural products from the Aguán Valley may have been exchanged to the coast. The coastal plain is very narrow and offers little space to grow plants on a large scale. However, the presence of

Bay Islands (Barbereta)

Aguán Valley

(Strong 1935: Plate 30e)

(Stone 1941: Fig. 36e)

Bay Islands (Guanaja)

(Craig 1977: 24)

Peroles Calientes

(Stone 1941: Fig. 19)

Bay Islands (Roatán)

(Goodwin 2011: Fig. 6.14)

Culmi Valley

(Begley 1999: Fig. 4.4.3)

Río Claro

(Healy 1993: Fig. 11.20c)

(Dennett 2007: Fig. 4.22)

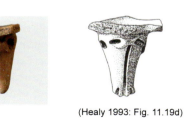

(Healy 1993: Fig. 11.19d)

(Dennett 2007: Fig. 4.22)

210   Ceramic fragments from different regions of northeast Honduras compared to ceramic from Guadalupe. The sherds with a gray background were found in Guadalupe (F. Fecher). Doris Stone, *Archaeology of the North Coast of Honduras,* Memoirs of the Peabody Museum of Archaeology and Ethnology, Harvard University, vol. 9, no. 1, 1941, figure 19 and 36e. Reprinted courtesy of the Peabody Museum, Harvard University.

numerous manos and metates shows that agricultural products were consumed here. The presence of spindle whorls indicates that textile fibers were processed here, which may have also been cultivated in the Aguán Valley. It is also possible that other products from the valley were brought to the coast to transport them on to more distant places. Columbus' report of his encounter with the trading canoe testifies that such an exchange of goods by canoe existed.

This coastal network consists of close connections and strong ties that are reflected in regular exchange. It presumably represented an everyday environment, and contact between its agents certainly went beyond simple exchange relationships. Ideas and information were exchanged through objects, as is evident in the shared iconography. These connections formed a network that was based on and had access to both terrestrial and aquatic ecosystems; it could use and exchange resources from both regions. The people who were part of this system had access to a very efficient and stable food base because it involved different environments. It included marine resources, the lagoon, mangrove forests with their rich food supply, the forests of the cordillera, and agricultural products from a large fertile valley. Moreover, fresh water from mountain springs and the Aguán River was ubiquitous and could be used for subsistence, production, and agricultural activities. Water was undoubtedly an essential part of this system and did not act as a separating element but as a connecting one that enabled and promoted the exchange between people in the valley, on the coast, and on the islands. Coastal regions with favorable conditions have proven to be the driving forces for the origin of early societies in pre-Hispanic America, which attests to their productivity. The coastal interaction network seen here presumably has a certain temporal depth. Located at one of the passes leading from the valley to the coast, the Cuyamel Caves were used as prominent ritual sites during the Formative period and are an important indication of this.

How was this network organized, and was there a hierarchical connection between the settlements and their inhabitants? The archaeological evidence shows that there was a particular settlement hierarchy, at least in the Aguán Valley, in which large settlements can be interpreted as centers controlling smaller nearby settlements. Ethnohistorical sources confirm this system. They inform us that the area around Trujillo, where the Spaniards settled in 1525, was organized into different hierarchical levels. The sources tell of two geopolitical units located near Trujillo: Chapagua and Papayeca. They refer to these units as "provinces," although it is not entirely clear what this term implies. While the precise location of Chapagua remains unknown, Lara Pinto (1980: 72) was able to locate Papayeca in the Aguán Val-

ley. She assumes that the territory of this geopolitical entity included the Aguán Valley but probably extended beyond it. A second important element is that these "provinces" included various "*sujetos*," i.e., localities that were subject to them. This description suggests that there was at least a two-tiered political system. Furthermore, it is interesting that several "*señores*" or leaders are mentioned for each province (Lara Pinto 1980: 71). Thus, it seems as though the power was not held by a single person but distributed over several authorities. To what extent the settlements on the coast were integrated into this system is not clear from these sources.

The archaeological finds and features from the coastal sites make it difficult to interpret them in this respect because the Cocal period sites present themselves mainly in the form of ceramic concentrations and individual stone formations. Information about architecture from which we could infer the size of settlements is lacking at the moment. This is further complicated by the fact that most Cocal-period settlements are overbuilt by modern settlements. Thus, we mainly have to rely on finds to make statements about similarities and differences.

Which position did Guadalupe occupy within this network? Compared to the other coastal settlements, Guadalupe stands out due to several characteristics. There is an enormously large number of ceramics that is not seen in other sites on the mainland. The presence of Bay Island Polychrome is especially remarkable, which has not been found at any other settlement along the coast. The presence of metal bells and needles is not known anywhere else in this region either. However, the enormous amount of obsidian fragments that we registered in Guadalupe is especially surprising. Some of these observations are indeed based on the fact that excavations have not been carried out at the other sites, and they will surely be revised in the future. The abundance of pottery and obsidian, which is quite apparent even on Guadalupe's surface, has not been matched at any other sites during our surveys. The possible reasons for this are discussed in the following.

Guadalupe's context is complex. We have clear evidence for integration into extensive exchange networks (jade beads, metal objects, obsidian from various sources, and polychrome ceramics), but also for ritual activities that only reflect the final use of these objects. This only gives us an incomplete idea about how the objects found their way to Guadalupe and what their use was before they were deposited in the ritual context. This raises the question of whether we can attribute these special objects in Guadalupe to economic connections or whether they are more related to the ritual activities and festivities that were performed in Guadalupe. The two elements are not mutually exclusive and are often even closely linked. One need only consider pilgrimage destinations in medieval Europe, which also had an enormous economic factor and served as a trading center for various goods. It is precisely the combination of economic and cultural/ritual elements listed as criteria for the definition of international trade centers by Gasco and Berdan (2003). In the Bay Islands, the discovery of a diverse number of products is interpreted as an indication that the islanders were involved in far-reaching exchange networks (Nance 1965, cited in Goodwin 2011) and that they, therefore, enjoyed special privileges. This theory is mainly based on objects that we also found in Guadalupe. So, this theory might also apply to the inhabitants of Guadalupe. For Wild Cane Cay (Belize), a generally increased amount of exotic goods and a substantial amount of obsidian compared to the surrounding settlements is used as an argument to describe the location as a coastal trading port (McKillop 1989, 1996). Guadalupe's location can explain its economically important position. As a coastal settlement, Guadalupe acts as a link between the hinterland and the Bay Islands; it may have served as a kind of transshipment point for goods. In any case, goods from the Aguán Valley that were brought to the coast via land route had to be loaded into canoes in order to be transported by sea, which leads to the coastal settlements becoming a kind of hub or transshipment point, a nexus of economic interchange (Zeitlin 1978: 203).

Considering the entire situation in the context of network theory, it becomes even more apparent. The links to Mesoamerica can be understood in the sense of Granovetter's (1973) "weak tie," i.e., an infrequent interaction that has no increased importance for everyday life. Nevertheless, this link is an important connection because Granovetter shows that weak ties are especially important for the flow of information and resources. Guadalupe fulfills a crucial bridging function by connecting this network with the Mesoamerican network (and its subnetworks) due to its position as a node on the edge of the coastal interaction network. In the words of Ronald Burt (1992), Guadalupe serves as a "broker" that connects the two otherwise separate networks. These brokers have an advantage because they have access to different subnetworks and the information and resources exchanged via these networks. To a certain degree, they can decide to what extent and to whom they pass on this information or not. It is conceivable that Guadalupe's distinctiveness results from this strategic position within the network structure.

5.2.2 NORTHEAST INTERACTION NETWORK

The regional interaction network discussed above is embedded in a larger system and can be understood as a subnetwork of a more extended entity. Judging by the similarities in material culture, this extended network covers large parts of northeast Honduras. The definition of this area has already been addressed in chapter 4.1. Begley (1999: 259f) discusses its extent based on current data. However, the limits of this network are not clear due to the lack of available data. The data we have for this region mainly comprise research results from the first half of the 20th century. These include the expedition along the Patuca River by Strong (1934), the observations by Stone (1941) on the sites of Jamasquire, Peroles Calientes, and Los Andes, and the geographic reconnaissance trip by Helbig (1956). Helbig's journey led from Danlí to Dulce Nombre del Culmí, the Agalta Valley to the coast, and along the Paulaya River back to his starting point. In the second half of the 20th century, several expeditions were undertaken to the Mosquitia and the northeast (Lara Pinto / Hasemann 1991). Unfortunately, the research results were often not published, which makes it difficult to verify the data. Instead, we have to partially rely on personal statements. Furthermore, we have to rely on the principle of similarity since there are hardly any scientific analyses of material culture. For example, Hasemann, Lara Pinto, and Sandoval Cruz (2017: 152f), who participated in such expeditions, state that the mainland's ceramic traditions (in the Culmí, Paulaya, and Plátano areas) are very similar to those of the Bay Islands. Exceptions include the publication of Clark et al. (1982), which describes several sites along the Rio Tinto, the pottery analysis of Piedra Blanca by Véliz (1978), which is based on a collection from Spinden, and the studies of Begley in the Culmí Valley (1999), which is the only comprehensive settlement study in the area to date. This also includes the recently conducted studies in the Ciudad del Jaguar in the Mosquitia (Fisher et al. 2016). In addition to archaeological publications, museum collections are another means of reconstructing the information gathered during these surveys. Objects collected by Strong that are now stored at the NMNH were, for example, studied by Cuddy (2007). Figure 3 shows the sites known in the northeast, which could be assigned to the Cocal period. Outside of our study area, these sites are concentrated in the mouth of the Rio Tinto (also known as Black River), the Culmí Valley, and the headwaters of the Rio Patuca.

The Cocal-period site of Piedra Blanca is located east of Corocito in the Aguán Valley. The pottery found here is very similar in form, incisions, and appliqués to Guadalupe's. There are even identical motifs. The sites were presumably closely connected, and Piedra Blanca may have even been part of the coastal interaction network.

Clark et al. (1982) describe several sizeable settlements between the mouth of the Rio Tinto and the village of Sico. The area along the Rio Tinto seems to have been densely populated. In addition to surface concentrations of pottery and the discovery of several metates at different locations, the two sites, Aguacates and Antiguales de Claura, are described in detail. Aguacates consists of several rectangular and L-shaped mounds with a height of up to 4 m. Several stone statues were found during excavations and visits by the IHAH, including stone slabs and a carved stone owl. The pottery depicted in the publication dates to the Cocal period. It has strong similarities to the Guadalupe pottery, but there are also motifs not found in Guadalupe and vice versa. For example, the wave pattern, which is very common in Guadalupe, is not reported in Aguacates. Los Antiguales de Claura is located approximately 2 km to the west of Aguacates on the river of the same name. More than 30 rectangular mounds arranged in two parallel lines, resulting in an elongated shape, have been recorded here. More than 80 metate fragments were found in the settlement area, most of them three-legged and some decorated with geometric patterns. The chronology of the site is not entirely clear from the description of the material but probably dates to the Cocal phase as well.

Peroles Calientes and Los Andes are very close to these two settlements, and are described by Stone (1941). Peroles Calientes is an offertory site. Numerous vessels are deposited here near a hot spring. The presence of painted pottery and manatee lugs proves that it dates to the Selin phase. Rider lugs, as found in Río Claro (Dennett 2007), show that the site was also used during the Cocal phase to a lesser extent. Los Andes apparently dates to the Selin phase. The material from both sites is not very similar to Guadalupe's, which may be due to the differing chronology.

Begley (1999) registered 125 sites in the Culmí Valley near the headwaters of the Rio Plátano and Paulaya, which is about 100 km inland. The architecture consists of earthen mounds that reach up to 10 m in height and 200 m in length. Some are faced with cobbles. Most of the settlements date to the Selin period. Begley (1999: 194) assesses that the highest population density existed between AD 300 and 1200. In the Late Cocal period, the occupation seems to have declined. Begley uses Healy's existing typology to classify the pottery found throughout the Culmí Valley, which presupposes that he sees similarities to the pottery found on the northeast coast. We can see similarities in the few published images of the pottery, but the information is too limited to allow detailed comparative studies. Begley sees differences in the fabric and thus suggests local production. He also

reports finding many metates throughout his study area. At one of the sites, he finds thousands of miniature metates (Begley 1999: 161).

Near the headwaters of the Rio Patuca, the sites las Crucitas del Rio Aner and Wankybila are repeatedly mentioned as examples of important and impressive settlements, but published information is minimal. Hasemann investigated Las Crucitas in the 1970s, but the report was never published. Lara Pinto and Hasemann (1991) present some information about the settlement and provide a site plan. It is located near the Rio Wampú, a tributary of the Rio Patuca, and consists of several structures arranged around a central plaza. The authors describe the site as a monumental site. According to them, the material culture is very similar to that of the Rio Paulaya and Rio Plátano regions. Descriptions or illustrations of the material are not given. According to Begley, the settlement dates to the Cocal phase (1999: 192).

Wankybila is located on the confluence of the Rio Wampú and the Rio Patuca. Strong (1934) visited the site and carried out test excavations. He described at least 14 mounds that range up to 12 m long. Wankybila seems to have been inhabited during the Selin and Cocal phases, although Cuddy (2007) notes that the similarity to the other settlements in the northeast increases during the Cocal phase. Strong mentions more settlements along the upper tributaries of the Patuca River, which feature formally arranged mounds, monoliths, and paved causeways. Recently, LIDAR flights have discovered 19 settlements in the Valle de Fortaleza, also located on a tributary of the Patuca River near the Rio Plátano Biosphere Reserve (Fisher et al. 2016). The researchers assume a three-tiered settlement hierarchy. One of the largest settlements is Ciudad del Jaguar, where several rectangular mounds are distributed across terraces, with some of them having a square-pattern layout. In Ciudad de Jaguar, a cache with numerous ground stone objects like metates and stone bowls was found and dates to the Early Cocal phase. However, finds from sites in the Valle de Fortaleza that could be used in a stylistic comparison with the Guadalupe material have not yet been published.

In summary, all of the settlements presented here have a link to Guadalupe and the coastal interaction network. This is true of their architecture (paved walkways and earthen mounds) and material culture, especially regarding the presence of unpainted pottery decorated with incisions and appliqués, which exemplifies a certain stylistic similarity throughout the area. In Piedra Blanca, there are almost identical shapes to those found in Guadalupe, and therefore we can assume that there was a closer connection between these nodes. However, between the other locations, only a general similarity is noted but not the presence of common specific features. For example, in Antiguales, we find rider lugs that also exist in Río Claro but not Guadalupe. A network of waterways may have connected the sites along the Aguán River and the Rio Sico River. However, it is somewhat bold to reconstruct networks based on single features with so little available data.

Just as similarities between sites are of interest, differences are as well. The discovery of stone sculptures, slabs, and three-legged metates is mentioned for many sites in the northeast network. Deposits with hundreds of such objects were found at several sites. The presence of numerous ground stone artifacts seems to be a defining characteristic of the northeast interaction network. In Guadalupe, we found a fragment of a three-legged sculpted metate, while another carved metate in a private collection is said to have come from Betulia. The other metates found in Guadalupe and other settlements of the coastal interaction network are simple, undecorated metates without legs. Stone sculptures have not been registered on the coast either. This data suggests that Guadalupe was part of the northeast network but that the connections may not have been as intense as those with the coastal settlements. At the same time, we must bear in mind that metates and stone sculptures are sought-after objects for collectors and that the coastal region is more densely populated than the Mosquitia. Only further studies can provide clarity. They should include identification of settlements and extensive excavations to corroborate our statements about the existing networks. The publication of research data is of particular importance to provide a basis for comparative work.

Despite the limited data, can we still make statements about the type of interaction that characterized the northeast interaction network and led to the similarities in material culture? What kind of theories exist regarding this? Begley (1999: 15) sees an underlying cultural affiliation as the reason for the similarities in material culture, which he attributes to common ancestral tradition—cultural or biological. Cuddy (2007) goes a step further by assuming that the similarities in material culture can be traced back to a common identity related to the development of northeast Honduras within the framework of a paramount polity starting at about AD 300. "Northeast Honduras crafted its identity from, and tactfully in relation to, its stalwart and more renowned neighbors" (Cuddy 2007: 5). Furthermore, theories on the northeast culture region concern the nature of relations with neighboring culture areas and the reasons behind the emergence of social hierarchy. Begley sketches a scenario in which the elite consciously adopted elements from Mesoamerica in order to gain prestige. As examples of these elements, he cites ballcourts and architectural elements in particular. He argues that not only symbolism but also the underlying concepts and linked worldviews were adopted with them. Begley sees

this as a conscious strategy of the elite to gain prestige and maintain power through esoteric knowledge. Cuddy follows Begley in some aspects but emphasizes the inclusionary strategy of the elite. He emphasizes the role of political identity, which plays a major part in the region's cohesion and stability. In his eyes, however, the emulation of foreign elements does not necessarily imply the adoption of ideologies.

It is striking that these theories attribute an important role to the neighboring Mesoamerican culture area, directly or indirectly, for the internal developments of the societies in northeast Honduras. Furthermore, although the nature of the interactions between the agents (common ancestry and political strategies for inclusion) is considered, the possible nature of these interactions in practice is not. Were goods transferred and information exchanged? Which goods were produced, which resources were needed for this, and where were they found? What role did stone and greenstone, for example, play as raw materials? What meaning can be assigned to the deposits of ground stone implements? Are these also possible signs of feasting that functioned as a form of social interaction? Or were there other types of social interaction, such as conflicts? And what role did rivers play as connecting routes? Again, only careful future research can answer these questions. Until these fundamental questions are clarified, and we have a stable framework that also explains the temporal issues, we should evaluate the scope of the available data and ensure that the extent of the theories built on it correspond.

5.3 Towards the Identification of Interregional Networks

As described throughout the text, the societies in northeast Honduras were often characterized by their relations to neighboring culture regions. This section combines the available data with that from our investigations in Guadalupe to examine the evidence for existing links to Mesoamerica, Southern Central America, and the Caribbean. While these three regions were previously perceived as culture areas, they are understood as networks with respective subnetworks in this work (Figure 211). As of yet, northeast Honduras' relations with Mesoamerica have primarily been considered, while there are only a few systematic studies on the relations with Southern Central America. However, considerations of links to the Caribbean are new and have not yet been dealt with comprehensively. At this point, the analysis can no longer be conducted based on the connections between individual settlements. Instead, it

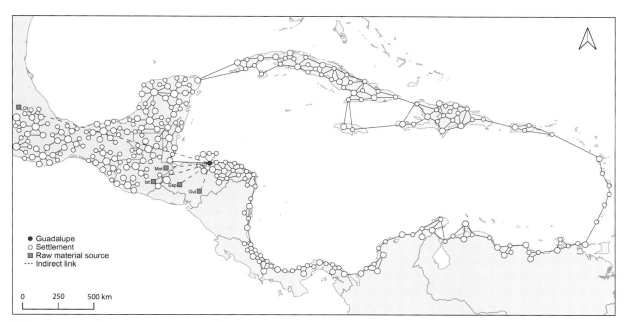

211   Schematic depiction of networks in Middle America. Note that the nodes do not represent the exact locations of settlements and that the graphs do not illustrate the actual network structure. They are to be understood as a schematic representation of the networks and their subnetworks. Note that the Mesoamerican networks are more centralized compared to the other networks. The emphasis is on the depiction of interaction along the coasts. Dotted lines indicate indirect links (F. Fecher).

is conducted on a more general level regarding the extent to which Guadalupe was related to these different networks.

5.3.1 Links to Mesoamerica

The relationship between northeast Honduras and Mesoamerica is most often discussed. It is based on a greater interest in the "complex societies" to the west but also on the fact that there is more data available in this region. Defining the southern border of the Maya's sphere of influence was one reason the first researchers came to Honduras (e.g., Spinden 1925; Strong 1935). With the conducted research in Guadalupe and the surrounding area, we can contribute new data that will allow us to make more precise statements about these interactions.

Previous research in Mesoamerica has shown that the exchange mechanisms in the Postclassic period differed from those of the Classic period (Freidel 1978: 239; Smith / Berdan 2003b; Stemp / Graham / Goulet 2011: 137). Current theories suggest that the collapse of elite networks at the end of the Classic led to a decentralization of exchange. This also brought about new opportunities for access to resources, and new trade routes were established. Exchange along the Atlantic coast played an increasingly important role: Various trading centers were identified (Andrews et al. 1988; Gasco / Berdan 2003; McKillop 1996; Simmons / Graham 2017), a shift of

population to the coast became apparent, and the volume and diversity of commodities increased. Some ethnohistorical sources indicate that western Honduras was involved in these exchange networks. Piña Chan (1978) compiles various sources that illustrate this. Among other things, he reports of a conversation between Maya traders and Cortés: "they told him they were merchants and understanding his intent they showed him a canvas, woven of cotton, (where) the road to Naco and Nito in Honduras and even to Nicaragua was painted" (Herrera y Tordesillas 1934-36, cited in Piña Chan 1978: 44). A Cocom-Maya lord escaped a massacre in Mayapán because he was on a trade journey to the Ulúa Valley (Landa 1978: 18). "In the town of Ichmul there were temples where the lords of Chichen Itza made sacrifices when they embarked on or returned from a commerce trip to Honduras" (Piña Chan 1978: 38). He also shows that there was a coastal route connecting Yucatán with western Honduras. One of the goods traded was cacao, which was cultivated in the Ulúa Valley and used as currency during the Postclassic period. Feathers were another commodity from west Honduras (Bergmann 1969; Healy 1974b: 442; Scholes / Roys 1968: 316). Some researchers also assume that the inhabitants of the Bay Islands were involved in trade with Mesoamerica, especially with the Maya (Epstein 1957: 3; Epstein / Véliz 1977; Nance 1965, cited in Goodwin 2011: 130). This is mainly confirmed by exotic archaeological finds such as metal objects, the discovery of a piece of Plumbate pottery (Véliz / Willey / Healy

1977), and Bay Island Polychrome vessels, whose iconography is similar to that of Mesoamerica. The excavations in Guadalupe have brought similar objects to light that show that the inhabitants were also involved in exchange relationships with the west, albeit to a lesser extent. Based on Guadalupe's data, we can assume that the exchange route described in ethnohistorical sources did not end in western Honduras but (possibly sporadically) extended further east. The presence of obsidian from the Ixtepeque source in present-day Guatemala and Otumba in Central Mexico is a clear indication. The piece from Otumba is a casual flake made from an exhausted blade core. It certainly reached Guadalupe indirectly via several stages. The available data suggest that obsidian from Ixtepeque was imported to Guadalupe in the form of finished blades. Whether the blades came to Guadalupe directly from Ixtepeque or another processing center is unclear. However, the raw material can be clearly attributed to the source. The obsidian was likely transported to the coast via the Rio Motagua and then reached Guadalupe by sea (Hammond 1972). Although blades from these sources found their way to Guadalupe in their finished state, we have evidence that prismatic blades were manufactured at Guadalupe from Güinope obsidian. This manufacturing technique is a Mesoamerican technology (Braswell 1997: 19). The fact that the inhabitants of Guadalupe adopted it shows that the interaction went beyond a mere exchange of goods. To learn and adopt a technique, people have to learn from each other, communicate with each other, and see the production process with their own eyes. At the same time, the process was not simply adopted but adapted to local conditions and needs; it was modified. The production of prismatic blades of Güinope obsidian is a perfect example of the confluence of different levels of interaction that we encounter in northeast Honduras and that define this region. Greenstone beads made of jade, which most likely originate from the Motagua Valley, are another indication of exchange relations with Mesoamerica. Again, it remains unclear where the beads were made. We know that raw material was exchanged from the Motagua Valley to other places (Kovacevich 2013; Wagner 2012). Nevertheless, based on the current data, production in Guadalupe cannot be confirmed. Greenstone beads are a product that was often crafted from leftovers of raw material from other production chains. Such objects were not found in Guadalupe. Other production waste or tools for processing greenstone were not encountered. Furthermore, one would expect a higher number of greenstone objects in a production center. Nevertheless, there was a greenstone processing tradition in northeast Honduras, as shown above, and it is conceivable that the beads were made in the area around Guadalupe. The presence of jade in Guadalupe is significant because it is

the first place in northeast Honduras where real jade has been identified. Other artifacts analyzed so far are all made of social jade, i.e., softer material such as muscovite, serpentine, or soapstone (Begley 1999: 175f; Cuddy 2007: 122; Strong 1935: 62). The presence of real jade in Guadalupe is an indication that the inhabitants had access to exotic material from long-distance exchange.

The origin of the metal objects is puzzling. The composition and style of the needle indicate an origin in the Central Mexican highlands. However, it is not clear how it found its way to Guadalupe. Regarding obsidian from Otumba, I would suspect less a direct exchange than an indirect contact, such as down-the-line exchange. Nevertheless, its presence is another indication that the inhabitants of Guadalupe had access to an exchange network that included distant regions in Mesoamerica. It represents a significant find, as only needles made of other materials such as bone have been found in sites in the northeast until now (Healy 1978b: 60f; Stone 1934a: 131). The bell also points more to Mesoamerica due to its copper composition, where such bells were a popular trading item during the Postclassic period. However, as long as it has not been confirmed if there was regional metal production in northeast or western Honduras, as ethnohistorical sources suggest, we cannot consider the bells as reliable evidence of an economic connection to Mesoamerica.

Another element to consider is the Bay Island Polychrome ceramic style, the name of which comes from its initial discovery on Roatán. However, the production location of the ceramics remains unknown. Its polychrome nature makes it stand out from otherwise unpainted ceramics. Some authors recognize a plumed serpent or serpent bird motif. This motif is an important theme in Mesoamerica with roots in the Formative period. Later, it is associated with Kukulcan by the Maya or Quetzalcoatl by the Aztecs. The symbol was widely spread during the Postclassic period and is regarded as part of the international style (Smith / Berdan 2003a: 4). Reyes Mazzoni (1976: 397) and Cuddy (2007: 137) see the Bay Island Polychrome Style as very similar to the Papagayo Polychrome Ceramics in Nicoya. However, as Cuddy correctly notes, the Bay Island Polychrome vessels also have local elements, especially in the shape and design of the handles. So, once again, these vessels testify to a confluence of different influences: Mesoamerican iconography represented on a local vessel form. Furthermore, this indicates that the connections to Mesoamerica went beyond the mere exchange of materials and techniques, but ideas and stories were also shared.

Another indication for the exchange of ideas is the identification of *patolli* game boards on Guanaja and in Sawacito in the Mosquitia. As described above, *patolli* is a game known from Mesoamerica where it was strongly tied to religious practice and cosmovision (Fecher 2019). The game occurs in the Maya region and central and western Mexico. It is known from different archaeological contexts and is depicted in codices. The design of the Guanaja *patollis* is very similar to a *patolli* game depicted in the Codex Borgia, whose origin is attributed to the Central Mexican highlands. So, I would assume that the inspiration for the *patollis* on Guanaja most likely comes from interaction with groups from the Central Mexican highlands during Period VI. However, data is very sparse here as well, and the interpretation is not certain. However, it is certain that the presence of the *patollis* once again shows us that the interaction extended beyond an economic level. Simultaneously, it illustrates how difficult it is to separate different types of networks or interactions from one another because economic interaction is always also social interaction if only because communication is needed to negotiate the values of items. Similar to the adoption of technologies, the adoption of games requires close interaction on a social level. The rules of the game must be communicated, and perhaps the game was played together. The discovery of at least five *patollis* on Guanaja (there are indications that there were more) suggests that the game was very popular and occupied an important role among the island's inhabitants. At the same time, it supports the hypothesis that the inhabitants of Guanaja and the islands, in general, were involved in exchange relationships. The discovery of a *patolli* game in the Mosquitia is surprising. It is not clear if it also found its way there through direct contact with inhabitants of the Mesoamerican culture area or, more likely, through a close exchange with the Bay Islanders or inhabitants of the northeast, who knew about the game and its rules. The extent to which religious practices and cosmovision associated with the game were also adopted remains open. Perhaps it was just a pastime.

A much-debated topic that also concerns interaction with the inhabitants of Mesoamerica is the question of Nahua presence. Some scholars believe that when the Spanish arrived, several Nahua enclaves in northeast Honduras were associated with the expansion of trade relations during Period VI. Lara Pinto and Hasemann (1988) even attribute the monumental architecture in the Mosquitia to immigrated Nahua groups. Other authors believe that the province of Papayeca was a Nahua enclave (Fowler 1983; Stone 1976: 194). The authors largely rely on ethnohistorical sources and linguistic data. In particular, the story of Cortés' interpreter, who may have been able to speak Nahuat and could communicate in the region, is cited as evidence. The problem is that such a presence has not yet been proven in an archaeological context. On the contrary, the material culture of northeast Honduras during Period VI differs greatly from that of its western neighbors but shows more similarity to the material culture of Costa Rica. Although some of the objects described above suggest a specific interaction with the Mexican highlands, I believe this is due to economic and social interaction in particular and not migratory movements. In my opinion, the ethnohistorical sources can at best be interpreted to the effect that northeast Honduras was integrated into a trade network, and Nahua possibly served as the lingua franca in this network, as initially suggested in earlier texts by Lara Pinto (1980).

In conclusion, the following picture emerges when considering interaction with Mesoamerica. The inhabitants of Guadalupe had access to one or more exchange networks that connected western Honduras to the Maya region and indirectly reached as far as Central Mexico. Based on the few objects that we can assign with certainty to a Mesoamerican origin, we must assume that this contact was somewhat sporadic and consisted of weak ties, that no large quantities of goods were traded, and that the inhabitants of Guadalupe relied mainly on local and regional raw materials and products. Of course, perishable materials may have played a more significant role in the exchange, but we cannot prove this at the moment. Furthermore, we can see that the interaction took place not only on an economic level but also on a social one, which is evident in the adoption of technologies, iconography, and games for which closer communication is needed.

Another important observation is that, due to objects such as metal items, real jade, and obsidian, Guadalupe occupies a unique position. These objects have not been found in such great quantities at any other locations within the coastal interaction network. Guadalupe is unique due to its location on the coast and its function as an important ritual site. Based on this observation, we can also assume that the exchange route that connected western Honduras with Mesoamerican societies extended further east along the coast and that the inhabitants of Guadalupe had access to this network.

Ultimately, it is clear that the economic and social interaction with the inhabitants of Mesoamerica did not leave any major cultural traces, which supports the observations of earlier authors (e.g., Goodwin 2011: 23; Healy 1984a). The style of material culture bears little resemblance to the adjacent culture area in the west. It shows much stronger similarities to the material culture further south. The contact did not apparently lead to the formation of an elite or an increase in the import of luxury goods or prestige objects from this region, as is sometimes argued. The extent to which the interaction has led to changes in architecture, as Begley (1999) suggests, needs to be examined more closely, as local developments are also conceivable here.

5.3.2 LINKS TO SOUTHERN CENTRAL AMERICA

In the pursuit of reconstructing connections to Southern Central America, detailed ethnohistorical sources are not available as they are for Mesoamerica. However, a few archaeological finds testify that during Period VI, there was exchange between the inhabitants of Mesoamerica and Southern Central America in both directions. As a prominent example, metal objects deposited in the Sacred Cenote in Chichen Itza are mentioned, whose distinctive style points to an origin in Costa Rica or Panama (Lothrop 1952). On the other hand, Plumbate ceramic fragments produced on the Pacific coast in the border area between Guatemala and Mexico have been found as far away as Panama (Evans 2008: 347f; Sharer / Traxler 2006: 583).

The existence of greenstone objects with Maya inscriptions in Costa Rica, which were reworked there, points to an existing network during earlier periods. However, there are few detailed theoretical models that characterize these exchange networks or consider the nature of the prevailing interaction. Apart from Dennett's publication (2007) that characterizes northeast Honduras as a frontier zone of Southern Central America, there are no models that look closer at the interaction between our research area and Southern Central America. The prevailing opinion that the inhabitants of northeast Honduras had a close connection to Southern Central America during the Cocal period can be confirmed by research in Guadalupe and its surroundings. Both the material culture and cultural traditions show striking similarities to this culture area. Based on the results of previous studies and our research data, we will look closer at the elements involved, identify whether we can define the interaction more precisely on a geographical level, and consider the nature of the interaction.

The first category of interest here is architecture. Due to the excavations in Guadalupe and the results of other projects, we already have a particular base of data that we can draw from. At the moment, it seems that stone buildings did not exist in northeast Honduras as we find them in Mesoamerica. Buildings were constructed from perishable materials like wood, clay, and palm leaves. Platforms are still preserved in the archaeological record today and give us information about the arrangement of buildings, rows of stones as structure foundations, and postholes, which yield information about the buildings' shape and size. Sometimes, as in Guadalupe, even remains of the daub are preserved. If we compare these elements with the architecture in Southern Central America, we notice some similarities. Elements that are widespread in large parts of Southern Central America and considered a defining part of it include, for example, the rather unplanned alignment of mounds loosely arranged around central spaces that often follow the topography. This stands in contrast to the typical rectangularly arranged courtyard groups that can be found in Mesoamerica. Unworked river cobbles are often used in Southern Central America to reinforce platforms, which serve as the basis for building houses or for other construction activities. Cut stone is not used here, as is the case in many Mesoamerican regions where stones were carved to build facades. The buildings themselves are usually made of perishable material (Hoopes 2001). Since we find all of these features in northeast Honduras as well, we can see a clear relation to Southern Central America in this regard. At the same time, the layout of some sites is particular to northeast Honduras. The existence of rectangularly arranged settlements in the Mosquitia must be investigated in more detail. This element does not necessarily have to be considered Mesoamerican but could also be a local characteristic. The presence of paved walkways is distinctive. These are paths paved with river cobbles located within and between settlements that connect them or lead to important points in the landscape, such as rivers or springs. These walkways can be found in many Southern Central American settlements, especially in Costa Rica, where they became increasingly common in Period VI. We find them, for example, in Guayabo de Turrialba (Stone 1977: 201), Las Mercedes (Snarskis 1984: 227), La Fábrica, La Cabaña and Anita Grande (Snarskis 1981), Murciélago (Drolet 1982-1983: 328f), Pozo Azul (Corrales Ulloa / Quintanilla Jiménez 1996), and Barriles in Panama (Ranere 2008: 205). Such walkways in northeast Honduras are known from the Culmí Valley (Begley 1999: 213f), Utila (Rose 1904, cited in Hasemann 1977), and Río Claro (Healy 1978a) and are mentioned for several settlements in the Mosquitia. The discovery of such paths in Betulia and the Aguán Valley expands our base of data and shows a clear connection to Southern Central America.

There are also clear similarities in the material culture of northeast Honduras and Southern Central America. In Guadalupe, a stone metate fragment that once represented the tongue of a zoomorphic head was found (see Figure 190a). Another sculpted metate with a zoomorphic head in a private collection in Trujillo is said to come from Betulia. As already discussed above, metates with sculpted heads belong to northeast Honduras' typical inventory of finds and are among the defining elements of the culture region. In Southern Central America, such decorated metates are frequently found. Jones (1992) shows that their geographical distribution is limited to this culture area, which is why she considers them important cultural features for Southern Central America. These metates are made from a single block of volcanic rock. While some are decorated with simple low relief, the so-called flying-panel metates feature masterfully crafted three-dimensional scenes below the grinding platform. While most of these metates were used to prepare plants and are, therefore, an indication of agriculture, some of the particularly elaborate specimens show no traces of use, so it is assumed that they were used for ritual purposes. Sometimes they are also referred to as "seats of power" (Begley 1999: 165). In Costa Rica, they are mainly found in Nicoya, the central highlands, and the Atlantic Watershed. In Nicaragua, they have only been found on the Pacific coast so far (Jones 1992). According to Jones, the metates in Southern Central America date to between AD 500 and the Spanish arrival. In northeast Honduras, they are mainly from Late Selin and Cocal contexts (Jones 1992: 181).

There are also clear parallels to Southern Central America in the processing of greenstone. Greenstone was a highly valued raw material in Mesoamerica as well as in Costa Rica. In the latter, axe gods (celt-shaped pendants with stylized zoomorph heads, mostly avian) are frequently found (Figure 212). They are connected to the expression of an animistic belief. Snarskis (1981: 29) associates them with the importance of agriculture due to their celt-like form. In northeast Honduras, such axe gods have been found at several sites. Although we have not found any in Guadalupe, they have been found in the Bay Islands, Jerico Farm (as described by Stone), and sites around the Guaimoreto Lagoon and in the Aguán Valley (Cuddy 2007: 125; Stone 1934a, 1941: 39, 52, Fig. 39)[24]. Numerous other axe gods of this kind can be found in the private collection of Rufino Galán in Trujillo. As some authors have already noted (Cuddy 2007; Lothrop 1955), specimens from northeast Honduras do not precisely correspond to those in Costa Rica. They differ in size, and the Honduran specimens are not as carefully and symmetrically crafted as those found in Costa Rica. It is, therefore, assumed that they are imitations. Cuddy (2007: 125) further that the artifacts from northeast Honduras were not manufactured in Costa Rica. Therefore, the axe gods from Honduras are not imports from Costa Rica but were most likely manufactured locally based on models from Costa Rica. To imitate objects, however, a model must be present in the form of a prototype or oral description. Although it is currently difficult to define the underlying reasons for the imitation of these objects, it is a further indication of close interaction between the inhabitants of these regions. In Costa Rica, where greenstone processing decreased by AD 700, the objects seem to date mainly to Periods IV and V, while their chronological context in northeast Honduras is not entirely clear.

0   2 cm

212   Jade axe god from Gran Nicoya (Museum Rietberg Zurich, inventory no. RMA 409, photo: R. Wolfsberger).

The similarities in material culture are most evident in ceramics. Cocal-period ceramics are generally similar to those of Southern Central America, especially in that they use incisions and appliqués for decoration. The appliqués are often shaped like animal heads. Furthermore, the tripod vessel form is widely used (see, e.g., Haberland 1976; Hartman 1901; Linares 1968; Lothrop 1926; MacCurdy 1911). Dennett (2007) demonstrates the similarity between Cocal ceramics from Río Claro and those from Costa Rica and Panama by comparing supports and handles. We can go beyond this overall similarity to the ceramics from Southern Central America and narrow it down to specific regions. Early researchers who had access to the finds from several countries in Central America and were able draw conclusions based on their first-hand observations noticed a particular similarity

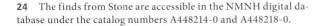

24   The finds from Stone are accessible in the NMNH digital database under the catalog numbers A448214-0 and A448218-0.

between the material from Costa Rica and northeast Honduras. This is especially true of the material from the central highlands and the Atlantic coast (Stone 1941: 95; Strong 1948c: 77). Strong specifies this by noting a similarity to the Highland Appliqué Ware defined by Lothrop (1926: 135) for Costa Rica. In his eyes, the similarities are so strong that he calls the ceramic style in northeast Honduras "North Coast Appliqué Style" in reference to the Costa Rican style. The Highland Appliqué Ware in Costa Rica is further divided into Curridabat, Tripod, Stone Cist, and Handled Ware (Strong 1948b: 135). According to Strong (1948b: 136), the Tripod and Stone Cist wares are "very characteristic of northeastern Honduras." While Strong was not able to chronologically classify these wares with certainty, later authors date them to Period VI (cf. Snarskis 2003: 190).

These similarities can be confirmed based on illustrations by Lothrop (1926) and Hartmann (1901) and those in online museum catalogs. They exist in form, modifications (appliqués and incised decoration), iconography, and style. In both publications, it is clear that the most common vessels forms are dishes and bowls, which correspond to form categories A and B as defined in this work. There are both insloping bowls (B-II-6) and bowls with a neck (B-III-1 and 3). A few hemispherical bowls are also represented. Most of the bowls are associated with tripods, as we assume the material from Guadalupe is as well. Other base shapes include ring bases, which we also found in Guadalupe but could not yet assign to any vessel shape. Another common form is the shallow tripod dish, some of which have a characteristic break like Form A-II. Large, deep vessels, such as those we found in Guadalupe (vases/jars), are rarely found here. The supports are mainly elongated and often have zoomorphic or anthropomorphic attributes, as is the case for the Guadalupe material. If there are appliqués near the rims, there are two, and they have a D-shape or include zoomorphic or anthropomorphic designs. Sometimes there are other three-dimensional appliqués on the vessel wall. These are more extensive in Costa Rican ceramics. In comparison, the ceramics from Guadalupe seem like a reduced version of this. Incisions are mainly located on the upper part of the vessel wall and consist of simple lines and geometric patterns in zigzag or cross shapes. Bands or appliqués that correspond to Appliqué Motif 27 are also common. In general, the style and technique of the appliqués are very similar. Instead of forming figures from a single piece of clay, they are built using several clay balls. This is done in such a way that the joints remain unblended, but the various components remain visible. Facial and body features are often indicated by punctures. In both ceramic traditions, the depictions are not lifelike and realistic but depict some level of abstraction. In both cases, perfect symmetry does not seem to be the predominant pattern of arrangement. In the following, these observations are illustrated with several concrete examples: Hartman (1901: Pl 24, Fig. 10; Pl 38, Fig. 2,3) shows several tripod dishes that are very similar in shape to those from Guadalupe. These are dishes almost identical to Form A-II-2, with a marked break and hollow and elongated supports. On Pl. 38 Fig. 3, the supports clearly indicate feet or paws (compare to Appliqué Motif 6). In Fig. 211 (p. 107), he presents a bowl with an appliqué that strongly resembles the abstract form of Appliqué Motif 18. In the Denver Art Museum[25], there are tripod dishes from the Central Highlands and the Atlantic Watershed that have elongated anthropomorphic supports that appear very similar to Motifs 9 and 10 and PAG-71-21 (see Figure 168t). Lothrop (1926: Fig. 240d) includes a bowl with handles that are strikingly similar to a combination of Appliqué Motif 17 and the bowl shape. A privately owned object from Guadalupe has an applied lizard on the bottom of the vessel (Figure 213). It resembles decorative elements in its design that Lothrop (1926) shows in Fig. 234. Lastly, these authors present frying pans/censers with decorated solid handles, which are reminiscent of those from Guadalupe in style and shape. These examples show that Cocal-period pottery from Guadalupe and northeast Honduras is similar to certain pottery traditions in Southern Central America with particularly pronounced parallels to those from the Central Highlands and the Atlantic Watershed of Costa Rica.

Interestingly, Costa Rica is also considered the core area of the Chibchan languages, to which the Pesh language also belongs (Hoopes / Fonseca 2003: 55f). Burial customs reveal that connections to this region go beyond similarities in material culture and possible economic contacts. The situation in Guadalupe has notable parallels. A very similar situation is described for the site Sitio Bolivar (AD 300–600) in central Costa Rica (Hoopes / Chenault 1994). This is a small settlement located on the shore of Lake Arenal. Nearby hilltops were used as burial grounds. The burials are associated with stone formations and deposits of ceramic fragments, lithic debitage, and other artifacts. The findings suggest that some of the artifacts were directly deposited and possibly destroyed intentionally. However, some of the artifacts were also deposited as fragments. According to the authors, the deposits accumulated due to periodic activities. Over a certain period, burials were interred here, whereby the cultural debris was partially relocated. The burials are

---

25 E.g. object ID 1993.465.

covered by a final deposit of ceramic sherds corresponding to a final dedicatory event. The deposit and intentional smashing of ceramics and other objects are interpreted as ritual and ceremonial acts. Feasting is also mentioned as a possible explanation. Similar to Guadalupe, however, the presence of artifacts indicating domestic use, such as spindle whorls, is surprising. As a possible explanation, the authors mention that these might be the personal belongings of the deceased. "Smashing and depositing them on top of the burials would have removed the objects of the deceased from common use – the psychological equivalent of placing them in the grave. This could explain both the domestic nature of the artifact deposit and the paucity of offerings within the tombs themselves" (Hoopes / Chenault 1994: 104). This situation is very similar to that in Guadalupe, where we have the same curious mixture of artifacts, some with a ritual nature and others with a domestic use. I assume that the findings in Costa Rica are also remnants of festivities related to the burials.

Ethnohistorical sources from Costa Rica also report on the importance of festivals. Bozzoli (1979) describes the so-called *chichadas* of the Bribri, a Chibcha-speaking ethnic group living today in southern Costa Rica. These are celebrations associated with a person's death that extend over several days and involve the consumption of a considerable amount of food and beverages. The name is derived from the excessive consumption of fermented *chicha*. The food consumed belongs to the deceased. A large celebration is held one year after the person's death when their second burial takes place. Pittier (1938: 24–26) reports of a ten-day festival with numerous intoxicated participants. Pablo Solano (cited in Bozzoli 1979: 118f) mentions a *baile de huesos*, a festival that ends only after all of the deceased's possessions have been consumed. He also reports of large pottery containers for *chicha* that can hold up to 50 liters. He states that the festivities can last up to three weeks. They are accompanied by music, singers, and dances. Gabb (1875: 500-503) witnessed the burial of the Bribri King Santiago. The festivities lasted for three weeks, during which time much was drunk, eaten, danced, and sung. Three cows and 12 pigs were slaughtered and eaten. He also observed how several *chicha* containers were ostentatiously broken during a procession. At the same time, he noticed that "nothing of real value" was destroyed (Gabb 1875: 502). In the descriptions of the archaeological context and the ethnohistorical sources, we find striking parallels to the findings in Guadalupe and the importance of funeral celebrations. Interestingly, the authors mention that the findings in Sitio Bolivar are not unique. In the Northwest Cordillera and the Atlantic Watershed, there are several sites where burials are associated with a layer of pottery sherds, which indicates that this phenomenon is widely distributed in this area.

213   Ceramic fragment with lizard appliqué (M. Müller).

The above-mentioned examples make it clear that the similarities of northeast Honduras to Southern Central America during the Cocal phase are much stronger than those to Mesoamerica. There is a particularly strong link to the central and Atlantic coast portions of Costa Rica. Although there are also similarities in the material culture, many of them relate to immaterial or immobile things such as language, burial rites, architecture, and iconography and thus go far beyond purely economic connections or exchange of goods. Although the presence of Costa Rican ceramics on the Bay Islands shows that objects were exchanged as well (Véliz / Willey / Healy 1977).

What were the underlying reasons for this connection, and what kind of interaction is represented? The existing theory of the frontier zone states that around AD 300, a group split off from the Chibchan core in present-day Costa Rica and migrated northwards, where it finally settled in northeast Honduras (Dennett 2007). It further assumes that the similarities in culture are due to the fact that the group continued to maintain contact with the core land. However, this does not quite fit the archaeological evidence, which shows that the connection to the south was particularly strong during the Cocal phase. If Dennett's theory is correct, the similarity should be greater during the Selin phase and decrease during the Cocal phase. The linguistic data do not support this theory either, as current hypotheses assume that the Pesh language already separated from the other Chibcha languages much earlier (Constenla Umaña 1995).

In Guadalupe, there is a continuity in the use of the settlement site and the ceramic style from the Transitional Selin to the Cocal. Although there are clear differences between the two phases, there are also similarities indicating a gradual change. Thus, the archaeological context indicates that the situation did not primarily consist of migrations but more of local developments with a shift in the intensity of interaction in different geographical directions. What was the reason for increased orientation towards interaction with Southern Central America, especially towards Costa Rica during the Cocal period? Although we cannot currently answer this question with any certainty, we can consider some possibilities.

The transition from the Selin to the Cocal period is an interesting time that was connected to fundamental changes in many parts of Central America. The most important event is probably the process that led to the decline of central authority in the Maya lowlands around AD 900. Due to the decline of the Maya centers, a power vacuum was created. The structure of the Maya polities corresponded to a relatively centralized network that was very sensitive to the failure of highly connected central nodes. The neighboring societies in Gualjoquito and the Sula Valley also seem to have been affected by these events, which demonstrates that they were connected to these networks. These regions experienced a substantial decrease in population during Period VI, and the Sula Valley seems to have been almost wholly depopulated during this time (Hasemann / Lara Pinto / Sandoval Cruz 2017: 148). The societies of northeast Honduras, on the other hand, do not appear to have been greatly affected by these changes. On the contrary, current research suggests that the Cocal phase was a period of growth in most regions, accompanied by the emergence of many new and large settlements. The loss of potential exchange partners in the west may have been a factor for the increasing orientation towards the south. The changes may have also been linked to the exchange of different resources. For example, Begley (1999: 177f) considers how the increase in social complexity in the Culmí Valley was related to the exploitation of greenstone sources in northeast Honduras. Balser (1993) shows that the presence of real jade from the Motagua Valley in Costa Rica decreased and the use of social jade increased towards the end of Period V. Begley considers the raw material deposits in the Mosquitia as possible sources that would partly explain the increasing interaction between the two regions. It is hypothetically possible that metal processing technology adopted from the south also played a role in the increased interaction. Hosler (1994: 15f) shows that with the adoption of metalworking technology in western Mexico from Colombia, cultural elements such as burial customs were also adopted.

In summary, the links to the Southern Central American network consist of strong ties, i.e., interaction that took place more frequently and shaped everyday life. What these strong ties actually consisted of, however, must be left to future research. Open questions regarding the interaction with Southern Central America also concern the role of Nicaragua in this network. The close links between coastal settlements in northeast Honduras and the Atlantic Watershed in Costa Rica suggest that the connections were established via a coastal route. One would expect that coastal settlements in Nicaragua were also part of this network. However, the poor state of research in this area leaves this question unanswered. Furthermore, chronological questions must be clarified. A better definition of the Selin phase in Honduras is necessary to make a well-founded comparison between the societies of the Selin and Cocal periods and to better evaluate the degree of difference between those periods. Moreover, some elements seem to occur earlier in Costa Rica than in Honduras, such as axe gods or metates. A stable chronological framework and the classification of these artifact traditions are necessary to better assess the existing relationships and networks.

5.3.3 LINKS TO THE CARIBBEAN

The Caribbean is the final geographic region considered in terms of interregional interaction. The idea of a Circum-Caribbean region was actually established early on (Steward 1948). However, after this point, research traditions in the Caribbean and on the Central American mainland diverged, and mutual influences and interactions were hardly considered. This is primarily because archaeologists were concerned with understanding the fundamental cultural developments in the respective culture areas (Rodríguez Ramos 2013). The idea of a Circum-Caribbean region has been revived in recent years, and the possible levels of interaction between mainland and islands are increasingly being discussed. However, the Greater and Lesser Antilles have not yet been seriously considered a possible direction of interaction for northeast Honduras. I cover this in the following and add a new spatial level to the discussion about possible networks.

Hoopes (2017: 56f) develops the concept of the "American Mediterranean." He assumes that the Caribbean Sea can be compared to the Mediterranean Sea and that the interaction and exchange between the adjoining agents were as intense as that of the inhabitants of the Mediterranean coast. The two systems are also comparable in terms of geographical dimensions. Rodriguez Ramos (2013) drafts an image of an Isthmo-Antillean Interaction Sphere by pointing out several indications for the connection between inhabitants of Southern Central America and the Antilles and calls for more attention to be paid to their mutual influences. In any case, it is clear that water did not serve as a barrier but as a link between the inhabitants. For example, on the Antilles, more intensive contact is observed between the inhabitants of opposite coasts than between the inhabitants of the same island (Hofman / Bright / Rodríguez Ramos 2010: 1; Wilson 2007: 14). An interesting story illustrates how mobile people were at that time and how quickly objects and information could spread: Only three days after the Spaniards went ashore for the first time during their voyage in 1492, they met a man in a canoe on their way south. He was carrying glass beads and two Spanish coins (Dunn / Kelley 1989: 85).

Fitzpatrick (2013) provides a good overview of the current state of knowledge regarding seafaring capabilities in the Caribbean. Only a few seafaring crafts have been found in archaeological contexts; most of the information comes from ethnohistorical reports. However, both sources show that the typical means of transport was a dugout canoe made from a single tree. These canoes could vary in size from smaller vessels used for fishing to impressive canoes that could be up to 20 m long and hold several dozen people. Some accounts speak of 50-60 people in a single canoe. Possible woods from which these canoes were made are those of the Mahogany family (*Meliaceae*), Ceiba (*Malvaceae*), or Cedar (e.g., *Cedrela odorata*). These canoes were powered with paddles. Questions as to whether the sail was yet invented have still not been resolved. However, there are currently no signs that confirm this, and it is assumed that paddling was the only means of propulsion. These technical requirements had significant consequences for the possible routes of travel since mobility was strongly dependent on the natural conditions of wind, weather, and currents. The use of canoes also played a role in the form of exchange and interaction. Theoretically, canoes can land anywhere with a flat shore. No harbors are necessary. In contrast to the Mediterranean, for example, major seaports were not necessary, and the routes and landing points could be chosen more flexibly. For us archaeologists, this means that canoe landing points are hardly identifiable, as they leave no archaeologically recognizable traces.

So, what are the indications for contact between the Caribbean islands and the mainland? While it has long been known and accepted that the inhabitants of the Lesser Antilles maintained intensive and constant contact with the inhabitants of the South American mainland, this has not yet been clarified for the inhabitants of the Greater Antilles. However, there are indications that they had contact with different regions of the mainland. There is also evidence that points to contact with Southern Central America.

The discussion begins with the question of settlement. From which regions were the islands settled around 4000 BC? Currently, several different regions are being discussed as the possible origin based on various evidence. The stylistic and technological similarity of stone artifacts indicates that the area was settled by those of today's Yucatán region (Wilson 2007: 27-33) or northern South America (Fitzpatrick 2013: 108). Linguistic data suggest that settlement would have come from Honduras. Granberry and Vescelius (2004: 48f, 125) raise the possibility that Tolan-speaking groups from Belize or Honduras may have populated the Greater Antilles. They base their observations on the similarity between the Tolan languages and Ciguayo, which was spoken when the Spanish arrived on Hispaniola. Early connections to the Southern Central American mainland are also visible in the paleoethnobotanical record. On the one hand, there are indications that certain plants from Southern Central America found their way to the Greater Antilles. On the other hand, food preparation methods were probably also adopted from there (Rodríguez Ramos 2013: 157). These early connections show that contact between the mainland and islands was possible from a technical point of view and occurred in very early stages.

In later periods, similarities become most apparent in architecture and material culture. Similar to Southern Central America, worked stones were not used for construction in the Caribbean. Here, too, buildings were made of perishable material or river cobbles. In the architectural layout of the stone-lined plazas (*bateys*), which are often found as an important component of settlements in the Greater Antilles, some authors see similarities to such plazas in Southern Central America and consider whether this could be due to influence from the latter region (Rodríguez Ramos 2013: 167; Rodríguez Ramos / Pagán Jiménez 2006: 124f; Snarskis 1984: 230). Stone paved walkways are also frequently found on the islands, connecting settlements to fresh water, among other things (Wilson 2007: 121, 126). Greenstone pendants found on Puerto Rico and attributed to the Huecoide culture (500 BC–AD 700) are often cited as examples of similarities in material culture. More precisely, these are ornithomorphic and frog-shaped pendants. In technique and iconography, they are similar to objects from Panama and the Atlantic Watershed in Costa Rica (Rodríguez Ramos 2013: Fig. 11.2). On Antigua, an axe god was found in the Costa Rican style. On the same island, greenstone objects were found whose raw material could be identified as jade from the Motagua Valley—a clear indication of exchange with the Central American mainland (Garcia-Casco et al. 2013; Reid / Curet 2014: 141). Interestingly, the importance of greenstone objects, just as observed for Costa Rica, also appears to decrease by AD 700 (Rodríguez Ramos / Pagán Jiménez 2006: 124; Snarskis 2003). Furthermore, there are three-legged sculpted metates on the Greater Antilles, which are quite similar to those from Costa Rica and northeast Hondu-ras (Rodríguez Ramos / Pagán Jiménez 2006: 124). In her dissertation, Paulsen (2019: Fig. 7.7) includes a wooden chair with a sculpted feline head from Haiti (AD 1000–1500) that also resembles these metates. Some of the metates from Costa Rica depict birds. Based on ethnohistorical sources, Balser (1954) argues that such birds played a significant role in fertility and procreation in Caribbean mythology and sees the same depictions in Costa Rica, which are also related to fertility scenes, as a link between the two regions. He sees further similarities between these two regions in stylistically similar stone statues and the use of tobacco.

Metal objects are often cited as signs of a connection. On the islands, objects made of *guanín*, a gold-copper alloy, were prized status symbols. According to all available indications, the inhabitants of the Antilles did not know about metal smelting techniques. Copper-gold alloys are known in Southern Central America as *tumbaga* and were produced there in large quantities. Therefore, it seems evident that the objects reached the islands from this region (Rodríguez Ramos 2013: 167; Valcárcel Rojas / Martinón-Torres 2013). A study by Laffoon et al. (2014) shows that pendants made from animal teeth found in the Antilles originate from the mainland. The observations are based on a sample from Puerto Rico that includes teeth from jaguars (*Panthera onca*), peccaries (*Tayassu pecari*), and tapirs (*Tapirus terrestris*). None of the animals are native to the islands. With the help of strontium and oxygen isotope analyses, their origin could be assigned to the South and Central American mainland. It could also be shown that the objects were exchanged over long distances. Further similarities are seen in ceremonial weapons (axes, celts, and daggers) from Costa Rica and Hispaniola (McGinnis 2004, cited in Wilson 2007: 151). When looking through the NMNH's Caribbean collection, I noticed that the elaborate design of stone pestles from the Atlantic Watershed in Costa Rica closely parallel specimens from the Caribbean (compare Graham 1981: Plate 60, 61 and NMNH catalog numbers A231421-0 and A231419-0).

Finally, Stone (1976: 204f) summarizes some ethnohistorical sources that point to a connection between Panama and the Antilles. Amodio (1991: 599) also states that ethnohistorical reports confirm direct contact between the Greater Antilles and the Central American mainland. Although it is assumed that the connections between the Antilles and Southern Central America have existed since early times, it is believed that they intensified during Period VI (Reid / Curet 2014: 141).

All of this evidence points to the fact that the inhabitants of the Caribbean were indeed in contact with people from Southern Central America. Further data

are needed to clarify chronological issues—especially for the Cocal phase—to define the interaction more precisely in regional terms, and to determine the reason for and nature of the interaction. However, it is interesting to note that some of the above elements emphasize a particular similarity of artifacts between Costa Rica (Highland / Atlantic Watershed) and the Greater Antilles. As noted in the previous chapter, some of the elements found in Costa Rica and cited here as indications of a connection to the Caribbean also occur in northeast Honduras. These include architectural traditions such as paved walkways, sculpted metates with zoomorphic heads, the importance of greenstone objects, and the presence of axe gods. I would like to add ceramics to these categories. It was already demonstrated above that the pottery from northeast Honduras has strong parallels in form, technique, and overall appearance to the so-called stone cist ware in Costa Rica. Some of the elements that were listed can also be found in the ceramics of the Caribbean. During Period VI, a change from painted ceramics to mostly unpainted ceramics with incisions and appliques also occurs here. A focus on anthropomorphic appliqués is a distinctive feature of Caribbean pottery, which were already widespread during earlier periods (Saladoid) (Waldron 2016). Some of the zoomorphic appliqués are very similar to those found in Guadalupe. Waldron (2016: 13), for example, shows the application of an ant-eater, which resembles Appliqué Motif 21. He mentions that—just like in Guadalupe—this motif can have the snout facing up or down. Dacal Moure and Rivero de la Calle (1996: Fig. 77) show ornitomorphic handles from Cuba that resemble Appliqué Motif 20. While Waldron's example is an appliqué from the Saladoid horizon, the similarities in the depictions of animals may be based on similar worldviews linked to an animistic belief. As Balser (1954) hypothesized, this may show that the regions were linked by a similar worldview. Cranial protuberances are another indication of this, which exist in both Guadalupe and Caribbean ceramics (see chapter 5.1.3.3).

While further research is certainly needed, the similarities in architectural elements and material culture in northeast Honduras, the Atlantic coast of Costa Rica, and the Caribbean indicate that the inhabitants of these regions were involved in the same interaction sphere in which objects, ideas, stories, and perhaps technologies circulated. Based on the available data, we can assume that an exchange network stretched along the Caribbean coast of Southern Central America and included the Greater Antilles and possibly parts of the South American mainland. Guadalupe's inhabitants were connected to this network, which I refer to in the following as the Caribbean coastal network.

5.3.4 Summary of Interregional Networks

As demonstrated in the last three chapters, the inhabitants of Guadalupe were participants and components of different interregional networks. The inhabitants were connected to an exchange network that included the Maya region and mainly operated along the Atlantic coast. Via this network, obsidian from Ixtepeque and jade from Motagua reached Guadalupe. The obsidian from Otumba and the metal needle found in Guadalupe show that this network also had links to the Central Mexican highlands. In addition to goods, technologies and ideas circulated in this network and its subnetworks. We see this in the production of prismatic blades in Guadalupe, the presence of *patolli* boards on Guanaja and in Sawacito, and the iconography of the Bay Island Polychrome vessels. Guadalupe obviously functioned as a kind of "broker" between the regional networks and this Mesoamerican network, which led to a distinct settlement position. Other networks existed that connected Guadalupe to southern and central Honduras. Obsidian reached Guadalupe from la Esperanza and Güinope. Whether these networks had levels other than an economic one is unclear at the moment because the regions from which the obsidian originates are not yet sufficiently explored. Nor do we know if these were direct links or if (more likely) the raw material passed through several stations before reaching Guadalupe.

Numerous elements indicate a close existing network with societies in Southern Central America, especially the Highland and Atlantic Watershed of Costa Rica. While the connections to Mesoamerica consisted of sporadic contacts from which individual elements were adopted, we see parallels to Southern Central America in many aspects of life. The existing connections must have been closer than those to the west. The strengthening of ties in this direction during the Cocal period is undoubtedly prevalent in the context of the decline of the Classic Maya centers in the west. The nature of this interaction regarding Costa Rica, such as whether they were primarily economic networks or whether the inhabitants of the regions had sociopolitical ties or were united by a common worldview, will have to be clarified by future studies. Finally, the data suggest that the inhabitants of Guadalupe were also in contact with the inhabitants of the Caribbean islands. A network seems to have connected the coastal regions of Southern Central America, the South American mainland, and the Caribbean islands in the sense of a Circum-Caribbean Area once defined by Steward (1948). The vectors of interaction suggest that the coast was a vital connection route for interaction with Mesoamerica and the Caribbean coastal network. The coastal location is one reason for the importance and uniqueness of Guadalupe in the settlement structure, which represents a central node and acts as a broker between the different networks.

It is now clear that the inhabitants of Guadalupe in particular and northeast Honduras in general by no means occupied a peripheral position but were involved in many networks on a local, regional, and interregional level. This interconnectedness is a critical element that defines Cocal-period society in northeast Honduras. Furthermore, it exists not only at geographic levels but also finds expression in the connection to the world of ancestors, who are honored through the celebration of feasts and thus are a vital part of social life and memory. In this case, network theory proves to be not only a mere tool but also a new perspective that focuses on the importance of precisely these interconnections in different areas of life. The situation in northeast Honduras is thus proving to be much more complex than previously assumed, and it becomes evident that we should study this region for its own sake and not regard it as a mere annex to one of the surrounding culture areas. Moreover, the concept of networks lends itself to replace the static and simplistic concept of the culture area, thus integrating a more dynamic and detailed understanding of conditions and replacing outdated concepts.

5.4 Future Research Strategies

In the present work, we have begun to identify networks and to reconstruct their nodes and links. However, this is just the beginning. In order to paint a more comprehensive picture of the existing networks, we have to define the scale and boundaries of these entities more precisely. It is also crucial to map more nodes in order to reconstruct a more precise network topography. For this purpose, it is necessary to identify as many settlements as possible and to assign them a temporal context, for example, through systematic settlement surveys. Can certain settlements be assigned a function? How can these settlements (and their inhabitants) be characterized? To better reconstruct the links, we need to gather more information on material culture, iconography, and cultural traditions. Extensive excavations are required for this. Shovel test pits or test excavations make it challenging to identify and interpret the relationships between archaeological features. At a regional level, this means extending studies along the coast, which is one of the future plans of the Archaeological Project Guadalupe. In particular, it must be clarified if Guadalupe is an individual case or if there are other settlements with similar finds and features. In addition to the coastal strip, research should be extended into the Aguán Valley and the Bay Islands to better define the nature of the links between these regions. In a further step, research in the northeast region is important, as it represents an area we still know very little about. Revision and publication of the existing but unpublished research data and museum collections would be useful. We need to better understand what united this region and what differences there were. On an interregional level, the role of Nicaragua in the existence of a coastal network is of particular interest. Research near the Atlantic coast would be necessary to evaluate connections with Costa Rica and the network form. Was it a continuous coastal network, or was Nicaragua excluded? If so, what were the reasons for this? Again, questions regarding possible connecting routes and natural conditions, such as ocean currents, etc., are important. Links with the Caribbean should also be given more attention. So far, we have found little definitive evidence of a relationship to the Caribbean during the Cocal period, but the connections during the earlier phases suggest that there were also links during this period. A better definition of the periods preceding the Cocal phase is central for understanding the culture developments in the phase itself. A better understanding of the material culture from these periods is vital to judging the extent to which the Cocal-period material differs. Once this basic framework is established, we can move on to a more thorough analysis of the existing networks and investigate their structure, e.g., thinking about how connections affect one another, what happens to a network when nodes are removed, etc.

It is also important not to carry out this analysis at the level of culture areas. Interaction did not occur between culture areas but between their inhabitants, who did not necessarily feel that they belonged to such a culture area. Network theory provides a good alternative here, as it offers a dynamic perspective. Instead of borders, it focuses on connections. Understanding archaeological landscapes as a formation of networks and subnetworks, which differ in their structure but can nevertheless connect, comes much closer to the reality of social relations than the concept of culture areas (Müller 2009). Research should also aim to go beyond naming "influences" or "connections" and ask questions about the nature and motivation of these connections, as has been partly pursued in the present work. New scientific methods, such as provenience analysis and isotope analysis of humans and plants, can help us to better understand the movements of objects and people. It is also crucial to look at connections in both directions. In this work, we have mainly observed elements from external regions that we encounter in northeast Honduras in order to reconstruct networks. However, elements from northeast Honduras that were found in the surrounding regions should also be examined. For this purpose, the comprehensive presentation and publication of the find material from this region is an essential step toward enabling the identification of imported products in other regions as well.

A specific research design is required to achieve these goals. Basic research and the generation of primary data remain particularly important in our field. It is essential to publish these data to provide future researchers with a basis for comparison. 3D scanners and online publications now provide us with new possibilities that allow us to generate research data quickly and accurately, to publish a larger amount of data, and at the same time to disseminate research data more easily and widely. Digital media can be used to facilitate and systematize access to research data. A good example is the online bibliography on archaeological research in Nicaragua, which was developed under the direction of Geoffrey McCafferty[26]. An online-accessible GIS, which can be used as an interactive map and simultaneously as an archive to collect data and make them available online, would also be a good strategy. A lot of previously unpublished data is stored in the IHAH archives, which has not yet been digitized. Digitizing this data and making it available to interested researchers would be an important step. The revision of objects in museums is also an important aspect that many large museums are meeting by digitizing their catalogs (see Appendix C for a list of museums that hold collections from northeast Honduras).

In order to achieve these goals, cooperation is essential at all levels. Archaeologists from different culture regions should work together more closely. Exchange with colleagues from the Caribbean would be especially fruitful. But also, close and mutually beneficial cooperation with Honduran archaeologists is necessary. Despite the existing difficulties, future projects should help to strengthen the national archaeology and raise awareness in the general population of archaeological remains and cultural heritage. Only in this way can we counteract the destruction of archaeological remains.

---

26 https://antharky.ucalgary.ca/mccafferty/nicaragua/bibliography, accessed on 08.03.2022.

6 Summary and Conclusion

The present study aimed at characterizing the pre-Hispanic cultural history of a poorly known and underresearched region and at reconstructing important aspects of its cultural history over the last 600 years before Spanish arrival. The question of which networks the inhabitants of northeast Honduras were involved in was investigated. For this purpose, the nodes, i.e., the different settlements, were examined in combination with their links, i.e., the interaction between the settlements. Guadalupe, occupied during the Transitional Selin and the entire Cocal period (AD 900–1525), was selected as a case study to characterize a typical settlement or node. The excavations revealed that several burials were interred in the settlement center around AD 1260 at the latest and that feasts were held in connection with these burials. The remains of the feasts were deposited close to the burials together with other objects as a kind of grave goods. These festivities were carried out periodically so that a clearly visible accumulation of pottery, bones and other objects had formed over time. This accumulation was present and visible at all times, acting as a monument for the commemoration of the deceased, who thus continued to occupy an important place in society.

The studies in Guadalupe have also provided us with information on local architectural traditions and have shown us that the inhabitants made intensive use of the area's available resources, not only to obtain foodstuffs but also to produce various goods. These goods played an important role in the emergence of networks within which they were exchanged. The inhabitants of Guadalupe were involved in many different networks of different types and intensities. On a regional level, a coastal network was part of the everyday life of the inhabitants and was characterized by close connections, made apparent by the strong similarity of material culture. A further-reaching network existed between the settlements of northeast Honduras. However, more data is needed to determine the nature of these relationships and reconstruct the network's topography in order to identify particularly close links as well as those that were less intense.

At the interregional level, there were connections to Mesoamerica. This was apparently an exchange network with less involved connections that seems to have had little impact on the local culture. However, there were closer links to Southern Central America. Architecture, burial rites, ceramics, and stone processing strongly point to Atlantic and Highland Costa Rica and to the Caribbean, which led to the identification of a Caribbean Coastal Network. The nature of and underlying reasons for this network need to be identified more precisely in the future. The cause for growing ties to the south may be due to the decline of the Classic Maya centers in the west. Through its integration into various networks, Guadalupe played a unique role in that it assumed the function of a broker, a connecting position between the networks.

The study also showed that simply assigning northeast Honduras to a culture area would be too simplistic and would not do justice to the situation's complexity. We can assume that the pre-Hispanic inhabitants of northeast Honduras did not define themselves as belonging to a culture area of Mesoamerica or Southern Central America, but that relations to other settlements or their inhabitants, especially on a local and regional level, played an important role. Network theory has proven to be a particularly appropriate framework because it focuses on these connections and their importance to society during the Cocal period. This approach also circumvents the notion that northeast Honduras is peripheral or less complex than the neighboring Mesoamerican societies. Instead, it provides a new, individual, and value-free approach for the investigation of the region.

Finally, making a connection to the present is a valuable exercise, as the past still affects the here and now. The archaeology of northeast Honduras can play an important role in the current cultural understanding of the country's inhabitants. Maya culture and its exploration have played a major role in the building of a national identity. Research in other areas of Honduras can help to raise awareness of cultural heritage. Celebrating the cultural and ethnic plurality of the past may contribute to the understanding and acceptance of cultural and ethnic plurality today.

Resumen en español

Investigación arqueológica en Guadalupe, noreste de Honduras: Redes de interacción durante el periodo prehispánico tardío (900-1525 d.C.)

Introducción

El noreste de Honduras ocupa una posición especial en la América Central prehispánica. Se encuentra en la confluencia de tres grandes áreas culturales: Mesoamérica, el sur de Centroamérica y el Caribe. A pesar de esta interesante ubicación, el noreste de Honduras ha sido poco estudiado arqueológicamente.

El presente trabajo tiene como objetivo contribuir a la investigación de esta región y estudiar su papel en la historia cultural prehispánica, examinando cuestiones como la caracterización de su cultura material y de los asentamientos, las relaciones culturales y económicas entre los habitantes de la región y el papel que desempeñó el noreste de Honduras en el intercambio de objetos e ideas entre las sociedades de América Central. Cronológicamente, se centra en los últimos 600 años antes de la llegada de los españoles a América.

Muchos de los estudios previos se han enfocado en la cuestión sobre qué influencias tuvieron las regiones culturales vecinas, especialmente Mesoamérica, en el noreste de Honduras. El reconocimiento de los desarrollos autóctonos y la percepción del noreste de Honduras como algo propio se relegaron a un segundo plano. En este trabajo se aplica por primera vez el método de análisis de redes o análisis reticular que permitirá establecer una nueva teoría desde una perspectiva diferente y poner el noreste de Honduras en el centro de atención.

Los análisis se basan en los hallazgos del asentamiento costero de Guadalupe (900-1525 d.C.), donde el Proyecto Arqueológico Guadalupe realizó investigaciones entre 2016 y 2020. Guadalupe se entiende como el vértice central de una red. A partir del análisis de la cultura material, la arquitectura y las costumbres funera-rias, se reconstruyen los vínculos de esta red con otros asentamientos y regiones. En este contexto, la cerámica, como categoría de hallazgo mayormente representada, desempeña un papel especial y se desarrolla una nueva clasificación. Las conexiones y redes se consideran a tres niveles: local, regional e interregional. Como aspecto novedoso, cabe destacar que se incorpora el estudio de las conexiones con el Caribe, que hasta ahora han recibido poca atención.

El Proyecto Arqueológico Guadalupe, dirigido por el Prof. Dr. Markus Reindel y el Dr. Peter Fux, es una cooperación entre la Universidad de Zúrich (UZH), el Instituto Arqueológico Alemán (DAI), el Museo Rietberg de Zúrich (MRZ) y el Instituto Hondureño de Antropología e Historia (IHAH).

Áreas culturales e historia cultural en América Central: Estado de la cuestión

Para llegar a entender el contexto del noreste de Honduras prehispánico, y comprender cómo su ubicación ha influenciado la investigación arqueológica en la región, es importante prestar atención a las áreas culturales circundantes, su definición y la historia de su investigación.

El área cultural de Mesoamérica fue definida por Paul Kirchhoff en 1943. En el norte se extiende hacia el Río Lerma. En el sur incluye tanto la parte oeste de Honduras como la Península de Guanacaste en Costa Rica. Su definición se basa en la idea de que todos los habitantes de esta área compartían las mismas tradiciones cul-

233

turales. Las culturas mesoamericanas, además, se caracterizan por el desarrollo de "sociedades complejas" con una organización sociopolítica a nivel de estado. De las tres áreas culturales consideradas aquí, Mesoamérica es la región más investigada con diferencia. Su historia cultural se caracteriza por la existencia de horizontes culturales que se extienden repetidamente por grandes áreas, manifestándose en el uso de elementos estilísticos comunes en el contexto arqueológico.

El sur de Centroamérica ha sido definido de varias maneras. Incluye la parte sur del puente terrestre centroamericano, es decir, las partes orientales de El Salvador y Honduras, Nicaragua, Costa Rica, Panamá y, en algunas definiciones, se incluyen también partes del continente sudamericano. Gordon Willey (1959) fue el primero en definirlo como área cultural coherente, usando el término "Àrea Intermedia". Especialmente en las investigaciones tempranas, la región se consideraba transitoria y marginal respecto a las complejas sociedades del norte (Mesoamérica) y del sur (Andes), y se creía que el desarrollo cultural estaba fuertemente influenciado por las civilizaciones vecinas. Esta percepción empezó a cambiar en los años 1980. También tuvo un impacto importante la definición del Área Istmo-Colombiana realizada por John Hoopes y Oscar Fonseca (2003). En este caso, el concepto se centra en los elementos comunes del área y demuestra que la región se caracterizó por menos movimientos migratorios e influencias externas de lo que se suponía. La intesidad de la investigación arqueológica varía entre países y regiones geográficas. En Costa Rica existe una arraigada tradición arqueológica nacional, mientras que en Honduras y Nigaragua, la arqueología se desarrolla más bien poco. El desarrollo cultural prehispánico en el sur de Centroamérica parece haber sido más regionalizado que en Mesoamérica. Todavía no se han identificado horizontes estilísticos de gran alcance, aunque la cultura material tiene elementos comunes en toda la región, un fenómeno que Hoopes y Fonseca denominan "unidad difusa".

El Caribe abarca todas las islas que están dentro del mar Caribe y toda la costa que lo rodea. Julian Steward (1948) definió el área cultural Circum-Caribe, la cual corresponde a esta delimitación geográfica. Sin embargo, en los años siguientes, las investigaciones tomaron otros rumbos y dieron lugar a una arqueología caribeña que se ocupaba principalmente de la historia cultural de las islas del Caribe, enfocándose en estudios regionalizados según sus condiciones geográficas. Las preguntas que surgen durante estas investigaciones y las estrategias vinculadas a ellas difieren entre las islas debido, en parte, a las numerosas naciones involucradas y a sus diferentes contextos políticos. En este caso, la atención se centra en cuestiones como el asentamiento de las islas y la interacción entre ellas.

El presente estudio se enfoca en el periodo entre 900 d.C. y 1525 d.C. En el noreste de Honduras, este lapso de tiempo corresponde al periodo Cocal, que normalmente se define empezando alrededor de 1000 d.C. Sin embargo, durante nuestra investigación quedó claro que el siglo anterior es importante para entender este periodo, ya que ahí es donde tienen sus raíces los fenómenos y características que lo definen, y por este motivo se incluye en el análisis. Fuentes etnohistóricas y datos arqueológicos demuestran que el último periodo antes de la Conquista fue muy dinámico. La mayoría de las regiones de América Central se caracterizan por un elevado crecimiento demográfico y por la existencia de grandes asentamientos. Los eventos de finales del periodo Clásico en el área maya provocan cambios significativos en el sistema económico, el cual ahora es más descentralizado. El intercambio de objetos a larga distancia cobra importancia, como se puede ver en el ejemplo de los *pochtecas* o en la distribución extensa del estilo internacional. Y las rutas marítimas, que ya se utilizaban con anterioridad, adquirieron un papel más importante durante este periodo tardío. Las fuentes etnohistóricas hablan también de numerosos movimientos migratorios de diferentes grupos, aunque, en este caso, no siempre se pueden verificar en el contexto arqueológico.

En el centro de estas grandes regiones culturales se encuentra nuestra zona de estudio, el noreste de Honduras. Según los conocimientos actuales, la región comprende las Islas de la Bahía, los departamentos Colón y Olancho y la parte oeste del departamento Gracias a Dios. Sin embargo, los límites no están claramente definidos y no hay un acuerdo entre autores. Algunos definen el noreste de Honduras como una región cultural propia, basándose principalmente en las fuertes similitudes de la cultura material. Las fuentes etnohistóricas también indican que la región era una entidad política antes de la Conquista.

Una de las características geográficas prominentes del noreste de Honduras es el ancho y fértil valle de Aguán, que se extiende paralelamente a la costa atlántica y que hoy en día se utiliza para la agricultura intensiva. Al norte, está delimitado por la cordillera Nombre de Dios, y más al norte de esta cordillera, se encuentra una estrecha franja costera que se ensancha hacia el este y finalmente se transforma en la Mosquitia, una zona de selva tropical poca desarrollada en cuanto a infraestructuras se refiere. En toda la zona domina un clima tropical caracterizado por estaciones secas y lluviosas.

La investigación arqueológica en el noreste de Honduras comenzó en la primera mitad del siglo XX. Al principio solía estar relacionada con expediciones de museos norteamericanos. Uno de los objetivos principales de estas expediciones fue la identificación de la frontera sur de la cultura maya. Una contribución importante fue la de William D. Strong (1934, 1935), que exploró las Islas de la Bahía y partes de la Mosquitia. Doris Stone (1934a, 1941) investigó principalmente sitios a lo largo de los ríos Aguán, Sico y Paulaya. Jeremiah Epstein (1957) fue el primero en establecer una cronología para la región, definiendo las sucesivas fases Selin (300-1000 d.C.) y Cocal (1000-1525 d.C.). Paul Healy añadió una fase temprana a la cronología (1350-400 a.C.) fundamentada en los hallazgos en las Cuevas de Cuyamel y fue el primero en confirmar la cronología mediante dataciones por radiocarbono (Healy 1984a). Hasta la actualidad, existe un lapso de tiempo, entre el 400 a.C. y el 300 d.C., para el cual no se han encontrado evidencias arqueológicas. Carrie Dennett (2007) hizo una importante contribución al conocimiento de la tipología cerámica de la fase Cocal. Además, se realizaron investigaciones bajo la dirección del Instituto Hondureño de Antropología e Historia (IHAH), principalmente en las Islas de la Bahía (Epstein/Véliz 1977; Hasemann 1977; Véliz/Willey/Healy 1977). Christopher Begley llevó a cabo extensas investigaciones en el valle de Culmi (Begley 1999), y Whitney Goodwin, que anteriormente trabajó en las Islas de la Bahía (Goodwin 2011) publicó recientemente un importante trabajo sobre el sitio de Selin Farm (Goodwin 2019). Otras investigaciones han sido realizadas por Vito Véliz (1978), Robert Sharer (Sharer/Sedat/Pezzati 2009), Operation Raleigh (Clark/Dawson/Drake 1982), Thomas Cuddy (2007), Alejandro Figueroa (2011) y Christopher Fisher (Fisher et al. 2016), entre otros.

A la llegada de los españoles, el territorio de la actual Honduras estaba poblado por diversos grupos lingüísticos y étnicos. La reconstrucción de estos grupos no está exenta de problemas, en parte porque la Conquista provocó el desplazamiento, la decimación y la desaparición de grupos indígenas. Hoy en día se supone que una gran parte del noreste de Honduras estaba habitada por grupos de habla pesh. El pesh pertenece a las lenguas chibchas, cuya región de origen se encuentra en Costa Rica y Panamá. Algunos investigadores también mencionan la posibilidad de la presencia de grupos jicaques, nahuas y tawahkas en partes del noreste de Honduras (Conzemius 1932:14; Fowler 1983; Stone 1941: 8).

Según las fuentes etnohistóricas del siglo XVI, la región de Trujillo desempeña un papel importante. Fue aquí donde Colón encontró tierra firme por primera vez en 1502. Algunas de las fuentes más importantes son los escritos de su hijo Fernando (1959 [1571]), Diego de Porras (1825-37) y Bartolomé de las Casa (1986). Un acontecimiento frecuentemente citado hace referencia a una canoa que Colón encontró en la isla de Guanaja. Además de varias personas, contenía numerosos bienes. Este pasaje se cita a menudo como evidencia de un intercambio con la región maya, aunque algunos investigadores han demostrado que esta información no está incluida en las

fuentes originales (Edwards 1978: 203; Lara Pinto 1980: 34-37). Sin embargo, esta historia demuestra que la ruta marítima era importante para el intercambio de bienes y que los habitantes de las Islas de la Bahía participaban en este intercambio. Además, las fuentes proporcionan información sobre que la zona de Trujillo era una región densamente poblada. La infraestructura existente fue aprovechada por los españoles para fundar la primera capital del país allí. También se menciona la existencia de diferentes provincias en el noreste de Honduras. Gloria Lara Pinto (1980) logró ubicar la provincia de Papayeca en lo que hoy es el valle de Aguán. El término Taguzgalpa también aparece con frecuencia, pero hay diferentes opiniones sobre la extensión de esta entidad geopolítica.

El posicionamiento del noreste de Honduras entre las grandes áreas culturales ha influido mucho en la perspectiva de la investigación arqueológica en Honduras. La zona se percibía como periférica en comparación con las "complejas culturas" de Mesoamérica. Influenciados por un enfoque difusionista, los primeros investigadores que fueron a esta zona buscaron influencias de la cultura maya vecina, intentando asignar la región a alguna de las áreas culturales adyacentes. En los últimos años, la zona se percibe cada vez más como una región con su propia entidad, y el enfoque de la investigación se ha desplazado hacia los desarrollos autóctonos (p. ej., Goodwin 2019; Hasemann/Lara Pinto 1993). A pesar de estas importantes contribuciones dedicadas a la comprensión de la sociedad local, en muchas publicaciones, el noreste de Honduras sigue siendo entendido como una zona intermedia entre las principales regiones culturales. La interacción se estudia a nivel de áreas culturales, y se asume que estas interacciones interregionales son las que crean identidad. Mesoamérica, en particular, se considera un área importante de influencia para innovaciones, mientras que la interacción con los habitantes del Caribe apenas se tiene en cuenta. Muchas publicaciones dedican un gran esfuerzo a la elaboración de teorías, aunque estas no siempre son apropiadas dada la limitada disponibilidad de datos subyacentes.

Redes de interacción en América Central: El marco conceptual

El objetivo de este trabajo es proporcionar una concepción diferente desde una perspectiva alternativa del noreste de Honduras y posicionar esta región desde la periferia al centro de la investigación. La interacción no se analizará con un enfoque "top-down" a nivel de áreas culturales, sino que se reconstruirá "bottom-up" desde la perspectiva de los habitantes del noreste de Honduras

235

como agentes activos. Esta debe considerarse no sólo a nivel interregional, sino sobre todo a nivel local y regional, y debe entenderse como bilateral y no en términos de influencias unilaterales.

Una revisión de las teorías de la interacción que se suelen aplicar en estudios arqueológicos deja claro que la mayoría de las teorías no ofrece un valor añadido para el análisis de la compleja situación de Honduras. Algunos enfoques consideran la interacción como unidireccional (p.ej. difusionismo), otros presuponen una relación jerárquica entre los diferentes actores de la interacción (p.ej. teoría del sistema-mundo), mientras que otros solo consideran tipos específicos de interacción (p.ej. esfera de interacción, estudios económicos). Además, algunos enfoques no pueden aplicarse de forma satisfactoria debido a la escasez de datos (p. ej., peer-polity interaction). Finalmente, se encontró un enfoque adecuado con el análisis de redes, que cumple con todos los requisitos necesarios para realizar un análisis significativo en la zona de estudio.

El análisis de redes se basa en la teoría matemática de los grafos. Los grafos están formados por vértices y aristas y pueden utilizarse para representar formalmente sistemas que existen en el mundo real, facilitando así su análisis. Antes de iniciar un análisis de redes es importante definir qué tipo de redes se van a estudiar y qué se entiende por vértices y aristas. En general, los vértices se entienden como actores y las aristas como la interacción entre ellos. Las posibilidades de análisis incluyen observaciones sobre la intensidad de aristas, sobre la centralidad o conectividad de vértices individuales, y sobre la topografía de la red entera.

En arqueología, a menudo nos encontramos con la limitación de las posibilidades de análisis debido a una base de datos incompleta. Muchas veces se trata más de la reconstrucción de redes que de su análisis detallado (Sindbaek 2013). En arqueología se estudian principalmente las redes materiales a partir de las observaciones sobre la cultura material. Los vértices pueden entenderse, por ejemplo, como sitios arqueológicos o fuentes de materias primas. Para reconstruir las interacciones, pueden aplicarse análisis estilísticos basados en los principios de similitud, así como análisis científicos como el de procedencia.

Para el noreste de Honduras, se analiza una red egocéntrica (ego-network) en la que Guadalupe se entiende como vértice central. A partir de los hallazgos y rasgos identificados en Guadalupe, se reconstruyen sus conexiones con otros sitios, fuentes de materias primas y regiones. El potencial de este enfoque para nuestra área de investigación es que se centra en las conexiones y subraya su importancia para la vida cotidiana, ofreciendo una perspectiva alternativa a los conceptos de áreas culturales y "sociedades complejas".

Los conceptos de "complejidad" y "áreas culturales" son reliquias de la historia de la investigación arqueológica, pero siguen utilizándose y, por tanto, siguen influyendo mucho en la práctica. Sin embargo, estos conceptos son muy simplificadores y consideramos que deben rebatirse por varias razones. El concepto de sociedades complejas se basa en ideas evolucionistas que caracterizan como estado ideal el desarrollo de una jerarquía sociopolítica marcada, acompañada de "logros civilizatorios" como la escritura, los edificios monumentales, etc. Además, esta yuxtaposición no tiene en cuenta las numerosas y diferentes formas de organización sociopolítica que se sitúan entre lo "complejo" y lo "no complejo". El concepto de áreas culturales igualmente crea una visión dicotómica y carece de flexibilidad. En cambio, el análisis de redes permite comparar diferentes estructuras sociales de una manera neutral. En lugar de contrastar áreas culturales delimitadas, las sociedades prehispánicas y sus interacciones pueden entenderse como redes y subredes, pudiendo examinar así sus interconexiones.

Nuevas investigaciones en la costa norte

La región de estudio se definió incluyendo la zona costera desde Betulia al oeste, Trujillo al este, el valle del Aguán al sur y las Islas de la Bahía al norte. En esta zona hay varios sitios arqueológicos aún no explorados. El sitio arqueológico de Guadalupe se encuentra a unos 15 km al oeste de Trujillo, dentro del moderno asentamiento del mismo nombre. En la superficie, concentraciones densas de cerámica dan testimonio a una ocupación prehispánica. Esta ocupación parece haberse concentrado en una terraza que se extiende hacia la costa como una prolongación de la cordillera costera. Directamente al este de esta terraza encontramos el cauce seco de un río. Y en el centro de esta terraza se encuentra el vestigio arqueológico mejor conservado, en forma de montículo, un área que hoy en día pertenece a la escuela primaria local.

Con el fin de investigar esta zona, se llevaron a cabo varios levantamientos topográficos. A continuación, se realizó una trinchera de 2x12 m en el montículo en dirección oeste-este. Esta se dividió en cuatro secciones (Unidades 1-4), con numeración ascendente hacia el este. La estratigrafía del montículo puede dividirse en dos secciones. La parte superior consiste en una capa de aproximadamente 1m de grosor, compuesta por tierra oscura y muchos fragmentos de cerámica de gran tamaño. Además, contiene numerosos huesos, conchas y otros hallazgos. Debajo de esta concentración hay varias capas que pueden interpretarse como horizontes de asentamiento. En la zona central del montículo destacamos, como rasgos importantes, varias fosas, así como dos suelos rojos de ladrillo y un fogón.

Además, se registraron varias concentraciones de bajareque en la periferia del montículo. Por debajo de estas concentraciones había enterramientos de al menos cinco individuos. Las observaciones estratigráficas y los resultados de la datación por C14 sugieren que los enterramientos, las concentraciones de bajareque y la acumulación de cerámica están temporalmente relacionados. La mayor parte de las dataciones C14 se sitúan entre el 900 y el 1525 d.C.

Basándose en la observación de los rasgos, se asume que el yacimiento estuvo ocupado, como muy tarde, a partir del periodo Selin Transicional. Los hoyos de poste, los suelos y un fogón dan testimonio de las actividades de asentamiento. Alrededor del 1260 d.C., se empezó a utilizar el lugar como cementerio y, en relación con estos entierros, se realizaban festividades en las que el consumo de comida y bebida desempeñaba un papel importante. Los restos de la comida se depositaban junto con los recipientes de cerámica cerca de los enterramientos. Se trataba de actividades recurrentes, por lo que en el transcurso del periodo Cocal se desarrolló una acumulación claramente reconocible de tiestos y otros objetos.

Además de los trabajos de excavación, se realizaron recorridos por la zona de estudio definida anteriormente con el objetivo de reconstruir el sistema de asentamiento durante el periodo Cocal. Con la ayuda del IHAH y de informantes locales, se identificaron 16 sitios arqueológicos. Los sitios costeros se sitúan mayormente cerca de ríos y de depresiones en la Cordillera Nombre de Dios que permiten el paso al valle del Aguán. En la propia cordillera, también se encontraron asentamientos a lo largo de estos pasos. En Río Arriba 1 y 2, ubicados en la zona norte del valle del Aguán, se registraron asentamientos de dimensiones hasta ahora desconocidas. Cuentan con montículos de hasta 80 m de longitud, terrazas artificiales y caminos empedrados que llevan a la costa. La región costera probablemente estaba en comunicación activa con los asentamientos del valle del Aguán a través de los pasos de la cordillera. Por otro lado, en Plan Grande, en la isla de Guanaja, se identificaron petroglifos *patolli*, lo que indica una conexión con Mesoamérica.

El estudio de los hallazgos de las excavaciones en Guadalupe proporciona información sobre las redes materiales durante el periodo Cocal. Entre ellos, la cerámica representa la categoría más abundante. La mayoría no es cerámica pintada, sino que se caracteriza por decoraciones incisas y aplicaciones. Para el análisis de la cerámica se desarrolla un nuevo sistema de clasificación basado en el trabajo de Iken Paap (2002). Su enfoque se basa en la definición de atributos, los cuales se documentan para cada fragmento individual. Un tipo se define por la asociación frecuente de estos atributos. Para aplicar este método al material de Guadalupe se hicieron algunos ajustes.

Mientras Paap examina las categorías tradicionales de "pasta", "forma" y "decoración", para el material de Guadalupe se definieron las categorías "forma" y "modificaciones". El tema de la pasta se trata en detalle en la tesis doctoral de Mike Lyons. La categoría "forma" contiene los atributos de proporción (de altura y diámetro), composición (composición geométrica / número de cambios), posición del borde, forma del borde, labio y base. La categoría "modificaciones" incluye todas las modificaciones que se realizan después de la producción del cuerpo básico de una vasija y se divide, a su vez, en incisiones, aplicaciones y pintura. Esta división se basa en el hecho de que las aplicaciones desempeñan un papel importante en el material de Guadalupe. Sin embargo, no pueden atribuirse claramente a las categorías tradicionales de forma o decoración, por lo que se creó un esquema nuevo que se orienta en la secuencia de producción de una vasija cerámica. También se definieron atributos para la documentación de las modificaciones que incluyen principalmente su posición en la vasija y los motivos representados. Para la documentación de los atributos, se elaboró un sistema y una clave. Como base de análisis se utiliza una muestra de 868 fragmentos provenientes de la Unidad 2.

La figura 69 ilustra las formas de vasijas representadas en la muestra. El 28% de los fragmentos examinados llevan incisiones y se encuentran frecuentemente en la zona del borde. Los motivos en forma de aspa y ondas son especialmente comunes, así como diversas combinaciones de líneas y puntos. El 54% de los fragmentos cuentan con aplicaciones, que son mayormente asas y soportes. Las asas en forma de D son las más comunes. Existen soportes cónicos en diferentes variantes, algunos tienen forma de pies humanos, otros probablemente representan aletas. También existen soportes en forma de cabezas antropomórficas en versiones cónicas y hemisféricas, tanto detalladas como estilizadas. Especialmente común es el motivo de la serpiente, que se encuentra en diversas formas bien como asa o como soporte. Otros motivos zoomórficos incluyen aves y mamíferos (posiblemente coatíes u osos hormigueros). Sólo unos pocos fragmentos tienen pintura y estos se pueden dividir en pintura polícroma, pintura monocroma y engobe. Todos los fragmentos pintados polícromos corresponden al tipo Islas de la Bahía Polícromo.

La combinación frecuente de los atributos observados en las categorías de forma y modificación es la base para la definición de tipos. Para Guadalupe se definen 14 tipos. Se puede observar una evolución estilística en la secuencia estratigráfica de atributos y tipos, lo que confirma que el conjunto cerámico se creó durante un cierto periodo de tiempo. La ocurrencia de algunos atributos y tipos está espacialmente limitada. Los tipos 9 y 13, por ejemplo, se acumulan en la parte superior de la concentración cerámica, mientras que los tipos 10 y 14 se observan principalmente en la parte inferior. La forma A-II-1, la forma de borde 6 y las incisiones 7, 13, 16 y 18 sólo aparecen en los horizontes de asentamiento y, por tanto, son fenómenos tempranos. Sin embargo, también hay elementos que se observan en todos los contextos, indicando que las transiciones entre las diferentes fases no eran muy abuptas, sino fluidas.

Para evaluar si se podían atribuir patrones de uso a las categorías definidas por el análisis tipocronológico se llevó a cabo un estudio de residuos[27]. Se analizaron 23 fragmentos con respecto a residuos de fosfatos, carbonatos, proteínas, hidratos de carbono, ácidos grasos y de pH, lo que permitió realizar observaciones semicuantitativas de su concentración. A partir del análisis se dedujo que todos los fragmentos analizados tuvieron un contacto intensivo con alimentos. Parece que las vasijas del tipo 1 ("sartén") no se utilizaban como incensario, como se suponía anteriormente, sino para la preparación de alimentos y que las vasijas del tipo 14 (vasijas grandes decoradas) se utilizaban como recipientes para bebidas alcohólicas (chicha). Además de las vasijas, también se encontraron otros objetos de cerámica, entre ellos, ocarinas, mayormente en forma de tortugas, figuritas zoomorfas, sellos cilíndricos, husos de hilar y vasijas en miniatura.

La obsidiana representa otra de las grandes categorías de hallazgos y se presta, especialmente bien, para la investigación de redes de intercambio. En Guadalupe, se encontraron 767 objetos de obsidiana, la mayoría, navajas prismáticas, pero también puntas de proyectiles y un núcleo. Hasta ahora, no se había reportado tal cantidad de obsidiana en ningún otro sitio del noreste de Honduras. Se analizó la composición química y la tecnología de producción de 355 objetos[28]. Con el fin de investigar la procedencia geológica de los fragmentos, su análisis químico se realizó con la metodología XRF. Además, se examinaron varios casos dudosos mediante análisis visual. La combinación de estos métodos reveló que 223 piezas provienen de la fuente de Güinope (Honduras), 122 de La Esperanza (Honduras), 9 de Ixtepeque (Guatemala) y 1 de Otumba (México).

El estudio, además, demostró que los habitantes de Guadalupe estuvieron involucrados en diferentes redes de intercambio. La obsidiana de Güinope se usaba para la producción local de navajas prismáticas y de Ixtepeque y La Esperanza se importaban las navajas prismáticas ya listas para su uso. Los datos de Guadalupe evidencian, por primera vez, tal producción in situ de material proveniente de Güinope. La producción de navajas prismáticas es una tecnología mesoamericana que se considera un rasgo cultural distintivo. El hecho de que esta tecnología se utilizara en Guadalupe es una prueba del contacto con esta región y revela la transferencia tecnológica entre zonas. La tecnología mesoamericana se adaptó a las necesidades locales y, en este caso, se desarrolló como un método manual.

En Guadalupe se encontraron nueve objetos de piedra verde. La mayoría de estos objetos son pequeñas cuentas cilíndricas. Ocho de los nueve objetos se analizaron mediante espectroscopia Raman, la cual demostró que todos son de jadeíta[29]. La fuente más cercana de jade se encuentra en el Valle del Motagua, Guatemala, y es muy probable que estos objetos procedieran de allí. Algunos autores suponen que existe otra fuente de jade en Costa Rica, aunque esta hipótesis aún no se ha confirmado y hace poco se descubrieron otras fuentes de jade en Cuba e Hispaniola (García Casco et al. 2009; Schertl et al. 2012; Schertl/Maresch/Krebs 2007). El jade y otras piedras verdes son materias primas altamente apreciadas entre las sociedades prehispánicas de Centroamérica y el Caribe. También se conocen varios artefactos de piedra verde del noreste de Honduras, aunque la mayoría se encuentran en colecciones privadas y son de procedencia incierta. También se han encontrado varios ejemplares del "dios hacha", una forma muy común en Costa Rica. El gran número de artefactos de piedra verde encontrados en el noreste de Honduras demuestra que existía una tradición propia regional de manufactura de piedra verde. La presencia de jade real en Guadalupe es puntual y singular, ya que los otros hallazgos que se han analizado son de jade social, es decir, de piedra verde más suave, como serpentina o muscovita. Se han identificado fuentes de estas piedras en las Islas de la Bahía (Feachem 1940) y en la Mosquitia (Begley 1999).

Además de obsidiana y piedra verde, se encontraron 116 objetos de piedra, entre ellos, 13 hachas, la mayoría, ejemplares muy pequeños y bien pulidos. El hacha más pequeña mide solamente 2.3 x 2.2 cm. Otros objetos parecidos, identificados de diferentes contextos de Centro-

---

27 El análisis se realizó bajo la dirección de Luis Barba Pingarrón (Uiversidad Nacional Autónoma de México).
28 El análisis se realizó bajo la dirección de Geoffrey Braswell, con la colaboración de Luke Stroth y Raquel Otto. Los resultados presentados aquí se basan principalmente en Stroth (2019) y Otto (2019).

29 El análisis se realizó bajo la dirección de Ulrich A. Glasmacher (ThermoArchaeo, Instituto de Geosciencias, Universidad de Heidelberg).

américa, se encontraron en Río Claro y Roatán. Estudios de traceología revelaron que este tipo de hachas se usaban para tallar madera (Aoyama et al. 2017). Se encontraron dos fragmentos de trituradoras de corteza. Estas herramientas se utilizaban para machacar la corteza de los árboles y producir telas de corteza. Hasta la década de 1960, los pesh utilizaban la corteza del árbol *tunu* para fabricar telas (Griffin et al. 2009: 64f). También se encontraron 29 fragmentos de manos y siete fragmentos de metates, los cuales se usaban para moler alimentos. Uno de los fragmentos pertenece a un metate decorado con tres soportes y representa la lengua de un reptil. Estos metates, normalmente muy elaborados, se encuentran en el sur de Centroamérica. Otros objetos de piedra incluyen morteros, guijarros, que probablemente se usarían para alisar cerámica, piedra pómez con acanaladuras, que posiblemente se utilizarían para afilar astiles de flechas, y piedras pequeñas de cuarzo blanco que hoy en día se insertan en tablas de madera para rallar yuca.

Entre los hallazgos había también tres objetos de metal: una aguja y dos cascabeles. Se examinó la composición química de la aguja y de uno de los cascabeles[30] y los análisis demostraron que la aguja es de bronce de estaño y el cascabel de cobre. La asignación a una zona geográfica de origen no es tan fácil en este caso como con el jade o la obsidiana. Durante el periodo prehispánico tardío existían centros de producción de metal en el oeste de México y el sur de Centroamérica. Recientemente, también se han encontrado pruebas de la producción de metales en las tierras bajas mayas (Simmons/Shugar 2013a). Algunos investigadores sugieren que también hubo una zona de producción de metales en el sur de Mesoamérica, posiblemente en Honduras (Hosler 2003; Lothrop 1952: 22; Simmons/Shugar 2013b). Esta teoría se ve respaldada por el descubrimiento de cientos de cascabeles de metal y cobre nativo en la Cueva de Quimistán en el Valle de Naco. En la región existen yacimientos de cobre y se ha comprobado arqueológicamente la existencia de varios pasos de producción de cobre (Urban et al. 2013). Las fuentes etnohistóricas sugieren que también se procesaba metal en el noreste de Honduras y es posible que hubiera producción de cascabeles. Sin embargo, estos se encuentran en toda Centroamérica durante el periodo prehispánico tardío, ya que eran un producto muy apreciado, y la composición del cobre, así como las observaciones estilísticas, podrían apuntar también a una producción en México. El estilo y la composición de la aguja apuntan al oeste de México. Sin embargo, la procedencia de los objetos no puede determinarse de forma concluyente con los datos disponibles.

Otra categoría de hallazgos son los restos faunísticos, los cuales fueron muy numerosos en Guadalupe. Los restos de animales pueden proporcionarnos información sobre la subsistencia y sobre las redes económicas existentes. En cuanto a la fauna vertebrada, sólo se ha podido realizar un análisis preliminar partiendo de 755 objetos[31]. La identificación taxonómica de los objetos se realizó según el Número de Especímenes Identificados (NISP). El grupo de animales más abundante es el de los peces con un 63,31% (NISP = 478), seguido de los mamíferos con un 22,91% (NISP = 173). Los reptiles, con un 13,25% del total de la muestra (NISP = 100), fueron un grupo minoritario, y las aves, con sólo un 0,53% (NISP = 4), fueron el grupo menos representado en el conjunto zooarqueológico (Tabla 4). Algunos huesos presentan marcas de afectación térmica como la quema y la calcinación. Algunos huesos también fueron usados como materia prima para la fabricación de artefactos. Entre ellos se encontraron huesos con incisiones, dientes con perforaciones que probablemente se utilizaron como colgantes y una figurilla antropomorfa de hueso.

La muestra de la fauna invertebrada comprendía 4309 objetos y el análisis taxonómico también se realizó según el número de especímenes identificados (NISP)[32]. Los moluscos no estaban tan bien conservados como los huesos, pero también se observaron efectos térmicos, que aparentemente, en algunos casos, se debieron al contacto directo con el fuego. Los moluscos pueden asignarse a 37 familias diferentes. Las más comunes, con diferencia, son los bivalvos de la familia Ostreidae (especialmente *Crassostrea* sp.). También son comunes los restos de las familias Glycimeridae (*Glycymeris* sp.), Strombidae (*Strombus pugilis*), Turbinellidae (*Turbinella angulata*), Neritidae (*Nereina* cf. *Punctulata*) y Veneridae (Tabla 5 y 6). Los moluscos proceden de diferentes biotopos, que se distinguen por su salinidad. También aparecen representados moluscos de aguas dulces (2,7%), estuarinos (82,5%) y marinos (14,8%). Destaca el uso intensivo de especies estuarinas. Respecto a los moluscos marinos, a pesar de que hay menor porcentaje, se observa una mayor diversidad de especies, las cuales se pueden encontrar en diferentes profundidades, incluyendo cuatro ejemplares del género Spondylus. Muchos moluscos presentan marcas de procesamiento, la mayoría de las cuales se deben a la extracción de la carne como alimento. Sin embargo, se encontraron huellas no relacionadas con la extracción de alimento en 84 objetos. Algunos bivalvos tienen una perforación en el centro y probablemente representan pesos de redes de pesca. Otros bivalvos presentan marcas de

---

30 Los estudios fueron realizados por Andreas Hauptmann (Museo Alemán de Minería en Bochum) utilizando un microscopio electrónico de barrido.

31 Análisis realizado por Nayeli Jiménez Cano (Universidad Autónoma de Yucatán).

32 Análisis realizado por Nayeli Jiménez Cano (Universidad Autónoma de Yucatán) y Annkatrin Benz (Universidad de Bonn).

raspadura a lo largo de sus bordes, lo que sugiere que estos objetos se utilizaban como herramientas para raspar o rayar. Las conchas de los grandes gasterópodos marinos también se utilizaron para la producción de artefactos. Se realizaron artefactos alargados de forma ovalada, trapezoidal y en forma de L, aunque su uso no está claro. Otros especímenes representan picos y perforadores y los objetos de carácter ornamental incluyen conchas *Oliva* trabajadas como pendientes.

Este análisis de los restos faunísticos manifiesta que se trata de una muestra taxonómicamente muy diversa. Al parecer, los habitantes de Guadalupe utilizaban varios ambientes de su entorno donde los recursos marinos desempeñaban un papel especialmente importante. Estos recursos no sólo se utilizaban para el consumo, sino que también los transformaban en herramientas y otros artefactos.

Discusión

Los resultados de las excavaciones en Guadalupe sirven de base para investigar la participación de sus habitantes en diversas redes de interacción durante el periodo prehispánico tardío (900-1525 d.C.). Guadalupe se entiende como el vértice central de una red egocéntrica. Fue ocupado al menos desde el año 900 d.C. y se convirtió en un importante centro ceremonial a mediados del siglo XIII, cuando los difuntos fueron enterrados en el centro del asentamiento. En relación con estos enterramientos, periódicamente se celebraban fiestas y se depositaban los restos de estas festividades, de modo que con el tiempo se formaba una acumulación claramente visible.

En cuanto a la subsistencia de los habitantes, es evidente que la base alimenticia muestra un alto grado de diversidad. Se utilizaron todas las ecozonas circundantes para obtener alimentos, lo que permitió una estrategia de subsistencia amplia y equilibrada. Los recursos marinos desempeñaron un papel especial. También estaban representados los mamíferos y los reptiles, mientras que las aves no parecen haber ocupado un papel importante en la subsistencia. Además, la presencia de numerosos metates, manos y morteros indica que las plantas también eran importantes para la alimentación. En cuanto a los restos animales, se observó un patrón similar para Selin Farm (Healy 1983) y no parece haber ocurrido un cambio marcado en la subsistencia en comparación con el periodo Selin.

En cuanto a la producción de objetos, podemos suponer que la cerámica se producía en Guadalupe o en sus alrededores. Hay depósitos de arcilla en la zona y durante la excavación se encontraron deshechos de cerámica relacionados con el proceso de producción. Dado que la cerámica no muestra una elevada estandarización, es de suponer que se trataba de una producción descentralizada, posiblemente a nivel doméstico. Los fuertes vestigios de uso en la cerámica indican que esta no fue producida específicamente para la deposición ritual, sino que previamente fue utilizada de forma intensiva. Otros artefactos producidos en Guadalupe incluyen navajas de obsidiana, hechas con obsidiana proveniente de Güinope, herramientas fabricadas de moluscos y posiblemente herramientas de piedra. Las herramientas como los husos de hilar, los trituradores de corteza y las agujas también indican la producción de textiles. Las fuentes etnográficas demuestran que los pesh utilizaban antiguamente la corteza del árbol *tunu* para fabricar telas de corteza (Griffin/Escobar Martínez/Hernández Torres 2009). El tamaño de los husos sugiere que se procesaron fibras finas, posiblemente de algodón. Es probable que este se haya cultivado en el Valle de Aguán. Además de estos productos, los materiales perecederos que no se conservan en el contexto arqueológico (como la madera para la arquitectura y la construcción de canoas, las hojas de palma y el zacate para fabricar cuerdas y cestas, los tintes, las resinas, las plumas, las pieles, etc.) desempeñaron, sin duda, un papel muy importante en la vida cotidiana de los habitantes. Los datos existentes demuestran que la abundancia de recursos en un entorno diverso garantizaba el abastecimiento de la población y no requería la importación de alimentos básicos. Al mismo tiempo, los bienes producidos eran un factor esencial para la creación de redes de intercambio.

Los hallazgos y rasgos de Guadalupe, junto con la información de las fuentes etnológicas, permiten hacerse una idea sobre la arquitectura prehispánica (Mattes 2019). Como base de una casa se disponían hileras de piedras. Postes verticales de madera, posiblemente cañas, estaban arriostrados con otros palos horizontales y todo esto se cubría posteriormente con arcilla. El suelo de la casa era de tierra pisada, el techo probablemente de hojas de palmera. El tamaño de las casas no está claro. Se identificaron plataformas de hasta 80 m de longitud en el noreste de Honduras, que podrían tratarse de casas largas en las que vivían varias familias juntas o familias extensas.

Un aspecto que sin duda desempeñaba un papel central en la vida de los habitantes eran los entierros y las fiestas que se celebraban en relación a ellos. Hasta la fecha, sólo se han documentado unos pocos enterramientos en el noreste de Honduras. Entre ellos, se incluyen entierros en urnas (Strong 1935: 20-28), entierros dentro de un montículo en Utila (Epstein 1957: 22-33), posibles cementerios en Roatán (Begley 1999: 178; Cruz Castillo/Orellana 2000) y entierros individuales cerca de Trujillo (Epstein 1957: 45f; Healy 1975: 65; Spinden 1925: 534; Stone 1934a). Según algunas descripciones, estos enterramientos se asocian a una acumulación de tierra oscura, fragmentos de cerámica, huesos y otros artefactos, lo que los hace similares al sitio de Guadalupe. Strong describe una situación muy similar para el Sitio 1 de Indian Hill en Barbereta y el Dixon Site en Roatán (1935: 51-72 y 86-111) e interpreta estos hallazgos como signos de actividades ceremoniales periódicas a largo plazo. Podemos definir estas actividades con mayor precisión y estamos convencidos de que estos hallazgos son los resultados de festejos. Las fiestas se entienden como eventos constituidos esencialmente por el consumo comunitario de comida y bebida para una ocasión especial (Dietler/Hayden 2001: 3). Como forma particular de interacción social, los festejos adquieren un papel importante y pueden servir, entre otras cosas, para negociar o reforzar los vínculos sociales. Otros yacimientos arqueológicos que se han interpretado como lugares de fiesta muestran fuertes similitudes con Guadalupe, especialmente por la presencia de una gran cantidad de cerámica destruida intencionalmente, restos de comida y objetos rituales como incensarios e instrumentos musicales. En Guadalupe sorprende la presencia adicional de objetos como husos, herramientas de piedra, etc., que a primera vista no se asocian con festividades, pero que posiblemente sirvieron como una especie de ofrenda funeraria. Las fuentes etnográficas confirman estas observaciones (Chapman 1958; Conzemius 1927; Griffin/Escobar Martínez/Hernández Torres 2009) y apuntan que los pesh realizaban periódicamente festividades relacionadas con la muerte de una persona, que implicaban el consumo comunitario de alimentos y la realización de rituales. Los restos de las fiestas se recogían y se depositaban en un lugar concreto. El ajuar funerario solía estar compuesto por las posesiones del difunto y, en muchas ocasiones, consistía en objetos rotos o de poca utilidad. Para los sumu y miskito también se describe un uso secundario de los entierros (Conzemius 1932), como probablemente ocurría en Guadalupe. Las fiestas en el centro del asentamiento prehispánico de Guadalupe debieron ser eventos visibles y acústicos, acontecimientos importantes, cuya preparación y ejecución influyó en la vida comunal de una manera determinada. No sólo se celebraba la interacción entre los vivos, sino también la conexión con los difuntos, que parecen haber sido parte integral de la sociedad. Además, la acumulación de los restos de la fiesta estaba siempre presente y visible para los habitantes de Guadalupe. Formaba parte de la vida cotidiana y, al igual que un monumento, mantenía vivo el recuerdo de los ancestros. Los hallazgos en Selin Farm, que Goodwin (2019) también interpreta como restos de fiestas rituales, indican que estas celebraciones tienen una larga tradición en el noreste de Honduras y que no son sólo un fenómeno del periodo Cocal.

Las fiestas están estrechamente relacionadas con el sistema de creencias de una sociedad, lo que muchas veces se expresa en la iconografía. En la cerámica de Guadalupe, el entorno natural juega un papel esencial. En cuanto a los animales, se representan principalmente aquellos que no eran de gran importancia para la subsistencia, como las aves, las serpientes y los felinos. Dado que en las vasijas de cerámica se representan igualmente los animales y los humanos, no parece haber existido una separación estricta entre ellos. Un fenómeno similar se da en la cerámica de la región amazónica, donde los humanos y los animales tienen el mismo estatus y no representan dos categorías diferentes como en nuestra visión occidental (Bonomo/Politis 2016). La destacada tematización del entorno natural en la cerámica muestra la estrecha conexión entre el hombre y la naturaleza, lo que podría relacionarse con una visión animista del mundo y con mitos cuyo significado se ha perdido en la actualidad.

Para describir la organización sociopolítica de las sociedades del sur de Centroamérica y el Caribe, a menudo se usa el término "cacicazgo". Sin embargo, este término conlleva dificultades. Proviene de una tradición que entiende la historia humana como un desarrollo evolutivo en un orden fijo, comparando sobre todo la complejidad, es decir, la jerarquía vertical de diferentes rangos sociales. Sin embargo, aparte de estas etapas de desarrollo, existen numerosas formas de organización sociopolítica. El concepto de cacicazgo es, por tanto, muy simplista y tiene poco valor analítico. Más bien hay que examinar los mecanismos que subyacen a una organización sociopolítica y tener en cuenta distintos sistemas de organización alternativos, ya que la complejidad también puede adoptar otras formas además de la jerarquía social. En el caso de Guadalupe, hay poca evidencia disponible que sugiera una sociedad jerárquica en el sentido clásico. Existían otros elementos que desempeñaban un papel importante en la sociedad y que eran necesarios para su organización, como la celebración de fiestas que reforzaban los vínculos entre la gente y sus antepasados, a los que se rendía culto y se conmemoraba colectivamente.

Redes de interacción regional

Se identifican al menos dos redes de interacción a nivel regional que estaban estrechamente relacionadas entre sí: una red de interacción del noreste de Honduras y una red de interacción costera, la cual representa una subred dentro de la primera. El sistema de interacción costera se extiende desde Betulia, al oeste, hasta la Laguna Guaimoreto, al este, e incluye las Islas de la Bahía en el norte y el Valle de Aguán en el sur. Así pues, todo el entorno inmediato de Guadalupe alcanzable en un día queda incluido y éste se caracteriza por los fuertes lazos entre sus habitantes. En la costa, los asentamientos se sitúan cada cierto intervalo, preferentemente cerca de ríos y donde es posible el paso al Valle del Aguán. En el Valle del Aguán existen numerosos asentamientos prehispánicos, hasta ahora no registrados, de dimensiones sorprendentes. Se puede suponer que el valle fértil estaba densamente poblado durante el periodo Cocal y que se utilizaba intensamente para la agricultura, probablemente para el cultivo de cacao o algodón. Las fuentes etnohistóricas (Lara Pinto 1980: 63) también confirman esta imagen. Es muy probable que los habitantes del Valle del Aguán y los de la costa mantuvieran estrechos vínculos y que los pasajes de la Cordillera fueran utilizados como vías de comunicación, sobre todo porque se registraron caminos empedrados y asentamientos a lo largo de estas rutas. Sin duda, las Islas de la Bahía también formaban parte de esta red. En un día despejado, estas islas son visibles desde la costa. También en este caso las fuentes etnohistóricas dan cuenta de una estrecha relación entre los habitantes de las islas y de la tierra firme (Lara Pinto 1980: 78, 1991: 234). Con respecto a las evidencias arqueológicas, la intensidad de la interacción puede determinarse sobre todo por la gran similitud de la cultura material.

El área cubierta por la red incluye varios nichos ecológicos y el intercambio de productos entre estos nichos debe haber sido beneficioso. Así, cabe imaginar que los recursos marinos se traían desde la costa y las islas hasta el Valle de Aguán y, en cambio, los productos agrícolas, como los alimentos o el algodón, llegaban a la costa desde el interior. Los datos actuales sugieren que no era una red muy centralizada. No obstante, es evidente que existía una cierta jerarquía y, sobre todo en el Valle de Aguán, había centros más grandes que controlaban los asentamientos circundantes. Guadalupe se distingue claramente de los demás asentamientos por la cantidad (especialmente de cerámica y obsidiana) y la naturaleza de los hallazgos (objetos de jade y metal y la presencia de fragmentos de Islas de la Bahía Polícromo). Esta posición especial puede ser el resultado de una función de bróker dentro de la red (Burt 1992). Los brókeres tienen la ventaja de tener acceso a diferentes subredes y a la información y los recursos que se intercambian a través de ellas. En este caso, son especialmente importantes los denominados "lazos débiles", que, a pesar de consistir en una interacción poco frecuente, son importantes para el intercambio de información. Los brókeres pueden decidir hasta qué punto y a quién transmiten esta información o no, de lo que resulta su posición privilegiada.

Esta red de interacción costera estaba integrada como subred en una red más amplia que cubría gran parte del noreste de Honduras. Los límites de esta red aún no se pueden definir con precisión debido a la escasa investigación y a que gran parte de los resultados no se han publicado. Hasta la fecha, la investigación arqueológica se ha centrado en observaciones de sitios a lo largo del Río Tinto, el Valle de Culmi y el curso superior del Río Patuca. Los asentamientos de estas regiones muestran una gran similitud en cuanto a la arquitectura (caminos empedrados y plataformas de tierra) y la cultura material, especialmente en lo que se refiere al estilo cerámico, el tallado de la piedra verde y la presencia de numerosas esculturas de piedra, incluidos metates zoomorfos. Al mismo tiempo, existen claras diferencias regionales. Las opiniones predominantes asignan un papel importante a las sociedades mesoamericanas vecinas en el surgimiento de una identidad común expresada en la cultura material (Begley 1999; Cuddy 2007). Sin embargo, en este caso, se deben poner en primer plano los procesos regionales y plantear preguntas sobre la naturaleza de la interacción dentro del noreste de Honduras, incluyendo los aspectos económicos, la interacción social y la presencia de rutas de intercambio.

Redes de interacción interregional

Los habitantes de Guadalupe también participaban en diferentes redes interregionales. Estaban conectados a una red de intercambio que incluía la región maya y que operaba principalmente a lo largo de la costa atlántica. Esta conexión está relacionada con la descentralización de la red de intercambio en la región maya durante el periodo prehispánico tardío. Las fuentes etnohistóricas documentan las relaciones de intercambio entre la región maya y el oeste de Honduras. Basándose en los hallazgos de Guadalupe, se puede deducir que esta red se extendía más al este. A través de ella, llegaba a Guadalupe la obsidiana de Ixtepeque y el jade de Motagua. La obsidiana de Otumba y la aguja encontrada en Guadalupe sugieren que los vínculos de esta red llegaban incluso hasta el altiplano central mexicano. Además de los objetos, en estas redes y subredes también circulaban tecnologías e ideas. Esto se observa en la producción de navajas prismáticas en Guadalupe, en la iconografía de las vasijas del estilo Islas de la Bahía Polícromo y en la presencia de tableros de *patolli* en Guanaja. Algunos autores, basándose principalmente en fuentes etnohistóricas, consideran que en el noreste de Honduras había una importante población de habla nahua durante el periodo prehispánico tardío. Sin embargo, el contexto arqueológico no apoya esta teoría. Más bien, basado en los pocos objetos que podemos asignar con certeza a un origen mesoamericano, parece que este contacto fue algo esporádico y con lazos débiles, que no se intercambiaban grandes cantidades de bienes, y que los habitantes de

Guadalupe dependían mayormente de materias primas y de productos locales y regionales. Por supuesto, los materiales perecederos pueden haber desempeñado un papel más importante en el intercambio, pero por el momento no se ha podido comprobar. Obviamente, Guadalupe funcionó como un tipo de bróker entre las redes regionales y esta red mesoamericana, lo que le llevó a ocupar una posición distinta dentro de la red de interacción costera descrita anteriormente. Existían otras redes que conectaban Guadalupe con el sur y el centro de Honduras. La obsidiana llegaba desde la Esperanza y Güinope, pero no está claro si estas redes tenían otros niveles, además del económico, ya que las regiones de las que procede la obsidiana aún no están suficientemente exploradas.

Numerosos indicios señalan la existencia de una estrecha interacción con las sociedades del sur de Centroamérica, especialmente con las de las tierras altas y la vertiente atlántica de Costa Rica. Mientras las conexiones con Mesoamérica consistieron en contactos esporádicos de los que se adoptaron elementos individuales, se observan paralelismos con el sur de Centroamérica en muchos aspectos de la vida cotidiana. Esto incluye una gran similitud en la arquitectura, por ejemplo, el uso de material perecedero para la construcción de las casas, la adaptación de los montículos y plataformas a la topografía, y la presencia de caminos empedrados. En la cultura material, lo más notable es la presencia de metates elaborados, con frecuencia zoomorfos, que se consideran un rasgo cultural importante del sur de Centroamérica (Jones 1992). La piedra verde también era una materia prima muy valorada en ambas regiones. En el noreste de Honduras se encuentran imitaciones de los llamados "dioses hacha", que eran muy comunes en el sur de Centroamérica, especialmente en Costa Rica. También se observan claras similitudes en la cerámica, especialmente en la Highland Appliqué Ware de Costa Rica, como ya señaló Strong (1948b). Además, parecen existir paralelismos en las costumbres de enterramiento, como muestran informes etnológicos y arqueológicos (Bozzoli 1979; Gabb 1875; Hoopes/Chenault 1994). Por último, cabe señalar que Costa Rica se considera la zona de origen de las lenguas chibchas, a la cual también pertenece la lengua pesh (Hoopes/Fonseca 2003).Las conexiones con el sur de Centroamérica no se observan solamente en objetos móviles, sino también en la cultura material inmóvil y en tradiciones inmateriales. Por lo tanto, los lazos con el sur de Centroamérica deben haber sido más fuertes que las conexiones con el oeste. El fortalecimiento de las interconexiones en esta dirección durante el periodo Cocal probablemente fue causa del declive de los centros mayas del Clásico.

Respecto a la cuestión sobre la naturaleza de la interacción con Costa Rica, por ejemplo, si se trataba de re-

des principalmente económicas o si los habitantes de las regiones tenían lazos sociopolíticos o estaban unidos por una cosmovisión común y un marco cronológico estable para estas interacciones, queda pendiente de ser respondida por futuros estudios.

Por último, los datos sugieren que los habitantes de Guadalupe también estaban en contacto con los habitantes de las islas del Caribe. El estado actual de los conocimientos sugiere que la vela no se conocía en la época prehispánica y que la canoa era el medio de transporte típico y es muy probable que las rutas de viaje fueran principalmente a lo largo de las costas. Son también las similitudes en la arquitectura y la cultura material, como la cerámica o la presencia de ciertos objetos de piedra verde, así como reportes en las fuentes etnohistóricas, las que aportan pruebas del contacto entre los habitantes de estas regiones. Las similitudes indican que participaban en una misma esfera de interacción en la que circulaban objetos, ideas, historias y tecnologías. Basándose en los datos disponibles, se puede suponer que una red de intercambio conectaba la costa caribeña del sur de Centroamérica, el continente sudamericano y las islas del Caribe, coincidiendo con el área circum-caribe ya definida por Steward (1948).

A partir de estas observaciones, queda claro que los habitantes de Guadalupe, en particular, y del noreste de Honduras, en general, no ocupaban una posición periférica, sino que estaban involucrados en varias redes de interacción a nivel local, regional e interregional. Esta interconexión es un elemento crítico que define la sociedad del periodo Cocal en el noreste de Honduras. Además, no sólo existe a nivel geográfico, sino que también encuentra su expresión en la conexión con el mundo de los antepasados, a los que se honra mediante la celebración de fiestas y, por tanto, son una parte esencial de la vida social y de su memoria histórica. En este caso, el análisis de las redes resulta ser, no sólo una mera herramienta, sino también una nueva perspectiva que se centra en la importancia de estas interconexiones en diferentes ámbitos de la vida. La situación en el noreste de Honduras está demostrando ser mucho más compleja de lo que se suponía, y queda patente que esta región, en sí misma, tiene suficiente entidad, valía y complejidad para estudiarla de forma independiente y no considerarla como un mero anexo de una de las áreas culturales circundantes. Además, el concepto de redes de interacción se presta a sustituir el concepto estático y simplista de área cultural, integrando así una comprensión más dinámica y detallada de las condiciones y sustituyendo conceptos obsoletos.

Futuras estrategias de investigación

Para comprender mejor las redes de interacción aquí definidas, es necesario profundizar en su investigación. En un primer paso, la investigación debería centrarse en la reconstrucción de la topografía de las redes, es decir, identificar el mayor número posible de vértices o sitios arqueológicos y definir mejor la extensión de las respectivas redes. Para entender mejor las conexiones entre los vértices se requiere más información sobre la cultura material, la iconografía y las tradiciones culturales. Ambos objetivos sólo pueden alcanzarse mediante una combinación de prospecciones y excavaciones extensivas. También es importante que la investigación no se realice a nivel de áreas culturales aisladas. Enfocarse en las conexiones y entender los paisajes arqueológicos como una formación de redes y subredes que difieren en su estructura pero que, sin embargo, pueden conectarse, se acerca mucho más a la realidad de las relaciones sociales que el concepto de áreas culturales

(Müller 2009). En el noreste de Honduras, donde nos encontramos a nivel de investigación básica, la publicación de datos primarios juega un papel fundamental. En particular, la ilustración de los hallazgos es importante para poder hacer comparaciones. La cooperación internacional también tiene un papel especial que desempeñar, debe contribuir al fortalecimiento de la arqueología nacional en Honduras para promover la formación de futuros arqueólogos y arqueólogas y aumentar la conciencia pública sobre el patrimonio cultural. Asimismo, la arqueología del noreste de Honduras puede contribuir a la comprensión de la cultura actual de los habitantes del país. La cultura maya y su exploración han cumplido un rol importante en la construcción de la identidad nacional, así pues, la investigación en otras zonas de Honduras puede colaborar también a la concienciación sobre el patrimonio cultural. Entender la pluralidad cultural y étnica del pasado facilita la comprensión y aceptación de la pluralidad cultural y étnica del presente.

Appendix A: Ocarina Acoustic Analysis (P. Bayer)

Seven ocarinas were found during excavations in Guadalupe, two of which are completely preserved. The larger ocarina (PAG-43-1, Figure 173c) is still well playable, while the smaller (PAG-57-1, Figure 173d) only sounds to a limited extent.

Systematic recordings were made of these two ocarinas in order to determine the sounds they produce (Table 6, 7). An audio recorder[33] was used for the recordings, and the analyses were carried out using the Audacity software[34].

PAG-43-1				
Finger combination		soft	normal	strong
16	○○ / ○○ / ∧	G#6 -10	G#6 +6	G#6 +41 / 1701 Hz
15	○○ / ○● / ∧	F#6 -12	F#6 +6	F#6 +48
14	○○ / ●○ / ∧	F#6 +15	F#6 +45	G6 -38
13	○● / ○○ / ∧	F#6 -8	F#6 +44	G6 -10
12	●○ / ○○ / ∧	F#6 -14	F#6 +31	F#6 +50
11	○○ / ●● / ∧	E6 +31	E6 +38	F6 -25
10	○● / ●○ / ∧	E6 + 43	F6 -43	F6 -14
9	●○ / ○● / ∧	E6 -6	E6 +9	E6 +47
8	●○ / ●○ / ∧	E6 +11	E6 +24	E6 +40
7	○● / ○● / ∧	E6 +29	E6 +45	E6 +49
6	●● / ○○ / ∧	E6 -1	E6 +24	E6 +49

33 Zoom H1, the recordings were saved in lossless WAV format.   **34** https://www.audacity.de/

5	○ ● ● ● ∧	D6 -44	D6 -41	D6 -4
4	● ○ ● ● ∧	C#6 + 36	C#6 +48	C#6 +45
3	● ● ○ ● ∧	C#6 +18	C#6 +33	C#6 +36
2	● ● ● ○ ∧	C#6 +39	C#6 +37	D6 -29
1	● ● ● ● ∧	A5 -8 876 Hz	A5 +22	A#5 -31

Table 6   Recording scheme of ocarina PAG-43-1 (P. Bayer).

PAG-57-1		
Finger combination		
15	○ ○ ○ ● ∧	B7 -43 3855 Hz
14	○ ○ ● ○ ∧	A7 -24
11	○ ○ ● ● ∧	A7 -5
7	○ ● ○ ● ∧	A#7 +43
5	○ ● ● ● ∧	G7 -40
1	● ● ● ● ∧	F#7 +15 2985 Hz

Table 7   Recording scheme of ocarina PAG-57-1 (P. Bayer).

The recording scheme and their presentation are based on Healy et al. (2011: 46–50) so that all possible combinations of the instruments' four finger holes are included. The arrow below the stylized holes in the tables (black = closed, white = open) indicates the position of the mouthpiece. Three variants were also recorded for the more playable instrument: weak, medium, and strong blowing. These values are subjective but are intended to show the resulting variations in the sound produced. The tones can be altered by eighth to quarter tones by adjusting the blowing pressure. This allows minor irregularities in the instrument to be compensated for. A constant tone lasting about two seconds was used for the analysis.

The tonal range of PAG-43-1 is close to the octave[35], similar to the six ocarinas from northeast Honduras published by Healy et al. (2011), which are also instruments with four finger holes. While the producible tones of the ocarinas do not coincide, the intervals do when considering the possibility of tone correction through stronger or weaker blowing. Thus, the same melodies could have been played with these instruments, although not necessarily in polyphony.

The tables show the tonal range of the two ocarinas. For PAG-43-1, all finger combinations produced evaluable sounds. For PAG-57-1, only Combination 1 produced a clear tone, while the other combinations produced peaks in the sound spectrum, which were not always prominent enough for a reasonably sure result.

---

35 Doubling of the pitch, the frequency ratio between the lowest and highest note is 1:2. On string instruments this is achieved by halving the length of the strings.

Appendix B: Petrography of Green Stone Artifacts from Honduras (D. Oestreich, U. Glasmacher)

Daniela B. Oestreich, M.Sc.; Prof. Dr. Ulrich A. Glasmacher

Institute of Earth Sciences, Research group Thermochronology and Archaeometry, Heidelberg University

1. Introduction

The following report presents a brief overview and the results of material analyses on eight artifacts from Honduras (Archaeological Project Guadalupe). The aim of the material analyses was to identify the petrographic composition of the green artifacts. Published data from other green artefacts of Honduras indicated jade/jadeite, serpentine, or albite as the major mineral composition (Gockel 2006). Nevertheless, no large analytical study dealing with the petrography of green artefacts of Honduras has been published so far. The mineral composition of the green artefacts is important for the search of the original ancient mining side, where the rocks were taken to manufacture the artefacts.

2. Artefacts and analytical methods

The eight artefacts differ in shape and colour (Table 8). The colour of seven artefacts varies from light yellow green to dark green. The artefact PAG-33-Pi-2 has a grey-green colour. Seven artefacts are elongated rounded with a hole in the middle part and might have been worn as part of a jewellery chain neckless. The artefact PAG-33-Pi-2 is flat with no hole.

No.	Inv. No.		Image	Mineral+Gas comp.
861	5	PAG-5-Pi-1		Jadeite, Muscovite, Quartz, org. matter, CO, H_2S, C_3H_8, CH_4, H_2O, OH
861	5	PAG-5-Pi-2		Jadeite, Albite, Muscovite, Quartz, Serpentinite, org. matter, CO, H_2S, C_3H_8, CH_4, H_2O, OH
862	7	PAG-7-Pi-1		Jadeite, Albite, Muscovite, Quartz, org. matter, CO, H_2S, C_3H_8, CH_4, H_2O, OH
866	12	PAG-12-Pi-1		Jadeite, Albite, Muscovite, Quartz, Serpentinite, org. matter, CO, H_2S, C_3H_8, CH_4, H_2O, OH

No.	Inv. No.		Image	Mineral+Gas comp.
869	15	PAG-15-Pi1		Jadeite, Albite, Muscovite, Quartz, Serpentinite, org. matter, CO, H_2S, C_3H_8, CH_4, H_2O, OH
1449	33	PAG-33-Pi-2		Jadeite, Albite, Muscovite, org. matter CO, H_2S, C_3H_8, CH_4, H_2O, OH
1449	33	PAG-33-Pi-3		Jadeite, Albite, org. matter, CO, H_2S, C_3H_8, CH_4, H_2O, OH
2228	42	PAG-42-Pi-1		Jadeite, Albite, org. matter, CO, H_2S, C_3H_8, CH_4, H_2O, OH
			0 2 cm	

Table 8   Artifact numbers, images and mineral and gas composition revealed by Raman spectroscopy (D. Oestreich, U. Glasmacher).

Non-destructive determination of the mineral composition of ancient artefacts uses Raman spectroscopy for analytical purpose. The following results were gained by applying a confocal Raman system consisting of a Horiba iHR 320 Pelitier-cooled spectrometer and a Quantum Laser of 532 nm wavelength. Standardization of the system was performed by using a calcite crystal and an artificial Si-plate. Prior to each analyses the calcite and the Si-plate were analyzed. To be able to compare the individual spectra of each artefact, the following equipment settings were continually applied:

Objective	50x
Laser	532 nm
Front entrance	100 μm (98 μm)
Measuring range	100 – 4000 cm^{-1}
Slit	1800

The artefacts were first analyzed by Raman spectroscopy as received, i.e. no cleaning of the artefacts were applied prior to the analysis (Figures 214, 215). The Raman spectra revealed many different organic components. As the possible minerals (like jadeite, serpentine, albite etc.) normally do not bear organic components, the possibility that the surface of the green artefacts was covered by grease was considered. The grease might have been stained on the surface of the artefacts by handling the artefacts without using gloves. Also, the grease might represent the type of use of the artefacts in the past. To test the hypothesis of grease on the surface, the artefacts were cleaned with ethanol and methanol. Raman spectra obtained after the cleaning process was significant different form the Raman spectra revealed before cleaning. (Figures 214, 215).

This analytical result clearly indicate that the surface of the artefacts is stained by grease. The origin of the grease is not clear. As the importance of the surface staining is not known the Ramana spectra with organic components are presented and interpreted. If, however, the grease is related to recent handling with bear hands, all organic carbon bearing components can be eliminated from the Raman spectra. The Raman spectra were interpreted by comparing the spectra with spectra stored in the RUFF-data bank (Lafuente et al. 2015). nevertheless, it must be considered that minerals vary in their composition and therefore, also vary in the shape of the Raman spectra.

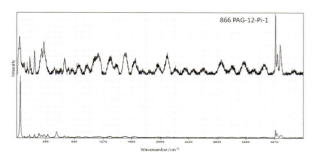

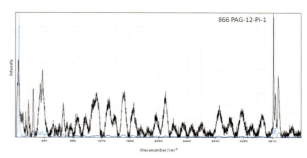

214   Raman spectra of sample 866 PAG-12-Pi-1. The upper spectrum is the spectrum of the non-cleaned artefact. The lower spectrum is the spectrum of the artefact cleaned with ethanol and methanol. All analytical conditions were kept the same (D. Oestreich, U. Glasmacher).

215   Raman spectra of the non-cleaned and cleaned artefact 866 PAG-12-Pi-1 superimposed. Black is the original spectrum of the non-cleaned sample, blue the spectrum of the sample cleaned with ethanol and methanol (D. Oestreich, U. Glasmacher).

3.   Results

The Raman spectra indicated jadeite, muscovite, quartz, org. substances and various carbon-bearing gas phases (Table 8, Figures 216-223). The H_2O and OH is related to the OH-bearing mineral phases such as muscovite and serpentinite or fluid inclusions in the mineral phases. Artefact PAG-5-Pi-1 consists of jadeite, muscovite, and quartz as mineral phases (Figure 216). It is the only artefact without the feldspar albite. All others bear albite together with jadeite as a major mineral phase.

The minerals muscovite and quartz occur in the artefacts PAG-7-Pi-1 (Figure 217), PAG-5-Pi-2 (Figure 218), PAG-12-Pi-1 (Figure 219), PAG-15-Pi-1 (Figure 220). PAG-33-Pi-2 (Figure 221) bears muscovite but no quartz. Important to notice is the occurrence of serpentinite in the artefacts PAG-5-Pi-2, PAG-12-Pi-1, PAG-15-Pi-1. Artefacts PAG-33-Pi-3 (Figure 222), and PAG-42-Pi-1 (Figure 223) consists of jadeite and albite, only.

From Honduras other objects and artefacts consisting of jade/jadeite, serpentine or albite are described by Gockel (2006). Nevertheless, the mining site of the rocks are unknown. If, however, a search would be initiated metamorphosed ultramafic to mafic rocks would be the potential source rocks for the artefacts. It also could be possible that boulders of this type of rocks were found in rivers and were used to produce the artefacts.

Furthermore, organic substances, CO, H_2S, C_3H_8, CH_4, H_2O and OH can be assigned to the Raman bands in the spectra. A possibility would be that the samples are covered with a kind of lipid. As informed by Dr. M. Reindel, at the place of the sampling among other things food remains were found, which would confirm this assumption.

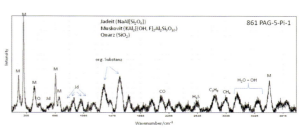

216   Raman spectrum of PAG-5-Pi-1. Marks the identified minerals and phases. Jd: Jadeite, M: Muscovite, Q: Quartz (D. Oestreich, U. Glasmacher).

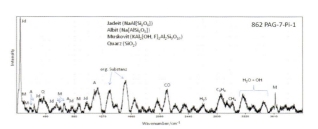

217   Raman spectrum of PAG-7-Pi-1. Marks the identified minerals and phases. Jd = Jadeite, A = Albite, M = Muscovite, Q = Quartz (D. Oestreich, U. Glasmacher).

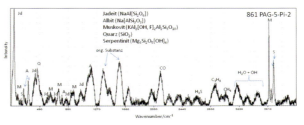

218   Raman spectrum of PAG-5-Pi-2. Marks the identified minerals and phases. Jd: Jadeite, A: Albite, M: Muscovite, Q: Quartz, S: Serpentinite (D. Oestreich, U. Glasmacher).

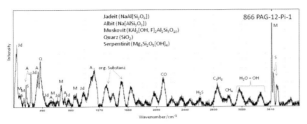

219   Raman spectrum of PAG-12-Pi-1. Marks the identified minerals and phases. Jd: Jadeite, A: Albite, M: Muscovite, Q: Quartz, S: Serpentinite (D. Oestreich, U. Glasmacher).

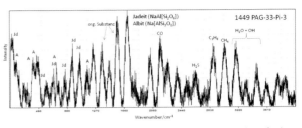

222   Raman spectrum of PAG-33-Pi-3. Marks the identified minerals and phases. Jd: Jadeite, A: Albite (D. Oestreich, U. Glasmacher).

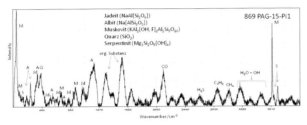

220   Raman spectrum of PAG-15-Pi-1. Marks the identified minerals and phases. Jd: Jadeite, A: Albite, M: Muscovite, Q: Quartz, S: Serpentinite (D. Oestreich, U. Glasmacher).

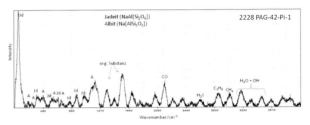

223   Raman spectrum of PAG-42-Pi-1. Marks the identified minerals and phases. Jd: Jadeite, A: Albite (D. Oestreich, U. Glasmacher).

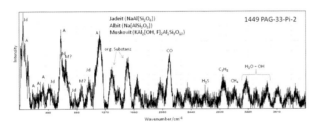

221   Raman spectrum of PAG-33-Pi-2. Marks the identified minerals and phases. Jd: Jadeite, A: Albite, M: Muscovite (D. Oestreich, U. Glasmacher).

Appendix C: List of Museum Collections with Objects from Northeast Honduras

1. **Fortaleza de Santa Bárbara, Trujillo, Honduras**
   Objects from the region around Trujillo

2. **Museo de Antropología e Historia de San Pedro Sula, Honduras**
   Objects from different parts of Honduras

3. **Museum of Archaeology and Anthropology, Cambridge, UK**
   Objects from the Bay Islands (collections Lord Moyne and R. W. Feachem)

4. **The British Museum, London, UK**
   Objects from the Bay Islands and the region around Trujllo (collection Baron Moyne)

5. **Smithsonian National Museum of Natural History, Washington D.C., USA**
   Objects from the Bay Islands and Dep. Colón (collection W. D. Strong)

6. **National Museum of the American Indian, Washington D.C., USA**
   Objects from the Bay Islands and Dep. Olancho (collection F. A. Mitchell-Hedges)

7. **American Museum of Natural History, New York, USA**
   Objects from northeast Honduras (collection A. George and Ekholm/Kidder/Stromsvik)

8. **Peabody Museum of Archaeology and Ethnology, Cambridge, MA, USA**
   Objects from the Bay Islands and Dep. Colón (collection D. Stone, W. Popenoe, H. Spinden, W. D. Strong, L. Wylie, R. H. Davis; some objects donated by H. J. Boekelman, P. Healy and United Fruit Company)

9. **Middle American Research Institute, Tulane University, New Orleans, USA**
   Objects from Dep. Colón, Gracias a Dios and Olancho (collection D. Stone; some objects dontated by H. J. Boekelman and A. C. Weyerstal)

10. **Phoebe A. Heast Museum of Anthropology, Berkeley, CA, USA**
    Objects from Roatán (collection D. K. Evans)

11. **Hood Museum of Art at Dartmouth College, Hanover, NH, USA**
    Objects from northeast Honduras (collection V. M. Cutter and H. J. Boekelman)

12. **Museum am Rothenbaum, Hamburg, Germany**
    Objects from northeast Honduras (collections O. Staudinger and G. de Lopez)

Bibliography

Abbas Shatto, Rahilla Corinne
1998 Maritime Trade and Seafaring of the Precolumbian Maya. MA Thesis, Texas A&M University.

Abbott, Robert T. / Morris, Percy A.
1995 A field Guide to Shells: Atlantic and Gulf Coast and the West Indies. The Peterson Field Guide Series 3. Boston.

Abbott, Robert T.
1974 American seashells: The marine mollusca of the Atlantic and Pacific Coast of North America. New York.

Abel-Vidor, Suzanne / Bakker, Dirk (eds.)
1981 Between Continents/Between Seas: Precolumbian Art of Costa Rica. New York, [Detroit].

Agurcia Fasquelle, Ricardo
1978 Las figurillas de Playa de los Muertos, Honduras. In: Yaxkin 2 (4): 221–240.

Alcina Franch, José
1958 Las "pintaderas" mejicanas y sus relaciones. Madrid.

Amodio, Emanuele
1991 Relaciones interétnicas en el Caribe indígena: Una reconstrucción a partir de los primeros testimonios europeos. In: Revista de Indias 51 (193): 571–606.

Andrews, Anthony P. / Gallareta Negrón, Tomás / Robles Castellanos, Fernando / Cobos Palma, Rafael / Cervera Rivero, Pura
1988 Isla Cerritos: An Itzá Trading Port on the North Coast of Yucatán, Mexico. In: National Geographic Research 4 (2): 196–207.

Andrews, E. W.
1969 The archaeological use and distribution of Mollusca in the Maya lowlands. Tulane University. Middle American Research Institute. Publication 34. New Orleans.

Andrews, E. W. / Lange, Frederick W.
1995 Doris Zemurray Stone 1909–1994. In: Ancient Mesoamerica 6: 95–99.

Antczak, Andrzej
1991 La Pesca Marina Prehispanica en el Archipielago de Los Roques, Venezuela: El Caso del Yacimiento de la Isla Dos Mosquises. In: Proceedings of the 14th IACA Congress, Barbados: 504–518.
1998 Late Prehistoric Economy and Society of the Islands off the Coast of Venezuela: A Contextual Interpretation of the Non-Ceramic Evidence. Ph.D. Thesis, University College.

Antczak, Maria M. / Antczak, Andrzej
2006 Los Ídolos de Las Islas Prometidas: Arqueología Prehispánica del Archipielago de Los Roques (Venezuela).

Aoyama, Kazuo / Inomata, Takeshi / Pinzón, Flory / Palomo, Juan Manuel
2017 Polished greenstone celt caches from Ceibal: the development of Maya public rituals. In: Antiquity 91 (357): 701–717.

Aoyama, Kazuo / Tashiro, Toshiharu / Glascock, Michael D.
1999 A pre-Columbian obsidian source in San Luis, Honduras: Implications for the relationship between classic Maya political boundaries and the boundaries of obsidian exchange networks. In: Ancient Mesoamerica 10 (2): 237–249.

Ashmore, Wendy
1987 Excavaciones en el sitio central de Gualjoquito, Santa Barbara, Honduras, 1983-1985. In: Yaxkin 10 (2): 89–104.

Balser, Carlos
1954 A Fertility Vase from the Old Line, Costa Rica. In: American Antiquity 20 (4): 384–387.
1993 Precolumbian Soft Stone Carvings Found in Costa Rica. In: Lange, Frederick W. (ed.), Precolumbian Jade. New Geological und Cultural Interpretations, pp. 260–268. Salt Lake City.

Barba Pingarrón, Luis / Rodríguez Suárez, Roberto / Córdova Frunz, José L.
1991 Manual de técnicas microquímicas de campo para la arqueología. Cuadernos de investigación. México.

Bard, Samuel
1855 Waikna: Or, Adventures on the Mosquito Shore. London.

Bar-Yam, Yaneer
2003 Dynamics of complex systems. Advanced book program. Boulder, Colordo, Oxford.

Baudez, Claude F.
1963 Cultural Development in Lower Central America. In: Meggers, Betty J. / Evans, Clifford (eds.), Aboriginal Cultural Development in Latin America. An Interpretative Review. Smithsonian Institution Publication 4517, pp. 45–54. Washington, D.C.

Bauer, Alexander A. / Agbe-Davies, Anna
2010 Trade and Interaction in Archaeology. In: Bauer, Alexander A. / Agbe-Davies, Anna (eds.), Social Archaeologies of Trade and Exchange. Exploring Relationships Among People, Places, and Things, pp. 29–48. London.

Bauer, Ingolf / Endres, Werner / Kerkhoff-Hader, Bärbel / Koch, Robert / Stephan, Hans-Georg
1993 Leitfaden zur Keramikbeschreibung (Mittelalter - Neuzeit): Terminologie - Typologie – Technologie. Kataloge der Prähistorischen Staatssammlung Beiheft 2. Kallmünz/Opf.

Beaudry-Corbett, Marilyn
1995 Final Report, Ceramic Analysis, Talgua Archaeological Project 1995: Manuscript on file at the Instituto Hondureno de Antropología e Historia. Tegucigalpa.

Beaudry-Corbett, Marilyn / Henderson, John S. / Joyce, Rosemary A.
1993 Approaches to the Analysis of Pre-Columbian Honduran Ceramics. In: Henderson, John S. / Beaudry-Corbett, Marilyn (eds.), Pottery of Prehistoric Honduras. Regional Classification and Analysis, pp. 3–6. Los Angeles.

Beaudry-Corbett, Marilyn / McCafferty, Sharisse
2002 Spindle Whorls: Households Specialization at Ceren. In: Ardren, Traci (ed.), Ancient Maya women. Gender and Archaeology Series, pp. 52–67. Walnut Creek, CA.

Begley, Christopher
1999 Elite Power Strategies and External Connections in Ancient Eastern Honduras. Ph.D. Dissertation, University of Chicago.
2020 Eastern Honduran Region. Online article, https://archaeomosquitia.wordpress.com/the-prehistoric-mosquito-coast-how-extensive-was-this-area/ (accessed August 17, 2020).
2002 El Clásico Tardío y el Postclásico Temprano en el Oriente de Honduras. In: Laporte, Juan P. (ed.), XV Simposio de Investigaciones Arqueológicas en Guatemala, 2001, pp. 41–52.
2004 Intercambio interregional, conexiones externas y estrategias de poder en el Oriente de Honduras durante los períodos V y VI. In: Instituto Hondureño de Antropología e Historia (ed.), Memorias del VII Seminario de Antropología Hondureña 'Dr. George Hasemann', pp. 287–302. Tegucigalpa.

Bell, Charles N.
1899 Tangweera: Life and Adventures Among Gentle Savages. London.

Berdan, Frances F.
2003 The Economy of Postclassic Mesoamerica. In: Smith, Michael E. / Berdan, Frances F. (eds.), The Postclassic Mesoamerican World, pp. 93–95. Salt Lake City.

Bergmann, John
1969 The Distribution of Cacao Cultivation in Precolumbian America. In: Annals of the Association of American Geographers 59 (1): 85–96.

Bernbeck, Reinhard
1997 Theorien in der Archäologie. Uni-Taschenbücher 1964. Tübingen.

Bernier, Hélène
2009 Music in the Ancient Andes. Online article, https://www.metmuseum.org/toah/hd/muan/hd_muan.htm (accessed August 17, 2020).

Bhabha, Homi
1996 Culture's in-between. In: Hall, Stuart / Du Gay, Paul (eds.), Questions of cultural identity, pp. 53–60. London.

Bishop, Ronald / Lange, Frederick W.
1988 Abstraction and Jade Exchange in Precolumbian Southern Mesoamerica and Lower Central America. In: Lange, Frederick W. (ed.), Costa Rican Art and Archaeology. Essays in Honor of Frederick R. Mayer, pp. 65–88. Boulder.

Bishop, Ronald / Sayre, Edward / Mishara, Joan
1993 Compositional and Structural Characterization of Maya and Costa Rican Jadeitites. In: Lange, Frederick W. (ed.), Precolumbian Jade. New Geological und Cultural Interpretations, pp. 30–60. Salt Lake City.

Blackiston, Andrew H.
1910 Recent Discoveries in Honduras. In: American Anthropologist 12 (4): 536–541.

Blanton, Richard E. / Feinman, Gary M.
1984 The Mesoamerican World System. In: American Anthropologist 86 (3): 673–682.

Blanton, Richard E. / Feinman, Gary M. / Kowalewski, Stephen A. / Peregrine, Peter N.
1996 A dual-processual theory for the evolution of Mesoamerican civilization. In: Current Anthropology 37 (1): 1–14.

BoneID. Website, http://www.boneid.net/ (accessed August 17, 2020).

Bonomo, Mariano
2012 Historia Prehispánica de Entre Ríos. Buenos Aires.

Bonomo, Mariano / Politis, Gustavo
2016 Humanized Nature: Fauna in Pottery from the Middle and Lower Paraná River (Argentina). World Archaeological Conference. Kyoto.

Boone, Elizabeth H. / Smith, Michael E.
2003 Postclassic International Styles and Symbol Sets. In: Smith, Michael E. / Berdan, Frances F. (eds.), The Postclassic Mesoamerican World, pp. 186–193. Salt Lake City.

Bovallius, Carl Erik Alexander
1886 Nicaraguan Antiquities. Stockholm.

Bozzoli, Maria E.
1979 El nacimiento v la muerte entre los Bribris. San José, Costa Rica.

Braswell, Geoffrey E.
1997 El intercambio comercial entre los pueblos prehispánicos de Mesomérica y la Gran Nicoya. In: Revista de la Universidad del Valle de Guatemala 6: 17–29.
1999 La producción y comercio de obsidiana en Centroamérica.
2003 Obsidian Exchange Spheres. In: Smith, Michael E. / Berdan, Frances F. (eds.), The Postclassic Mesoamerican World, pp. 131–158. Salt Lake City.

Bray, Warwick
1985 Ancient American Metallurgy: Five Hundred Years of Study. In: Jones, Julie / Kerr, Justin (eds.), The art of Precolumbian gold. The Jan Mitchell Collection, pp. 76–84. London.

Brown, Linda
2001 Feasting on the Periphery: The Production of Ritual Feasting and Village Festivals at the Cerén Site, El Salvador. In: Dietler, Michael / Hayden, Brian (eds.), Feasts. Archaeological and ethnographic perspectives on food, politics, and power. Smithsonian series in archaeological inquiry, pp. 368–390. Washington, D.C.

Burt, Ronald
1992 Structural Holes: The Social Structure of Competition. Cambridge.

Caldwell, Joseph R.
1964 Interaction Spheres in Prehistory. In: Caldwell, Joseph R. / Hall, Robert L. (eds.), Hopewellian studies. Scientific papers (Illinois State Museum) 12, pp. 134–143. Springfield.

Callaghan, Richard T.
2003 Comments on the Mainland Origins of the Preceramic Cultures of the Greater Antilles. In: Latin American Antiquity 14 (3): 323–338.

Campbell, Lyle
1976 The linguistic prehistory of the southern Mesoamerican periphery, Las fronteras de Mesoamérica. Sociedad Mexicana de Antropología, Mesa Redonda 14, pp. 157–183.

Campbell, Roderick B.
2009 Toward a Networks and Boundaries Approach to Early Complex Polities. In: Current Anthropology 50 (6): 821–848.

Carmack, Robert M. / Salgado González, Silvia
2006 A World-Systems Perspective on the Archaeology and Ethnohistory of the Mesoamerican/Lower Central American Border. In: Ancient Mesoamerica 17 (2): 219–229.

Chacon, Richard J. / Mendoza, Rubén G. (eds.)
2017 Feast, Famine or Fighting?: Multiple Pathways to Social Complexity. Studies in Human Ecology and Adaptation 8. Cham.

Chapman, Anne

1957 Port of Trade Enclaves in the Aztec and Maya Civilizations. In: Polanyi, Karl / Arensberg, Conrad M. / Pearson, Harry W. (eds.), Trade and Market in the Early Empires, pp. 114–153. Chicago.

1958 An Historical Analysis of the Tropical Forest Tribes on the Southern Border of Mesoamerica. Ph.D. Thesis, Columbia University.

Ciofalo, A. J. / Sinelli, P. T. / Hofman, C. L.

2020 Starchy shells: Residue analysis of precolonial northern Caribbean culinary practices. In: Archaeometry 62 (2): 362–380.

Clark, Catherine M. / Dawson, Frank G. / Drake, Jonathan C.

1982 Archaeology on the Mosquito Coast: A Reconnaissance of the Precolumbian and Historic Settlement Along the Rio Tinto. Occasional publication 4. Cambridge.

Clark, John E.

1988 The lithic artifacts of La Libertad, Chiapas, Mexico: An economic perspective. Papers of the New World Archaeological Foundation 52. Provo, Utah.

Clemente-Conte, Ignacio / Gassiot Ballbé, Ermengol / Lechado Ríos, Leonardo

2009 Shellmiddens of the Atlantic Coast of Nicaragua: Something more than Mounds, Humans. Evolution and Environment. BAR international series 2026, pp. 285–294. Oxford.

Collar, Anna / Coward, Fiona / Brughmans, Tom / Mills, Barbara J.

2015 Networks in Archaeology: Phenomena, Abstraction, Representation. In: Journal of Archaeological Method and Theory 22 (1): 1–32.

Colón, Fernando

1959 The Life of the Admiral Christopher Columbus by his Son Ferdinand: Translated and annotated by Benjamin Keen. New Brunswick, New Jersey.

Constenla Umaña, Adolfo

1991 Las lenguas del área intermedia: Introducción a su estudio areal. San José.

1995 Sobre el estudio diacrónico de las lenguas chibchenses y su contribución al conocimiento del pasado de sus hablantes. In: Boletín del Museo del Oro (38-39): 13–55.

Conzemius, Eduard

1927 Los Indios Payas de Honduras: Estudio geográfico, histórico, etnográfico y lingüístico. In: Journal de la Societe des Americanistes 19: 245–302.

1928 On the Aborigines of the Bay Islands (Honduras), Proceedings of the Twenty-second International Congress of Americanists, pp. 57–68.

1932 Ethnographical Survey of the Miskito and Sumu Indians of Honduras and Nicaragua. Bureau of American Ethnology Bulletin 106. Washington, D.C.

Cooke, Richard

2005 Prehistory of Native Americans on the Central American Land Bridge: Colonization, Dispersal, and Divergence. In: Journal of Archaeological Research 13 (2): 129–187.

Corrales Ulloa, Francisco / Badilla, Adrián

2018 Sociedades Jerárquicas tardías en el delta del Diquís, sureste de Costa Rica. In: Cuadernos de Antropología 28 (2): 1–23.

Corrales Ulloa, Francisco / Quintanilla Jiménez, Ifigenia

1996 The Archaeology of the Central Pacific Coast of Costa Rica. In: Lange, Frederick W. (ed.), Paths to Central American Prehistory, pp. 93–117. Niwot.

Cortés, Hernán

1866 Cartas y relaciones de Hernán Cortés al Emperador Carlos V: colegidas e ilustradas por Pascual de Gayangos. Paris.

Coward, Fiona

2013 Grounding the Net: Social Networks, Material Culture and Geography in the Epipalaeolithic and Early Neolithic of the Near East (~21,000-6,000 cal bce). In: Knappett, Carl (ed.), Network Analysis in Archaeology. New Approaches to Regional Interaction, pp. 246–280. Oxford.

Craig, Alan K.

1977 Contribución a la prehistoria de las Islas de la Bahía. In: Yaxkin 2 (1): 19–27.

Cruz Castillo, Oscar Neil

2007 Informe final del proyecto de arqueología histórica en Trujillo, Colón. Unpublished document in the archives of the Instituto Hondureño de Antropología e Historia.

Cruz Castillo, Oscar Neil / Juárez Silva, Ranferi

2006 La pieza olmeca en Cueva Hato Viejo Olancho, Honduras. In: Arqueología Mexicana 81: 75–82.

Cruz Castillo, Oscar Neil / Orellana, Idelfonso
2000 Informe final de las excavaciones arqueológicas en Charlie Brown, Roatán, Islas de la Bahía. Unpublished document in the archives of the Instituto Hondureño de Antropología e Historia.

Cuddy, Thomas W.
2007 Political Identity and Archaeology in Northeast Honduras. Boulder, Colorado.

Curet, L. Antonio
2003 Issues on the Diversity and Emergence of Middle-Range Societies of the Ancient Caribbean: A Critique. In: Journal of Archaeological Research 11: 1–42.
2014 The Taino: Phenomena, Concepts, and Terms. In: Ethnohistory 61 (3): 467–495.

Curtiss, Brian
1993 Visible and Near-Infrared Spectroscopy for Jade Artifact Analysis. In: Lange, Frederick W. (ed.), Precolumbian Jade. New Geological und Cultural Interpretations, pp. 73–81. Salt Lake City.

Dacal Moure, Ramón / Rivero de la Calle, Manuel
1996 Art and archaeology of pre-Columbian Cuba. Pitt Latin American series. Pittsburgh.

Dennett, Carrie L.
2007 The Río Claro Site (AD 1000-1530), Northeast Honduras: A Ceramic Classification and Examination of External Connections. M. A. Thesis, Trent University.

Descola, Philippe
1997 Beyond Nature and Culture. Chicago.

Diehl, Richard A.
2004 The Olmecs: America's first civilization. Ancient peoples and places 112. London.

Dietler, Michael
2001 Theorizing the Feast: Rituals of Consumption, Commensal Politics, and Power in African Contexts. In: Dietler, Michael / Hayden, Brian (eds.), Feasts. Archaeological and ethnographic perspectives on food, politics, and power. Smithsonian series in archaeological inquiry, pp. 65–114. Washington, D.C.

Dietler, Michael / Hayden, Brian
2001 Digesting the Feast: Good to eat, good to drink, good to think. In: Dietler, Michael / Hayden, Brian (eds.), Feasts. Archaeological and ethnographic perspectives on food, politics, and power. Smithsonian series in archaeological inquiry, pp. 1–20. Washington, D.C.

Digby, Adrian
1972 Maya Jades. London.

Dixon, Boyd
1987 Conflict Along the Southeast Mesoamerican Periphery: A Defensive Wall System at the Site of Tenampua. In: Robinson, Eugenia J. (ed.), Interaction on the Southeast Mesoamerican Frontier. Prehistoric and Historic Honduras and El Salvador. BAR international series 327, pp. 142–153. Oxford.

Drolet, Robert
1982-83 Social Grouping and Residential Activities within a Late Phase Polity Network: Diquís Valley. In: Lange, Frederick W. / Norr, Lynette (eds.), Prehistoric Settlement Patterns in Costa Rica. Journal of the Steward Anthropological Society, pp. 325–338.

Dunn, Oliver / Kelley, James (eds.)
1989 The Diario of Christopher Columbus's first voyage to America: 1492-1493. The American exploration and travel series 70. Norman, Okla.

Dunnell, Robert C.
1971 Sabloff and Smith's "The Importance of Both Analytic and Taxonomic Classification in the Type-Variety System". In: American Antiquity 36 (1): 115–118.

Durán, Diego
1971 Book of the Gods and Rites and the Ancient Calendar. Translated and edited by Fernando Horcasitas and Doris Heyden. Civilization of the American Indian series 102. Norman.

Durando, Ottavio
1959 Primer estudio químico y geoquímica de artefactos encontrados en tumbas de indios de Costa Rica, Actas del XXXIII Congreso Internacional de Americanistas, San José, 20-27 Julio 1958, pp. 327–338. San José, Costa Rica.

Easby, Elizabeth K.
1968 Pre-Columbian Jade from Costa Rica. New York, N.Y.

Edwards, Clinton R.
1978 Pre-Columbian Maritime Trade in Mesoamerica. In: Lee, Thomas A. Jr. / Navarrete, Carlos (eds.), Mesoamerican Communication Routes and Cultural Contacts. New World Archaeological Foundation Papers 40, pp. 199–209. Provo, UT.

Eggert, Manfred K. H.
2012 Prähistorische Archäologie: Konzepte und Methoden. Tübingen.

Elvir, Wilmer / Goodwin, Whitney A.
2018 Guía de identificación de especies arqueomalacológicas y su medio ambiente en el Atlántico noreste de Honduras.

Epstein, Jeremiah F.
1957 Late Ceramic Horizons in Northeast Honduras. Ph.D. Thesis, Department of Anthropology, University of Pennsylvania.
1959 Dating the Ulua Polychrome Complex. In: American Antiquity 25 (1): 125–129.
1978 Problemas en el estudio de le prehistoria de las Islas de la Bahía. In: Yaxkin 2 (3): 149–159.

Epstein, Jeremiah F. / Véliz, Vito
1977 Reconocimiento arqueológico en la Isla de Roatán, Honduras. In: Yaxkin 2 (1): 28–39.

Evans, Susan T.
2008 Ancient Mexico and Central America: Archaeology and Culture History. London.

Fash, William L.
2001 Scribes, Warriors and Kings: The City of Copán and the Ancient Maya. London, New York.

Feachem, R. W.
1940 The Bay Islands, Gulf of Honduras. In: The Geographical Journal 96: 181–189.

Fecher, Franziska
2019 Patolli Petroglyphs in Northeast Honduras. In: Latin American Antiquity 30 (03): 624–629.

Fecher, Franziska / Reindel, Markus / Fux, Peter / Gubler, Brigitte / Mara, Hubert / Bayer, Paul / Lyons, Mike
2020 The ceramic finds from Guadalupe, Honduras: Optimizing archaeological documentation with a combination of digital and analog techniques. In: Journal of Global Archaeology 1: § 1-54.

Fernández Esquivel, Patricia
2010 Metalurgia de Costa Rica: Produccion Local e Identificacion de Relaciones Sociales entre Panama, Costa Rica, y Nicaragua. St. Louis, MO.

Feuer, Bryan A.
2016 Boundaries, borders and frontiers in archaeology: A study of spatial relationships. Jefferson, North Carolina.

Fewkes, Jesse W.
1922 A prehistoric island culture area of America. In: Thirty-fourth annual report of the Bureau of American Ethnology, 1912-1913, pp. 35–271. Washington.

Field, Frederick V.
1967 Thoughts on the Meaning and Use of Pre-Hispanic Mexican Sellos. Studies in Pre-Columbian Art and Archaeology 3. Washington, D.C.

Figueroa, Alejandro J.
2011 The Clash of Heritage and Development on the Island of Roatán, Honduras. M. A. Thesis, University of South Florida.

Filloy Nadal, Laura
2017 Forests of jade: Luxury arts and symbols of excellence in Mesoamerica. In: Pillsbury, Joanne / Potts, Timothy / Richter, Kim N. (eds.), Golden Kingdoms. Luxury Arts in the Ancient Americas, pp. 66-77. Los Angeles.

Fisher, Christopher T. / Fernández-Diaz, Juan C. / Cohen, Anna S. / Neil Cruz, Oscar / Gonzáles, Alicia M. / Leisz, Stephen J. / Pezzutti, Florencia / Shrestha, Ramesh / Carter, William
2016 Identifying Ancient Settlement Patterns through LiDAR in the Mosquitia Region of Honduras. In: PloS one 11 (8).

Fitzpatrick, Scott M.
2013 Seafaring Capabilities in the Pre-Columbian Caribbean. In: Journal of Maritime Archaeology (8): 101–138.
2015 The Pre-Columbian Caribbean: Colonization, Population Dispersal, and Island Adaptations. In: PaleoAmerica 1 (4): 305–331.

Fonseca, Oscar M.
1992 Historia antigua de Costa Rica: Surgimiento y caracterización de la primera civilización costarricense. San José.

Fonseca, Oscar M. / Cooke, Richard
1993 El sur de América Central: Contribución al estudio de la región histórica Chibcha. In: Carmack, Robert M. (ed.), Historia Antigua. Historia general de Centroamérica 1, pp. 217-282. Madrid.

Foster, Lynn V. (ed.)
2002 Handbook to Life in the Ancient Maya World. New York.

Fowler, William R.
1983 La distribución prehistórica e histórica de los pipiles. In: Mesoamérica 4 (6): 348–372.

Fowles, Severin
2018 The evolution of simple society. In: Asian Archaeology 2 (1): 19–32.

Freidel, David A.
1978 Maritime Adaptation and the Rise of Maya Civilization: The View from Cerros, Belize. In: Stark, Barbara L. / Voorhies, Barbara (eds.), Prehistoric Coastal Adaptations. The Economy and Ecology of Maritime Middle America. Studies in Archaeology, pp. 239–265. New York.

Freund, Kyle P. / Batist, Zack
2014 Sardinian Obsidian Circulation and Early Maritime Navigation in the Neolithic as Shown Through Social Network Analysis. In: The Journal of Island and Coastal Archaeology 9 (3): 364–380.

Gabb, William M.
1875 On the Indian Tribes and Languages of Costa Rica. In: Proceedings of the American Philosophical Society 14: 483–602.

Gamble, Clive / Gowlett, John / Dunbar, Robin
2015 Evolution, Denken, Kultur: Das soziale Gehirn und die Entstehung des Menschlichen. Berlin.

García Casco, Antonio
2009 A new jadeitite jade locality (Sierra del Convento, Cuba): First report and some petrological and archeological implications. In: Contributions to Mineralogy and Petrology (158): 1–16.

García Cubas, Antonio / Reguero, Martha
2004 Catálogo ilustrado de moluscos gasterópodos del Golfo de México y Mar Caribe. México.
2007 Catálogo ilustrado de moluscos bivalvos del Golfo de México y Mar Caribe. México.

Garcia-Casco, Antonio / Knippenberg, Sebastiaan / Rodríguez Ramos, Reniel / Harlow, George E. / Hofman, Corinne / Pomo, José Carlos / Blanco-Quintero, Idael F.
2013 Pre-Columbian jadeitite artifacts from the Golden Rock Site, St. Eustatius, Lesser Antilles, with special reference to jadeitite artifacts from Elliot's, Antigua: implications for potential source regions and long-distance exchange networks in the Greater Caribbean. In: Journal of Archaeological Science 40 (8): 3153–3169.

Gasco, Janine / Berdan, Frances F.
2003 International Trade Centers. In: Smith, Michael E. / Berdan, Frances F. (eds.), The Postclassic Mesoamerican World, pp. 109–116. Salt Lake City.

Gassiot Ballbé, Ermengol
2006 Prehistoric Settlement of the Atlantic Coast of Nicaragua: Absolute Chronology of Pearl Lagoon & Bluefields Shellmiddens, Change in the Andes. Origins of social complexity, pastoralism and agriculture: Préhistoire de l'Amérique : sessions générales = American prehistory : general sessions. BAR international series 1524, pp. 233–241. Oxford.

Geurds, Alexander
2011 The Social in the Circum-Caribbean: Toward a transcontextual order. In: Hofman, Corinne L. / van Duijvenbode, Anne (eds.), Communities in Contact. Essays in Archaeology, Ethnohistory & Ethnography of the Amerindian Circum-Caribbean, pp. 45–60. Leiden.
2018 Prehistory of Southern Central America. In: Smith, Claire (ed.), Encyclopedia of Global Archaeology, pp. 1–20. New York.

Gifford, James C.
1976 Prehistoric pottery analysis and the ceramics of Barton Ramie in the Belize Valley. Memoirs of the Peabody Museum of Archaeology and Ethnology, Harvard University 18.

Gilbert, Miles
2003 Mammalian Osteology. Columbia.

Gilbert, Miles / Martin, L. / Savage, H.
1996 Avian Osteology. Columbia.

Gilliland, Marion S.
1965 The material culture of Key Marco, Florida. MA Thesis, University of Florida.

Gockel, Wolfgang
2006 Guatemala, Belize, Honduras und El Salvador: Maya-Städte und Kolonialarchitektur in Mittelamerika. Köln.

Golitko, Mark / Feinman, Gary M.
2015 Procurement and Distribution of Pre-Hispanic Mesoamerican Obsidian 900 BC–AD 1520: A Social Network Analysis. In: Journal of Archaeological Method and Theory 22 (1): 206–247.

Golitko, Mark / Meierhoff, James / Feinman, Gary M. / Williams, Patrick Ryan
2012 Complexities of collapse: The evidence of Maya obsidian as revealed by social network graphical analysis. In: Antiquity 86 (332): 507–523.

Goodwin, Whitney A.
2011 Archaeology and Indigeneity, Past and Present: A View from the Island of Roatán, Honduras. M. A. Thesis, Department of Anthropology, University of South Florida.
2019 Communities of Consumption on the Southeastern Mesoamerican Border: Style, Feasting, and Identity Negotiation in Prehispanic Northeastern Honduras, Southern Methodist University.

Graham, Mark M.
1981 Traditions of Stone Sculpture in Costa Rica. In: Abel-Vidor, Suzanne / Bakker, Dirk (eds.), Between Continents/Between Seas. Precolumbian Art of Costa Rica, pp. 113–134. New York, [Detroit].

Granberry, Julian / Vescelius, Gary S.
2004 Languages of the pre-Columbian Antilles. Tuscaloosa, AL.

Granovetter, Mark S.
1973 The Strength of Weak Ties. In: American Journal of Sociology 78 (6): 1360–1380.

Griffin, Wendy / Escobar Martínez, Hernán / Hernández Torres, Juana Carolina
2009 Los Pech de Honduras: Una etnia que vive. Tegucigalpa.

Grove, David C.
2010 Olmec Culture. In: Evans, Susan T. / Webster, David (eds.), Archaeology of Ancient Mexico and Central America. An Encyclopedia, pp. 554–557. New York.

Gutiérrrez Castillo, Yeny
2015 Análisis de artefactos malacológicos provenientes del sitio arqueológico El Zotz, Petén, Guatemala. Tesis de Licenciatura, Universidad de San Carlos de Guatemala.

Haberland, Wolfgang
1976 Gran Chiriquí. In: Vinculos 1: 115–121.

Hall, Thomas D. / Kardulias, P. N. / Chase-Dunn, Christopher
2011 World-Systems Analysis and Archaeology: Continuing the Dialogue. In: Journal of Archaeological Research 19 (3): 233–279.

Hammond, Norman
1972 Obsidian trade routes in the mayan area. In: Science 178 (4065): 1092–1093.

Harding, Anthony
2013 World Systems, Cores, and Peripheries in Prehistoric Europe. In: European Journal of Archaeology 16 (3): 378–400.

Harlow, George
1993 Middle American Jade: Geologic and Petrologic Perspectives on Variability and Source. In: Lange, Frederick W. (ed.), Precolumbian Jade. New Geological und Cultural Interpretations, pp. 9–29. Salt Lake City.

Hartman, Carl V.
1901 Archaeological Researches in Costa Rica. Stockholm.

Hasemann, George
1977 Reconocimiento arqueológico de Utila. In: Yaxkin 2 (1): 40–76.

Hasemann, George / Lara Pinto, Gloria
1993 La Zona Central: Regionalismo e interacción. In: Carmack, Robert M. (ed.), Historia Antigua. Historia general de Centroamérica 1, pp. 135–216. Madrid.

Hasemann, George / Lara Pinto, Gloria / Sandoval Cruz, Fernando
2017 Los indios de Centroamérica. Tegucigalpa.

Hatt, Gudmund
1924 Archaeology of the Virgin Islands, In: International Congress of Americanists, Proceedings 21: 29-42. The Hague.

Hauff, Phoebe L.
1993 The Enigma of Jade, with Mineralogical Reference to Central American Source Materials. In: Lange, Frederick W. (ed.), Precolumbian Jade. New Geological und Cultural Interpretations, pp. 82–103. Salt Lake City.

Hayden, Brian
2001 Fabulous Feasts: A Prolegomenon to the Importance of Feasting. In: Dietler, Michael / Hayden,

Brian (eds.), Feasts. Archaeological and ethno-graphic perspectives on food, politics, and power. Smithsonian series in archaeological inquiry, pp. 23–64. Washington, D.C.

Healy, Paul F.
1974a An Olmec Vessel from Northeast Honduras. In: Katunob 8 (4): 73–79.
1974b The Cuyamel Caves: Preclassic Sites in North-east Honduras. In: American Antiquity 39 (3): 435–447.
1975 H-CN-4 (Williams Ranch Site): Preliminary Report on a Selin Period Site in the Department of Colon, Northeast Honduras. In: Vinculos 1 (2): 61–71.
1978a Excavations at Rio Claro, Northeast Honduras: Preliminary Report. In: Journal of Field Archaeology 5 (1): 15–28.
1978b Excavations at Selin Farm (H-CN-5), Colon, Northeast Honduras. In: Vinculos 4 (2): 57–79.
1983 The Paleoecology of the Selin Farm Site (H-CN-5), Colón, Northeast Honduras. In: Willey, Gordon R. / Leventhal, Richard M. / Kolata, Alan L. (eds.), Civilization in the Ancient Americas. Essays in Honor of Gordon R. Willey, pp. 35–54. Albuquer-que, N.M, Cambridge, Mass.
1984a Northeast Honduras: A Precolumbian Frontier Zone. In: Lange, Frederick W. / Hammond, Nor-man (eds.), Recent Developments in Isthmian Ar-chaeology. Advances in the Prehistory of Lower Central America. Proceedings of the 44th International Congress of Americanists, Manchester, 1982, pp. 227–241. Oxford, England.
1984b The Archaeology of Honduras. In: Lange, Fred-erick W. / Stone, Doris (eds.), The Archaeology of Lower Central America. School of American Re-search advanced seminar series, pp. 113–161. Albu-querque, N.M.
1993 Northeastern Honduras. In: Henderson, John S. / Beaudry-Corbett, Marilyn (eds.), Pottery of Prehis-toric Honduras. Regional Classification and Analy-sis, pp. 194–213. Los Angeles.

Healy, Paul F. / Asaro, Frank / Stross, Fred / Michel, Helen
1996 Precolumbian Obsidian Trade in the Northern Intermediate Area: Elemental Analysis of Artifacts From Honduras and Nicaragua. In: Lange, Freder-ick W. (ed.), Paths to Central American Prehistory, pp. 271–284. Niwot.

Healy, Paul F. / Dennett, Carrie L. / Harris, Mary H. / Both, Arnd Adje
2010 A Musical Nature: Pre Columbian Ceramic Flutes of Northeast Honduras. In: Hickmann, Ellen /

Eichmann, Ricardo / Koch, Lars-Christian (eds.), Musical Perceptions. Past and Present. On Ethno-graphic Analogy in Music Archaeology. Studien zur Musikarchäologie, pp. 189–212. Rahden, Westf. [Germany].

Healy, Paul F. / Pohl, Mary
1980 Archaeology of the Rivas region, Nicaragua. Wa-terloo, Ont.

Hecht, Niels
2013 A Relative Sequence of Nasca Style Pottery from Palpa, Peru. PhD Thesis, Rheinische Friedrich-Wil-helms-Universität Bonn.

Helbig, Karl
1956 Antiguales (Altertümer) der Paya-Region und die Paya-Indianer von Nordost-Honduras: (auf Grund einer geografischen Erkundungsreise im Jahre 1953). Beiträge zur mittelamerikanischen Völk-erkunde 3. Hamburg.

Helms, Mary
1979 Ancient Panama: Chiefs in Search of Power. Austin.

Henderson, John S.
1978 El noroeste de Honduras y la frontera oriental maya. In: Yaxkin 2 (4): 241–253.

Henderson, John S. / Beaudry-Corbett, Marilyn (eds.)
1993 Pottery of Prehistoric Honduras: Regional Classi-fication and Analysis. Los Angeles.

Hendon, Julia A.
2003 Feasting at Home: Community and House Soli-darity among the Maya of Southeastern Mesoamer-ica. In: Bray, Tamara L. (ed.), The Archaeology and Politics of Food and Feasting in Early States and Empires, pp. 203–234.

Hicks, David W. / Tunnell, John W. / Withers, Kim
2010 Encyclopedia of Texas seashells: Identification, ecology, distribution, and history. Harte Research Institute for Gulf of Mexico Studies series. College Station.

Hillson, Simon
1999 Mammal Bones and Teeth. Dorset.

Hirth, Kenneth
1988 Beyond the Maya Frontier: Cultural Interaction and Syncretism along the Central Honduran Corri-dor. In: Boone, Elizabeth H. / Willey, Gordon R. (eds.), The Southeast Classic Maya Zone. A Sympo-

sium at Dumbarton Oaks, 6th and 7th October 1984. Washington, D.C.

2010 Cajón, El (Honduras). In: Evans, Susan T. / Webster, David (eds.), Archaeology of Ancient Mexico and Central America. An Encyclopedia, p. 88. New York.

2012 Markets, Merchants, and Systems of Exchange. In: Nichols, Deborah L. (ed.), The Oxford Handbook of Mesoamerican Archaeology, pp. 639–652. New York, Oxford.

Hirth, Kenneth / Grant Hirth, Susan

1993 Ancient Currency: The Style and Use of Jade and Marble Carvings in Central Honduras. In: Lange, Frederick W. (ed.), Precolumbian Jade. New Geological und Cultural Interpretations, pp. 173–190. Salt Lake City.

Hofman, Corinne L.

2013 The Post-Saladoid in the Lesser Antilles (A.D. 600/800-1492). In: Keegan, William F. / Hofman, Corinne L. / Rodríguez Ramos, Reniel (eds.), The Oxford Handbook of Caribbean Archaeology. Oxford handbooks, pp. 205–220. Oxford [etc.].

Hofman, Corinne L. / Bright, Alistair J. / Boomert, Arie / Knippenberg, Sebastiaan

2007 Island Rhythms: The Web of Social Relationships and Interaction Networks in the Lesser Antillean Archipelago between 400 B.C. and A.D. 1492. In: Latin American Antiquity 18 (3): 243–268.

Hofman, Corinne L. / Bright, Alistair J. / Rodríguez Ramos, Reniel

2010 Crossing the Caribbean Sea: Towards a holistic view of pre-Colonial mobility and exchange. In: Journal of Caribbean Archaeology: 1-18.

Hofman, Corinne L. / Mol, Angus / Rodríguez Ramos, Reniel / Knippenberg, Sebastiaan

2014 Networks Set in Stone: Archaic-Ceramic interaction in the early prehistoric northeastern Caribbean. In: Bérard, Benoît / Losier, Catherine (eds.), Archéologie Caraïbe. Taboui no. 2, pp. 119–132. Leiden.

Holt, Dennis / Bright, William

1976 La lengua paya y las fronteras lingüísticas de Mesoamérica, Las fronteras de Mesoamérica. Sociedad Mexicana de Antropología, Mesa Redonda 14, pp. 149–156.

Hoopes, John W.

2001 Late Chibcha. In: Peregrine, Peter N. (ed.), Encyclopedia of Prehistory. Volume 5 Middle America. Encyclopedia of prehistory 5, pp. 239–256. New York.

2005 The Emergence of Social Complexity in the Chibchan World of Southern Central America and Northern Colombia, AD 300-600. In: Journal of Archaeological Research 13 (1): 1–47.

2007 Sorcery and the Taking of Trophy Heads in Ancient Costa Rica. In: Chacon, Richard J. / Dye, David H. (eds.), The Taking and Displaying of Human Body Parts as Trophies by Amerindians. Interdisciplinary contributions to Archaeology, pp. 444–480. Boston, MA.

2017 Magical Substances in the land between the Seas: Luxury Arts in Northern South America and Central America. In: Pillsbury, Joanne / Potts, Timothy / Richter, Kim N. (eds.), Golden Kingdoms. Luxury Arts in the Ancient Americas, pp. 55–66. Los Angeles.

Hoopes, John W. / Chenault, Mark L.

1994 Excavations at Sitio Bolívar: A Late Formative village in the Arenal basin. In: Sheets, Payson D. / McKee, Brian R. (eds.), Archaeology, volcanism, and remote sensing in the Arenal region, Costa Rica, pp. 87–105. Austin.

Hoopes, John W. / Fonseca, Oscar M.

2003 Goldwork and Chibchan Identity: Endogenous Change and Diffuse Unity in the Isthmo-Colombian Area. In: Quilter, Jeffrey / Hoopes, John W. (eds.), Gold and Power in Ancient Costa Rica, Panama and Colombia. A Symposium at Dumbarton Oaks, 9 and 10 October 1999, pp. 49–89. Washington, D.C.

Hosler, Dorothy

1988 Ancient West Mexican Metallurgy: South and Central American Origins and West Mexican Transformations. In: American Anthropologist (90): 823–855.

1994 Sounds and Colors of Power: The Sacred Metallurgical Technology of Ancient West Mexico. Cambridge, Mass.

1997 Los orígenes andinos de la metalurgia del occidente de México. In: Boletín del Museo del Oro (42): 3–25.

1999 Recent insights into the metallurgical technologies of ancient mesoamerica. In: Journal of The Minerals, Metals & Materials Society 51 (5): 11–14.

2003 Metal Production. In: Smith, Michael E. / Berdan, Frances F. (eds.), The Postclassic Mesoamerican World, pp. 159–171. Salt Lake City.

2010 Metal: Tools, Techniques, and Products. In: Evans, Susan T. / Webster, David (eds.), Archaeology of Ancient Mexico and Central America. An Encyclopedia, pp. 454–457. New York.

2013 Mesoamerican Metallurgy Today. In: Shugar, Aaron N. / Simmons, Scott E. (eds.), Archaeometallurgy in Mesoamerica. Current Approaches and New Perspectives, pp. 227-246. Boulder.

Hosler, Dorothy / Macfarlane, Andrew
1996 Copper Sources, Metal Production, and Metals Trade in Late Postclassic Mesoamerica. In: Science 273 (5283): 1819–1824.

Hudson, Kathryn M. / Henderson, John S.
2014 Life on the Edge: Identity and Interaction in the Land of Ulúa and the Maya World. In: Ikäheimo, Janne / Salmi, Anna-Kaisa / Äikäs, Tiina (eds.), Sounds like Theory. Monographs of the Archaeological Society of Finland 2, pp. 157–171.

Humfrey, Michael
1975 Sea shells of the West Indies: A guide to the marine molluscs of the Caribbean. New York.

Inomata, Takeshi / Triadan, Daniela
2015 Middle Preclassic Caches from Ceibal, Guatemala. Maya Archaeology 3. San Francisco.

Jenkins, David
2001 A network analysis of Inka roads, administrative centers, and storage facilities. In: Ethnohistory 48 (4): 655–687.

Jones, Julie / Kerr, Justin (eds.)
1985 The art of Precolumbian gold: The Jan Mitchell Collection. London.

Jones, Ursula
1992 Decorated metates in Prehispanic Lower Central America. Ph.D. Thesis, University College.

Joyce, Rosemary A.
2001 Stone, Doris Zemurray. In: Murray, Tim (ed.), Encyclopedia of Archaeology Part 2. History and Discoveries, pp. 1212–1214. Santa Barbara-CA.

Joyce, Rosemary A. / Henderson, John S.
2001 Beginnings of Village Life in Eastern Mesoamerica. In: Latin American Antiquity 12 (1): 5–23.

Junker, Laura L.
2001 The Evolution of Ritual Feasting Systems in Prehispanic Philippine Chiefdoms. In: Dietler, Michael / Hayden, Brian (eds.), Feasts. Archaeological and ethnographic perspectives on food, politics, and power. Smithsonian series in archaeological inquiry, pp. 267–310. Washington, D.C.

Karstens, Karsten
1994 Allgemeine Systematik der einfachen Gefässformen. Münchener Universitätsschriften, Philosophische Fakultät 12. München/Wien.

Keegan, Lindsay T. / Keegan, William F. / Carlson, Lisbeth A. / Altes, Christopher
2009 Shell Net Weights from Florida and Puerto Rico. In: Rebovich, S. (ed.), Proceedings of the XXIII Congress of the International Association for Caribbean Archaeology, pp. 1–11. Antigua.

Keegan, William F.
2013 The "Classic" Taíno. In: Keegan, William F. / Hofman, Corinne L. / Rodríguez Ramos, Reniel (eds.), The Oxford Handbook of Caribbean Archaeology. Oxford handbooks, pp. 70–83. Oxford.

Keegan, William F. / Rodríguez Ramos, Reniel
2005 Sin Rodeo. In: El Caribe Arqueológico 8: 8–13.

Keen, Angeline M.
1971 Sea shells of tropical West America: Marine mollusks from Baja California to Peru. Stanford.

Kepecs, Susan / Kohl, Philip
2003 Conceptualizing Macroregional Interaction: World-Systems Theory and the Archaeological Record. In: Smith, Michael E. / Berdan, Frances F. (eds.), The Postclassic Mesoamerican World, pp. 14–20. Salt Lake City.

Kirchhoff, Paul
1943 Mesoamérica: Sus límites geográficos, composición étnica y carácteres culturales. In: Acta Americana 1 (1): 92–107.

Knappett, Carl
2013a Introduction: Why Networks? In: Knappett, Carl (ed.), Network Analysis in Archaeology. New Approaches to Regional Interaction, pp. 3–16. Oxford.

Knappett, Carl (ed.)
2013b Network Analysis in Archaeology: New Approaches to Regional Interaction. Oxford.

Kovacevich, Brigitte
2013 Craft Production and Distribution in the Maya Lowlands: A Jade Case Study. In: Hirth, Kenneth G. / Pillsbury, Joanne (eds.), Merchants, Markets, and Exchange in the Pre-Columbian World. Dumbarton Oaks Pre-Columbian symposia and colloquia, pp. 255–282. Washington, DC.

Kunow, Jürgen
1986 Vorschläge zur systematischen Beschreibung von Keramik = Suggestions for the systematic recording of pottery = Propositions pour une description systématique des céramiques. Kunst und Altertum am Rhein 124. Köln.

Laffoon, Jason E. / Rodríguez Ramos, Reniel / Chanlatte Baik, Luis / Narganes Storde, Yvonne / Rodríguez Lopez,

Miguel / Davies, Gareth R. / Hofman, Corinne L.
2014 Long-distance exchange in the precolonial Circum-Caribbean: A multi-isotope study of animal tooth pendants from Puerto Rico. In: Journal of Anthropological Archaeology 35: 220–233.

Lafuente, Barbara / Downs, Robert T. / Yang, Hexiong / Stone, Nate
2015 The power of databases: the RRUFF project. In: Armbruster, Thomas / Danisi, Rosa Micaela (eds.), Highlights in Mineralogical Crystallography, pp. 1-30. Berlin.

Landa, Diego d.
1978 Relación de las cosas de Yucatán. Mexiko.

Lange, Frederick W.
1984a Cultural Geography of Pre-Columbian Lower Central America. In: Lange, Frederick W. / Stone, Doris (eds.), The Archaeology of Lower Central America. School of American Research advanced seminar series, pp. 33–62. Albuquerque, N.M.
1984b The Greater Nicoya Archaeological Subarea. In: Lange, Frederick W. / Stone, Doris (eds.), The Archaeology of Lower Central America. School of American Research advanced seminar series, pp. 165–194. Albuquerque, N.M.
1993a Introduction. In: Lange, Frederick W. (ed.), Precolumbian Jade. New Geological und Cultural Interpretations, pp. 1–6. Salt Lake City.

Lange, Frederick W. (ed.)
1993b Precolumbian Jade: New Geological und Cultural Interpretations. Salt Lake City.

Lange, Frederick W. / Sheets, Payson / Martínez, Aníbal / Abel-Vidor, Suzanne. (eds.)
1992 The Archaeology of Pacific Nicaragua. Albuquerque.

Lange, Frederick W. / Stone, Doris (eds.)
1984 The Archaeology of Lower Central America. School of American Research advanced seminar series. Albuquerque, N.M.

Lara Pinto, Gloria
1980 Beiträge zur indianischen Ethnographie von Honduras in der 1. Hälfte des 16. Jahrhunderts, unter besonderer Berücksichtigung der historischen Demographie. Ph.D. Thesis, University of Hamburg.
1991 Change for Survival: The Case of the Sixteenth-Century Indigenous Populations of Northeast and Mideast Honduras. In: Thomas, David H. (ed.), Columbian Consequences 3, pp. 227–243. Washington, DC.

Lara Pinto, Gloria / Hasemann, George
1988 La sociedad indígena del Noreste de Honduras en el siglo XVI: Son la etnohistoria y la arqueología contradictorias? In: Yaxkin 11 (2): 5–28.
1991 Leyendas y arqueología: Cuantas ciudades blancas hay en la Mosquitia? In: Murphy, Vicente (ed.), La Reserva de la Biósfera del Río Plátano. Herencia de nuestro pasado, pp. 16–19. Tegucigalpa.

Las Casas, Bartolomé de
1986 Historia de las Indias. Edited by André Saint-Lu. Caracas.

Lathrap, Donald W.
1973 The antiquity and importance of long-distance trade relationships in the moist tropics of pre-Columbian South America. In: World Archaeology 5 (2): 170–186.

Lau, George F.
2002 Feasting and Ancestor Veneration at Chinchawas, North Highlands of Ancash, Peru. In: Latin American Antiquity 13 (3): 279–304.

LeCount, Lisa J.
2001 Like Water for Chocolate: Feasting and Political Ritual among the Late Classic Maya at Xunantunich, Belize. In: American Anthropologist 103 (4): 935–953.

Lightfoot, Kent G. / Martinez, Antoinette
1995 Frontiers and Boundaries in Archaeological Perspective. In: Annual Review of Anthropology 24: 471–492.

Linares, Olga F.
1968 Ceramic Phases for Chiriqui, Panama, and Their Relationship to Neighboring Sequences. In: American Antiquity 33 (2): 216–225.
1979 What is Lower Central American Archaeology? In: Annual Review of Anthropology 8: 21–43.

López, Adolfo / Urcuyo, Janina
2008 Bivalvos. Moluscos de Nicaragua / Adolfo López, Janina Urcuyo ; 1. Managua.
2009 Gastrópodos. Moluscos de Nicaragua / Adolfo López, Janina Urcuyo ; 2. Managua.

Lothrop, Samuel K.
1955 Jade and String Sawing in Northeastern Costa Rica. In: American Antiquity 21 (1): 43–51.
1926 Pottery of Costa Rica and Nicaragua. Museum of the American Indian: Heye Foundation Contributions 8. New York, N.Y.
1937 Coclé: An Archaeological Study of Central Panama. Vol. I: Historical Background. Excavations at the Sitio Conte. Artifacts and Ornaments. Peabody Museum of American Archaeology and Ethnology Memoirs 7. Cambridge-MA.
1939 The Southeastern Frontier of the Maya. In: American Anthropologist 41 (1): 42–54.
1950 Archaeology of southern Veraguas, Panama: With appendices by W. C. Root, Eleanor B. Adams and Doris Stone. Memoirs of the Peabody Museum of Archaeology and Ethnology, Harvard University, v. 9, no. 3. Cambridge.
1952 Metals from the Cenote of Sacrifice, Chichén Itzá Yucatán. Memoirs of the Peabody Museum 10. Cambridge, Mass.
1963 Archaeology of the Diquís Delta, Costa Rica. Peabody Museum of American Archaeology and Ethnology Papers Vol. 51. Cambridge-MA.

M. W.
1752 The Mosqueto Indian and His Golden River; being a Familiar Description of the Mosqueto Kingdom in America, etc.: A Collection of Voyages and Travels Vol. VI. London.

MacCurdy, George G.
1911 A study of Chiriquian antiquities. Connecticut Academy of Arts and Sciences (New Haven-CT): memoirs 3. New Haven-CT.

MacNeish, Richard S.
1967-72 The Prehistory of the Tehuacan Valley. Austin.
2010 Archaic Period (c. 8000-2000 B.C.). In: Evans, Susan T. / Webster, David (eds.), Archaeology of Ancient Mexico and Central America. An Encyclopedia, pp. 30–33. New York.

Magnus, Richard
1974 The Prehistory of the Miskito Coast of Nicaragua: A Study in Cultural Relationships. Ph.D. Thesis, Yale University.

1978 The Prehistoric and Modern Subsistence Patterns of the Atlantic Coast of Nicaragua: A Comparison. In: Stark, Barbara L. / Voorhies, Barbara (eds.), Prehistoric Coastal Adaptations. The Economy and Ecology of Maritime Middle America. Studies in Archaeology, pp. 61-80. New York.

Martens, Eduard von
1890-1901 Biologia Centrali-Americana. Land and Freshwater Mollusca. London.

Mattes, Jill
2019 Präkolumbische Architektur in Nordost-Honduras. BA Thesis, Department of Archaeology, University of Zurich.

McAnany, Patricia A.
2004 Appropriative economies: Labor obligations and luxury goods in ancient Maya societies. In: Feinman, Gary M. / Nicholas, Linda M. (eds.), Archaeological Perspectives on Political Economies, pp. 145–165. Salt Lake City.

McCafferty, Geoffrey
2015 The Mexican legacy in Nicaragua, or problems when data behave badly. In: Archaeological Papers of the American Anthropological Association: 110–118.

McCafferty, Geoffrey / Esteban Amador, Fabio / Salgado Gonzalez, Silvia / Dennett, Carrie Lynd
2012 Archaeology on Mesoamerica's Southern Frontier. In: Nichols, Deborah L. (ed.), The Oxford Handbook of Mesoamerican Archaeology, pp. 83–105. New York, Oxford.

McCafferty, Sharisse / McCafferty, Geoffrey
2010 Textile Production in Postclassic Cholula, Mexico. In: Ancient Mesoamerica 11 (1): 39–54.

McGimsey, Charles R.
1956 Cerro Mangote: A Preceramic Site in Panama. In: American Antiquity 22 (2): 151–161.

McKillop, Heather
1989 Coastal Maya Trade: Obsidian Densities at Wild Cane Cay, Belize. In: Research in Economic Anthropology, Supplement 4: 17–56.
1996 Ancient Maya Trading Ports and the Integration of Long-Distance and Regional Economies: Wild Cane Cay in South-Coastal Belize. In: Ancient Mesoamerica 7 (1): 49–62.

McLeod, B. H.
1945 Examination of Copper Objects from Culiacán. In: Kelly, Isabel (ed.), Excavations at Culiacán,Sinaloa, pp. 180–186. Berkeley, California.

McOmish, David
1996 East Chisenbury: Ritual and rubbish at the British Bronze Age-Iron Age transition. In: Antiquity 70 (267): 68–76.

Mills, Barbara J.
2017 Social Network Analysis in Archaeology. In: Annual Review of Anthropology 46 (1): 379–397.

Minc, Leah
2010 Pottery. In: Evans, Susan T. / Webster, David (eds.), Archaeology of Ancient Mexico and Central America. An Encyclopedia, pp. 603–610. New York.

Mol, Angus
2014 The connected Caribbean: A socio-material network approach to patterns of homogeneity and diversity in the pre-colonial Period. Leiden.

Mol, Angus / Mans, Jimmy
2013 Old-Boy Networks in the Indigenous Caribbean. In: Knappett, Carl (ed.), Network Analysis in Archaeology. New Approaches to Regional Interaction, pp. 307–332. Oxford.

Mora Marín, David / Reents-Budet, Dorie / Fields, Virginia M.
2017 Costa Rica and the Maya: Prestige Goods and International Relations. In: Patton, M. / Manion J. (eds.), Trading Spaces. The Archaeology of Interaction, Migration and Exchange. Proceedings of the 46th Annual Chacmool Conference. Calgary, Alberta.

Moreno, Pedro
1525 Relación e información del viaje que hizo el Bachiller Pedro Moreno a las Higueras.

Mountjoy, Joseph B.
2001 Patolli. In: Carrasco, David (ed.), The Oxford Encyclopedia of Mesoamerican Cultures. The Civilizations of Mexico and Central America, p. 448. Oxford.
2005 Algunos patollis abreviados encontrados entre los petrograbados de Jalisco. In: Los Petrograbados del Norte de México, pp. 181–186.

Müller, Ulrich
2009 Netzwerkanalysen in der historischen Archäologie: Begriffe und Beispiele. In: Geuenich, Dieter et al. (eds.), Historia Archaeologica. Festschrift für Heiko Steuer zum 70. Geburtstag. Ergänzungsbände zum Reallexikon der germanischen Altertumskunde 70, pp. 735–754. Berlin, New York.

Murra, John V.
1962 Cloth and Its Functions in the Inca State. In: American Anthropologist 64 (4): 710–728.

NASA / METI / AIST / Japan Spacesystems and U.S. / Japan ASTER Science Team
2019 ASTER Global Digital Elevation Model V003 [Data set]. NASA EOSDIS Land Processes DAAC. Accessed 2021-04-20 from https://doi.org/10.5067/ASTER/ASTGTM.003

Nance, James
1965 Pre-Spanish Trade in the Bay Islands: An Analysis of the Archeological Evidence.

Nietschmann, Bernard
1973 Between land and water: The subsistence ecology of the Miskito Indians, eastern Nicaragua. New York.

Oberg, Kalervo
1955 Types of Social Structure among the Lowland Tribes of South and Central America. In: American Anthropologist 3 (1): 472–487.

Oliver, José
2005 The Proto-Taíno Monumental Cemís of Caguana: A Political-Religious 'Manifesto'. In: Siegel, Peter E. (ed.), Ancient Borinquen. Archaeology and Ethnohistory of Native Puerto Rico, pp. 230–284. Tuscaloosa, AL.
2009 Caciques and Cemí idols: The web spun by Taíno rulers between Hispaniola and Puerto Rico.Caribbean archaeology and ethnohistory. Tuscaloosa.

Olsen, Stanley J.
1964 Mammal remains from archaeological sites. Papers of the Peabody Museum of Archaeology and Ethnology 56 (1). Cambridge, MA.
1968 Fish, amphibian and reptile remains from archaeological sites. Papers of the Peabody Museum of Archaeology and Ethnology 56 (2). Cambridge, MA.
1982 An osteology of some Maya mammals. Papers of the Peabody Museum of Archaeology and Ethnology 73. Cambridge, MA.

Otto, Raquel
2019 Análisis tecnológico y de procedencia de la obsidiana del sitio Guadalupe, Colón, Honduras. BA Thesis, Universidad Nacional Autónoma de Honduras.

Paap, Iken
2002 Die Keramik von Khyinga: Mustang District, Nepal. Ph.D. Thesis, Rheinische Friedrich-Wilhelms-Universität Bonn.

Pahl, Gary W. (ed.)
1987 The Periphery of the Southeastern Classic Maya Realm. Los Angeles.

Pailes, R. A. / Whitecotton, Joseph W.
1979 The Greater Southwest and Mesoamerican 'World' System: an explanatory model of frontier relationships. In: Savage, William W. / Thompson, Stephen I. (eds.), The frontier. Comparative studies, pp. 105–121. Norman.

Parkinson, William A. / Galaty, Michael L.
2007 Secondary States in Perspective: An Integrated Approach to State Formation in the Prehistoric Aegean. In: American Anthropologist 109 (1): 113–129.

Parsons, Mary H.
1972 Spindle Whorls from the Teotihuacan Valley, Mexico. In: Spence, Michael W. / Parsons, Jeffrey R. / Parsons, Mary H. (eds.), Miscellaneous studies in Mexican prehistory. Anthropological papers / Museum of Anthropology Univ. of Michigan 45, pp. 45–80. Ann Arbor, Mich.

Pastrana, Alejandro / Domínguez, Silvia
2009 Cambios en la estrategia de la explotación de la obsidiana de Pachuca: Teotihuacan, Tula y la Triple Alianza. In: Ancient Mesoamerica 20 (1): 129–148.

Paulsen, Eva
2019 Everything has its Jaguar: A narratological approach to conceptualising Caribbean Saladoid animal imagery. PhD Thesis, Faculty of Archaeology, Leiden University.

Peabody Museum of Archaeology and Ethnology
What is an Ocarina? Online article, https://www.peabody.harvard.edu/node/2607 (accessed August 17, 2020).

Peeples, Matthew A. / Mills, Barbara J. / Haas, Randall W. / Clark, Jeffery J. / Roberts, John
2016 Analytical Challenges for the Application of Social Network Analysis in Archaeology. In: Brughmans,

Tom / Collar, Anna / Coward, Fiona S. (eds.), The connected past. Challenges to network studies in archaeology and history, pp. 59–84. Oxford.

Peregrine, Peter
1991 A Graph-Theoretic Approach to the Evolution of Cahokia. In: American Antiquity 56 (1): 66–75.

Piddocke, Stuart
1965 The Potlatch System of the Southern Kwakiutl: A New Perspective. In: Southwestern Journal of Anthropology 21 (3): 244–264.

Piña Chan, Román
1978 Commerce in the Yucatán Peninsula: The Conquest and Colonial Period. In: Lee, Thomas A. Jr. / Navarrete, Carlos (eds.), Mesoamerican Communication Routes and Cultural Contacts. New World Archaeological Foundation Papers 40, pp. 27–36. Provo, UT.

Pittier, Henri
1938 Apuntaciones etnológicas sobre los indios Bribri. Serie etnológica 1. San José.

Polanyi, Karl / Arensberg, Conrad M. / Pearson, Harry W. (eds.)
1957 Trade and Market in the Early Empires. Chicago.

Politis, Gustavo
2016 Bonescapes: Engaging People and Land with Animal Bones among South American Tropical Foragers. In: Lovis, William A. / Whallon, Robert (eds.), Marking the land. Hunter-gatherer creation of meaning in their environment. Routledge studies in archaeology, pp. 152–179. Abingdon, Oxon, New York, NY.

Pollock, Harry E.D. et al. (eds.)
1962 Mayapan, Yucatan, Mexico. Publication / Carnegie Institution of Washington 619. Washington, D.C.

Popenoe, Dorothy H.
1934 Some Excavations at Playa de los Muertos, Ulua River, Honduras. New York.

Porras, Diego d.
1825-37 Relación del viage é de la tierra agora nuevamente descubierta por el Almirante D. Cristóbal Colón. In: Navarrete, Martían F.d. (ed.), Colección de los viajes y descubrimientos que hicieron por mar los espanoles desde fines de siglo XV con varios documentos inéditos concernientes a la historia

de la marina castellana y de los establecimientos espanoles en Indias 1, pp. 282–287. Madrid.

Potthast, Barbara
1988 Die Mosquitoküste im Spannungsfeld britischer
und spanischer Politik, 1502-1821. Lateinamerikan-
ische Forschungen Bd. 16. Köln.

Prignano, Luce / Morer, Ignacio / Diaz-Guilera, Albert
2017 Wiring the Past: A Network Science Perspective
on the Challenge of Archeological Similarity Networks. In: Frontiers in Digital Humanities 4: 1–12.

Quesada Pacheco, Juan D.
2008 Las lenguas chibchas y sus hablantes: resistencia,
obsolescencia e indiferencia. Costa Rica.

Quilter, Jeffrey
2003 Introduction: The Golden Bridge of the Darien.
In: Quilter, Jeffrey / Hoopes, John W. (eds.), Gold
and Power in Ancient Costa Rica, Panama and Colombia. A Symposium at Dumbarton Oaks, 9 and
10 October 1999, pp. 1–14. Washington, D.C.

Ranere, Anthony
2008 Lower Central America. In: Pearsall, Deborah M.
(ed.), Encyclopedia of Archaeology, pp. 192–209.
Oxford, San Diego, Calif.

Rathje, William L. / Sabloff, Jeremy A.
1973 Ancient Maya Commercial Systems: A Research
Design for the Island of Cozumel, Mexico. In:
World Archaeology 5 (2): 221–231.

Reichel-Dolmatoff, Gerardo
1971 Amazonian Cosmos: The sexual and religious
symbolism of the Tukano Indians. Phoenix book
574. Chicago, Ill.

Reid, Basil A. / Curet, Antonio L.
2014 Elite Exchange in the Caribbean. In: Reid, Basil A. /
Gilmore, Richard G. (eds.), Encyclopedia of Caribbean Achaeology, pp. 140–141. Gainesville, Florida.

Renfrew, Colin
1986 Introduction: Peer polity interaction and socio-political change. In: Renfrew, Colin / Cherry,
John F. (eds.), Peer polity interaction and socio-political change. New direction in archaeology, pp.
1–18. Cambridge.

Renfrew, Colin / Cherry, John F. (eds.)
1986 Peer polity interaction and socio-political
change. New direction in archaeology. Cambridge.

Reyes Mazzoni, Roberto
1976 Introducción a la Arqueología de Honduras. Tegucigalpa.

Reyonard de Ruenes, Margarita
1993 A Possible Source of Raw Material for the Costa
Rican Lapidary Industry. In: Lange, Frederick W.
(ed.), Precolumbian Jade. New Geological und Cultural Interpretations, pp. 61–67. Salt Lake City.

Rice, Prudence M.
1987 Pottery Analysis: A Sourcebook. Chicago, London.

Robinson, Eugenia J. (ed.)
1987 Interaction on the Southeast Mesoamerican
Frontier: Prehistoric and Historic Honduras and El
Salvador. BAR international series 327. Oxford.

Robinson, Eugenia J.
1989 The Prehistoric Communities of the Sula Valley,
Honduras: Regional Interaction in the Southeast
Mesoamerican Frontier. Ph.D. Thesis, Department
of Anthropology, Tulane University.

Rodríguez Ramos, Reniel
2010 What is the Caribbean?: An Archaeological Perspective. In: Journal of Caribbean Archaeology (3):
19–51.
2013 Isthmo-Antillean Engagements. In: Keegan, William F. / Hofman, Corinne L. / Rodríguez Ramos,
Reniel (eds.), The Oxford Handbook of Caribbean
Archaeology. Oxford handbooks, pp. 155–170. Oxford.

Rodríguez Ramos, Reniel / Pagán Jiménez, Jaime
2006 Interacciones multivectoriales en el circum-caribe precolonial: Un vistazo desde las Antillas. In:
Caribbean Studies 34 (2): 99–139.

Root, William C.
1953 Report on Some Metal Objects from Zaculeu. In:
Woodbury, Richard B. / Trik, Aubrey S. (eds.), The
ruins of Zaculeu, Guatemala, pp. 266–268. New
York.

Rose, Richard H.
1904 Utila: Past and Present. Dansville, N.Y.

Rössler, Martin
1999 Wirtschaftsethnologie: Eine Einführung. Berlin.

Rouse, Irving
1964 Prehistory of the West Indies. In: Science (New
York, N.Y.) 144 (3618): 499–513.

Roys, Ralph
1943 The Indian Background of Colonial Yucatan. Carnegie Institution of Washington Publication 548. Washington.

Rue, David J.
1989 Archaic Middle American Agriculture and Settlement: Recent Pollen Data from Honduras. In: Journal of Field Archaeology 16 (2): 177–184.

Rye, Owen
1981 Pottery Technology: Principles and Reconstruction. Washington, D.C.

Sabloff, Jeremy A.
1975 Excavations at Seibal: Ceramics. Peabody Museum of American Archaeology and Ethnology Memoirs 13 (2). Cambridge, MA.

Sahagún, Bernardino d.
1938 Historia general de las cosas de Nueva España: Vol II. México, D.F.

Santley, Robert S.
2010 Classic Period. In: Evans, Susan T. / Webster, David (eds.), Archaeology of Ancient Mexico and Central America. An Encyclopedia, pp. 147–152. New York.

Schertl, Hans P. / Maresch, Walter V. / Krebs, M.
2007 The Rio San Juan serpentinite complex and its jadeitites (Dominican Republic). In: Martens, U. / Garcia-Casco, Antonio (eds.), High-pressure belts of Central Guatemala. The Motagua suture and the Chuacus Complex.

Schertl, Hans P. / Maresch, Walter V. / Stanek, Klaus P. / Hertwig, Andreas / Krebs, Martin / Baese, Rauno /

Sergeev, Sergey S.
2012 New occurrences of jadeitite, jadeite quartzite and jadeite-lawsonite quartzite in the Dominican-Republic, Hispaniola: Petrological and geochronological overview. In: European Journal of Mineralogy 24 (2): 199–216.

Schneider, Jane
1977 Was there e Precapitalist World-System? In: Peasant Studies 6 (1): 20–29.

Scholes, France V. / Roys, Ralph
1968 The Maya Chontal Indians of Acalan-Tixchel: A contribution to the history and ethnography of the Yucatan Peninsula. Norman, OK.

Scholnik, Jonathan B. / Munson, Jessica L. / Macri, Martha J.
2013 Positioning power in a multi-relational framework: A social network analysis of Classic Maya political rhetoric. In: Knappett, Carl (ed.), Network Analysis in Archaeology. New Approaches to Regional Interaction, pp. 95–124. Oxford.

Schortman, Edward M.
1989 Interregional Interaction in Prehistory: The Need for a New Perspective. In: American Antiquity 54 (01): 52–65.

Schortman, Edward M. / Urban, Patricia (eds.)
1986 The Southeast Maya Periphery. Austin.

Schortman, Edward M. / Urban, Patricia
1991 Patterns of Late Preclassic Interaction and the Formation of Complex Society in the Southeast Maya Periphery. In: Fowler, William R., JR. (ed.), The Formation of Complex Society in Southeastern Mesoamerica, pp. 121–142. Boca Raton.
1994 Living on the Edge: Core/Periphery Relations in Ancient Southeastern Mesoamerica. In: Current Anthropology 35 (4): 401–430.
2012 Networks, Cores, and Peripheries: New Frontiers in Interaction Studies. In: Nichols, Deborah L. (ed.), The Oxford Handbook of Mesoamerican Archaeology, pp. 471–481. New York, Oxford.
1987 Modeling Interregional Interaction in Prehistory. In: Schiffer, Michael B. (ed.), Advances in Archaeological Method and Theory, pp. 37–95. New York.

Seitz, Russel / Harlow, George E. / Sisson, Virginia B. / Taube, Karl E.
2001 'Olmec Blue' and Formative jade sources: New discoveries in Guatemala. In: Antiquity 75 (290): 687–688.

Service, Elman R.
1962 Primitive Social Organization: An Evolutionary Perspective. New York.

Sharer, Robert J. / Sedat, David W. / Pezzati, Alessandro
2009 Sitios arqueológicos en la costa norte de Honduras. In: Yaxkin 25 (1): 73–92.

Sharer, Robert J. / Traxler, Loa P.
2006 The Ancient Maya. Stanford, Calif.

Sheets, Payson
1992 The Pervasive Pejorative in Intermediate Area Studies. In: Lange, Frederick W. (ed.), Wealth and Hierarchy in the Intermediate Area. A Symposium

at Dumbarton Oaks 10th and 11th October 1987, pp. 15–42. Washington, D.C.

1994 Chipped Stone Artifacts from the Cordillera de Tilarán. In: Sheets, Payson D. / McKee, Brian R. (eds.), Archaeology, volcanism, and remote sensing in the Arenal region, Costa Rica, pp. 211–254. Austin.

Sheets, Payson / Hirth, Kenneth / Lange, Fred / Stross, Fred / Asaro, Frank / Michel, Helen

1990 Obsidian Sources and Elemental Analyses of Artifacts in Southern Mesoamerica and the Northern Intermediate Area. In: American Antiquity 55 (01): 144–158.

Simmons, Scott E. / Graham, Elizabeth

2017 Maya Coastal Adaptations in Classic and Postclassic Times on Ambergris Caye, Belize. In: Patton, M. / Manion J. (eds.), Trading Spaces. The Archaeology of Interaction, Migration and Exchange. Proceedings of the 46th Annual Chacmool Conference, pp. 167–180. Calgary, Alberta.

Simmons, Scott E. / Shugar, Aaron N.

2013a Archaeometallurgy at Lamanai, Belize: New Discoveries and Insights from the Southern Maya Lowland Area. In: Shugar, Aaron N. / Simmons, Scott E. (eds.), Archaeometallurgy in Mesoamerica. Current Approaches and New Perspectives. Boulder.

2013b Archaeometallurgy in Ancient Mesoamerica. In: Shugar, Aaron N. / Simmons, Scott E. (eds.), Archaeometallurgy in Mesoamerica. Current Approaches and New Perspectives, pp. 1–28. Boulder.

Sindbaek, Soren

2007 Networks and nodal points: The emergence of towns in early Viking Age Scandinavia. In: Antiquity 81: 119–132.

2013 Broken links and black boxes: Material affiliations and contextual network synthesis in the Viking world. In: Knappett, Carl (ed.), Network Analysis in Archaeology. New Approaches to Regional Interaction, pp. 71–94. Oxford.

Smith, Michael E.

1979 A Further Criticism of the Type-Variety System: The Data can't be Used. In: American Antiquity 44 (4): 822–826.

Smith, Michael E. / Berdan, Frances F.

2003a Postclassic Mesoamerica. In: Smith, Michael E. / Berdan, Frances F. (eds.), The Postclassic Mesoamerican World, pp. 3–13. Salt Lake City.

Smith, Michael E. / Berdan, Frances F. (eds.)

2003b The Postclassic Mesoamerican World. Salt Lake City.

Smith, Michael E. / Hirth, Kenneth

1988 The Development of Prehispanic Cotton-Spinning Technology in Western Morelos, Mexico. In: Journal of Field Archaeology 15 (3): 349–358.

Smith, Robert E. / Willey, Gordon R. / Gifford, James C.

1960 The type-variety concept as a basis for the analysis of Maya pottery. In: American Antiquity 30: 330–340.

Snarskis, Michael J.

1981 The Archaeology of Costa Rica. In: Abel-Vidor, Suzanne / Bakker, Dirk (eds.), Between Continents/ Between Seas. Precolumbian Art of Costa Rica, pp. 15–84. New York, [Detroit].

1984 Central America: The Lower Caribbean. In: Lange, Frederick W. / Stone, Doris (eds.), The Archaeology of Lower Central America. School of American Research advanced seminar series, pp. 195–232. Albuquerque, N.M.

2003 From Jade to Gold in Costa Rica: How, Why, and When. In: Quilter, Jeffrey / Hoopes, John W. (eds.), Gold and Power in Ancient Costa Rica, Panama and Colombia. A Symposium at Dumbarton Oaks, 9 and 10 October 1999, pp. 159–204. Washington, D.C.

Solórzano, Juan C.

2009 América antigua: Los pueblos precolombinos desde el poblamiento original hasta los inicios de la conquista española. San José.

Spinden, Herbert J.

1917 Ancient Civilizations of Ancient Mexico and Central America. Handbook Series 3. New York.

1925 The Chorotegan Culture Area, Proceedings of the Twentyfirst International Congress of Americanists, pp. 529–545. Leiden.

Spotila, James R.

2004 Sea turtles: A complete guide to their biology, behavior, and conservation. Baltimore.

Stein, Gil

1998 World System Theory and Alternative Modes of Interaction in the Archaeology of Culture Contact. In: Cusick, James G. (ed.), Studies in Culture Contact. Interaction, Culture Change, and Archaeology. Occasional Paper 25, p. 220–220. Carbondale.

1999 Rethinking World Systems: Power, Distances and Diasporas in the Dynamics of Interregional Interaction. In: Kardulias, P. N. (ed.), World Systems Theory in Practice. Leadership, Production, and Exchange, pp. 153–178. Lanham, Md.
2002 From Passive Periphery to Active Agents: Emerging Perspectives in the Archaeology of Interregional Interaction. In: American Anthropologist 104 (3): 903–916.

Steinbrenner, Larry L.
2010 Potting Traditions and Cultural Continuity in Pacific Nicaragua, AD 800-1350. Ph.D. Thesis, Department of Archaeology, Univerity of Calgary.

Stemp, W. J. / Graham, Elizabeth / Goulet, Jessica
2011 Coastal Maya Obsidian Trade in the Late Postclassic to Early Colonial Period: The View From San Pedro, Ambergris Caye, Belize. In: The Journal of Island and Coastal Archaeology 6 (1): 134–154.

Steward, Julian H. (ed.)
1948 Handbook of South American Indians: Vol. 4: The Circum-Caribbean Tribes. Washington.

Stone, Doris
1934a A Mound and a House-Site: On Jerico Farm, Near Trujillo, Honduras. In: Maya Research 1 (2): 129–132.
1934b A New Southernmost Maya City (Los Naranjos on Lake Yojoa, Honduras). In: Maya Research 1: 125–128.
1939 Delimitation of the Maya Area in Honduras and Certain Stylistic Resemblances Found in Costa Rica and Honduras, Actas y trabajos científicos del XXVII° Congreso Internacional de Americanistas, pp. 226–230. Lima.
1941 Archaeology of the North Coast of Honduras. Peabody Museum of American Archaeology and Ethnology Memoirs Vol. 9, No. 1. Cambridge.
1957 The Archaeology of Central and Southern Honduras. Peabody Museum of American Archaeology and Ethnology Papers Vol. 49, No. 3. Cambridge-MA.
1976 Pre-Columbian Man Finds Central America: The Archaeological Bridge. Cambridge, Mass.
1977 Pre-Columbian man in Costa Rica. Cambridge, Mass.
1993 Jade and Jade Objects in Precolumbian Costa Rica. In: Lange, Frederick W. (ed.),

Precolumbian Jade. New Geological und Cultural Interpretations, pp. 141–148. Salt Lake City.

Stone, Doris / Balser, Carlos
1958 The aboriginal metalwork in the Isthmian Region of America. San José.

Stone-Miller, Rebecca
1992 To weave for the sun: Andean textiles in the Museum of Fine Arts, Boston. Boston, MA.

Strong, William D.
1934 Hunting Ancient Ruins in Northeast Honduras. In: Explorations and Fieldwork of the Smithsonian Institution in 1933: 44–47.
1935 Archaeological Investigations in the Bay Islands, Spanish Honduras. Smithsonian Institution Publication 3290. Washington-DC.
1948a The Archaeology of Central America: An Introduction. In: Steward, Julian H. (ed.), Handbook of South American Indians. Vol. 4: The Circum-Caribbean Tribes, pp. 69–70. Washington.
1948b The Archaeology of Costa Rica and Nicaragua. In: Steward, Julian H. (ed.), Handbook of South American Indians. Vol. 4: The Circum-Caribbean Tribes, pp. 121–142. Washington.
1948c The Archaeology of Honduras. In: Steward, Julian H. (ed.), Handbook of South American Indians. Vol. 4: The Circum-Caribbean Tribes, pp. 71–120. Washington.

Strong, William D. / Kidder, Alfred / Paul, Anthony Joseph Drexel
1938 Preliminary Report on the Smithsonian Institution-Harvard University Archaeological Expedition to Northwestern Honduras, 1936. Washington.

Stroth, Luke
2019 Geochemical and Technological Analysis of Lithic Artifacts from Guadalupe, a Cocal Period (AD 1000 to 1530) Site in Northeast Honduras. MA Thesis, University of California.

Stroth, Luke / Otto, Raquel / Daniels, James T. / Braswell, Geoffrey E.
2019 Statistical artifacts: Critical approaches to the analysis of obsidian artifacts by portable X-ray

fluorescence. In: Journal of Archaeological Science: Reports 24: 738–747.

Taube, Karl A.
2005 The Symbolism of Jade in Classic Maya Religion. In: Ancient Mesoamerica 16 (1): 23–50.

Thompson, J. Eric
1970 The Eastern Boundary of the Maya Area: Placements and Displacements. In: Thompson, J. E. (ed.), Maya History and Religion. Civilization of the American Indian series v. 99, pp. 84–102. Norman.

Torres, Joshua M. / Wilson, Samuel S.
2014 Plazas and Bateys. In: Reid, Basil A. / Gilmore, Richard G. (eds.), Encyclopedia of Caribbean Achaeology, pp. 277–280. Gainesville, Florida.

Uhle, Max
1890 Verwandtschaften und Wanderungen der Tschibtscha. In: Actas del VII Congreso Internacional de Americanistas: 466–489.

Urban, Patricia A. / Shugar, Aaron N. / Richardson, Laura / Schortman, Edward M.
2013 The Production of Copper at El Coyote, Honduras: Processing, Dating and Political Economy. In: Shugar, Aaron N. / Simmons, Scott E. (eds.), Archaeometallurgy in Mesoamerica. Current Approaches and New Perspectives, pp. 77–112. Boulder.

Valcárcel Rojas, Roberto / Martinón-Torres, Marcos
2013 Metals in the Indigenous Societies of the Insular Caribbean. In: Keegan, William F. / Hofman, Corinne L. / Rodríguez Ramos, Reniel (eds.), The Oxford Handbook of Caribbean Archaeology. Oxford handbooks, pp. 504–522. Oxford.

Vallo, Michael
2000 Die Keramik von Xkipché. Ph.D. Thesis, Philosophische Fakultät, Rheinische Friedrich-Wilhelms-Universität Bonn.

Vaughn, Kevin J.
2004 Households, Crafts, and Feasting in the Ancient Andes: The Village Context of Early Nasca Craft Consumption. In: Latin American Antiquity 15 (1): 61–88.

Véliz, Vito
1978 An Analysis of Ceramics from the Piedra Blanca Site, Northeastern Honduras. Estudios antropológicos e históricos 1. Tegucigalpa.

Véliz, Vito / Willey, Gordon R. / Healy, Paul F.
1977 Clasificación descriptiva preliminar de cerámica de Roatán. In: Yaxkin 2 (1): 7–18.

Viel, René / Begley, Christopher
1992 La Secuencia Cerámica de Difficulty Hill, Roatan, Islas de la Bahia: Paper presented at the VI Seminario de La Arqueologia Hondurena, Zamarano, Honduras.

Vokes, Emily H. / Vokes, Harold E.
1983 Distribution of shallow-water marine Mollusca, Yucatan Peninsula, Mexico. Middle American Research Institute, Tulane University 54. New Orleans.

Wagner, Elisabeth
2012 Jade. In: Grube, Nikolai (ed.), Maya. Gottkönige im Regenwald. Köln.

Walden, John / Voorhies, Barbara
2017 Ancient Maya Patolli. In: Voorhies, Barbara (ed.), Prehistoric Games of North American Indians. Subarctic to Mesoamerica, pp. 197–218. Salt Lake City.

Waldron, Lawrence
2016 Handbook of Ceramic Animal Symbols in the Ancient Lesser Antilles. Florida Museum of Natural History: Ripley P. Bullen series. Gainesville.

Wallerstein, Immanuel M.
1974 The Modern World-System: Capitalist Agriculture and the Origins of the European World-Economy in the Sixteenth Century. Studies in social discontinuity. San Diego, New York.

Wetter, Angelika
2005 Paracas-Keramik aus Jauranga: Grundlagen zur Klassifikation formativzeitlicher Keramik der Südküste Perus. Magisterarbeit, Rheinische Friedrich-Wilhelms-Universität Bonn.

Wheat, Joe B. / Gifford, James C. / Wasley, William W.
1958 Ceramic Variety, Type Cluster, and Ceramic System in Southwestern Pottery Analysis. In: American Antiquity 24 (1): 34–47.

White, Leslie A.
1959 The evolution of culture: The Development of Civilization to the Fall of Rome. New York.

Willey, Gordon R.
1959 The Intermediate Area of Nuclear America: Its Prehistoric Relationships to Middle America and Peru, Actas del XXXIII Congreso Internacional de Americanistas, San José, 20-27 Julio 1958, pp. 184–191. San José, Costa Rica.
1984 A Summary of the Archaeology of Lower Central America. In: Lange, Frederick W. / Stone, Doris (eds.), The Archaeology of Lower Central America. School of American Research advanced seminar series, pp. 341–378. Albuquerque, N.M.

Willey, Gordon R. / Olsen, Stanley J.
1972 The artifacts of Altar de Sacrificios. Papers of the Peabody Museum of Archaeology and Ethnology / Harvard University Vol. 64, Nr. 1. Cambridge, Mass.

Wilson, Samuel S.
2007 The Archaeology of the Caribbean. Cambridge World Archaeology. Cambridge.

World Register of Marine Species. Website, http://www.marinespecies.org/ (accessed August 17, 2020).

Young, Thomas
1842 Narrative of a residence on the Mosquito Shore, During the Years 1839, 1840, & 1841: With an account of Truxillo, and the adjacent islands of Bonacca and Roatan; and a vocabulary of the Mosquitian language. London.

Zeitlin, Robert N.
1978 Long-Distance Exchange and the Growth of a Regional Center: An Example from the Southern Isthmus of Tehuantepec, Mexico. In: Stark, Barbara L. / Voorhies, Barbara (eds.), Prehistoric Coastal Adaptations. The Economy and Ecology of Maritime Middle America. Studies in Archaeology, pp. 183–210. New. York.

Ziemann, Andreas
2009 Systemtheorie. In: Kneer, Georg / Schroer, Markus (eds.), Handbuch soziologische Theorien, pp. 469–490. Wiesbaden.